MAKING U.S. FOREIGN POLICY TOWARD SOUTH ASIA

About the Editors

Lloyd I. Rudolph and Susanne Hoeber Rudolph are Professors Emeriti of Political Science, University of Chicago. In 1975 they directed an analysis of foreign policy making in South Asia for the National Commission on the Organization of the Government for the Conduct of Foreign Policy, a study that leads to the 1980 edition of this book. The Rudolphs have briefed successive US ambassadors designate to India and consulted with President Clinton's National Security Advisor on South Asia policy. Susanne Rudolph headed the Center for International Studies and the South Asia Languages and Area Studies Center at the University of Chicago, and served as President of the Association for Asian Studies and of the American Political Science Association. Lloyd Rudolph chaired the University of Chicago's Committee on International Relations and its college programs in International Studies and South Asian studies.

They are authors, among other writings, of *Postmodern Gandhi* (2006), *In Pursuit of Lakshmi* (1987), and *The Modernity of Tradition* (1967). Susanne Rudolph edited and contributed to *Transnational Religion and Fading States* (1997) and Lloyd Rudolph to *Reversing the Gaze* (2000).

About the Editors

Lloyd I. Rudolph and **Susanne Hoeber Rudolph** are Professors Emeriti of Political Science, University of Chicago. In 1975 they headed a study on foreign policy making in South Asia for the National Commission on the Organization of the Government for the Conduct of Foreign Policy, a study that leads to the 1980 edition of this book. The Rudolphs have briefed successive US ambassadors-designate to India and consulted with President Clinton's National Security Advisor on South Asia policy. Susanne Rudolph headed the Center for International Studies and the South Asia Language and Area Studies Center at the University of Chicago. She served as President of the Association for Asian Studies and of the American Political Science Association. Lloyd Rudolph chaired the University of Chicago's Committee on International Relations and its college programs in International Studies and South Asian Studies.

They are authors, among other writings, of *Postmodern Gandhi* (2006), *In Pursuit of Lakshmi* (1987), and *The Modernity of Tradition* (1967). Susanne Rudolph edited and contributed to *Transnational Religion and Fading States* (1997) and Lloyd Rudolph to *Experiencing the State* (2006).

MAKING U.S. FOREIGN POLICY TOWARD SOUTH ASIA

Regional Imperatives and the Imperial Presidency

LLOYD I. RUDOLPH
SUSANNE HOEBER RUDOLPH

CONCEPT PUBLISHING COMPANY, NEW DELHI-110059

Cataloging in Publication Data—DK
Courtesy: D.K. Agencies (P) Ltd. <docinfo@dkagencies.com>

Making U.S. foreign policy toward South Asia : regional imperatives and the imperial presidency / [editors], Lloyd I. Rudolph, Susanne Hoeber Rudolph. — 1st ed.

p. cm.

Contributed articles.

Revised and updated ed. of: The regional imperative : the administration of US foreign policy towards South Asia under presidents Johnson and Nixon.

Includes bibliographical references.

Includes index.

ISBN 13: 9788180694110

ISBN 10: 8180694119

1. United States—Foreign relations—South Asia. 2. South Asia—Foreign relations—United States. 3. United States— Foreign relations—20th century. 4. United States—Foreign relations—21st century. I. Rudolph, Lloyd I. (Lloyd Irving), 1927- II. Rudolph, Susanne Hoeber, 1930- III. Title: Regional imperative.

DDC 327.540 73 22

ISBN-13: 978-81-8069-411-0
ISBN-10: 81-8069-411-9

First Edition, 2008

Published and Printed by
Ashok Kumar Mittal
Concept Publishing Company
A/15-16, Commercial Block, Mohan Garden
NEW DELHI-110059 (India)

Phones: 25351460, 25351794
Fax: 091-11-25357103
Email: publishing@conceptpub.com

PREFACE

Making US Foreign Policy Toward South Asia: Regional Imperatives and the Imperial Presidency is a revised and updated edition of *The Regional Imperative: The Administration of US Foreign Policy Towards South Asia Under Presidents Johnson and Nixon*, published in 1980 by Concept Publishing Company, New Delhi and Humanities Press, Atlantic Highlands, NJ.

Making US Foreign Policy Toward South Asia includes four new contributions: a Prologue by Lloyd Rudolph and three new essays by Walter Anderson, Harold Gould and Arthur Rubinoff. In order to keep the new edition at a reasonable length, it has been necessary to drop the texts of eight of ten cases studies included in *The Regional Imperative*. However, all of the case studies are analyzed in Part II, "The Coordination of Complexity in South Asia." The two most salient cases for the theme of our subtitle, the imperial presidency, have been re-published in this edition: Philip Oldenburg's "The Breakup of Pakistan" and James Bjorkman's "Public Law 480 and the Policies of Self-Help and Short-Tether."

Our effort and that of our fellow contributors has been to take account of the experience and lessons of the 30 plus years since 1975 when *The Regional Imperative* was researched and written. Our goal is to improve the attentive public's understanding of the politics of making foreign policy. Of particular concern to us has been to show how the concepts of imperative and deliberative coordination help to explain the imperial presidencies of Lyndon Johnson, Richard Nixon and George W. Bush.

LLOYD I. RUDOLPH
SUSANNE HOEBER RUDOLPH
Barnard, Vermont
June 20, 2007

ACKNOWLEDGEMENTS

The transition from *The Regional Imperative to Making US Foreign Policy Toward South Asia* could not have been accomplished without the assiduous editorial attention of Jeannie Koops-Elson to new and old authors' manuscripts. Her editorial skills were only exceeded by her positive attitude and quotidian diplomacy. We thank Mr. Ashok Mittal and his editorial staff at Concept Publishing Company for their care and patience in bringing the project of a new edition to fruition.

LLOYD I. RUDOLPH
SUSANNE HOEBER RUDOLPH

CONTENTS

PROFILE OF THE CONTRIBUTORS

Walter K. Andersen served in a number of positions at the U.S. Department of State before joining the School of Advanced International Studies/John Hopkins University in late 2003 as the associate director of its South Asia Studies program. He was selected acting director of the program for the 2006-2007 academic year. He has written extensively on Indian domestic politics, including a book on Hindu nationalism, and on the international politics of South Asia.

James Warner Björkman, educated in political science at the University of Minnesota (B.A. summa-cum-laude 1966) and Yale University (M.Phil. 1969, Ph.D. 1976), is Professor of Public Policy and Administration at the Institute of Social Studies, The Hague, as well as Professor of Public Administration and Development at Leiden University, The Netherlands. Previously faculty member at the University of Wisconsin-Madison (U.S.A.), Director of the American Studies Research Centre in Hyderabad (India) and Executive Director of the International Institute of Comparative Government in Lausanne (Switzerland), he has held appointments in Sweden, England, Pakistan and India.

Harold A. Gould is a former Director of Asian Studies at the University of Illinois (Urbana-Champaign). He has specialized in the sociology and political anthropology of India since 1954. He has authored five books on Indian society and politics, and co-edited three other books on various aspects of South Asian politics. Since 1991, he has been a Visiting Scholar in the Center for South Asian Studies at the University of Virginia (Charlottesville). His email address is: Harold.gould4@verizon.net.

Philip Oldenburg is an Independent Scholar, who has taught most recently in the Department of Government, University of

Texas at Austin, and in the Political Science Department, Columbia University. He has been editor or co-editor of the last ten volumes in the Asia Society's *India Briefing* series.

Arthur Rubinoff (Ph.D. Chicago) is Professor of Political Science and South Asian Studies at the University of Toronto, where he has taught since 1972. He is writing a book on "The Role of Congress in the Formulation of U.S. South Asia Policy." In 2000 he was a Public Policy Fellow at the Woodrow Wilson Center for International Scholars in Washington, D.C.

PROLOGUE

— *Lloyd I. Rudolph*

Making US Foreign Policy Toward South Asia presents a revised, expanded version of *The Regional Imperative: US Foreign Policy Towards South Asian States Under the Administration of Presidents Johnson and Nixon.* First published in 1980 by Concept in India and by the Humanities Press in the U.S., *The Regional Imperative* made available to scholars and policy intellectuals the study Susanne Hoeber Rudolph and I had done in 1974 and 1975 for the National Commission on the Organization of the Government for the Conduct of Foreign Policy.[1]

The book featured the making of foreign policy for South Asia during the presidencies of Lyndon Johnson and Richard Nixon, presidencies that span the years 1963-1974. Arthur Schlesinger, Jr. characterized those years as the era of "the imperial presidency."[2] Imperial presidents practiced an extreme version of what we theorized in *The Regional Imperative* as imperative coordination. Imperative coordination, we argued, is based on hierarchy and command and executed by president's men who serve at the president's pleasure and are committed to his interests. Like the president, the president's men are attuned to the president's standing in the polls, the next election and geo-political and ideological perspectives. Nixon and Johnson practiced an extreme version of imperative coordination. It was extreme because it was not balanced by what we conceptualized in *The Regional Imperative* as deliberative coordination, i.e., coordination based on collegiality and persuasion and executed by foreign policy professionals attuned to the long run and knowledgeable about the regional and bi-lateral as well as the global dimensions of the national interest.

The Commission for which we and our fellow contributors wrote was convened at a time of unparalleled governmental crisis. In March 1968, Lyndon Johnson announced that he was abandoning his campaign for a second term. He had been driven from office for a variety of reasons including taking the country to war under false pretences and with wrong assumptions.[3] The Tonkin Bay Resolution, which used an unverified and ultimately non-existent naval attack on US vessels to persuade Congress to go to war, had functioned for Lyndon Johnson as the false weapons of mass destruction had for George Bush in April 2003 to justify going to war in Iraq.

In the face of certain impeachment, Richard Nixon resigned on August 9, 1974. Over-reaching had done him in too. He had failed to make good on his commitment during the 1972 presidential campaign to end the war in Vietnam, he had authorized a secret invasion of Cambodia and, most decisively, he had authorized a break-in to Democratic Headquarters in the Watergate complex.

Extreme versions of imperative coordination contributed to the failure of both imperial presidencies. James Bjorkman's chapter shows how Lyndon Johnson engaged in imperative coordination in the making of US policy with respect to PL-480 food aid to India; we and Philip Oldenburg show how President Nixon and Henry Kissinger ignored and repelled all attempts at deliberative coordination when they tilted towards Pakistan in 1971 during the Bangladesh crisis.

Imperative and deliberative coordination are ideal types, useful for raising questions but, like all models, problematic in that they posit dichotomies and polar opposites in a world that is full of middling conditions. In the text of this book we associate imperative coordination with global perspectives in foreign policy and deliberative with regional, in part because the location of presidents and their "men" leads them to adopt a global, geo-political perspective, in part because they tend to care less and know less abut regional and bi-lateral relations than the foreign policy professionals. But that does not mean that professionally shaped foreign policy cannot be both presidential and global. It was both most famously when the late George Kennan, a career professional *par excellence*, writing in *Foreign Affairs* as Mr. X in 1947, advanced a doctrine of containment to deal with Soviet geopolitical designs after World War II.[4]

Both in the 1980 text of this book and in the present Prologue, we feature the negative consequences of imperative coordination as practiced by Presidents Nixon, Johnson and George W. Bush. Yet imperative coordination can have positive consequences: Alexander Hamilton in Federalist 70 argued that a unitary executive such as the proposed US president would be able to act with energy and dispatch while a collective executive's deliberations would make it difficult for it to do so. Imperative coordination by the president's men in the name of the president is more swift than deliberative coordination. It can more effectively override the resistances of entrenched and parochial bureaucratic baronies. It can inspire. If a limitation of imperative coordination is lack of attention to the local knowledge essential to the conduct of regional and bi-lateral relationships, a strong point can be a propensity to look at the big picture and adopt a global perspective. And deliberative coordination has its limitations. If there can be global parochialism that ignores the local knowledge essential to regional and bi-lateral relationships, there can also be regional and bi-lateral parochialism that mistakenly believes that what is good for "them" is good for "us." Deliberative coordination can lead to stalemate. The professionals can go excessively native. And professionals are prone to bureaucratic vices such as excessive attachment to procedure and to its corollary, the displacement of goals.

The imperial presidency reached its apogee and began its fall during Richard Nixon's second term. The National Commission was conceived when Richard Nixon's imperial presidency was under siege and was constituted in the aftermath of its demise. Perceived failure in Vietnam and in the making of foreign policy generally led Congressional leaders such a Senate Majority Leader Mike Mansfield and Chairman of the Senate Foreign Relations Committee, William Fulbright, to move for a national commission to study the conduct of foreign policy and make recommendations for its improvement. The War Powers Resolution, an attempt by the Congress to reclaim from a rogue presidency its authority for the declaration of war, became law in November 1973. In 1974 Senator Frank Church took the lead in reigning in the CIA and establishing Congressional oversight committees for intelligence. The National Commission was created by an Act of Congress in 1973. By March 1974 the Commission had authorized a broad range of study programs, including one that led to the writing of this book, to make recommendations for the coordination of complexity in South Asia.

Our study began at a time when the leadership for the making of the country's foreign policy was in perilous condition. Following President's Nixon's resignation on August 9, 1974, Gerald Ford, an unelected vice-president,[5] became an unelected president. President Ford, in turn, selected Nelson Rockefeller to be his unelected vice-president. Henry Kissinger combined in his own person the offices of secretary of state and national security advisor.

There are several reasons for bringing out an expanded and updated edition of *The Regional Imperative*. One is its continued relevance. The pathologies of imperative coordination are as striking in the Bush presidency as they were in the Johnson and Nixon presidencies. We have renamed the book *Making US Foreign Policy Toward South Asia* because the revised version takes a broader perspective of foreign policy making than that found in *The Regional Imperative*. A second reason is the interest these essays on US foreign policy making in South Asia of the 1960s and 1970s have as bureaucratic politics and international history. For example Oldenburg analyzes the clash between foreign policy professionals and president's men, not the least of whom was Henry Kissinger, over the wisdom and viability of tilting toward Pakistan in the run-up to the Bangladesh war. Bjorkman reports Lyndon Johnson's use of a "short tether" in the allocation of food aid to India in order to bring pressure on "that little lady's" (i.e., Indira Gandhi's) policy toward Vietnam.

A third reason to bring out a new edition of *The Regional Imperative* is to update and to revise *The Regional Imperative's* contribution to the understanding of the relations between the US and the principal states of the South Asian region. We do this in part by supplying this Prologue and in part by adding three new essays, two by new contributors, Harold Gould and Arthur Rubinoff, and one by a previous contributor, Walter Andersen. Gould's essay deals with "The Reasons Why: America's Half-Century Struggle to Control the Political Agenda in South Asia." Rubinoff throws light on a subject too often left in the shadows, Congress's role: "From Congressional Indifference to Congressional Engagement: The Making of Foreign Policy for South Asia." Andersen updates our understanding of the bureaucratic politics for the South Asia region in "US Foreign Policy toward South Asia: A Continuing Tilt to the Functional."

In what follows, I relate the theories, concepts and explanations that we developed in *The Regional Imperative* to the making of foreign policy in South Asia in the years since the close of the Nixon presidency.

The intervening years, from the crisis era in the conduct of foreign policy examined in *The Regional Imperative* until the transformation wrought by the post 9/11 Bush presidency, spanned the presidencies of Gerald Ford (1974-1976), Jimmy Carter (1976-1980); Ronald Reagan (1980-1988); George Herbert Walker Bush (1988-1992); and Bill Clinton (1992-2000). With the exception of Ronald Reagan's second term when the Iran-Contra affair brought him to the brink of impeachment,[6] presidents by and large kept a rough balance at the global level between imperative and deliberative coordination.

During this era, with the possible exception of nuclear proliferation policy, US relations with the South Asia region generally and with India in particular were, in the parlance of the time, "on the back burner" "where normal diplomacy and bilateral relations can be carried on outside the glare of the presidential gaze."[7] Being on the back burner did not mean that South Asia was not part of America's global strategy. As I will explain at greater length below, from the Baghdad Pact (1952-1955), to CENTO (1955-1979) to opposing the Soviet invasion and occupation of Afghanistan (1979-1989), i.e., until the close of the Cold War and the Soviet withdrawal from Afghanistan in 1989, the US acted as "an off-shore balancer" for the South Asia region by supporting Pakistan against India.[8] An off shore balancer casts its weight from a distance into another region's balance of power. In the case of South Asia, the US de-stabilized South Asia by blocking India, by far the region's most powerful country, from becoming the region's hegemon.[9]

For most of that era, 1952 through 1989, Pakistan played a key role in America's global strategy. The consequence for the South Asia region of making it possible for Pakistan to claim "parity" with India was to deny India the hegemony for which its attributes qualified it and to destabilize the region: Since Independence and Partition in 1947 India and Pakistan have fought four wars—in 1948; 1965; 1971; and 1999—the last three enabled by US military assistance to Pakistan. During the 1999 confrontation over the Kargil salient both sides were in possession of nuclear weapons.

Imperative and Deliberative Coordination and the Imperial Presidency

I have already alluded to how, in *The Regional Imperative*, Susanne Rudolph and I formulated two models for coordinating complexity in the making of foreign policy, an imperative coordination model and a deliberative coordination model.[10] The models grew out of the bureaucratic politics literature.[11] That literature stands in marked contrast with what is taken to be Max Weber's view that bureaucrats faithfully and efficiently follow rules and carry out commands because they have internalized them; as Weber put it, they act *as if* they had willed the rules and the commands.[12] According to one version of the bureaucratic politics literature,[13] bureaucrats use the opportunities their position makes available to pursue power, status, jurisdiction and resources. In Allison's epigram, where you stand depends on where you sit.

Our models like the bureaucratic politics literature down play explanations of state behavior that assume the US government (USG) is a unified national or rational actor. From this perspective, states should not be read as anthropomorphic entities, i.e., as persons who can know and pursue a national interest.[14] If states rarely act as unified rational entities it follows that they can not be theorized as a "black box" whose actions are structurally determined by a need to survive in an anarchic world of aggressively self-interested and self-serving states.[15] Instead we invoked Richard Neustadt's two images of presidential power, one of a president in sneakers figuratively padding down the corridors of power in search of leverage and allies in a world of departmental baronies and Congressionally embedded "iron triangles," and one of a president in boots and spurs whose commands are obeyed with alacrity and without question. The two images posed a perennial question, how to achieve a balance between a Hamiltonian and a Madisonian presidency, i.e., between a presidency of energy and initiative and a presidency constrained by constitutional checks and balances.[16]

Neustadt's account is of interest because it provides a prehistory of the extreme version of imperative coordination, a version that correlates with the rise of the imperial presidency. Neustadt wrote about the president in sneakers with Harry Truman in mind.[17] It was the early days of the Cold War and of the National Security State when the president did not yet have "president's men" to help him over-awe departmental heads let alone ride roughshod over them in the manner of Johnson and Nixon.

What were some of the pre-conditions that allowed for the rise of the imperial presidency and the practice of imperative coordination? In order to answer this question I have to go back to the days just before World War II. In 1939, in the waning days of Franklin Roosevelt's second term, it was already clear that, as Louis Brownlow famously put it, "the president needs help." After considerable controversy, he was given help in the form of six "anonymous" assistants who were to serve as his "eyes and ears," and an Executive Office of the President that included a Bureau of the Budget.[18] In 1947, after the death of Roosevelt, the end of World War II, and the beginning of Harry Truman's presidency and the Cold War, the president was given a lot more help. The National Security Act of 1947 created a National Security Council with a national security assistant and a small staff and a Central

Intelligence Agency whose Director reported directly to the President.[19] The Act added numbers, layers and missions to the six anonymous helpers whom Brownlow had recommended serve as the president's eyes and ears.[20] Over the subsequent years the White House staff and the Executive Office of the President grew rapidly. In the Nixon years a crisis of scale led to the upgrading of the Bureau of the Budget into an Office of Management and Budget and to using the 3000 plus "plum" political appointments available to the president to colonize the departments and agencies with president's men. The executive branch had become, in Hugh Heclo's apt phrase, "a government of strangers"[21] and the president's six helpers a government within the government capable, on occasion, of becoming a Frankenstein's monster that threatened to destroy its creators.

The strengthening of the presidency enabled presidents to face up to departmental baronies with sufficient effect that they could do so without the risk of being overrun. The burgeoning of a Cold War national security state from Truman through Eisenhower to Kennedy greatly strengthened the president's bargaining advantages. By Kennedy's time the president could practice deliberative or imperative coordination to his advantage, as President Kennedy did during the Cuban missile crisis. By Johnson's and Nixon's time presidents had acquired bargaining advantages not only from the presidential staffs and bureaucracies at their command but also from the perception that they were high priests whose esoteric knowledge could ward off an imminent nuclear Armageddon. They said *mantras* about mutually assured destruction (MAD) while keeping their finger on the nuclear trigger. Increasingly, they and the president's men at their side came to believe that what is good for the president is good for the nation.[22]

After 9/11 the Bush administration created a particularly virulent version of the imperial presidency and of imperative coordination. The ground had been prepared by the prior organizational and political aggrandizement of presidential power. Twenty-five years before 9/11 in the Introduction to *The Regional Imperative* we put it this way:

> As Truman gave way to Eisenhower and Eisenhower gave to Kennedy, presidents became, relatively, more powerful and barons less. "Bargaining advantages" were, increasingly, held by the president and his men. In the policy arena of foreign affairs particularly, Congress and its leadership surrendered the bargaining advantages that lay at the roots of their power. In the federal bureaucracy, officials who offered non-presidential alternatives, or more commonly, suggested the costs and the dangers associated with presidential strategies, became increasingly suspect. Presidents came to live in a world of asymmetrical power relations, isolated from the kind of peership and collegiality that sustain argument and rational discourse in the professions and the academic world. . . . Relying on the president for coherence made certain assumptions about him: his voice spoke for the people; his will expressed the national interest. But these assumptions proved at best only partially true. The president had his own political interests. The search for "immediate gains visible during his current term",[23] the personal desire for honor and historical immortality, and the need to prove himself politically and personally too often lead to "an activism divorced from the national purpose and interest."[24]

We contrasted this version of the imperative coordination model with a deliberative coordination model. It featured persuasion and bargaining among knowledgeable and experienced professionals representing diverse views and interests. It helps deliberative coordination if a spirit of collegiality and shared purpose is available in some degree to counter the tendency to please the boss and to be on the winning side (the effectiveness trap)[25] and to not rock the boat and to get along by going along ("group think").[26]

Deliberative coordination, we argued, could mitigate if not eliminate the negative effects associated with administrative hierarchy and presidential power. We argued that "if presidents are able to practice imperative coordination without any attention to the benefits of deliberative coordination, the conduct of foreign policy will lack the kind of knowledge and accountability available to lawyers, legislators, politicians and academics." "The benefits of deliberation in professional life," we wrote, "are needed in the conduct of foreign policy." Lawyers carry on their work in the context of adversary procedures. Their briefs and arguments are disciplined by the precedents the law provides and the arguments of their opponents. Legislators deliberate by examining proposals in committee, in reports and, to an extent, on the floor through debates and conference procedures. Politicians formulate and debate issues, defend their record and criticize their opponents' record. Scholars debate the validity of arguments and evidence; their published work is subject to peer review. Doctors are held accountable by medical boards. Without the presence of deliberative processes found in professional and academic life, presidents and president's men can make foreign policy relatively unconstrained by the kind of procedures and knowledge that discipline professional and academic life. Bush's presidents' men spoke of "creating the reality" that others reported.

Imperative Coordination Illustrated

The Bay of Pigs fiasco (April 17-19, 1961) near the beginning of the Kennedy administration provides a good example of the perils of imperative coordination. The fiasco was the result of a presidentially sanctioned CIA covert operation. It involved landing a small force of 1200 Cuban exiles at Playa Giron, a flat swampy area, with the expectation that they would easily succeed because they would be welcomed as liberators from Fidel Castro's tyranny. But the CIA had grossly underestimated Fidel Castro's popularity. Like the expectation 42 years later that US forces invading Iraq would be welcomed with flowers as liberators,[27] the expectation that the people of Cuba would rise against Castro proved false.

Treated as invaders, the landing force was resisted, overcome and abandoned by its CIA handlers. Conceived by the CIA at the fag end of an outgoing Eisenhower administration, the Bay of Pigs operation was sold to a recently inaugurated young and inexperienced president concerned to prove himself and then "tightly held" by CIA Director Allen Dulles, Deputy Director Richard Bissell and a small coterie of top level officials. Roger

Hillsman, Director of the State Department's Bureau of Intelligence and Research, wasn't consulted. Nor was the State Department's Cuba Desk Officer, Robert Hurwitch. "There was," he said, ". . . a divorce between the people who daily or minute by minute had access to information as to what was going on, and the people who were making plans and policy decisions."[28]

The failure of the Bay of Pigs operation illustrates the dangers of relying solely on imperative coordination. Absent some contribution from deliberative coordination, there was no way to take account of the kind of local, regional and professional knowledge that Susanne Rudolph and I argued for in *The Regional Imperative*. The Bay of Pigs fiasco was reminiscent of the imperial presidency under Presidents Johnson and Nixon when, in the context of South Asia, we found that the making of foreign policy "reflected (presidents') personal and strategic predispositions and concerns . . . The result . . . was the confusion of presidential with national interest, global over-determination in the assessment of other states' intentions and actions, and poorly informed and managed coordination of policy." (vi) We infer that President Kennedy's handling in October 1962 of the Cuban missile crisis and China's invasion of India just 18 months after the Bay of Pigs fiasco showed that he had learned from his mistakes at the Bay of Pigs to use deliberative coordination.[29]

George Bush's post 9/11 presidency brought back an extreme version of imperative coordination. President's men in the White House, the Vice-President's office and in the Defense Department (particularly its Office of Special Plans) regarded knowledgeable professionals in the State Department (particularly its Intelligence and Research Bureau (INR)), the CIA and the Defense Department's Defense Intelligence Agency (DIA) not as colleagues but as, in Richard Neustadt's telling phrase, "natural enemies."[30] The 9/11 attacks provided an unprecedented opportunity for the committed neo-conservatives in the Bush administration to seize power. The response to the attacks, they argued, required a war on terrorism,[31] a war they tried to use to justify unlimited use of executive power.[32]

Soon after the 9/11 attack, the media began to document the "us" versus "them" practices of the president's men in a tightly scripted Bush administration. Among the first to go was Bush's Secretary of the Treasury, Paul O'Neill, who wrongly thought his views about tax and fiscal policy should be heard.[33] O'Neill spoke of Dick Cheney, now the vice-president but O'Neill's subordinate when he ran OMB for Richard Nixon's White House, heading a "praetorian guard that encircled the president to block out contrary views."[34] Ron Suskind reports O'Neill as saying in *The Price of Loyalty* that "the president did not make decisions in a methodical way: there was no free flow of ideas or open debate."[35] Robert Woodward's *Plan of Attack* about the rush to war in Iraq told a similar story of "them" and "us" worlds of the president's men and career professionals.

Secretary of State Colin Powell, the only member of the Bush cabinet member with independent political standing, proved to be another victim of the post-9/11 coup. Powell told Woodward that the government had been seized by a "Gestapo office" of neo-conservatives directed by Cheney and running from the Pentagon to the vice-president's office. Woodward, reflecting Powell's view, writes that "It was a separate little government that was out there."[36]

Three Examples of Post-9/11 Imperative Coordination

Three examples from the post-9/11 Bush administration will illuminate the consequences for the making of foreign policy of ideologically driven president's men practicing imperative coordination. They did so by avoiding deliberative exchanges with experienced professionals in the State and Defense Departments, the US Army and the CIA. The three key policy arenas are: (1) the status and treatment of prisoners; (2) the claim that Saddam Hussein had or was making nuclear weapons; and (3) the size of the armed forces required to defeat, occupy and govern Iraq. After updating the imperative and deliberative coordination models by examining these three policy arenas I will return to how the models apply to the making of foreign policy for South Asia.

The Treatment of Prisoners

Making policy for the interrogation of prisoners generated a great deal of attention because the policy's consequences shocked the country and the world. Photographs of prisoners being tortured at Abu Ghraib prison near Baghdad appeared on television screens and front pages around the globe. Less dramatic visually but equally destructive of US credibility and respect as a beacon of liberty and a government of laws was news of the imprisonment without habeas corpus rights of about 600 so-called enemy combatants in the US naval base at Guantanamo Bay, Cuba. The interrogation policy reveals how the president's men in the White House, the Justice Department and the Department of Defense were able to use imperative coordination to prevail over the voices and views of knowledgeable and responsible professionals, including lawyers in the State Department and the military lawyers of the services' Judge Advocate General branches.

A Defense Department memorandum of March 6, 2003 circulated in the name of Secretary of Defense Donald Rumsfeld and entitled "Working Group Report on Defense Interrogations in the Global War on Terrorism: Assessment of Legal, Historical, Policy, and Operational Considerations,"[37] claimed unlimited power to interrogate prisoners:

> In order to respect the President's inherent constitutional authority to manage a military campaign . . . (the prohibition against torture) must be construed as inapplicable to interrogations undertaken pursuant to his Commander-in-Chief authority. . . . Congress may no more regulate the President's ability to detain and interrogate enemy combatants than it may regulate his ability to direct troop movements in the battlefield. . . . Any effort by Congress to regulate the interrogation of unlawful combatants (terrorists) would violate the Constitution's sole vesting (sic) of the Commander-in-Chief authority of the President.

Having overcome to their own satisfaction domestic obstacles created by the U.S. Constitution to the unrestrained interrogation of prisoners, the president's men still faced international obstacles. The most important of those obstacles was the Third Geneva Convention, including its call for a mechanism for deciding whether someone in custody is a soldier, a saboteur, a "terrorist" or an innocent civilian. The convention calls for the matter to be decided by a hearing before a "competent tribunal." According to John Yoo's memorandum of January 9, 2002, the Third Geneva Convention dealt only with state citizens or subjects. Al Qaeda was declared to be a non-state actor and Afghanistan under a Taliban government, a "failed state."[38] These thoughts led President Bush to decide that the Third Geneva Convention didn't apply to the prisoners held at Guantanamo.

When Secretary of State Colin Powell learned about the President's finding he asked the President to reconsider his decision. In a memorandum dated January 26, 2002 to White House Counsel Alberto Gonzales and to Condoleezza Rice, the National Security Adviser, Powell argued that the use of the "competent tribunal" required by Third Geneva Convention should apply to those captured in the Afghanistan war. Prisoners could be found to be "unlawful" or "enemy" combatants but only after a hearing before a competent tribunal.[39] Not applying the Geneva Convention to prisoners held at Guantanamo would "reverse over a century of US policy and practice. . . . And undermine the protections of the law of war for our troops."[40] William H. Taft IV, General Counsel, Department of State, pressed the State Department's case with a memorandum to Alberto Gonzales on February 2, 2004. Taft argued that using "competent tribunals" as required by the Geneva Convention would show that the United States "bases its conduct on its international legal obligations and the rule of law, not just on its policy preferences."[41]

At the heart of the imperative coordination cabal (as they called themselves) was David Addington, Counsel to Vice-President Dick Cheney.[42] A long-time Cheney aide, Addington had "an indistinct portfolio and no real staff. . . ." Although not well known in government, "he would become legendary. . ." because of his "wide influence over military, intelligence and other matters. In a matter of months, he would make a mark as one of the most important architects of the administration's legal strategy against foreign terrorism."[43]

Soon after the September 11, 2001 attacks White House Counsel Alberto F. Gonzales set up what appeared to be a deliberative coordination mechanism, an interagency group to draw up options for interrogating and prosecuting terrorists. Pierre-Richard Prosper, the State Department's ambassador-at-large for war crimes issues, was assigned to lead the group. Prosper had earned a reputation as a crime fighter; he was expected to favor criminal courts over military tribunals as the best means to prosecute terrorists but Gonzales, who had created the task force, made it clear from the beginning that he favored military commissions or tribunals. Although in previous wars military tribunals had followed prevailing standards of military justice, military commissions had no statutory rules. Bush administration civilian lawyers saw no reason why procedures couldn't be invented that would lower standards of proof, expand the scope for secrecy and make it easier to apply the death penalty to deal with the Al Qaeda operatives they confidently expected to be locked up in Guantanamo.

"In past administrations," Tim Golden wrote, the White House's Office of Legal Counsel ". . . usually weighed in with opinions on questions that had already been deliberated by the legal staffs of the agencies involved." But by late October 2001, Bush administration lawyers led by Deputy White House Counsel Timothy Flanigan had had enough of Prosper's efforts to practice deliberative coordination. Golden tells it this way:

> "With the White House in charge . . . the planning for tribunals moved forward more quickly, and more secretly. Whole agencies were left out of the discussion. So were most of the governments experts in military and international law. The Justice Department's Michael Chertoff (later Secretary of Homeland Security), who had argued for trying terror suspects in federal courts, saw the military order only when it was

> published. . . . Many of the Pentagons experts on military justice, uniformed lawyers who had spent their careers working on (military justice) . . . issues, were mostly kept in the dark. . . . Senior officials of the State Department and the National Security Council staff were excluded from final discussions of the policy."[44]

Dick Cheney at a private lunch with the president showed him the draft of the order authorizing military commissions and the president signed it on November 13, 2001.[45] The Bush administration's circumventing of deliberative coordination in making policy for the treatment of prisoners taken during the war in Afghanistan and subsequently in Iraq contributed to disastrous consequences at Abu Ghraib and Guantanamo for America's standing and credibility in the world.[46]

Saddam Hussein's Nuclear Weapons

My next story about favoring imperative over deliberative coordination has to do with the Bush administration's claim that Saddam Hussein had or was making nuclear weapons.[47] The claim lay at the heart of the administration's case for war against Iraq; Saddam Hussein, it was said, threatened the US with a mushroom cloud. And he could do so because Saddam and bin Laden's Al-Qaeda were allies who helped each other. The implication was that the next time Al-Qaeda struck the US it could do so with nuclear bombs supplied by Saddam Hussein.

The claim that Saddam's nuclear weapons threatened the US with a mushroom cloud was made often in many forums and contexts but perhaps no more notoriously than by National Security Adviser, Condoleezza Rice when she said "We don't want the 'smoking gun' to be a mushroom cloud," and by President Bush himself when he said in his 2003 State of the Union address that "America must not ignore the threat gathering against us. Facing clear evidence of peril, we cannot wait for the final proof—the smoking gun—that could come in the form of a mushroom cloud."[48]

Evidence of the nuclear peril was supplied in 16 words in President Bush's 2003 State of the Union address: "The British government has learned that Saddam Hussein recently sought significant quantities of uranium from Africa." We have a pretty good idea of why these words appeared in the President's address—he and his president's men were seeking reasons to go to war with Iraq—but *how* did this false intelligence enter the president's speech?

The Bush administration's abandonment of deliberative coordination with respect to the intelligence process helps to explain how the 16 words happened.

The story centers on Joseph Wilson. Five months after the president's state of the union address, Wilson blew the whistle on the 16 words in an op-ed piece in the *New York Times* of July 6, 2003. Wilson is a retired career foreign service office who served *inter alia* under Presidents George Herbert Walker Bush and Bill Clinton. As *charge d'affaires* in Baghdad in 1990 he was the last American diplomat to meet Saddam Hussein. Wilson served as US ambassador to several African countries and on the "Africa desk" of the National Security Council during the Clinton administration. He knew Niger, the alleged source in Africa of the uranium oxide (called yellow cake), well. He is, as Gilbert and Sullivan might have put it, the very model of the model knowledgeable professional. His story suggests why president's men regard knowledgeable professionals as "natural enemies" of the president.

In February 2002, four months after 9/11 when, in retrospect, we know the president's men had already decided to attack Iraq,[49] Wilson was told by CIA officials that Vice-President Dick Cheney's office had questions about "a particular intelligence report."[50] Again, in retrospect we know that Dick Cheney and Secretary of Defense Donald Rumsfeld had begun to seek intelligence to justify an attack on Iraq.[51] With no awareness that he was being "set up," Wilson returned to Africa to visit Niger where, as a former ambassador to two nearby African countries, he was familiar with the situation on the ground.[52] Wilson carefully re-visited the structure of uranium production in Niger and conducted further investigation. Like US Ambassador to Niger, Barbro Owens-Kirkpatrick, who had already denied reports of uranium sales to Iraq in her reports, Wilson concluded that it is "highly doubtful that any such transaction had ever taken place."[53] Returning to Washington in early March, Wilson provided a detailed briefing to the CIA and shared his conclusions with the State Department's African Affairs Bureau. Wilson thought the Niger matter was closed but in September 2002 the British government published a "white paper" asserting that Saddam Hussein's "unconventional arms" posed an "immediate danger" as proved by the fact that Iraq had attempted to purchase uranium from an African country. In January President Bush, "citing the British dossier, repeated the. charges about Iraqi efforts to buy uranium from Africa." Wilson says that:

> the vice-president's office asked a serious question. I was asked to formulate the answer. I did so, and *I have every confidence that the answer I provided was circulated to the appropriate officials within our government*. . . . The question . . . is how that answer was or was not used by our political leadership. . . . If . . . the information was ignored because it did not fit certain preconceptions about Iraq, then a legitimate argument can be made that we went to war under false pretenses. . . . At a minimum, Congress, which authorized the use of military force at the president's behest, should want to know if the assertions about Iraq were warranted. . . . America's foreign policy . . . depends on the sanctity of its information. For this reason, questioning the selective use of intelligence to justify the war in Iraq is neither idle sniping nor 'revisionist history', as Mr. Bush has suggested. The act of war is the last option of a democracy, taken when there is grave danger to our national security.[54]

Very soon Joseph Wilson learned that he had to pay a price for supposing the Bush White House wanted to practice deliberative coordination. On July 14, 2003 Robert Novak published a column in which he said that two "senior officials"—president's men—of the Bush administration had told him that Wilson's wife, Valerie Plame, was a CIA "operative"[55] who worked on weapons of mass destruction. Later he implied that she had somehow arranged for her husband's assignment. The "senior officials" apparent objective in leaking this information through Novak was to discredit Wilson's report on Niger yellow cake and to intimidate other knowledgeable professionals who might consider speaking truth to power.[56]

We may surmise that Cheney and Rumsfeld ignored or misread Wilson's report because it wasn't the kind of intelligence they wanted. Soon after 9/11, Rumsfeld arranged to get the kind of intelligence he and Dick Cheney wanted by creating his own intelligence operation in the Department of Defense, the Office of Special Plans.

Seymour Hersh puts it this way:

> Special Plans was created in order to find evidence of what (Paul) Wolfowitz and his boss, Defense Secretary, Donald Rumsfeld, believed to be true—that Saddam Hussein had close ties to Al Qaeda, and that Iraq had an enormous arsenal of chemical, biological, and possibly even nuclear weapons. . . . By the fall of 2002, the operation rivaled the CIA and the Pentagon's own Defense Intelligence Agency, the DIA, as President Bush's main source of intelligence regarding Iraq's possible possession of . . . weapons of mass destruction and connection with Al Qaeda.

Hersh quotes Patrick Lang, former chief of Middle East intelligence at DIA, as saying that the Pentagon had "banded together to dominate the government's foreign policy, and they've pulled it off. . . . The DIA has been intimidated and beaten to a pulp. And there's no guts at all in the CIA."[57] While some in the Bush administration continued to maintain that the intelligence for the 16 words justified their use, there seems little doubt that the words suited the "cabal's" efforts to practice imperative coordination.

Those efforts were thwarted in the short run by Wilson's July 6, 2003 op-ed. On July 7, 2003, the day after his op-ed, White House Press Secretary Ari Fleischer said, ". . . the information on yellow cake did, indeed, turn out to be incorrect."[58] Three days after Wilson's article, Secretary of State Colon Powell said

"President Bush should not have made the Iraq-Niger assertion."[59] On July 11, 2003 National Security Adviser, Condoleezza Rice, at a White House press briefing "acknowledged that the 16 words were, in retrospect, a mistake. . . . Knowing what we now know, that some of the Niger documents were apparently forged, we wouldn't have put this in the President's speech. . . ." The same day, CIA Director George Tenet said "These 16 words should never have been included in the text written for the President."[60]

Despite these admissions the cabal persisted. The 16 words found their way into the president's state of the union address in part because the professional intelligence agencies, the CIA, the DOD's DIA and the State Department's INR (Bureau of Intelligence and Research) were intimidated or by-passed by the president's men in the Office of Special Plans.[61]

Seymour Hersh tells us the cabal's operatives, Abram Shulsky, the "Straussian"[62] Director of the Office of Special Plans, William Luti, a retired Navy captain and protégé of Richard Perle serving as Deputy Secretary of Defense for Near East and South Asian Affairs, and Douglas Feith,[63] Under Secretary of Defense for Policy ". . . see everybody not 100 percent with them as 100 percent against them—it's a very Manichaean world. . . . They see themselves as outsiders. There's a high degree of paranoia. They've convinced themselves that they're on the side of the angels, and everybody else in government is a fool."[64]

In the State Department John Bolton's office for Arms Control and International Security was an outpost of the DOD centered cabal but Bolton's Secretary, Colin Powell, often found himself opposed to the cabal's top leaders, Donald Rumsfeld and Dick Cheney. Early on in the Bush administration Powell assigned Greg Thielmann of the Department's INR to be Bolton's daily intelligence liaison. When it became clear that Thielmann was not telling Bolton "what he wanted to hear" he was intercepted at the door of (Bolton's) office and told, "the undersecretary doesn't need you to attend this (daily) meeting any more."[65] Thielmann's intelligence didn't please Bolton because it reflected INR's view that there ". . . is no persuasive evidence that the Iraqi nuclear program is being reconstituted."[66]

Bolton, like Wolfowitz in DOD, was reluctant to let the military and civilian analysts on the staff vet the intelligence "that the Office of Special Plans was producing." Hersh reports a former aid to Cheney telling him that "it was an unbelievably closed and small group,"[67] *them vs us*, president's men against their natural enemies.

The Size of the Forces Needed in Iraq

The third and last policy arena for examining the effects of imperative and deliberative coordination on the making of foreign policy is the size of the armed forces required to defeat, occupy and govern Iraq. This time my story centers on General Eric Shinseki, Army Chief of Staff from 1999 to 2003. The central event was his testimony before the Senate Armed Services Committee on February 25, 2003. Shinseki told the Senators that "something on the order of several hundred thousand soldiers" would be required for an occupation of Iraq. Two days later, on February 27, 2003, Paul Wolfowitz, Deputy Secretary of Defense, in testimony before the House Budget Committee, said that Shinseki's estimate was "wildly off the mark." "I am reasonably certain," Wolfowitz told the committee, "that they (the people of Iraq) will greet us (the US invading and occupying forces) as liberators and that will help us to keep the requirements down."[68]

The Iraqis, Wolfowitz believed, would welcome liberation from Saddam Hussein's tyranny; American troops would be greeted, as they were in Paris at the end of World War II, by cheering crowds offering bouquets of flowers. According to James Fallows, Wolfowitz "went out of his way essentially to slap Shinseki in the face" by saying that he was "wildly off the mark." It would be almost impossible to imagine, Wolfowitz argued, "that it would be harder, and take more troops, to occupy Iraq than to conquer it."[69]

Wolfowitz' public rebuke of Shinseki was, according to Fallows, "probably the most direct public dressing-down of a military officer, a four star general, by a civilian superior since Harry Truman . . ." dressed down Douglas MacArthur 50 years ago. Calling Shinseki's recommendation "wildly off the mark" "was not the way that generals and Pentagon superiors talked to each other."[70] Nor was Secretary of Defense Donald Rumsfeld's response to his Chief of the Army Staff (Shinseki's) offer of professional advice on a variety of questions, including the "several hundred thousand" properly trained and equipped soldiers required for the occupation of Iraq.

Rumsfeld like Wolfowitz not only humiliated Shinseki, he also undermined his authority by announcing his successor as chief of staff fourteen months before his term was up on June 11, 2003, a move that violated a long standing convention that the announcement of a successor is made at the very last minute to avoid turning the incumbent into a lame duck. This was only one of a series of "apparently calculated and intentional insults" by the president's men at the top of the Defense Department.[71]

This clash between a knowledgeable military professional like Shinseki and key president's men like Wolfowitz and Rumsfeld reveals how the victory of imperative over deliberative coordination can make a difference for the relative success or failure of policy. Shinseki had served for more than ten years in Europe,[72] including as the commander of the NATO Force in Bosnia and Kosovo where he had learned about the importance of adequate numbers of appropriately trained occupation forces. His recommendation was also based on extensive studies done at the Army War College. They showed that "there was a crucial moment just after the fall of a regime when the potential for disorder was enormous." If disorder was allowed to happen in the first days or weeks after the regime was defeated, "there would be a ripple effect for years to come." As a result, the Army War College study concluded "it was best to go in heavier than you actually needed to be, so that at the beginning of the postwar period your presence would be so intimidating that nobody would dare to challenge you." It was better, the study argued, to go in heavy, set the tone, and then draw down rapidly than to do the reverse.[73]

The differences between the Pentagon's top civilians and top generals precede the question of how many and what kind of troops would be needed to occupy Iraq. In late July 2002, the

Washington Post reported that the then Chairman of the Joint Chiefs Staff, Henry Shelton, other members of the Joint Chiefs and other "top generals and admirals" believed that Saddam Hussein's regime "poses no immediate threat and that the United States should continue its policy of containment rather than invade Iraq to force a change of leadership in Baghdad."

Even if an invasion was successful, top military commanders warned that the aftermath could see "mass instability, requiring tens of thousands of US troops to maintain peace, prop up a post-Saddam government, and prevent fragmentation of Iraq."[74] Richard Perle, then the Chairman of the Defense Policy Board and, like Paul Wolfowitz, a veteran neo-conservative and core member of the "cabal," warned the military professionals that the decision of whether or not to go to war against Iraq is "a political decision that these guys aren't competent to make."[75] "The hawks in and around the Administration, including Paul Wolfowitz and Richard Perle, were arguing . . . that any show of force would immediately trigger a revolt against Saddam within Iraq, and that it would quickly expand."[76] Again, according to the *Washington Post* the split between the White House, the Vice-President's office and civilian Pentagon leadership (Rumsfeld, Wolfowitz, Perle, *et al.*) on the one hand, and top military officers on the other, over going to war with Iraq created "an unusual alliance between the State Department and the uniformed side of the Pentagon, elements of the government that more often seem to oppose each other in foreign policy debates."[77]

During the fall and winter of 2002 many senior retired military officials spoke out against the Bush administration's talk of attacking Iraq. In mid-January 2003 *Time* magazine estimated that "as many as 1 in 3 senior officers questions the wisdom of a pre-emptive war with Iraq." They argued that "the US military is already stretched across the globe, the war against Osama bin Laden is unfinished, and a long postwar occupation looks inevitable."[78]

The war against Iraq was launched on March 19, 2003. Rumsfeld and his inner circle of advisers not only had successfully pushed for war but also pushed the military aside in the war's management.

> Rumsfeld repeatedly overruled the senior Pentagon planners on the Joint Staff, the operating arm of the Joint Chiefs of Staff. . . . On at least six occasions. . . . He insisted that the number of troops be sharply reduced. Rumsfeld's faith in precision bombing and his insistence on streamlined military operations has had profound consequences for the ability of the Armed Forces to fight effectively overseas.[79]

Rumsfeld was personally contemptuous of senior generals and admirals who gained senior rank during the Clinton administration. He generated an atmosphere of derision and challenge. "One witness to a meeting recalled Rumsfeld confronting General Eric Shinseki, the Army Chief of Staff, in front of many junior officers. 'He was looking at the Chief and waving his hand,' the witness said, 'saying, "Are you getting this yet? Are you getting this yet?"'"[80] Seymour Hersh says that according to a dozen or so military men he spoke to, "Rumsfeld simply failed to anticipate the consequences of protracted warfare. He put Army and Marine units in the field with few reserves and insufficient number of tanks and other armored vehicles."[81]

Most serious was Rumsfeld's failure, in the face of Shinseki's professional advice, to anticipate and prepare for the occupation of Iraq. Niall Ferguson, an admirer of empire who keeps hoping the Yanks will learn from the Brits, says that Britain in 1920 successfully crushed the insurgency in Mesopotamia (today's Iraq) with 120,000 (mostly Indian) troops,[82] a few less than the US had in Iraq in May 2005, but that the ratio of British troops to population (3 million) was 1: 23 while the ratio of US troops to population (24 million) is 1: 174. Counting this way, Ferguson says the US would need about one million troops to prevail in Iraq.[83] By these calculations, Shinseki, it seems, had it right.

The first mistake was to assume that Iraqi military units would surrender and, after removing the politically tainted top layer, would be available as a security force. Whether intentionally or not, the Iraqi army "melted away" and then, inexplicably, according to General Jay Garner, the first and short-lived US Administrator in Iraq, the army was "decommissioned" by his successor, Ambassador Paul Bremer III.

Even worse was the vicious cycle loosed by wrong assumptions, lack of preparation and trained personnel. US armed forces failed to respond to looting and to stop destruction of property and infrastructure such as the power grid and oil pipe lines. The opening scene after the staged pulling down of Saddam Hussein's statue, looting of antiquities from the Baghdad museum, was emblematic. Hospitals and schools were stripped bare and government ministries were wrecked. Because there were no troops to patrol the borders, wanted persons escaped and unwanted persons entered the country. Fallows argues that "because the US wasn't ready to guarantee security in the month after the war, Iraq started off on a path that got worse . . . as opposed to a path that got better. . . ."[84] It is still coping with the consequences of solely following the views of ideologically motivated generalists, i.e., president's men, Rumsfeld and Wolfowitz, while ignoring the recommendations of military professionals such as Generals Shinseki and Shelton.

Concluding Remarks about Imperative and Deliberative Coordination

I conclude this account of the role of imperative and deliberative coordination in the making of US foreign policy in the post-World War II era by reporting that, unlike Lyndon Johnson, Richard Nixon and, marginally, Ronald Reagan, George W. Bush as of late-2007 had not been driven from office by the unrestrained practice of imperative coordination. Instead, he was elected to a second term in the November 2004 presidential election. His party, the Republican Party, increased its majorities in the US House of Representatives and in the US Senate. The Republicans won the 2004 presidential and congressional elections in the face of admitted failures to find weapons of mass destruction in Iraq and failure to find evidence that Saddam Hussein had anything to do with the 9/11 attacks or links with Osama bin Laden. The ostensible justifications for going to war against Iraq had proven false. Only after the election was more evidence allowed to surface that Bush administration negligence and incompetence helped to make the 9/11 attacks possible.[85]

The pundits will be sorting out for some time why and how George W. Bush won the 2004 presidential election. Most analysts agree that an important reason was his ability to persuade enough American voters that American troops fighting in Iraq were fighting the terrorists who attacked and threatened the US. He also convinced enough of them that he was a better commander in chief than his much decorated war veteran Democratic opponent, John Kerry.[86]

In the face of his administration's admitted failure to find weapons of mass destruction, connect Saddam Hussein to the 9/11 attacks and anticipate that the US forces would be received as occupiers rather than as liberators, President Bush claimed legitimacy for his foreign policy record by claiming that the election's outcome was an "accountability moment." A more convincing accountability moment came with the 2006 Congressional election when the Democrats wrested control of the House and Senate from the Republicans. The story of the Bush administration's war in Iraq has not ended. As of winter 2007 US troops were still fighting and dying in Iraq with few signs of when and how they would leave. And the President's approval ratings and the level of support for the war in Iraq continued to slide downward.

South Asia Moves from Back to Front Burner

How has the making of US foreign policy for South Asia changed in the 30 years since *The Regional Imperative* was researched and written? The first thing to notice is how much has changed with respect to the context of "governmental pluralism" that conditions the making of foreign policy for South Asia. Susanne Rudolph and I organized our analysis of governmental pluralism in *The Regional Imperative* around the State Department's construction of the geo-strategic world into regional bureaus. In the mid-1970s there were departmental bureaus for Africa, East Asia, Europe, Near East and South Asia and Latin America. Each region, we argued, "can be profitably dealt with as a separate policy arena with a distinguishable 'government'."[87] Each has a distinctive constellation of salient bureaus and agencies,

Congressional committees, interest groups, policy NGOs, attentive publics, and security, economic and cultural determinants. The constellations wax and wane depending on the changing universe of economic and security issues. For example, the geo-political exigencies of the Cold War elevated the European Bureau to a pre-eminent position for almost six decades. The Near East and South Asia Bureau also attracted a great deal of attention because of the strategic value of oil resources located in and around the Persian Gulf and the US' special relationship with Israel. NEA's South Asia appendage appeared only rarely on US policy makers' radar screen.

Enormous changes have occurred since 1975 in the context and parameters of the South Asia regional government. In the mid-1970s South Asia as a region and India and Pakistan as countries were on the back burner. In 1998 they moved to the front burner after India and Pakistan tested nuclear weapons in May and June. Since then, in 1999 in connection with Pakistan's military occupation of the Kargil salient in Kashmir, and in early 2002 following a terrorist attack in December 2001 on the Indian Parliament by a Pakistan based group, the nuclear rivals have engaged in conventional and nuclear military confrontations. When, on March 2, 2006, the US President, George Bush, and the Indian Prime Minister, Manmohan Singh, concluded a nuclear agreement that legitimized India's standing as a nuclear power and gave it access to nuclear technology and fuel, India moved to center stage in the drama of the global balance of power.[88]

Like the dramatic changes in India's strategic significance, changes in its economic performance and condition have also made India globally more visible. In the years since 1991, the year India launched its economic liberalization policy, its economy has grown rapidly reaching as high as 8 percent of GDP per annum; its middle class consumers are estimated at 250,000,000; it has attracted high levels of foreign direct and portfolio investment; its rapidly growing information technology firms are setting world standards; and jobs in India's business process outsourcing firms became an issue in America's 2004 presidential election.[89]

Major changes in the Indian diaspora also have enhanced India's visibility in the US. In the intervening years, it has grown from half a million to almost two million. The Indian-American community not only has the highest proportion of college and advanced degrees and the highest median family income of any ethnic group in the US,[90] it also has one of the most effective foreign policy lobbying groups, US-INPAC (US-India Political Action Committee) and the largest country caucus in the U.S. House of Representatives (155 members).[91] Indo-Americans are now visible and effective players in US politics and in the making of US foreign policy.

Since 1975, the State Department has been reorganized in ways that take into account of the increased significance of India and the South Asia region in US foreign policy concerns. In our 1975 report to the National Commission on the Organization of the Government for the Conduct of Foreign Policy Susanne Rudolph and I had recommended separating South Asia from the Near East and locating the region in a separate South Asia Bureau. On August 24, 1992 a Bureau of South Asia Affairs was created as a result of Congressional legislation.[92] We note too that, in line with our argument in *The Regional Imperative*, the South Asian Affairs Bureau as well as the Near Eastern Affairs Bureau have created an Office of Regional Affairs that, hopefully, tries to promote the sort of inter-regional coordination which was missing at the time of our report on "the coordination of complexity in South Asia."

Another arena of change has been America's relation with South Asian states since the September 11, 2001, attacks on the World Trade Center and the Pentagon. As we have noted, during the Cold War US administrations pursued a global policy of containment. Starting in 1952, containment in South Asia meant Pakistan's participation in the Middle East Treaty Organization or Baghdad Pact, later CENTO. India meanwhile took a leading role in organizing and leading the non-aligned movement. Starting with Dwight Eisenhower's Secretary of State, John Foster Dulles, US administrations, particularly Republican administrations, followed

Dulles' view that if a country isn't with us, it is against us. That made India as a practitioner of non-alignment suspect.

In rationalizing its de facto support for Pakistan in South Asia during the Cold War the US often spoke of parity of treatment for Pakistan and India. Parity and beyond parity, tilting toward Pakistan, denied India the possibility of becoming the regional hegemon, a role which India's size, population, endowments and capabilities made possible. In effect the US acted as an "offshore balancer" for the South Asia region. Selig Harrison put it this way: "During the Cold War, American policy assigned a clear priority to relations with Pakistan by providing a total of $3.8 billion in military aid to Pakistani military rulers that was nominally directed against the communist powers but was in practice used to strengthen Pakistan relative to India."[93] Weighing in in support of Pakistan had the effect of destabilizing the region. Parity and the military support to Pakistan that it entailed bear a good deal of the responsibility for regional instability in South Asia, including three of the four wars that destabilized the region between 1948 and 1999.

CENTO's collapse in early1979 after the Khomeini-led Iranian revolution and the flight of Shah Reza Pahlavi was soon followed by the Soviet invasion of Afghanistan. Overnight, Pakistan became a "front line state." Once again, as in the heyday of CENTO in the 1950s, billions of dollars of military and economic aid became available to Pakistan, ostensibly for supporting the resistance movement to the Soviet invasion and occupation of Afghanistan. Ten years later, after the Soviet defeat and withdrawal from Afghanistan in 1989, Pakistan for a short time moved to the back burner, away from the presidential attention and largesse.

Then came the attacks of September 11, 2001, and President Bush's call for a war on terrorism. Pakistan turned on a dime.[94] It had been the sponsor, mentor and patron (with US money and weapons) of a Taliban regime in Afghanistan that provided Pakistan with "strategic depth" and harbored and protected Al Qaeda leader, Osama bin Laden. Now it again became a front line state for the US in an American led war against terrorism, a war that included Pakistan's erstwhile ally, Afghanistan's Taliban government. Again the US was "tilting" to Pakistan in the South

Asian region by supplying Pakistan with military and economic aid. The US in the name of a presidential global strategy was again poised to de-stabilize the South Asia region by challenging India's potential hegemonic role. Pakistan again became the vehicle for the US to engage in offshore balancing in the South Asia region.[95] But there was a difference; this time as we will see in greater detail below, the US was trying to enlist India as well as Pakistan in a common cause, a "war against terrorism."

Sir Olaf Caroe Invents Offshore Balancing in South Asia

Why and how did offshore balancing come to the South Asia region? Its origin can be found in the geo-strategic ideas of Sir Olaf Caroe, the last foreign secretary for the British *raj* in India (1939-45). The British ruled an undivided Indian subcontinent. Winston Churchill thought India was the heart of the British empire and that Britain's capacity to be a world power depended on its rule in India. He succeeded in blocking the Viceroy, Lord Irwin's, the Prime Minister Ramsay MacDonald's and the leader of the Conservative Party, Stanley Baldwin's, effort in 1929-30 to grant dominion status to India.[96] The power and influence of British India reached into Central, Southeast and West Asia, not least into the Persian Gulf and the Arabian peninsula; Burma, Sri Lanka and Singapore; Afghanistan and Tibet; and into East Africa and the Eastern Mediterranean. The *raj*'s Political Service[97] made foreign and security policy for this vast trans-regional space and the British Indian Army backed it up.

In the dying days of the *raj* at the close of World War II, Caroe began to worry about what he came to call in a prescient phrase, "the wells of power," the oil resources of the Middle East in general and of the Gulf and the Arabian peninsula in particular. For a variety reasons he facilitated, then welcomed the partition of India into successor states, India and Pakistan. Indian independence was expected to bring the anti-imperialist Jawaharlal Nehru to power, an eventuality that Caroe feared not least because Nehru couldn't be trusted[98] to use the diplomatic and military resources of an independent India to secure Middle East oil for British use and, more broadly, for the use of the Atlanticist world of America and Europe.

Caroe was attracted to Jinnah's theory of two nations and to his plan to partition the subcontinent into a Muslim Pakistan and a Hindu India. Like Kipling before him, Caroe was attracted to Muslim character and culture[99] and sympathized with Mohammed Ali Jinnah's call for a Muslim state on the sub-continent. A Jinnah-led Pakistan would be a more suitable vehicle to help secure the "wells of power." He would understand the importance of the spheres of influence, buffer states and protectorates that Caroe and *raj* foreign secretaries before him had developed into a fine art of imperial security policy. Although the last Viceroy, Lord Louis Mountbatten, was an admirer of Jawaharlal Nehru's political ideas and leadership, he, like his principal, Britain's Labour Government, was bent on extricating Britain from India at as early a date as possible, a result that could best be realized by agreeing to India's partition. By creating an independent Muslim state of Pakistan, partition favored Caroe's evolving geo-political ideas about how to secure "the wells of power."

At about this time some in Washington were looking for ways to secure the oil resources and practice containment in the Middle East. The formulations of Sir Olaf Caroe attracted attention and soon found favor in official circles.[100] His article in the March 1949 number or *Round Table* and his 1951 book, *Wells of Power*, led to invitations from the State and Defense Departments to visit Washington. In his *Round Table* article he argued that military operations in Mesopotamia (Iraq) and Persia (Iran) during World War I and World War II "were made possible from the Indian base", (i.e., by the use of the Indian Army). The partition of India into independent India and Pakistan "entails a new approach to old problems." His new approach substituted Pakistan for Imperial India. "Pakistan," he argued, "has succeeded to much of (undivided British) India's responsibility for the Indian peninsula" [!] "the Northwest Frontier" [e.g., Afghanistan and its surround] and "the Gulf" [i.e., the Arabian Sea as well as the Persian Gulf]. Karachi commands the Gulf, a "Muslim lake" whose "littoral states control the fuel on which European powers increasingly depend." Defending the wells of power merged with George Kennan's recently articulated containment policy. In Caroe's formulation—the littoral states' security is threatened as "shadows lengthen from the north."

By 1951, when Caroe published *Wells of Power* he was disillusioned with Nehru's anti-colonialism and non-alignment. India, he announced, "is no longer an obvious base for Middle East defense. It stands on the fringe of the defense periphery. Pakistan on the other hand lies well within the grouping of Southwestern Asia."[101]

Caroe wrote *The Wells of Power* for American consumption. It encouraged the US to step forward as an offshore balancer. The book was an attempt, he said, "to catch and save a way of thought known to many who saw these things from the East [a euphemism for the British empire in India] but now in danger of being lost." "New workers in the vineyard," he wrote, "may find [his perspective] . . . something worth regard" as they face "the imminence of Soviet Russia towering over these lands."[102] The Great Game in Asia was being redefined: The British game with Russia in (Central, West and South) Asia was now to be played with substitutes, America and Pakistan, as a weary and weakened Britain benched itself and Nehru's India fouled out.

Caroe's hopes were soon richly rewarded. Among his early important disciples was Henry Byroade. In December 1951, he had become Assistant Secretary of State for the Near East, South Asia and Africa. A West Point graduate with a military career behind him,[103] he knew very little about the regions and states for which he was responsible. In May 1952, Byroade met Caroe in Washington, and as Caroe tells it, he persuaded not only Byroade but also the new U.S. Secretary of State, John Foster Dulles, of the soundness of his views about the role Pakistan should play in the geo-politics of West, Central and South Asia.

> My Pakistani friends regard me as the inventor of the Baghdad Pact! I went on a tour of the US for the British FO (Foreign Office) in 1952 and had talks with State Department officials and others on these lines, and perhaps some of the exchanges

we had were not without effect. Indeed I have more than once ventured to flatter myself that J.F. Dulles' phrase "The Northern Tier" and his association of the US with the "Baghdad" countries in Asia were influenced by the thinking in *Wells of Power*. In that book I called those countries 'The Northern Screen'—the same idea really.

It is in this context that we can say that Sir Olaf Caroe used the circumstance of India' s partition to help launch Pakistan on a 50 year career as the vehicle of America's practice of offshore balancing against Indian hegemony in the South Asia region. While this outcome was not necessarily Caroe's overt objective, he did mean to make Pakistan the fulcrum of his strategy to protect the "wells of power" and to contain Soviet Russia and he did mean to sideline Jawaharlal Nehru's India.

An End and a Beginning in South Asia: India as Regional Hegemon and US Ally?

For roughly 50 years, the US destabilized the South Asia region by acting as an offshore balancer. Its actions allowed Pakistan to realize its goal of "parity" with its much bigger neighbor and to try to best that neighbor in several wars. With the end of the Cold War (1989), the Soviet withdrawal from Afghanistan (1989) and the collapse of the Soviet Union (1991), little was left to justify the US acting as an offshore balancer in South Asia. By President Clinton's second term the US saw no need for a special relationship with Pakistan. As Strobe Talbott, Clinton's Deputy Secretary of State, makes clear in his account of his protracted negotiations with India's External Affairs Minister, Jaswant Singh, US diplomacy with India during the Clinton years was deliberately coordinated by knowledgeable professionals. "It was," he says, "an extraordinarily collegial process, and it helped keep to a minimum the personal backbiting, bureaucratic warfare, and mischievous leaks that too often accompany policy-making."[104]

Talbott's procedure and attitude capture the essence of deliberative coordination. In preparation for extended discussions with India's External Affairs Minister, Jaswant Singh, about nuclear proliferation Talbott tells us that he "... convened a series of meetings with the team that had been working on India and Pakistan the past several years, a mixture of regionalists and functionalists from the key departments and agencies of the US government. The core members from State were Bob Einhorn and Rick Inderfurth, along with Rick's senior adviser, Matt Daley; Walter Andersen, a career South Asia Analyst in the Bureau of Intelligence and Research; and Phil Goldberg, a versatile foreign service officer on my staff who had the unenviable job of meshing the many moving parts of the process and managing my role in it. . . . These gatherings became a regular, often daily feature of our lives for the next two years. . . ."[105]

We see a new era in Indo-US relations beginning with President Clinton's very successful visit to India in March 2000. Notoriously, the President spent five days in India and five hours in Pakistan. His visit to India was widely acclaimed and much celebrated, his visit to Pakistan, tense and censorious. Strobe Talbott, Deputy Secretary of State for most of the Clinton years, put it this way: "Clinton's visit to India—the first by an American president in twenty-two years—was, by any standard and in almost very respect, one of the most successful trips ever, not just because of the rhapsodic reception he received, but because it marked a pivotal moment in an important and vexed relationship."[106] The pivotal moment was marked by Prime Minister Atal Bihari Vajpayee when, in his reply to Clinton's widely acclaimed speech to the Indian parliament and nation, he referred to the US and India as "natural allies."[107]

The president's trip to Pakistan stands in stark contrast. Although 9/11 was 18 months in the future, Al Qaeda attacks on US embassies in East Africa and the presumed presence of Osama bin Laden in Taliban-ruled Afghanistan, led to Secret Service concern about a threat to the President's safety. As a result, Air Force One leapfrogged ahead to Muscat, Oman. Clinton traveled into Islamabad aboard an unmarked Gulfstream executive jet with another Gulfstream executive jet painted with Air Force One's colors and the words "United States of America," leading the way. The idea was to deceive terrorists armed with surface-to-air missiles. In a 15 minute speech to Pakistan's parliament broadcast live Clinton told his national audience that Pakistan "can fulfill its destiny as a beacon of democracy in the Muslim world. . . ." His message in private to General Pervez Musharaff, who had recently overthrown Nawaz Sharif's democratically elected government, was different: return to democracy; show restraint in Kashmir; exert pressure on terrorist groups; and help in capturing bin Laden.[108] The events of Clinton's visit to South Asia in March 2000 signaled that the US now recognized Indian hegemony in the region.

The events of September 11, 2001, by restoring Pakistan to front line status in a "war against terrorism," challenged the Clinton administration's policy of treating Pakistan as a failing and an incipient pariah state[109] and recognizing India as the hegemonic state in South Asia. 9/11 also challenged the corollary of these policies, the Vajpayee government's decision to recognize the US as a "natural ally."

Soon after 9/11, in anticipation of waging war in Afghanistan, the Bush administration restored Pakistan to its role as a front line state. As we have seen, Pakistan responded overnight to an American ultimatum to abandon its support for the Taliban regime in Afghanistan and its accommodation of Osama bin Laden's al Qaeda in Afghanistan and to join America's "war on terrorism." The US rewarded the Musharaff government with large scale military and economic assistance.[110] Because the amount and quality of the military equipment went well beyond what was needed for the war on terrorism, many analysts in India, the US and elsewhere saw the massive military aid to Pakistan as rekindling an arms race with India. From the perspective of this Prologue, it looked as though the US was resuming its role as an offshore balancer in South Asia.

But there was a difference; this time the US was trying to enlist India as well as Pakistan in a common cause, the "war against terrorism."[111] The US, according to Ashley Tellis, a quasi-official voice located somewhere between the world of career professionals and president's men,[112] "would invest the energy and resources to enable India—*the pre-eminent regional state* . . . to secure as trouble free an ascent to *great power status* as possible."[113] (*emphasis added*)

Tellis was trying to persuade India to join Pakistan as an ally of the US, the world's only super-power.[114] In the language of Stephen Walt, India was being asked to bandwagon[115] with the US, i.e., to gain the benefits and prestige that go with joining the most powerful and, putatively, the winning side. Another grand strategy that many Indian policy-makers are considering is for India to balance against what they perceive to be a unilateralist and imperial US. Whether India should bandwagon with the US or balance against the US depends in part on the answer to another question. Should India regard China as more of a threat than the US? If so, to bandwagon with the US is not only to join what appears to be the winning side but also to balance against an increasingly powerful and allegedly dangerous Asian neighbor, China.[116] A third grand strategy for India to consider is to work with like-minded actors (such as the EU generally and France and Germany in particular; the six nation China, Russia and Central Asia states Shanghai Cooperation Organization; Brazil; and South Africa) to promote a multipolar balance of power. Such a strategy would be consistent with India's non-alignment policy during the Cold War era and with the Clinton administration's orientation to the South Asia region.

In the spring of 2005, New Delhi seemed to be taking with a grain of salt Washington's blandishments about being a "pre-eminent regional state" and a "great power"[117] and its offers of access to what the US labeled "advanced defense equipment."[118] Sometimes India seemed inclined to bandwagon with the US, sometimes to balance against it and sometimes to act on its own in a multipolar world.

India acting on its own hasn't always suited the Bush administration's global agenda. When Secretary of State Condoleezza Rice visited New Delhi on March 16, 2005, she made it clear that America's global security interests took priority over India's efforts to become more energy independent and to do so in ways that encouraged regional cooperation. According to the April 2005 number of *India Review*, a publication of the Embassy of India,

Washington, D.C., "The two sides differed over their approach to Iran, with Secretary Rice expressing her country's concern over India's move to source natural gas from Iran through a proposed $5 billion pipeline that would run through Pakistan." Not only would the gas pipeline project help India meet its increasingly severe need for additional sources of energy[119] but also it would break with five decades of Indian and Pakistani intransigence about regional economic and security cooperation. Indian and Pakistani inter-dependence and mutual benefit on the gas pipe line project would require cooperation and reduce the risk of regional war between the nuclear armed neighbors.[120]

Since its inception in 1985, the South Asian Association for Regional Cooperation (SAARC) has belied its name and fallen short of its purpose, regional cooperation. As India's Foreign Secretary, Shyam Saran, put it in March 2005 on the eve of the pipeline agreement, ". . . SAARC is still largely a consultative body . . . (it) has shied away from undertaking even a single collaborative project in its 20 years of existence. In fact there is a deep resistance to doing anything that could be collaborative." The Iran-Pakistan-India pipeline project and other planned pipeline projects such as those linking India to Turkestan through Afghanistan and Pakistan and to Myanmar through Bangladesh give promise of widening circles of mutual benefit and regional interdependence.

But there is a fly in the ointment. According to some president's men in the Bush administration Iran is a hostile country, an "axis of evil" country, a country that kept US citizens hostage for 79 days, a country that seeks nuclear weapons[121] and to enhance its power in the Middle East and Central Asia, a country that threatens our close ally, Israel, a country that is home for Muslim extremists and state sponsored terrorism, a country that is against "us" in a global war against terrorism.[122] The goal of US policy for some president's men in Bush's second term, and that seemed to include Secretary of State, Condoleezza Rice as well as UN representative John Bolton, appeared to be to punish Iran, perhaps to change its regime. Some professionals read the situation differently. They saw a pipeline agreement as not only contributing to regional stability in South Asia but also to strengthening democracy and reform in Iran.

At the end of June 2005, the Indian and US Defence Ministers, Pranab Mukerjee and Donald Rumsfeld, signed "a new framework for the US-India defence relationship for the next ten years." The agreement was designed to strengthen "our countries' security, reinforce our strategic partnership, and build greater understanding between our defence establishments."[123] And on July 18, 2005 and March 2, 2006 Prime Minister Manmohan Singh and President George W. Bush signed historic agreements that eventuated in December 2006 in the US India Peaceful Atomic Energy Cooperation Act, or Hyde Act. Even though India was not a signatory of the NPT [Nuclear Proliferation Treaty] and had tested and possessed nuclear weapons, the Hyde Act opened the way for India to gain access to nuclear fuel and technology.[124]

Did this effort to bandwagon with the world's sole super-power preclude India from moving ahead with the Iran—and other—gas pipeline projects? At the time, nothing was said about India's pipeline negotiations. Pranab Mukerjee, India's then Minister of Defence, went out of his way in the context of signing the ten year defence relationship agreement with Washington to remind the US that India would continue its long-standing arms purchase relationship with Russia. And the Indo-US Joint Statements of July 18, 2005 and March 2, 2006 were silent on the subject of India's efforts to negotiate gas pipeline agreements.

In August 2005 when Prime Minister Manmohan Singh visited Afghan President Hamid Karzai in Kabul, India was able to practice a grand strategy of balancing in a multipolar world. It was the first visit by an Indian Prime Minister in 29 years. The President and the Prime Minister not only agreed to implement both the Iran and Turkmenistan gas pipeline projects but also that Afghanistan, a country closely tied to the US and the EU, should join SAARC (South Asia Association for Regional Cooperation). At a joint press conference Karzai "said he was . . . glad to have had the same positive response from President Musharaff of Pakistan" as he had from Prime Minister Manmohan Singh of

India."[125] India and Pakistan seemed to be poised to cooperate on the economic and security future of Afghanistan.

By November 2007 it was clear that India's effort simultaneously to bandwagon with the sole super power and to balance against it was in trouble. Negotiations to consummate a "strategic partnership" with the US via a nuclear agreement were stalled; the odds on salvaging it seemed low. On October 17, Prakash Karat, CPI-M Politbureau member and spokesperson for the left parties supporting Congress Prime Minister Manmohan Singh's coalition government, declared that "It is inconceivable that a government supported by the Left would allow the Indo-US nuclear deal to go through because it's part of a larger strategic alliance [with that country]."[126] The nuclear agreement, Karat charged, would make "India subservient to US foreign policy." On October 12 Sonia Gandhi, the Congress party president, ended months of speculation about whether she would support the Prime Minister's plan to counter Karat's threat by calling a mid-term election. "We are not," she told the country, "in favour of early elections. . . I don't think the Left is being unreasonable."[127] In so as the nuclear agreement was meant to establish a "strategic partnership" between India and the US, that partnership appeared dead for in the short to medium if not the for long term.

By the end of 2007, there seemed to be a good prospect that India's policy of using "pipelines of power" to promote interdependence and cooperation in South Asia might successfully challenge Sir Olaf Caroe's "wells of power" as the dominant geo-political strategy in South Asia. If "pipelines of power" could displace "wells of power" as Pakistan's as well as India's orienting strategy it seemed possible that the 50 year reign of "offshore balancing" by the US and its consequence, regional instability, could be brought to a close.[128]

Acknowledgements

The transition from *The Regional Imperative* to *Making US Foreign Policy Toward South Asia* could not have been accomplished without the assiduous editorial attention of Jeannie Koops-Elson to new and old authors' manuscripts. Her editorial skills were only exceeded by her positive attitude and quotidian diplomacy.

We thank Mr. Ashok Mittal and his editorial staff at Concept Publishing Company for their care and patience in bringing the project of a new, enlarged edition to fruition.

NOTES AND REFERENCES

1. Our study was published along with the National Commission's *Report* in June 1975 as Appendix V of Volume 7 by the Superintendent of Documents, US Government Printing Office, Washington D.C.
2. Arthur M. Schlesinger, Jr., *The Imperial Presidency* (Boston, MA: Houghton Mifflin Company, 1973).
3. Johnson was in the grip of a Cold War world view that pictured a global zero-sum struggle between a free world and a communist world. It led him to pursue the then hegemonic containment policy and to invent a corollary, the theory/metaphor of falling dominos: if Vietnam fell, other countries in South East Asia and in neighboring regions would fall to "Communism." That fear led the Johnson administration to, in effect, resume France's colonial war against the Vietnamese nationalism of Ho Chi Min. In retrospect, it seems clear that what a handful of knowledgeable career professionals and area experts said at the time was true, Ho Chi Min's anti-colonial nationalism was wary of rather than receptive to the embrace of the Communist regimes in China and the Soviet Union.
4. The single document that best illustrated suspicion of Soviet aspirations and how to respond to them was George Kennan's famous *Long Telegram* of 1946. The *Long Telegram* articulating what became known as the containment policy was perhaps the most cited and most influential statement of the early years of the Cold War.

   The essence of Kennan's telegram was published in *Foreign Affairs* in 1947 as *The Sources of Soviet Conduct* and circulated everywhere. The article was signed by "X" although everyone in the know knew that the authorship was Kennan's.

   Kennan's containment policy article makes clear that a professional can be instrumental in the practice of imperative coordination.
5. Following the resignation of Vice-President Spiro Agnew in 1973, Gerald Ford was nominated as Vice-President by President Richard Nixon and approved by both houses of Congress (not just the Senate, as is the procedure for Cabinet members, Supreme Court justices and most other federal officials) in keeping with the provisions of the 25th Amendment to the Constitution. Ford had been Minority Leader of the House of Representatives when Nixon chose him to be Vice-President.
6. Wittingly or unwittingly, President Reagan formally agreed to and informally acquiesced in illegal actions by presidents' men working in his National Security Staff. Emblematic was the colorful figure of Oliver

North, a rogue operative working out of a White House basement office. Reagan survived two investigations in part because North's boss, President Reagan's National Security Advisor, Admiral John M. Poindexter, fell on his sword by testifying that he had "... deliberately withheld information from President Reagan (with respect to illegal arms shipments to Iran and illegal payments to the Nicaraguan contras)." He did so he said because "... I wanted the President to have some deniability so that he would be protected."

Unlike Richard Nixon and Lyndon Johnson before him, Ronald Reagan escaped the ignominy of being driven from office, in part because Admiral Poindexter and Oliver North protected him, in part because he steadfastly maintained that he "repeatedly told his aids to obey the law and he was unaware of their criminal acts." Citation from ex-president Reagan's seven hour videotaped deposition made at Poindexter's request at his trial before the US Court of Appeals for the District of Columbia.

See *Final Report of the Independent Counsel for Iran/Contra Matters. Volume 1: Investigations and Prosecutions, Lawrence E. Walsh, Independent Counsel*, August 4, 1993, Washington, D.C.: United States Court of Appeals for the District of Columbia Circuit, Division for the Purpose of Appointing Independent Counsel, Division No. 86-6. Quote from Part IV. Investigations and Cases: The National Security Council Staff Chapter 3. U.S. John M. Poindexter, p. 105. Poindexter destroyed the only existing presidential Finding that was intended to authorize retroactively CIA involvement in the November 1985 Hawk shipment to Iran. Oliver North witnessed the destruction but, in an effort to protect his boss, Poindexter, denied he knew it was a presidential finding. North's testimony on this point was not believed by the Court.

7. The term "back burner" and its relation to the conduct of US policy is elaborated in Lloyd I. Rudolph, "Back to the Back Burner; India's Role in South Asia—A United States Perspective," in Vernon L.B. Mendis, Editor, *India's Role in South Asia* (Colombo: Bandaranaike Centre for International Studies, S.W.R.D. Bandaranaike National Memorial Foundation, 1992), pp. 29-41.
8. We take the term "offshore balancer" from John Mearsheimer's, *The Tragedy of Great Power Politics* (New York: W.W. Norton, 2002).

   Michel C. Desch shows *inter alia* in *When the Third World Matters: Latin America and United States Grand Strategy* (Baltimore, MD: Johns Hopkins University Press, 1993), how important a condition it was for the US becoming a world power that no European great power was successful in checking US hegemony in the Americas by being an offshore balancer.
9. See Lloyd I. Rudolph and Susanne Hoeber Rudolph, "The United States, India and South Asia," "Table 3. Indicators of Regional Hegemony: Leading-Country Shares of Regional Aggregates," in John P. Lewis and Valeriana Kallab, editors, *U.S. Foreign Policy and the Third World, Agenda 1983* (New York: Praeger Publishers, 1983), p. 107. Table 3

compares five regions, South Asia, the Middle East, Latin America, Africa (south of the Sahara) and Southeast Asia, on country proportion of six regional aggregates, GNP, Population, Armed Forces, Military Expenditure, Installed Energy, and World Trade (Exports and Imports). India's proportions of its region's aggregates range from 63 percent and 68 percent of World Trade and Armed Forces to 87 percent, 81 percent. 79 percent, 76 percent of Installed Energy, Military Expenditures, GNP and Population. India's proportion of regional aggregates exceeds those of the leading countries in the other four regions by two to four times. We conclude that, indicated by objective determinants of regional hegemony, India was—and is—more likely to be the hegemon in South Asia than Iran or Egypt in the Middle East; Brazil, Mexico or Argentina in Latin America; Nigeria or South Africa in Africa; or Indonesia, Philippines or Thailand in Southeast Asia.

10. For a more elaborate account of how the models were formulated and applied in the context of the coordination of complexity see the Introduction, "Part III Defining Coordination, A. Imperative and Deliberative Coordination of Complexity," pp. 10-18.
11. See Introduction, footnote 7 for the scholars who contributed to the first and second waves of the bureaucratic politics literature. Graham Allison's second wave study of the Cuban missile crisis, *The Essence of Decision*, was particularly influential in the formulation of our models and in guiding the case studies included in this volume.
12. For our critique and reformulation of Weber's view of bureaucracy see our "Authority and Power in Bureaucratic and Patrimonial Administration: A Revisionist Interpretation of Weber on Bureaucracy," *World Politics*, Vol. XXXI, No. 2 (January 1979).
13. We have in mind Allison's Model II where bureaucratic politics is featured. His Model III features conflicts arising out of standard operating procedures.
14. For more on why and how we reject the unified national and/or rational actor model see Part II of the Introduction, "The Present Context of Organizational Change," where, *inter alia*, we discuss Graham Allison's *The Essence of Decision: Explaining the Cuban Missile Crisis* (Boston: Little Brown, 1971); I.M. Destler, *Presidents, Bureaucrats and Foreign Policy* (Princeton, NJ: Princeton University Press, 1972); and Morton Halperin, *Bureaucratic Politics and Foreign Policy* (Washington, D.C.: Brookings Institution, 1974). We recognize that much organizational analysis has flowed over the dam since these books were written and critiqued but, for our purposes here, they stand the test of time in establishing the "bureaucratic politics" framework for our models of imperative and deliberative coordination.
15. Here we have in mind the world of "neo-realist" theory where the work of Kenneth Waltz, *Theory of International Politics* (Reading, Mass.: Addison-Wesley, 1979); John J. Mearsheimer, *The Tragedy of Great Power Politics* (New York: W.W. Norton, 2003), and Stephen M. Walt, *The Origins of Alliances* (Ithaca, NY: Cornell University Press, 1987) appears.

Mearsheimer's recent qualification of his neo-realist position in *Great Power Politics* does not diminish the state-centric orientation of his analysis. For a recent critique of Mearsheimer's position that helps to explain why India has not become a regional hegemon see Colin Elman, "Extending Offensive Realism: The Louisiana Purchase and America's Rise to Regional Hegemony," *American Political Science Review*, Vol. 98, No. 1 (November 2004).

16. The texts for these two views of the presidency can be found in *The Federalist Papers*, Isaac Kramnick, ed. (Penguin Books, 1987). For Hamilton see particularly Federalist Paper 70 and for Madison Federalist Paper 51.
17. Richard Neustadt, *Presidential Power* (New York: John Wiley, 1960), p. 9.
18. See Barry Karl, *Executive Reorganization and Reform in the New Deal: The Genesis of Administrative Reform* (Cambridge, MA: Harvard University Press, 1963).

    In the 25 years between Louis Brownlow's image of six anonymous assistants who were to be the president's eyes and ears and a National Security Council under Henry Kissinger's direction and control, the president's helpers had morphed into president's men, the "us" who confronted the rest of the executive branch "them."
19. For an account of the Act by a participant in the process see Carroll French Miles, *The Office of the Secretary of Defense, 1947-1953* (New York: Garland, 1988). Athan G. Theoharis argues that the 1947 National Security Act provided the slippery slope that led to the imperial presidency. See his *The Truman Presidency: The Origins of the Imperial Presidency and the National Security State* (Standfordville, NY: Earl M. Coleman Enterprises, Inc., Publishers, 1979).
20. For a critical account of the National Security Council's growing role in the making and conduct of U.S. foreign policy as illustrated in the Iran-Contra affair and its subsequent investigation by the Tower Commission, two Congressional Committees and an independent counsel see Harold H. Koh, *The National Security Constitution: Sharing Power After the Iran-Contra Affair* (New Haven, CT: Yale University Press, 1990).
21. See Hugh Heclo, *A Government of Strangers: Executive Politics in Washington* (Washington, D.C.: The Brookings Institution, 1977), particularly Ch 1. "People in Government," and Ch 3. "Political Executives: A Government of Strangers," pp. 1-19; 84-112, for a sophisticated account of the "us *vs* them" version of the president's and the president's men relationship to the departments and agencies. These constitute the baronies that presidents are enjoined by the Constitution to administer in conjunction with a Congress that has constitutional authority to authorize, appropriate and oversee the departments and agencies of the executive branch.
22. See by contrast Forrest McDonald's account of the "clerk" view of the president (i.e., the constitutional injunction that the president "shall faithfully execute the laws") in his *The American Presidency; An Intellectual*

History (Lawrence, KA: University Press of Kansas, 1994). Ch. 12. "President and Administration", pp. 315-45.

Edward S. Corwin speaks of the president as clerk and of an "invitation to struggle" with the Congress, particularly over control of war and foreign policy in Corwin's *The President: Office and Powers*, 5th Revised Edition by Randall Bland *et al.* (New York: New York University Press, 1984).

Harold Seidman and Robert Gilmour illustrate the struggle in *Politics, Position and Power: From the Positive to the Regulatory State*. Fourth Edition (New York: Oxford University Press, 1986).

23. The characterization is from I. M. Destler, *Presidents, Bureaucrats, and Foreign Policy* (Princeton, NJ: Princeton University Press, 1972), p. 87.
24. Language from Morton Halperin, *Bureaucratic Politics and Foreign Policy* (Washington, D.C.: The Brookings Institution, 1974). Chapter 4, "The Presidential Interest." The blocked quotation is from *The Regional Imperative*, p. 12.
25. For the "effectiveness trap" see James C. Thomson, "How Could Vietnam Happen?" *The Atlantic*, 1968.
26. See Irving Janis, *Group Think* (Boston: Houghton Mifflin, 1982), 2nd edition. *The 9/11 Commission Report* gave considerable weight to this term in explaining how collective misperceptions and mistakes happened.
27. The view that the US forces sent to invade and occupy Iraq would be treated as liberators and greeted with flowers was something of a leitmotif of the Bush administration. Paul Wolfowitz, Deputy Secretary of Defense, was, perhaps, its most articulate spokesman. See http://www.washingtonpost.com/wp-dyn/articles/A25454-2004Dec1.html
28. Quoted in Henry Raymont, "Kennedy Library Documents, Opened to Two Scholars, Illuminate Policies on Cuba. . .," *The New York Times*, August 17, 1970, p. 16.
29. The Cuban missile crisis may be the most studied event in the conduct of foreign policy, starting with Graham Allison's *The Essence of Decision* (Boston, MA: Little Brown, 1968). Retrospective analyses that include the views of Soviet and US actors can be found in Raymond Garthhoff, *Reflections on the Cuban Missile Crisis*, rev. ed. (Washington, D.C.: Brookings Institution, 1987, 1989), and James G. Blight, *On the Brink: Americans and Soviets Reexamine the Cuban Missile Crisis* (New York: Hill and Wang, 1989).

    For the best account of how the Kennedy administration made foreign policy in response to China's invasion of India in 1962 see John Kenneth Galbraith, *Ambassador's Journal* (Boston, MA: Houghton Mifflin, 1969).
30. Neustadt, *Presidential Power*, p. 9.
31. There was an alternative discourse to "war" available about the 9/11 attacks. Writing in *The New Yorker* as early as September 24, 2001, Hendrick Hertzberg, for one, argued that Al Qaeda was a non-state actor and should be treated accordingly. According to Hertzberg, treating the al Qaeda attacks as acts of war "is a category mistake. The metaphor of war—and it is more metaphor than description—ascribes to the

perpetrators a dignity they do not merit, a status they cannot claim, and a strength they do not possess. Worse," he continues, "it points to a set of responses that could prove futile and counter productive (such as going to war against Iraq in March 2003) . . . (A) more useful metaphor than war is crime. The terrorists of September 11 are outlaws within a global polity . . . they do not constitute or control a state. . . .Their status and numbers are such that the task of dealing with them should be viewed as a police matter, of the most urgent kind. As with all criminal fugitives, the essential job is to find out who and where they are."

32. Perhaps the most clear expression of this view can be found in John C. Yoo's September 25, 2001 memorandum for Timothy Flanigan, Deputy Counsel to the President, entitled "The President's Constitutional Authority to Conduct Military Operations Against Terrorists and Nations Supporting Them." As against the provision of Article I, section 8 giving Congress exclusive power to declare war, Yoo wrote, "that the President has broad constitutional power to use military force. . . . The President has the constitutional power not only to retaliate against any person, organization, or State *suspected* of involvement in terrorist attacks on the United States, but also against foreign states *suspected* of harboring or supporting such organizations. Finally, the President may deploy military force pre-emptively against terrorist organizations or the States that harbor or support them, whether or not they can be linked to the specific terrorist incidents of September 11." Karen Greenberg and Joshua L. Dratel, eds., *The Torture Papers: The Road to Abu Ghraib* (New York: Cambridge University Press, 2003). Memo 1, p. 3. *My emphasis.*
33. According to Leslie Stahl's interview with Paul O'Neill on January 11, 2004, after Ron Suskind's book, *The Price of Loyalty*, had appeared, O'Neill thought the President's trillions of dollars tax cuts for the very rich "should have been the end. After 9/11 and the war in Afghanistan, the budget deficit was growing. So at a meeting with the vice-president (Dick Cheney) after the mid-term elections in 2002, Suskind writes that O'Neill argued against a second round of tax cuts. . . . Cheney . . . says 'You know, Paul, Reagan proved that deficits don't matter. We won the mid-term elections, this is our due'. . . . O'Neill is speechless. . . . 'It was not just about not wanting the tax cut. It was about how to use the nation's resources to improve the condition of our society', says O'Neill. 'And I thought the weight of working on Social Security and fundamental tax reform was a lot more important than a tax reduction'." Leslie Stahl interview, *CBS News*, January 11, 2004.
34. *CBS News*, Lesley Stahl interview with Paul O'Neill, January 11, 2004.
35. Ron Suskind, *The Price of Loyalty: George W. Bush, the White House, and the Education of Paul O'Neill* (New York: Simon and Shuster, 2004).
36. Bob Woodward, *Plan of Attack* (New York: Simon Shuster, 2004).
37. The Working Group Report numbered 26 in Greenberg and Dratel, eds., *The Torture Papers*, was designated "Draft" and classified by Secretary of Defense Donald Rumsfeld. It was based on Assistant Attorney General, U.S., Department of Justice, Jay S. Bybee's memorandum to

Alberto R. Gonzales, Counsel to the President, of August 1, 2002, entitled "Standards of Conduct for Interrogation under 18 U.S.C., paras 2340-2340A."

On March 1, 2005 the American Civil Liberties Union (ACLU) filed a suit in a federal court in Illinois charging that Secretary of Defense Rumsfeld bears direct responsibility for the torture and abuse of detainees in U.S. military custody. The suit seeks a court declaration that Secretary Rumsfeld violated the U.S. Constitution and international laws.

38. John Yoo was emblematic of Bush administration presidents' men. According to Tim Golden, Yoo, a 34-year old Bush appointee had a "glittering resume and a reputation as perhaps the most intellectually aggressive among a small group of legal scholars who had challenged what they saw as the United States' excessive deference to international law." Yoo was on leave from the University of California Law School and located in the Justice Department's Office of Legal Counsel. Tim Golden, "Threats and Responses: Tough Justice; After Terror, a Secret Rewriting of Military Law," *New York Times*, October 24, 2004.
39. Memo 8. "Draft Decision Memorandum for the President on the Applicability of the Geneva Convention to the Conflict in Afghanistan," in Greenberg and Dratel, *The Torture Papers*, p. 122ff.
40. Memo 8. Powell, January 26, 2002, ". . . Applicability of the Geneva Convention. . .," in Greenberg and Dratel, eds., *The Torture Papers*, p. 122ff.
41. Anthony Lewis, "Making Torture Legal," *The New York Times*, July 15, 2004.
42. Seymour Hersh tells us that "cabal" is a self-designation: "They call themselves, self-mockingly, the Cabal, a small cluster of policy advisers who were based in the Pentagon's Office of Special Plans. In the debate leading up to the Iraq war, their operation, which was conceived by Paul Wolfowitz, brought about crucial change of direction in the American intelligence community. These advisers and analysts, who began their work in the days after September 11, 2001, produced a skein of intelligence reviews that helped shape public opinion and American policy toward Iraq." Seymour M. Hersh, *Chain of Command: The Road from 9/11 to Abu Ghraib* (New York: Harper Collins, 2004), p. 207.

    Paul O'Neill according to Ron Suskind spoke of a "praetorian guard" around Dick Cheney and Colin Powell, according to Bob Woodward, of a "Gestapo office" directed by Cheney that ran from the Pentagon to the vice-president's office.
43. The narrative and language of the story about the use of imperative coordination to make policy for prisoners taken as a result of the war in Afghanistan—follows closely the account in Golden, "Threats and Responses. . . ."

    For the characterization of David Addington see Golden, "Threats and Responses. . .," p. 3.
44. Golden, "Threats and Responses. . .," p. 4 and 5.

45. The order drew immediate and intense criticism. Many saw the order as a way to escape the standards of the criminal justice system: the president or his representatives would define the crimes, set the rules for trial, and choose the judges, juries and appellate panels. Some compared the tribunals to the English crown's Star Chamber proceedings that were abolished in 1641 as a result of the English civil war. Many of the Pentagon's uniformed lawyers in the respective services' judge advocate branches saw the tribunals as destructive of the due process standards and defendants rights embedded in the Uniform Code of Military Justice.
46. The order allowed the military to detain and prosecute any foreigner whom the president or his representative determined to have "engaged in, aided or abetted, or conspired to commit" terrorism. "There was no mention of public trials, no right to remain silent, no presumption of innocence. . . . Guilt did not necessarily have to be proven beyond reasonable doubt and a death sentence could be imposed even with a divided verdict." Golden, "Threats and Responses. . .," p. 6.
47. I focus on nuclear weapons in part because it simplifies without weakening the story about the Bush administration's self-destructive use of imperative coordination. I recognize but put aside consideration of the Bush administration's sweeping claims about Iraq possessing biological and chemical weapons of mass destruction.
48. For Condoleezza Rice's "smoking gun" quote see www.cnn.com/2003/US/01/10/wbr.smoking gun/ Wolf Blitzer interviewing Condoleezza Rice, Friday, January 10, 2003. For President Bush's use, see www.whitehouse.gov/news/releases/2003/01/20030128-19.htm Office of the Press Secretary.
49. The top secret "Downing Street Memo" for Prime Minister Tony Blair dated July 23, 2002 and published in a front page article by Matthew Rycroft in *The Sunday Times* on May 1, 2005, revealed that the Bush administration had decided to use "military action" to remove Saddam Hussein. Military action was to be "justified by the conjunction of terrorism and WMD." But, the memo went to say, "the intelligence and facts were being fixed around the policy."
50. Wilson, "What I Didn't Find in Africa," *New York Times*, July 6, 2003.
51. See chapter V. "Who Lied to Whom?" in Seymour Hersh, *Chain of Command.*
52. According to Wilson, Niger's uranium business consists of two mines, Somair and Cominak, which are run by a consortium of foreign interests. If the government wanted to remove uranium from a mine, it would have to notify the consortium, which in turn is strictly monitored by the International Atomic Energy Agency (IAEA) and by the Niger government whose chain of command for uranium sales includes the Minister for Mines, the Prime Minister and the President. Wilson, *New York Times*, July 6, 2003.
53. Wilson, *New York Times*, July 6, 2003.
54. Wilson, *New York Times*, July 6, 2003.

55. It is a criminal offense under the Intelligence Identification Protection Act of 1982 to intentionally reveal the identity of a clandestine CIA official. Novak said the high level officials used the word "operative;" an operative is not an "analyst," the word used for CIA employees who are not undercover. Analysts are not clandestine employees but operatives might be. At the time of this writing, a Justice Department Special Prosecutor, Patrick J. Fitzgerald, was looking into whether or not a crime had been committed.
56. Mark Kleiman writing in "Open Source Politics: United States Politics," on September 2, 2003, said that "The Valerie Plame affair has all the elements needed for a major, Administration-shaking scandal: Clear violations of law, undertaken by high officials, for discreditable motives, and with significant damage to the national security."

    Novak's July 14, 2003 column carried the assertion that Wilson had been recruited for the mission at the instigation of his wife, Valerie Plame. That assertion was sourced to "two senior administration officials," and was accompanied by the un-sourced assertion that "Wilson never worked for the CIA, but his wife, Valerie Plame, is an Agency operative on weapons of mass destruction."

    Wilson publicly has said that he thought Carl Rove, the president's political adviser, was behind the effort to discredit him via his wife and should, in accordance with the President's pledge to fire anyone involved in leaking in the Wilson case, be fired. *MSNBC Today Show*, July 14, 2005. http://msnbc.msn.com/id/8568216
57. Hersh, *Chain of Command*, pp. 207-08.
58. FactCheck.org, "Bush's '16 Words' on Iraq & Uranium," July 26, 2004. Modified August 23, 2004.
59. McNeil/Lehrer Productions, "False Claims?" July 20, 2004.
60. FactCheck.org, Bush's "16 Words. . . ."

    Seymour Hersh reports that "George Tenet clearly was ambivalent about the information in early October (2002), he intervened to prevent the President from referring to Niger in a speech in Cincinnati. But Tenet then seemed to give up the fight, and Saddam Hussein's desire for uranium from Niger soon became part of the Administration's public case for going to war." Hersh, *Chain of Command*, p. 233.
61. Hersh, *Chain of Command*, pp. 207-08; 223-34.
62. For the best account of the "Straussians" see Anne Norton, *Leo Strauss and the Politics of American Empire* (New Haven: Yale University Press, 2004), particularly Ch. 11. "The Sicilian Expedition," an allusion to Thucydides' account in Books VI-VIII of Athens' ill-fated effort to conquer Syracuse.

    Norton tells us that the nuclear strategist, Albert Wohlstetter, like the eminent political theorist, Leo Strauss, a professor in the University of Chicago's Department of Political Science, "offered the Straussians an ally in the field of international relations. He marked the possibility that one might move out of the academy and acquire other forms of influence.

He had taught Paul Wolfowitz. . . . Wolfowitz was part of a cohort who came to Strauss, and to Chicago, from Allan Bloom. That group included . . . Abram Shulsky, who was thought—at least by the students—to be the cleverest of the cohort." Norton explains that the Straussians abandoned Wohlstetter's conventional geo-politics of deterrence for ". . . an enthusiasm for empire and a determination to exploit American imperial hegemony. . . . This is the program of the Project for a New American Century. . . . The aim (of the Project) is to make the world in America's image. . .," p. 183 and p. 186.

63. For characterizations of Douglas Feith see Chris Suellentrop, "What has the Pentagon's third man done wrong? Everything," *Slate*, Posted May 20, 2004, and Jeffrey Goldberg, "What Douglas Feith knew, and when he knew it," *The New Yorker*, May 9, 2005.

"Why is Feith involved with all these foul-ups?" Suellentrop asks. "How could one man be so consistently in error? Nearly every critique of the Pentagon's plan for Iraq occupation blames the blinders imposed by ideology. For example, . . . Feith intentionally excluded experts with experience in postwar nation-building, out of fear that their pessimistic, worst-case scenarios would leak and damage the case for war." Another example is Feith's reaction to complaints by military Judge Advocate General lawyers about new interrogation rules (at Guantanamo Bay, Cuba). "'They said he had a dismissive, if not derisive, attitude toward the Geneva Conventions', Scott Horton, a lawyer who was approached by six outraged JAG officer last year, told the Chicago Tribune. 'One of them said he calls it (the Geneva Convention) law in the service of terror'."

64. Hersh, *Chain of Command*, pp. 221-22.
65. Hersh, *Chain of Command*, p. 222.
66. Hersh, *Chain of Command*, p. 225.
67. Hersh, *Chain of Command*, p. 228.
68. Quoted from Thomas E. Ricks, "U.S. Troop Level in Iraq to Grow," *Washington Post*, December 1, 2004. http://www.washingtonpost.com/wpdyn/articles/A25454-2004Dec1.html
69. This account draws on the transcript of an interview with James Fallows on the PBS program, *Frontline*, posted February 26, 2004. http://www.pbs.org/wgbh/pages/frontline/shows/invasion/interviews/fallows.html
70. Fallows, *Frontline*, February 26, 2004.
71. John Kerry claimed in the first and second 2004 presidential debate that Chief of the Army Staff, General Eric Shinseki, was retired for saying before the invasion of Iraq that more troops were needed than the administration was planning to send. As we have seen, Shinseki wasn't prematurely retired but he was prematurely made into a lame duck Chief of the Army Staff. The *Washington Times* reported that Shinseki was going to retire on April 19, 2002. His retirement date was June 11, 2003. FactCheck.org, October 9, 2004. Modified November 8, 2004.

72. *Inter alia* he had extensive experience in the mid-1990s with occupation requirements as commander of the US Army in Europe and the allied land forces in Central Europe.
73. This account of General Shinseki's experience with occupation forces in Bosnia and Kosovo and of the Army War College study of occupations is based on Fallows, *Frontline*, posted February 26, 2004. http://www.pbs.org/wgbhlpages/frontline/shows/invasion/interviews/fallows.html
74. *Washington Post*, July 28, 2002.
75. *Washington Post*, July 28, 2002.
76. Hersh, *Chain of Command*, 182.
77. *Washington Post*, August 1, 2002. Condoleezza Rice, the National Security Adviser, who should have been in a position to mediate the dispute between the Pentagon civilians on the one side and the top military and the State Department (Colin Powell and Richard Armitage, the Secretary and Deputy Secretary of State) on the other was handicapped by the absence during these critical months of a senior Iraq expert on her staff. Hersh, *Chain of Command*, pp. 177-79.
78. *Time*, January 19, 2003. Retired military leaders who spoke out against a pre-emptive war against Iraq included Wesley Clark, Joseph Hoar, John M. Shalikashvili, Tony McPeak, James L. Jones, Norman Schwarzkopf, Anthony Zinni, Henry H. Shelton, Thomas G. McInerney and Kim Holmes. Recently retired Chairman of the Joint Chiefs of Staff, Henry Shelton, put it this way: "If we get drawn into something in Iraq, then our focus will go very heavily there, and it will be hard to sustain the momentum in the war against terrorism." *Washington Post*, September 1, 2002.
79. Hersh, *Chain of Command*, p. 251.
80. Hersh, *Chain of Command*, p. 252.
81. Hersh, *Chain of Command*, p. 252.
82. Ferguson is being misleading here. There was no Iraq at the time and thus no Iraq insurgency. Winston Churchill, recently appointed Secretary of State for the Colonies, created the "Middle East powder keg" with which, as of this writing in August 2005, the "Iraqis" and the US are grappling when he carved a space out of the defeated Ottoman empire, pasted together disparate peoples (Kurds, Sunnis, Shias, etc.) and imposed an alien Hashemite monarch, Feisal, on a synthetic entity called Iraq. See Christopher Catherwood, *Churchill's Folly: How Winston Churchill Created Modern Iraq* (New York: Avalon/Carroll and Graf, 2004).
83. Niall Ferguson, "Cowboys and Indians," *The New York Times*, May 24, 2005. Ferguson asks, "How did the British address the manpower problem in 1920? By bringing in soldiers from India (i.e., the Indian Army), who accounted for more than 87 percent of troops in the counter insurgency campaign. . . . The United Kingdom had the Indian Army, the United States does not. . . ." Ferguson continues: ". . . it is time to acknowledge how thinly stretched American forces in Iraq are and to address the problem . . ." by, for example sending "Condoleezza Rice to

New Delhi?. . ." As we shall see in our conclusion, these may not be idle words as the US woos India to bandwagon with it in its war against terrorism.

84. Fallows, *Frontline*, February 26, 2004.

85. The failure of the FBI, the CIA and other USG agencies "to connect the dots" was amply documented in the 9/11 Commission Report. Here we draw the reader's attention to the fact that the Bush administration delayed the release of the 9/11 Commission's chapter on the failures of the FAA to anticipate and prevent the 9/11 attacks until three months after the election. See Eric Lichtblau's story in *The New York Times* of February 10, 2005, "9/11 Report Cites Many Warnings About Hijackings." The story's lead sentence reads: "In the months before the 9/11 attacks, federal aviation officials reviewed dozens of intelligence reports that warned about Osama bin Laden and Al Qaeda, some of which specifically discussed airline hijackings and suicide operations, according to a previously undisclosed report from the 9/11 commission."

    On June 10, 2005 a *New York Times* story further elaborated on what had been withheld from the 9/11 Commission. "The FBI missed at least five chances in the months before September 11, 2001, to find two hijackers as they prepared for attacks and settled in San Diego, the Justice Department inspector general said in a report made public on Thursday (June 9) after being kept secret for a year." This means that the Bush administration kept this information out of the 2004 presidential election.

86. The Democratic Party's effort to portray war-hero John Kerry as a more effective commander-in-chief than the "draft dodging" "hooky playing" George Bush failed when Republican party inspired TV advertisements alleged that Swift Boat commander Kerry had been a coward rather than a hero and a CBS program showing George Bush's failure to meet his Air National Guard obligations was discredited by CBS's use of unverifiable letters.

87. For our concept of "governmental pluralism" see pp. 89-91 of the Introduction to *The Regional Imperative* and for our analysis of "regional governments" as policy arenas see pp. 81-83 of the Introduction to *The Regional Imperative*.

88. For a detailed account of the Kargil crisis and President Clinton's role in defusing it, see Strobe Talbott's intimate and insightful account in chapter eight, "From Kargil to Blair House," in his *Engaging India: Democracy, Diplomacy and the Bomb* (New Delhi: Viking/Penguin, 2004). At the height of the Kargil crisis, Pakistan's Prime Minister, Nawaz Sharif, initiated a visit to Washington in July 1999. The conversations, Talbott says, convinced Clinton that "the world was closer even than during the Cuban missile crisis to a nuclear war. Unlike Kennedy and Krushchev in 1962, Vajpayee and Sharif did not realize how close they were to the brink, so there was an even greater risk that they would blindly stumble across it," p. 167.

89. See Matthew C.J. Rudolph, *et al*, "Kerry's not scary," *The Hindu* (Chennai), October 27, 2004.

90. http://www.asian-nation.org/demographics.shtml
91. The Indian community is not always in agreement. It split in March 2005 over the proposed visit of Gujarat Chief Minister, Narendra Modi. Modi had been invited to address the Asian-American Hotel Owners Associations (many of whom are Patels from Gujarat) in Fort Lauderdale, Florida, and the Association of Indian-Americans of North America in Madison Square Garden, New York City. Secularists who held Modi responsible for the deaths of as many as 2000 Muslims in 2002 following the event at Godhra waged an email and lobbying campaign against his visit that eventuated in the United States Government denying him a visa under the US Immigration and Nationality Act. The Act prohibits anybody who was "responsible for, or directly carried out, at any time, particularly severe violations of religious freedom from entering the US."
92. The "country desk" offices in the Bureau of South Asian Affairs were: Afghanistan; India, Nepal and Sri Lanka; and Pakistan and Bangladesh. In addition to the Office of Regional Affairs there is also a fifth Office of Public Diplomacy.

    Under the second Bush administration, the Bureau was reorganized as the Bureau of South and Central Asian Affairs. It included not only the seven South Asian states and Afghanistan but also five former Soviet Republics, Kazakstan, Kyrgyzstan, Tazikistan, Turkmenistan and Uzbekistan.
93. Selig Harrison, "The United States and South Asia: Trapped by the Past?"
94. Here is how *The 9/11 Commission Report* put it:" (National Security Adviser) Rice chaired a Principals Committee meeting on September 13 (2001) . . . to refine how the fight against Al Qaeda would be conducted. . . . The Principals also focused on Pakistan and what it could do to turn the Taliban against Al Qaeda. *They concluded that if Pakistan decided not to help the United States. it too would be at risk.* [my emphasis] . . . The same day Deputy Secretary of State Richard Armitage met with the Pakistan Ambassador to the United States, Maheela Lodhi, and the visiting head of Pakistan's military intelligence service, Mahmud Ahmed. Armitage said that the United States wanted Pakistan to take seven steps." In effect Pakistan was asked to reverse course—to break relations with the Taliban government in Afghanistan and cooperate militarily with the US in hunting down bin Laden in Afghanistan.

    "Pakistan made its decision swiftly. That afternoon, Secretary of State Powell announced at the beginning of an NSA meeting that Musharaff had agreed to every US request for support in the war on terrorism." *The 9/11 Commission Report* (New York: W.W. Norton, 2004), p. 331.
95. Peter Gowan in "A Calculus of Power," *New Left Review*, July/August 2002, No. 47, critiques the concept of off-shore balancer as it appears in John Mearsheimer's, *The Tragedy of Great Power Politics* (New York: W.W. Norton, 2002).
96. See William Manchester, *Winston Spencer Churchill: The Last Lion, Vol. 1: Visions of Glory, 1874-1932* (New York: Delta, 1983). The debate in the House of Commons on Irwin's declaration (that India should be

granted Dominion Status) began on Friday, November 8, 1929. Prime Minister Ramsay MacDonald spoke for it. "... (Stanley) Baldwin announced that the Conservatives supported (MacDonald) ... Davidson estimated that at least a third of the Tory MPs would vote against the declaration. They had listened glumly to their leader; their applause for him had been perfunctory.... The diehards were much upset (and) violently opposed to it.... Winston was almost demented with fury...." Churchill's first attack came a week later in the columns of the *Daily Mail*. Britain, he said "had rescued India from ages of barbarism ... its slow but ceaseless march to civilization (constituted) ... the finest achievement of our history. Self-government was unthinkable for a community which treats sixty million of its members ... as Untouchables ... and it was absurd to contemplate (Dominion Status) while India is prey to fierce racial and religious dissension.... If the viceregal proposal were adopted the British raj would be replaced by a Gandhi Raj...," p. 845-46. In the end Churchill succeeded in blocking Dominion Status and paid the price for doing so by being sent into the political wilderness by his party leader, Stanley Baldwin.

For a more detailed and nuanced study see S.G. Ghosh, *Decision-making and Power in the British Conservative Party: A Study of the Indian Problem*, Kolkata: Oceania Publishing House, 1972.

97. See Terrence Creagh Coen, *The Indian Political Service: A Study in Indirect Rule* (London: Chatto and Windus, 1971).

98. Caroe served as Governor of the Northwest Frontier Province (NWFP) in 1946-47. Caroe wrote to Lord Wavell, the Viceroy, that Jawaharlal Nehru, then the acting prime minister of an interim government, was lucky not to have been killed by Muslim League activists and the tribal followers of the Mullah of Manki when, as minister of tribal relations, he toured the NWFP. Caroe told the viceroy that he made no effort to restrain the Mullah and the League because Nehru's tour "was obviously designed to push the Congress cause" and to have done so "would certainly have led to disturbances." Caroe to Wavell, 23 October 1946, as quoted and cited in Anita Inder Singh, *The Origins of the Partition of India, 1936-1947* in *The Partition Omnibus* (New Delhi: Oxford University Press, 2002), p. 204.

99. Caroe's admiration for Muslim India, particularly the Pathans of the NWFP, was expressed in his book, *The Pathans, 550 B.C.-A.D. 1957*.

100. We draw freely in what follows about Sir Olaf Caroe from Lloyd I. Rudolph, "The Great Game in Asia: Revisited and Revised," *Crossroads: An International Socio-Political Journal* (New York: Crane Russak), No. 16, 1985. For an historical account of the great game see Peter Hopkirk, *The Great Game: The Struggle for Empire in Central Asia* (New York: Kodansha America, 1992). Sir Olaf's career is documented in Peter John Probst, *The Future of the Great Game: Sir Olaf Caroe, India's Independence, and the Defense of Asia* (Akron, OH: University of Akron Press, 2005).

101. Olaf Caroe, "The Persian Gulf—A Romance." *Round Table*, Vol. XXXIX, No. 154, p. 135, and Olaf Caroe, *Wells of Power: The Oilfields of South—Western Asia—A Regional and Global Study* (London: Macmillan, 1951).
102. Caroe, *Wells of Power*, p. ix.
103. Byroade had served with George Marshall in China.
104. Strobe Talbott, *Engaging India: Diplomacy, Democracy and the Bomb* (New Delhi: Penguin/Viking, 2004). Talbott got on well with his Secretary, Madeleine Albright, the National Security Adviser, Sandy Berger, his Assistant Secretary of State for South Asia, Karl Inderfurth, and State's non-proliferation specialist, Robert Einhorn.

    When Warren Christopher, President Clinton's Secretary of State in his first term, made Talbott his Deputy Secretary in early 1994, he inaugurated "morning senior staff meetings that brought all the assistant secretaries together in my conference room," p. 29.
105. Talbott, *Engaging India*, p. 92.
106. Talbott, *Engaging India*, p. 193. Clinton's visit had been preceded by his resolution of the Kargil crisis in July 1999, i.e., getting Prime Minister Nawaz Sharif to order the Pakistan Army to withdraw unconditionally. His handling of the Kargil crisis had " 'greatly diminished' Indian distrust of the United States's strategic orientation in South Asia. . . ." According to Indian External Affairs Minister Jaswant Singh, "There is more good will toward the United States of America in India today than I've ever known in my life." Talbott, *Engaging India*, p. 175.
107. Talbott, *Engaging India*, p. 200.
108. Talbott, *Engaging India*, p. 205.
109. Pakistan's "sins" were numerous : A.Q. Khan's sale of nuclear technology, including to North Korea and Iran; state sponsored cross-border terrorism in Kashmir; indirect responsibility for the terrorist attack on the Indian parliament: continued if now underground support for the Taliban in Afghanistan; a military coup replacing democracy with authoritarian rule.
110. The Bush administration's *quid pro quo* for Pakistan was a $3 billion economic and military assistance package, support for international assistance in reforming education and health and increasing "state penetration in the Federally Administered Tribal Area" (where bin Laden might be hiding), and sale of an unlimited number of F-16 aircraft equipped with the AIM-120 AMRAAM, "the best active radar missile in service anywhere in the world." Also made available were P-3C Orions, TOW antitank missiles, and Phalanx terminal defense systems.

    The F-16 sale thus expands the access to US weapons systems that Islamabad has enjoyed since the beginning of counter terrorism operations in Afghanistan. Previous transfers included C-130 transport aircraft, helicopters, and communications and electronic equipment.
111. India had reasons to participate in the war against terrorism. It alleged that a terrorist attack on India's Parliament in December 2001, just three months after the 9/11 attacks in the US, originated in Pakistan and that Pakistan was supporting cross border terrorism in Kashmir. Even before the 9/11 attacks President Clinton in his March 2000 visits to India and

Pakistan told Pakistan to stop supporting cross border attacks in Kashmir. The Bush administration with even more leverage made the same demands on Pakistan. The reduction if not elimination of cross-border attacks contributed to the resumption of peace talks between India and Pakistan. See Strobe Talbott, *Engaging India*, Chapter 9. "A Guest in the Parliament," and chapter 10: "Unfinished Business," pp. 170-232.

112. Ashley Tellis is a senior associate at the Carnegie Endowment for International Peace in Washington, D.C. Previously, he served as a senior adviser to Robert Blackwill, US ambassador to India and on the National Security Council staff. For eight years he was a senior policy analyst at RAND.

113. Ashley J. Tellis, "South Asian Seesaw: A New U.S. Policy on the Subcontinent," Carnegie Endowment for International Peace: Policy Brief, May 2005." http://www.carnegieendowment.org/files/PB38.pdf. The warrant for Tellis' assertion here is "senior officials" who "revealed through a background briefing on the day (March 25, 2005) . . . of the president's phone call (about the sale of F-16s to Pakistan) to (India's Prime Minister Dr Manmohan) . . . Singh, that the United States had in fact reached the decision to 'help India become a major power in the twenty-first century'." (*emphasis supplied*) Tellis, "South Asian Seesaw," p. 1.

114. According to Tellis, the Bush administration believes it can preserve "good relations with both India and Pakistan simultaneously" despite its decision to resume the sale of F-16 fighter aircraft to Pakistan, "because of the conviction that both countries represent different kinds of strategic opportunities for the United States; as Secretary of State Condoleezza Rice put it, 'India . . . is looking to grow its influence into a global influence . . . and Pakistan . . . is looking to a settled neighborhood so that it can deal with extremism inside its own border'." Tellis, "South Asian Seesaw," pp. 1-2. Tellis is presenting the scripts that the US expects India and Pakistan to follow.

115. For the concept of band-wagoning and its use see Stephen Walt, *Revolution and War* (Ithaca, NY: Cornell University Press, 1996).

116. There continue to be voices asking for cooperation, even collaboration, between India and China. Visiting Chinese Premier Wen Jiabao on Sunday, April 10, 2005, told executives of India's biggest software exporter, Tata Consultancy Services, in Bangalore that cooperation between India and China in the information technology industry will help the two nations lead the world in the sector and collaboration by the neighbors will signify the coming of the Asian century in the IT field. PTI, "Wen in Bangalore" April 11, 2005. Mani Shankar Aiyar, India's Petroleum Minister, was keen to persuade China to cooperate rather than to compete for oil and gas abroad. Somini Sengupta, "Hunger for Energy Transforms How India Operates, *New York Times*, June 5, 2005.

See also Zheng Bijian, " 'Peacefully Rising' to Great-Power Status," *Foreign Affairs*, September/October 2005, for arguments why China is and will remain committed to cooperation rather than confrontation. Bijian, Chair of the China Reform Forum, a Chinese "NGO," concludes:

"China's development depends on world peace—a peace that its development will in turn reinforce," p. 24.

Kishore Mahbubani, Dean of the Lee Kuan-Yew School of Public Policy in Singapore, also takes a sanguine view of China's emergence as a world power in "Understanding China," in the same issue of *Foreign Affairs*.

David Zweig and Bi Jianhai of Hong Kong University of Science and Technology, in "China's Global Hunt for Energy," same issue of *Foreign Affairs*, are less sanguine. Both access to energy resources and the need for secure sea lanes to bring those resources to China can bring China into conflict with a variety of countries, not least India. ". . . Beijing believes," they write, "that China would face an energy crisis if its oil supply lines were disrupted and whoever controls the Strait of Malacca and the Indian Ocean could block China's oil transport route," p. 33.

117. The question is how should India interpret American talk about recognizing India as a world power? Can American words make India a "great power"? Is the US prepared to back India's claim for a permanent seat on the UN's Security Council? What does it mean for US officials to call India a "strategic partner"? Can India expect tangible benefits from participating in succeeding rounds of the "Next Steps in Strategic Partnership (NSSP)", an initiative aimed at cooperation in the space and nuclear fields, hi-tech trade and missile defense, and if so at what cost?

118. The heart of the offer of "advanced defense equipment" seems to have been access to F-16s, including possible co-production. *Outlook's* cover story on the offer was headlined "No thanks, Mr. Bush." *Outlook* gave five reasons the Indian Air Force was "not keen on the US fighter: Setting up maintenance facilities for the F-16 could cost nearly Rs 10000 crore (a crore = 10 million; $1.00 = Rs. 45). This is above the Rs. 13,500 crore that has to be budgeted to purchase the 126 multi-role aircraft; the US has low reliability on supply of spares and after sales support. . .; the F-16 is a 30 year old design. The US air force no longer purchases the aircraft; there are better or comparable aircraft in the reckoning which could cost less to induct in the long run; the Mirage 2000-05, which the air force is keen on, comes with a modular design which can easily be upgraded. It can be put to use till 2015. The F-16 cannot be upgraded." *Outlook*, April 11, 2005, p. 40.

119. In 2005 India was the world's fifth largest consumer of energy. It was importing 70 percent of its rapidly mounting oil consumption. In another 20 years the Indian government estimates it will be importing 85 percent, "Hunger for Energy, . . ." *The New York Times*, June 5, 2005.

120. See George Perkovich and Revati Prasad, "A Pipeline for Peace," op-ed in the *New York Times*, April 18, 2005. *The Hindu* (Chennai) editorialized on March 17, 2005, the day after Secretary Rice's Press Conference in New Delhi, that India should "Stand Firm on the Iran Pipeline." Gas supplied by the pipeline, *The Hindu* argued, would be vital for India's search for energy security, "opens up a new and potentially exciting chapter in the bilateral relations between Islamabad and New Delhi" and

"engenders stability and predictability in the political equation." On February 11, 2005 *The Hindu* reported that the government of India would not link the gas pipeline to other issues such as through transit of Indian goods to Iran and Central Asia and on March 13, 2005 it reported that Pakistan Prime Minister Shaukat Aziz said he was under no pressure from the US to go slow on the Iran-Pakistan-India pipeline project and that he was inviting the Indian Petroleum Minister (Mani Shanker Aiyar) and the Iranian Petroleum Minister for talks.

The pipeline had its risks and its opponents. Would Pakistan for example be able to insure the safety of the pipeline "across vast, restive Baluchistan province where disgruntled tribal armies routinely attack gas installations"? "Hunger for Energy, . . ." The *New York Times*, June 5, 2005. Nationalist voices in India and Pakistan spoke forcefully against the agreement. Here is the voice of Brahma Chellaney, whose distrust of the Pakistani other was echoed by his counterparts across the border: "The pipeline-through-Pakistan business makes little strategic or commercial sense, yet there is an unseemly rush to blunder. Seeking energy security by sourcing India's main gas imports through an adversarial State committed to this country's unraveling is a contradiction in itself." *The Hindustan Times*, February 23, 2005.

121. In the spring of 2006 there were on-going negotiations with Iran by Britain, France and Germany on the question of whether Iran's nuclear program is peaceful and can be relied upon to remain so. The Bush administration seemed to insist that it was not or would not remain peaceful. There is, the *New York Times* reports, a ". . . widespread sense of national pride (that) complicates any attempt to persuade Iran's leaders to give up parts of the nuclear program, as European negotiators have been trying to prevail upon them to do. Only a small group, mostly hard-line revolutionaries, wants Iran to withdraw from the (NPT) treaty and try to develop nuclear weapons." "Across Iran, Nuclear Power Is a Matter of Pride," *The New York Times*, May 29, 2005.

122. For a recent assessment critical of the Bush administration position see Christopher de Bellaigue, "Think Again: Iran," *Foreign Policy*, May/June 2005, pp. 18-24. Kenneth Pollack's, *The Persian Puzzle: The Conflict Between Iran and America* (New York: Random House, 2005) shows, with few exceptions, how mistaken US policy in Iran has been since the CIA engineered the overthrow of Mohammed Mossadegh in 1953 down to the present day.

123. T.V. Parasurma, "Bond in the USA: India, Uncle Sam Ink Defence Pact," *The Economic Times on Line*, June 30, 2005.

124. The opposition to the nuclear agreement was compounded by concerns that provisions of the Hyde Act and of the follow on "123 Agreement" would compromise India's nuclear sovereignty and require it to adhere to US policy toward Iran. President Bush tried to allay such fears by invoking a version of his imperial presidency, the "signing statement." His signing statement on December 26, 2006 for the US-India Peaceful

Atomic Energy Cooperation Act or Hyde Act countermanded provisions of the Hyde Act. Most important was a provision that if India tested nuclear weapons the US would halt all nuclear exports. Another was a requirement that India adhere to US policy toward Iran.

The President's signing statement took the view that several provisions of the Hyde Act [such as Section 103 and Section 104 (d)(2)] . . . "are only advisory and will not be my foreign policy." "My approval of the act," he continued, "does not constitute my adoption of the statements of policy as US foreign policy. . . ." *IBN Live*, December 18, 2006.

For an analysis of the relationship between the provisions of the Hyde Act and of the August 2007 implementing "123 Agreement" between India and the US—an agreement for which the Bush administration expected to seek Congressional approval in early 2008—see "This Law is Your Law: What if Hyde Act and 123 came into conflict? Opinions in the US are as split as in India," *Outlook*, October 22, 2007.

125. *The Hindu*, August 29, 2005.
http://www.thehindu.com/2005/08/29/stories/2005082916590100.htm
126. *Outlook*, October 29, 2007, p. 42.
127. *India Today International*, October 29, 2007, p. 10.
128. India will soon have to position itself with respect to the China led and Russia supported Shanghai Cooperation Organization for central Asian states. The SCO has called for the US to withdraw from military bases in Kyrgyzstan and Uzbekistan. A key member of the SCO, Russian President Vladimir Putin, strongly endorsed the SCOs call for US to close its bases in Kyrgyzstan and Uzbekistan. It remains to be seen how India will relate to the SCO.

INTRODUCTION TO *THE REGIONAL IMPERATIVE [1980]*

This work first appeared in 1975 as one of twenty-four studies prepared by consulting scholars for the national Commission on the Organization of the Government for the Conduct of Foreign Policy. The Commission was created in 1973 on the initiative of the U.S. Senate's Foreign Relations Committee by an act of Congress. Chaired by Robert Murphy, the Commission was composed of twelve members equally chosen by the Senate, the House of Representatives and the President. It included the Vice-president, Senators, Congressmen, educationists, businessmen and professionals. The Commission's mandate was "to submit findings and recommendations to provide a more effective system for the formulation and implementation of the nation's foreign policy."

In March, 1974, the Commission authorized a study program. We were asked at the time to prepare a study responsive to one of the program's objectives, i.e. to evaluate "the capacity of the U.S. to maintain coordination between a large number of policies impinging on a . . . region." It was published along with the Commission's *Report*, and six additional volumes of appendices in June, 1975 as Appendix V of Volume 7 by the Superintendent of Documents, U.S. Government Printing Office, Washington D.C. and is published here as *Making U.S. Foreign Policy Toward South Asia.* We are pleased that Concept Publishing Company in India and Humanities Press in the United States are making it available to wider publics by bringing out trade editions.

The Commission was created at a time when the imperial presidency had reached its apogee with the beginning of Richard Nixon's second administration in January, 1972. It carried on its work during the Presidency's most serious crisis, the President's unprecedented resignation in August, 1974, and the incumbencies of an unelected President and Vice-president, Gerald Ford and

Nelson Rockefeller. The Commission concluded its efforts in 1975 under the influence of primaries for the 1976 presidential election. It was during this period too that Henry Kissinger, as the President's assistant for national security affairs, invoked executive privilege to declare himself immune to Congressional inquiries or accountability and became simultaneously Secretary of State, again unprecedental situations that influenced the creation of the Commission and its work.

The conduct of U.S. foreign policy towards the states of South Asia in the high noon of the imperial presidency under Presidents Johnson and Nixon reflected their personal and strategic predispositions and concerns. The result detailed in our overview and in the case studies by Oldenburg, Bjorkman and Moulton, was the confusion of presidential with national interest, global over-determination in the assessment of other states' intentions and actions, and poorly informed and managed imperative coordination of policy. Henry Kissinger's after-the-fact justification of the Nixon administration's response to the Bangladesh independence crisis in *White House Years* (1979) rationalizes its failure to deal effectively which Pakistan's genocidal civil war and the Indo-Pakistan war that followed. Kissinger's retrospective rationalizations of 1979 continue to reflect the conceptual and organizational inadequacies of the Nixon-Kissinger era. Happily, we have been able to append Christopher Van Hollen's telling and informed critique of Kissinger's interpretation of these events, "The Tilt Policy Revisited: Nixon-Kissinger Geo-Politics and South Asia," which appeared in the April, 1980 number of *Asian Survey*. Van Hollen, Deputy Assistant Secretary of State for South Asia at the time of the Bangladesh crisis, deals particularly well with the effects of global over-determination on national objectives and on the intentions and capabilities of global as against regional actors.

Making U.S. Foreign Policy Toward South Asia is the result of extensive research carried out in 1974 under our direction. It examines the capacity of the U.S. Government to maintain coordination among a large number of policies affecting the states of South Asia over the ten years (1965-1974) spanned by the Johnson and Nixon administrations. Our overview and the ten case studies examine the difficulties of coordination policies across several divides: from crises to more routine situations; from one function to another; from one state to another within the region; from one region to other regions; and from regional and functional to global or strategic considerations.

Of the ten case studies three (Cohen, Oldenburg and Rubin) deal with national security; four (Bjorkman, Hadden, Kochanek, and Moulton) with economic policy; and two (Andersen and Lenth) with people-to-people aspects of American policy making and execution as they related to South Asian states. Our overview, *inter alia*, comments on these cases and proposes organizational modifications to improve the policy process. We argue that regional considerations often were given less consideration than they require and propose conceptual, normative and organizational changes designed to promote better approximations of the national interest. We have kept the recommendations of the original report because they are an integral part of its analysis and explanation.

The studies in this volume were written under the influence of the literature on bureaucratic politics, particularly Graham Allison's study of the Cuban missile crisis, *The Essence of Decision*. Its influence was negative as much as positive, i.e. the concepts and explanations used here were as much in tension as in accord with a bureaucratic politics framework. Other conceptual dimensions such as world views encompassing ideological predispositions and national character stereotypes; cognitive categories that select and organize knowledge about international politics; and psychological processes that affect organizational, particularly small group, relationships, are among the additional determinants that shaped our analysis and recommendations.

Perhaps the least familiar of these determinants are the psychological processes that affect organizational relationships among those who formulate and manage policy, relationships we designated with the contrasting concepts imperative and deliberative coordination. We were less concerned with minimizing the irrationality that can result from "group think" and "effectiveness traps" than with maximizing the rationality that can result from deliberative coordination among knowledgeable and experienced colleagues. We recognize that administrative hierarchies, particularly those affected by presidential attention, are meant to produce results more desired by those higher than by those lower in the hierarchy. We also recognize that deliberation among colleagues across vertical and lateral differences can result in better informed and more rational decision-making and policy management. Organizational arrangements that promote collegiality and deliberation at the expense of hierarchy and command most of the time produce better approximations of the national interest.

The contradictions between hierarchy and collegiality will remain powerful as long as President's men seeking to promote the President's interest resist incorporating in their understanding of the national interest the knowledge and judgment independent career professionals can provide. Two years is a long time in a President's term. He needs results sooner rather than later. The opening to China (July, 1971) was well timed for the November election but the South Asia crisis with which it coincided was an unwanted irritant and embarrassment.

The mechanics of mounting and coordinating the studies in this volume were fairly straight forward. The project was funded by a grant from the Commission to us, the principal investigators. We in turn recruited knowledgeable and experienced academic colleagues, research assistants and clerical staff. A preliminary conference of participants formulated an agreed framework of analysis, division of labor and schedule of work. At a second conference draft studies were critiqued and subsequently revised. The revised papers were read and criticized by us and by the Commission study directors, who also critiqued our draft overview paper. At a final conference, this time in Washington rather than Chicago, the re-written papers, which had been circulated beforehand, were critically discussed by outside experts, mostly academic but some governmental, and Commission representatives. The papers were then put in their final form.

Under the terms of the legislation creating the Commission, consulting scholars with security clearance were given access to classified material on the understanding that it would be used only to inform judgments and make evaluations. Serving officials were expected to be forthcoming in the many interviews conducted in Washington and in South Asia. These arrangements, as might be expected, were only moderately successful.

A wide range of interviews were conducted, not only on diplomatic activities (State) but also on strategic (Department of Defense, Central Intelligence Agency and the White House's own state department, the National Security Council), economic (Treasury, Agricultural, Commerce) and people-to-people (United States Information Agency, Bureau of Educational and Cultural Affairs, now combined in the International Communication Agency). Information is a source of power as well as knowledge. Scholars and officials have overlapping but divergent interests with respect to information and this difference affected what we and our colleagues could learn. Kissinger loyalists for example, may have left some things unsaid not only because it was convenient to do so but also because they shared his world view.

The Commission's study directors, Peter Szanton and William I. Bacchus, were helpful throughout. Bacchus, who had primary responsibility for our study, greatly facilitated access to records and arrangements for interviews in Washington and made many valuable substantive and analytic suggestions to us and our colleagues. Overall, the Commission framework provided a unique opportunity to do research on foreign policy.

Chronology, the order of events, in fact orders events. It too is an important determinant of foreign policy. Reading Joan Landy Erdman's "A Chronology of Events in South Asia Bearing on the Conduct of Foreign Policy," which appears as an Annex, makes this abundantly clear.

Philip Oldenburg managed the flow of people and papers with aplomb and made important contributions to editing manuscripts.

Susan Lenth, who managed the office and finances with finesse, remained calm and charming throughout the hectic months of 1974 and 1975 that it took to complete the project.

"Fernworth"
Landour Cantonment

LLOYD I. RUDOLPH
SUSANNE HOEBER RUDOLPH
Mussoorie, Uttar Pradesh
21 April 1980

PART I

LOOKING BACK, LOOKING FORWARD

1

U.S. FOREIGN POLICY TOWARD SOUTH ASIA
A Continuing Tilt to the Functional

— Walter Andersen

The formulation of foreign policy in Washington D.C. very often involves a competitive relationship between regional specialists who manage bilateral relations and those who handle functional issues (e.g., terrorism, nonproliferation, etc.). Competition is almost inevitable if these two sets of policy makers are in bureaucratically separate offices, as is the case within the U.S. State Department. In a crisis, functionalists addressing geo-strategic issues usually dominate the policy process. In the South Asian case, bilateral relations have been derivative of large functional requirements for decades, even in non-crisis periods. The problem is that realities on the ground—the provenance of country/regional experts—often are distorted when regional considerations are secondary in the formulation of policy. This distortion can lead to situations that actually undermine larger U.S. geo-strategic considerations. My argument is that U.S. policy in South Asia today risks undermining the war on terrorism, the most important geo-strategic item currently on the Bush administration's U.S. foreign policy agenda and an issue that will likely remain a long-term concern of the U.S.

A basic reason for the secondary role of regionalists in the conduct of U.S. foreign policy towards South Asia—and towards other regions as well—is that the State Department, the primary bureaucratic repository of regional expertise in the federal bureaucracy, is itself often a secondary and ineffective player in the bureaucratic battles within the executive branch of the federal government. Numerous studies have shown that the State Department is structurally hobbled from asserting itself. I will focus on two such studies that make this point, one that addresses U.S. South Asia policy and the other a broader critique of the conduct of U.S. foreign policy. The first study, The *Regional Imperative* by Lloyd and Susanne H. Rudolph,[1] is an analysis of the conduct of U.S. foreign policy toward South Asia in the Johnson and Nixon administrations (1965-75). The second, released 20 years later, is the bipartisan *Commission on National Security/ 21st Century*, more commonly known as the Hart-Rudman Commission after its two co-chairs, Senators Gary Hart and Warren Rudman.[2]

The Rudolphs writing some 25 years ago argued that the secondary influence of country/regional experts was a significant cause for a policy that in many respects worked against the U.S. interest in a stable South Asia. The Iraq crisis demonstrates that this general problem persists some three decades later, and for much the same reason.

What appears to have motivated the Rudolphs to analyze the conduct of U.S. foreign policy was the "tilt" toward Pakistan before and during the 1971 Indo-Pakistani war. Henry Kissinger, in his recollection of the period in his book, *The White House Years* frankly admits that the opening to China prompted a "tilt" in U.S. policy favorable to Pakistan, and the chapter that discusses U.S. policy toward the region is appropriately titled "The Tilt".[3] Christopher Van Hollen, deputy assistant secretary for South Asia in the State Department at the time, wrote a highly critical analysis of Kissinger's "tilt" policy, arguing that U.S. policy makers repeatedly misread regional events, in part because regional expertise was often ignored.[4] The Rudolphs and others also discovered that the regional assumptions informing U.S. policy at the time were often significantly off the mark, perhaps the most egregious being the assumption that the military rulers of Pakistan did not have to make concessions to political forces demanding autonomy of the eastern wing of the country to avoid a civil war.

The Rudolphs and other contributors to their study discovered that the State Department and its regional specialists were repeatedly overruled during the South Asia crisis of the early 1970s,[5] a situation that was to happen again and again in the conduct of U.S. foreign policy towards South Asia over the next two decades.

The Rudolph critique regarding the consequences of the reduced influence of the State Department and of regional experts within it during the 1960s and 1970s could be applied to U.S. policy toward South Asia in the 1980s, when the center of the Cold War shifted to Afghanistan following the move of Soviet troops into that country in the late 1970s. At that time, the U.S. extended almost unqualified support to radical pan-Islamic forces because they were among the most effective fighters against the occupying Soviet troops, ignoring the advice of regional experts who urged caution because the ideology of these groups would prompt them to create a pan-Islamic jihadi state in Afghanistan and to undermine secularism elsewhere in South Asia. These radical forces did in fact cause political havoc in Afghanistan and Pakistan, assuming control in the former and turning it into an international training center for terrorism, and plunging Pakistan into a cauldron of bloody sectarian strife. Osama bin Laden honed his skills in the Afghan war and later trained a terrorist cadre that organized the September 11, 2001 attack on the U.S. Individuals associated with these groups in Pakistan today target foreigners and members of various religious minority groups, in addition to those Muslims presumed to be unorthodox. They carry out ethnic cleansing operations against minority Hindus and Sikhs in the Muslim majority Indian state of Kashmir and attack symbols of Indian authority in New Delhi and elsewhere; many of them have close links with Osama bin Laden's al-Qaeda network that carried out the 9/11 atrocities.

This secondary role of regional expertise continues to be a problem in the conduct of U.S. policy toward Pakistan, critically important because it is a frontline state in the fight against terrorism as it was earlier a frontline state against the Soviet presence in Afghanistan in the final decade of the Cold War. Pakistan has been a haven for and training ground of terrorist groups that operate in the Indian state of Kashmir and elsewhere in India. The U.S. has formally designated some of these groups as Foreign Terrorist Organizations.[6] Activities of such Pakistan-based terrorist groups brought India and Pakistan to the verge of war in the summer of 2002 and the chances are good that they will again try to trigger a war between the two countries; such a conflict would severely undermine the larger fight against terrorism and threaten the long term U.S. interest in a strategic relationship with India. Yet, the U.S. has been reluctant either to criticize Pakistani President Musharraf publicly for his reluctance to crack down hard on anti-Indian terrorist groups or to impose any formal conditions on the generous military and economic assistance that is extended as a reward for his backing of Operation Enduring Freedom and the global war on terrorism. Concerns regarding cross border terrorism were reportedly conveyed to Musharraf by senior U.S. officials during his June 2003 visit to Washington DC, but subsequently there have been no formal conditions attached to that assistance.[7] Musharraf might reasonably conclude from this reticence that the U.S. either is not serious about its opposition to Pakistan-based terrorist attacks against Indian targets or is unwilling to take him to task for this because of his critical role in the war on terrorism.[8]

Musharraf might also reasonably conclude that the US is willing to condone continued military rule, even though it formally advocates a transition to democracy. The US only mildly criticized him when he sought to sideline an independently-minded Supreme Court Chief Justice in early 2007, a move that backfired on him with massive pro-democracy demonstrations. It was virtually silent when he was re-elected in October 2007 by sitting representatives of the national and provincial assemblies (the electorate), elected in 2002 in polling widely regarded as rigged, rather than waiting for the new assemblies to be elected in January 2008. While the US repeatedly warned Musharraf privately and publicly not to declare a state of emergency in the wake of scheduled national elections in January 2008, he ignored this advice and declared a state of emergency on November 3 and again sought to dismiss a restored Supreme Court Chief Justice who was on the verge of ruling on the legality of Musharraf's re-election as president. He almost certainly has concluded that the war on terrorism trumps democracy in American calculations.

This absence of formal conditions on assistance to Pakistan prompted criticism from members of Congress and resulted in the introduction of legislation mandating that Congress, which must annually approve the money allocated to Pakistan, investigate the country's record on cross-border terrorism—and other issues—when the next proposed appropriation for Pakistan comes before it. Delegate Eni Faleomavaega (D-Somoa), a non-vote wielding member of Congress and a ranking member of the House Sub-committee on Asia and the Pacific, submitted an amendment that was unanimously approved by the House International Relations Committee on May 7, 2003.[9] It stipulated that:

> For each of fiscal years 2004 and 2005, the U.S. president shall prepare and transmit to the appropriate congressional committee a report that contains a description of the extent to which the government of Pakistan: (1) has closed all known terrorist training camps operating in Pakistan and Pakistani-held Kashmir; (2) has established serious and identifiable measures to prohibit the infiltration of Islamic extremists across the "Line of Control" into India; (3) has ceased the transfer of weapons of mass destruction, including any associated technologies, to any third country or terrorist organization.[10]

The actual bill was passed by the full house by a vote of 382 to 42 on July 15, 2003. The measure is only advisory and the recommended conditions have not been implemented by the Bush administration.

Reforming the State Department to Strengthen Its Role in Foreign Policy

Much of the criticism of the conduct of U.S. foreign policy regarding Iraq echoes the arguments raised by the Rudolphs about policy toward South Asia over 25 years ago. In both cases, regional expertise has played a secondary role. In both cases, policy makers have misread the political consequences in the region. On Iraq, this misreading has given rise to criticism that military steps were taken without serious—or informed—thought to their political consequences. American action has triggered a debate about how U.S. foreign policy should be conducted and which parts of the government should take the lead role.[11] On the one side are those who oppose U.S. unilateral military action and call for the return to close engagement with international institutions and other countries. This is a task preeminently for the State Department. The Department of Defense as the ultimate "functional" policy-making "bureau" is superb in planning and making war, but it is not well qualified to deal with the political consequences of war-making, a task that by default usually falls to other parts of the bureaucracy in the wake of military action. The strategic vision of the Defense Department is usually focused on the immediate task of battle and not on the longer term one of what happens politically after the battle. Brady Kiesling, the U.S. foreign service officer who resigned from the State Department in protest against U.S. policy on Iraq, is one of many critics who have argued that there is a tendency to replace diplomacy—carried out by the State Department—with military solutions which claim to advance U.S. geo-strategic interests.[12] Condoleezza Rice, since taking over as Secretary of State in the second Bush administration, has successfully asserted the role of the State Department in foreign policy decision-making. She has considerably closer relations with the President than her predecessor Colin Powell. However, the regional/functional problem within the State Department mentioned above has not been addressed, probably because the required restructuring of the State Department would set off terrific turf battles.

On the other side is the neoconservative case that has few qualms about using American power to advance such U.S. interests as democracy in the Middle East—and letting the Defense Department take the lead role in formulating policy that has both military and political consequences. Newt Gingrich, the former Republican speaker of the House of Representatives, has been the most prominent—and most publicized—neoconservative advocate of this position. In an April 22, 2003 speech at the American

Enterprise Institute, he charged that the State Department's handling of the Iraq issue again reveals that it is a "broken instrument of diplomacy," and explicitly contrasts the "pattern of diplomatic failure" of the State Department with what he describes as the successes of the Defense Department.[13] He calls for a major reform of the State Department to remedy the problem, arguing that, "Without bold dramatic change at the State Department, the United States will soon find itself on the defensive everywhere except militarily." Frank J. Gaffney Jr., contributing *National Review* editor, reiterated the Gingrich attack on the State Department even more bluntly by charging that foreign service officers tend to identify more closely with the interests of other countries than with the U.S., saying "They [foreign service officers] have a constituency of Middle East governments deeply opposed to democracy in Iraq."[14] In short, he charges they suffer from a severe—and probably "incurable"—case of "clientitis". Both critics also seem to be saying that the Department of Defense's geo-strategic vision, focused as it is on war making, is superior to the State Department's management of diplomacy.

The neoconservative critique of the State Department is not supported by the Hart-Rudman Commission, probably the most comprehensive study of the conduct of U.S. foreign policy since World War II. Hart-Rudman's critique is remarkably similar to that of the Rudolphs. Both studies want to make the State Department preeminent in the formulation and implementation of foreign policy so that regional expertise will again shape U.S. foreign policy. Both argue that this will not happen unless the State Department's present complex organizational structure is significantly simplified so it can speak with a clear and single voice. Finally, both argue that the key to simplification is to restore primacy to the regional bureaus by shifting functional responsibilities to the regional bureaus. Placing regional and functional specialists in a single bureau would force senior policymakers to synthesize both perspectives, thus getting around the present competitive atmosphere that characterizes so much of the interaction between regional and functional bureaus, a competitive atmosphere that is exacerbated by powerful turf and career considerations.

The effectiveness of the State Department has been undermined by the steady accretion of new bureaus, mostly dealing with functional issues such as human rights, democracy, law enforcement, narcotics, the environment, terrorism, nonproliferation, etc. With separate functional and regional offices advocating often competing policies, the State Department frequently speaks with multiple voices, which reduces its influence and credibility in dealing with other government departments, with the Congress, and abroad. This accretion has occurred at an accelerated pace since the Rudolph study 25 years ago in part because of the expanding set of international issues that the U.S. has chosen to address.[15] Hart-Rudman rightly points out "the State Department's present organizational structure works at cross-purposes with its foreign service culture. The Foreign Service thinks in terms of countries, and therein lays its invaluable expertise. But the most senior officials have functional responsibilities. The Department's organizational matrix makes it unclear who is responsible for policies with both regional and functional elements."[16]

Strengthened regional bureaus would, in addition, enable the State Department to handle more effectively crises that cover a whole region or parts of several regions, thus giving it a regional coverage comparable to the Department of Defense's CINCs, who are now better organized than the State Department to handle regional crises and thus in a better position to influence U.S. policy. Both the Rudolphs and Hart-Rudman observe that such regional planning needs to take place at headquarters. Embassies are not good mechanisms for such regional planning because the lines of communication tend to be between the overseas post and Washington rather than among regional embassies where there is often a competitive relationship among ambassadors.

The Rudolphs go further than Hart-Rudman in restricting the role of the National Security Council; they proposed that its responsibilities be confined to the preparation of defense budgets and military strategy, thus returning the Council to its original mandate. They argued that the National Security Council was over-weighted with representatives of the military and intelligence, thereby shifting "the concerns of foreign policy from diplomatic means and a political conception of the national interest to military means and a crisis-laden conception of national security."[17] Perhaps, Hart-Rudman take a less draconian approach because the formal representation of the military and intelligence inside the National Security Council is less an issue now.

Hart-Rudman and the Rudolphs also differ on whether there should be a separate Bureau of South Asia Affairs. Hart-Rudman recommend incorporating the South Asia regional bureau within the Near East Bureau, the traditional arrangement before congressional legislation creating a separate Bureau of South Asian Affairs on August 24, 1992, perhaps on grounds that a relatively small bureau with issues not at the top of the policy agenda faces marginalization in the policy arena. The Rudolphs argued that South Asia would get more attention in a separate bureau, an argument that is still valid. The Rudolphs recognized that size is a significant factor in attracting a talented cadre specializing in the region and suggested the addition of Southeast Asian countries to South Asia to create an expanded Bureau.[18] The Bureau was eventually expanded, but to include Central Asian rather than the Southeast Asian states. In 2006, the Central Asian states were added to create the new Bureau of South and Central Asian Affairs. The White House had to push against an often-recalcitrant State bureaucracy wary of changes that impact on the turf of powerful bureaus, as was the case here. President Bush and his new Secretary of State in the second administration, Condoleezza Rice, moved to enlarge the Bureau and appointed a highly talented foreign service officer to head it, Richard Boucher, formerly spokesperson of the State Department. These changes reflect the significantly enhanced importance of South Asia in U.S. foreign policy calculations and the appointment of someone with Boucher's status will give the newly expanded Bureau of South and Central Asian Affairs more clout within the State Department.

The Bureau of South Asia Affairs (with the recent addition of Central Asian republics), even though headed by very competent assistant secretaries, has had a running battle since its creation to protect its turf against functional bureaus, especially those addressing issues relating to weapons of mass destruction. The nuclear weapons program of India and Pakistan generated enormous bureaucratic attention in the U.S. Government during the 1990s and that issue played a significant role in shaping U.S. policy towards both countries and continues to be an important factor. The administration needs to be careful that the existential issue of terrorism does not put regionalist concerns on a backburner, as happened during the Cold War.

Following the May 1998 nuclear tests in India and Pakistan, Deputy Secretary of State Strobe Talbott, assisted by Karl F. Inderfurth, the Assistant Secretary of the Bureau of South Asian Affairs, asserted himself directly into the formulation of U.S. policy towards South Asia, and, in the process, restored a better balance between the regionalist and functional offices and shifted the focus of U.S. foreign policy to bilateral issues. Talbott organized intellectually stimulating brainstorming sessions within the State Department that often met on a daily basis to review the broad range of issues in the U.S. relationship with India and Pakistan—and to consider policy alternatives.[19] These meetings brought functionalists and regionalists together around the high table of decision making, which tended to bring out a synthesis of views in much less time and with much less acrimony than under "normal" circumstances.[20] His personal involvement enabled the State Department to speak clearly with one voice on South Asian nuclear issues and Indo-Pakistani tensions and thus enhanced the State Department's role in policy formulation. These in-house State Department discussions laid the groundwork for the substantive issues that came up in a series of some dozen meetings between Indian External Affairs Minister Jaswant Singh and Talbott, where Talbott effectively laid the groundwork for a significantly improved Indo-US relationship and for the very successful visit of President Clinton to India from March 20 to 25, 2000.[21] But the traditional dominance of geo-strategic considerations and functional bureaus returned in the wake of 9/11.

Following 9/11, the American approach to the region was significantly complicated by an effort to achieve two geo-strategic objectives: building a strategic relationship with India, while at the same time relying on Pakistan to be a front line state in the fight against terrorism.[22] The short-term approach towards Pakistan could undermine the other objective of achieving a strategic relationship with India, and could even threaten our longer-term objectives with Pakistan and, more broadly, the fight against terrorism. The second Bush administration moved to separate U.S. policy with India and that with Pakistan in part to get around this dilemma. The strategic importance of India was underscored by a decision of the second Bush administration to make India an exception to U.S. non-proliferation legislation—an exception denied to Pakistan—that prevents nuclear assistance to countries (like India and Pakistan) that have not signed the Nuclear Nonproliferation Treaty. This decision is part of a larger effort to build a stronger India that serves U.S. interest in a balance of power in Asia, and a closer relationship with an economically robust and democratically stable India, which is located in a critically important area along the Indian Ocean littoral. India stands out as a stable country in a very unstable area stretching from Saudi Arabia in the west to Indonesia in the east that still could be characterized as an "arc of crisis,"[23] a term that was coined by Zbigniew Brzezinski when he served in the Carter administration. The nuclear deal with India was kept on very close hold while it was being formulated, with the decision making group limited to the Secretary of State and a small group of trusted advisors. This tactic was almost certainly adopted upon to prevent the issue from getting bogged down by the functionalist bureaus of the State Department that address nonproliferation issues and the almost inevitable leaks that would have prompted the nonproliferation lobby in Washington to defeat or modify the proposal before it was proposed to the Indians. Nonproliferationist, functionalists, along with their allies outside the government, have sought to weight the proposed legislation with amendments that would alter the negotiated positions of Prime Minister Manmohan Singh and President Bush. These efforts to introduce killer amendments were defeated by large majorities and the Hyde Act mandating US negotiations with India on terms of civilian nuclear cooperation was signed into law by President Bush in December 2006.[24]

Consequences of a Weakened State Department: The South Asia Example

The 9/11 terrorists attacks on the U.S. made it inevitable that geo-strategic issues would again shape U.S. policy toward South Asia. The core of the threat is the amorphous al-Qaeda network, which is imbedded in the western parts of the region. But again decisions are often made with limited input from regional specialists either in the State Department or elsewhere, as happened during earlier crises involving South Asia. The resulting tendency to perceive regional events through functional lenses has had unintended—and sometimes dangerous—consequences for U.S. policy in South Asia, as was the case earlier when, the U.S. provided uncritical support for Islamic radicals fighting the Soviets in Afghanistan and thus helped lay the ground for the very terrorist menace now faced by the U.S.

U.S. public diplomacy in the wake of 9/11 involved lavish praise for both former Indian Prime Minister Vajpayee (voted out of power in 2004) and Pakistani President Musharraf, almost certainly because both were seen as important supporters of Operation Enduring Freedom. Given the widespread popular opposition to the U.S. fight against terrorism in Pakistan, Musharraf's personal support is probably essential to keep Pakistan committed to this effort. Indians on the other hand are generally supportive and any Indian leader is likely to back the anti-terrorism effort, as has Vajpayee's Congress Party successor Manmohan Singh. This praise of President Musharraf appears to have been calculated to bolster his popular standing in Pakistan. He came to power in a military coup, conducted elections widely regarded as rigged, and at loggerheads with a National Assembly on basic issues regarding his own power.[25] His support of the global war on terrorism is not popular in Pakistan, being considered by many Muslims as a war on Islam.[26]

Musharraf might reasonably draw the conclusion that U.S. silence on the issue of democracy—and the lavish praise heaped upon him—means that issues of governance are not significant factors in U.S. policy toward the region. He may also reasonably conclude that the U.S. perception of Pakistan's critical role as a front line state in the war against terrorism—and his own vital role in keeping Pakistan committed to this war—make it highly unlikely that the U.S. will push very hard on issues of terrorism that spills over into India.[27] In the absence of any U.S. pressure to democratize, the danger is that Musharraf will not take the politically risky steps required to strengthen democratic institutions. Not taking action on this is dangerous for him because he would inevitably be held personally responsible for economic, social and political failures, a situation that risks another bout of civil disorder in Pakistan. Such unrest would deal a blow to the fight against terrorism and would very likely strengthen Islamic radical forces that opposed Pakistan's participation in Operation Enduring Freedom and now oppose its support for the war on terrorism.

The proximate cause of an Indo-Pakistani confrontation would be an escalation of Pakistan-based terrorism within India. Musharraf might reasonably conclude, however, that the cautious U.S. approach means either that the U.S. is not serious or that he does not have to take the quiet entreaties of the U.S. very seriously.[28] Many Indians have come to this conclusion as well.[29] The issue has calmed since India and Pakistan agreed in late 2003 to a ceasefire along the line of control separating the two parts of Kashmir, and subsequently opened negotiations addressing all outstanding issues. Bombings in Delhi, a shooting spree in the city of Bangalore in late 2005 and the deadly July 11, 2006 bombings in Mumbai, however, underscore the continuing menace of terrorism, and the chances for a rapid deterioration in the bilateral relationship remain high. Bilateral relations are held hostage to terrorist activities, and Islamic militants are sure to continue such violent attacks as they do not want improved Indo-Pakistani relations. Indians widely believe that groups based in Pakistan are responsible for these and other acts of terrorism. The bombings in Delhi occurred in crowded market places on the eve of one of the most popular Hindu holidays. The shootout in Bangalore took place at a high-tech campus that is a showcase of India's growing technical prowess. The Mumbai bombings disrupted the city's busiest rail transit route, killing hundreds of people in a clear attempt to bring India's financial center to a halt.

The U.S. conduct of diplomacy in South Asia has always been complicated by the hostile Indo-Pakistani relationship. One side perceives any favorable U.S. steps toward the other as a setback. During the three decades after its independence in 1947, Pakistan agreed to cooperate in the U.S. led effort to contain communism, a policy that brought it substantial military and economic assistance from the U.S., even though the motivating reasons for Pakistani cooperation had almost nothing to do with containing communism. The objective was to get third party help against India, an objective not missed by the Indians. This assistance not only had an unsettling effect on the Indo-Pakistani relationship, which operated against the U.S. Cold War interests in a stable South Asia, but was also the cause of a long period of frigid Indo-US relations. This assistance also gave rise to unrealistic Pakistani assumptions about how far the U.S. would go to help them against India; a disappointed Pakistan repeatedly felt abandoned by Washington when the help did not materialize.

U.S. military assistance to Pakistan today also risks unsettling the Indo-Pakistani relationship. A major reason prompting the U.S. to work for better relations between India and Pakistan—the fight against terrorism—also risks producing a confrontation between the two powers. The U.S., seeking Musharraf's continued support in the fight against terrorism, is apparently wary of exerting significant pressure on him to crack down on terrorism that spills across the borders into India, presumably because that might undermine Musharraf's political standing in Pakistan, especially among the all important military corps commanders, or perhaps because of the perception that these attacks are something that India, the more powerful of the two countries, can absorb.

While the action of Pakistan-based terrorists would be the most likely trigger to a war, the issue that has sustained the tension between the two South Asian states is the unresolved Kashmir issue, now divided between the two countries as a result of the first Indo-Pakistani war soon after their independence in 1947. Kashmir was the proximate cause for still another war in 1965, a theater of action in the 1971 war and the reason for several confrontations that threatened war, most recently in 2002. The proximate cause for the most recent "near-war" was a surge in activity of Pakistan-based militant groups, most prominently the Laskhar-e-Taiba and the Jaish-e-Mohammed, inside the Indian state of Kashmir.[30] These groups, recruiting mainly non-Kashmiris and advocating a pan-Islamic jihad, have a record of attacks against civilians, especially Hindus and Sikhs remaining in the Valley of Kashmir. Their most egregious act—and the one that triggered the most recent military confrontation—was a December 13, 2001 terrorist attack on the Indian parliament while it was in session, one of several post 9/11 terrorist attacks outside of Kashmir. India quickly mobilized its troops along the frontier with Pakistan; Pakistan countered soon after with a similar mobilization. The Indian motivation was probably coercive diplomacy with the principle aim of getting the U.S. to put pressure on Musharraf to crack down on the terrorists using Pakistan as a safe haven.

War between India and Pakistan, however, seemed imminent following the May 2002 terrorist attack on the residential quarters of a military cantonment in Kashmir, in which a few dozen military dependents were killed. Indians were outraged and enormous pressure was put on Indian Prime Minister Vajpayee to take forceful steps to put an end to terrorist activity. Indian outrage energized the U.S., and Deputy Secretary of State Richard Armitage and Secretary of Defense Donald Rumsfeld were dispatched to the region in early June 2002. Armitage extracted a promise from Musharraf to halt cross border terrorist movement permanently, though Musharraf seemed to step back from this commitment a few weeks later in an interview with a prominent American journalist.[31] In any case, U.S. diplomacy had worked, for the moment, and India began to step back, announcing a withdrawal of troops from the international border. India on October 16, 2002, began to bring its troops back to their barracks, completing the stand-down over the course of the next two months. The Vajpayee government focused its efforts on year-end elections in Kashmir that brought to power a coalition representing the interests of the Muslim majority Vale of Kashmir and the Hindu majority Jammu area of the state.

While violence remained high in Kashmir after the June 2002 pledge to Armitage, Indian officials stated publicly that infiltration did drop off for a few months.[32] The U.S. called on the two sides to resume negotiations, though Prime Minister Vajpayee responded that negotiations with Pakistan would not resume until Pakistan demonstrated that it intended to stop supporting terrorist attacks inside India. President Musharraf in turn said he would be willing to resume negotiations immediately. The U.S. was criticized inside India for not exerting greater pressure on Pakistan to crack down on the movement of terrorists across the borders and to close down the training camps within Pakistan, with commentators arguing that the U.S. was displaying a double standard on the issue of terrorism. This perception not only works against the goal of developing a stronger Indo-US relationship, but also makes Indians less willing to follow American advice to show restraint in the face of terrorist provocations. Some Indians even argued that the country should take a leaf from the American strategic book and use preemptive action against a terrorist threat.[33] Former U.S. Ambassador to India Robert Blackwill, in a series of speeches in India at the end of his tenure in June and July 2003, addressed these concerns by stating that the U.S. is as concerned by terrorism in India as it is by terrorism in the U.S.[34] However, the Indian litmus test of these assertions will be the pressure exerted by the U.S. to stop terrorist activities in India.

While American officials have publicly stated on several occasions that Pakistan must do more to stop cross border terrorist activities, there is a reluctance to use any sticks to make sure this happens, even where there is evidence of backsliding.[35] Rather, sanctions imposed in the wake of May 1998 nuclear test explosions were lifted (as they were for India) as a reward for participation in the fight against terrorism. Several hundred million dollars in Pakistani debts were written off. Senior officials have repeatedly praised Musharraf for his statesmanship, which was witnessed in his June 23-24, 2003 visit to Washington. He was the first South Asian leader to be hosted by the president at Camp David. He was promised three billion dollars in assistance, half of it military, over the next five years. Pakistan subsequently was declared a non-

NATO ally and promised a sale of the desired F-16 aircraft. All this was done without any formal U.S. conditions stipulating steps Musharraf should take to ensure regional peace, a key regional objective in the war against terrorism. While India seems to have a fairly high tolerance for cross border terrorism, there are limits, as the December 2001 attack on Parliament demonstrated, and the terrorist groups undoubtedly see it in their interest to exacerbate tensions between India and Pakistan. The chances they will again try some outrageous attacks within India are therefore high. Terrorists within Pakistan, perhaps with support from the outside and with probable links to the al-Qaeda network, have also sought to kill Musharraf on at least two occasions, almost certainly because of his backing to Operating Enduring Freedom and the global war on terrorism.[36] The Prime Minister of Pakistan has been targeted, as has the military corps commander of Karachi. A selective crackdown on domestic terrorists is insufficient since there are links between groups with a foreign agenda (in India and Afghanistan) and those whose activities are domestically focused.

The extent to which U.S. policy makers are willing to go to reward Musharraf for his support in the war on terrorism and to strengthen his position at home surfaced in the bureaucratic debate over the supply of an updated F-16 fighter plane to Pakistan as part of the package of military assistance to be announced during his June 23-24, 2003 visit to Washington, his fourth to the U.S since September 11. This is a classic case of a view devoid of a regional context. The F-16 carries high symbolic value for both countries, and both view it as a sign of the U.S. relationship with them.[37] The Bush administration as part of its policy of de-hyphenating policies toward India and Pakistan made the decision in 2005 to sell the F-16s to Pakistan. The U.S. simultaneously decided to significantly upgrade its strategic relationship with India, a move that almost certainly led to the virtual Indian silence on the F-16 sale. The sale did not alter the military balance now in India's favor and more importantly under the new circumstances did not signal a U.S. move to strengthen Pakistan against India.

The U.S. has separate security interests in each country that call for different policies. Pakistan is an important tactical partner in the war on terrorism, India as an emerging power in Asia will play an increasingly important role in U.S. strategic thinking in the region, a major reason for the decision to make India an exception on U.S. nuclear nonproliferation legislation while not demanding that it simultaneously give up its nuclear weapons program. Lifting restrictions on the sale of nuclear materials and technology—to India and not to Pakistan—for the civilian nuclear program in an India that had not renounced its nuclear weapons was another indication of the U.S. refusal to club the two countries together in policy formulation. The U.S. has no intention of making a similar offer to Pakistan, whose record of safeguarding nuclear expertise is under a cloud because of the two-decade old nuclear bazaar managed by A.Q. Khan, who headed one of the country's major laboratories that developed Pakistan's nuclear weapon, The F-16 sale to Pakistan, however, is recognition of its important role as a frontline state in the war on terrorism; the nuclear deal with India underscores its strategic significance in the larger Asian context.

An F-16 delivery, however, could risk destabilizing Pakistani domestic politics. While delivery would strengthen Musharraf's status among the military corps commanders over the short term, the aircraft would do little to build his legitimacy among the larger public and the huge cost will reduce available funds needed for strengthening the domestic economy.[38] Musharraf's long term political survival and the prospects for stability within Pakistan depend on significantly greater investment that generates jobs, on much more money for schools that teach secular values, and on strengthening the democratic process and secular parties.

Chances are good that the U.S. policy in South Asia, especially the Pakistan policy, could result in the U.S. marching back to the situation in 1990, when the country came down hard on Pakistan (i.e., cutting off delivery of military equipment, included the contracted deal for 28 F-16s) for not following the nuances of U.S. decision making regarding Pakistan's development of nuclear weapons. Pakistan's lack of clairvoyance on this matter triggered the use of sanctions mandated by the Pressler Amendment. The U.S. had been less than firm on the nuclear weapons issue in the late 1980s, but began to focus more closely on the problem when it became strategically convenient to do so. Surprised and angry

Pakistanis interpreted the sanctions as another example of U.S. betrayal of an ally. In the present situation, terrorist groups operating out of Pakistan are likely to test the limits of Indian endurance and the U.S., facing prospect of a regional conflict, may find itself forced again to consider formalizing unstated "conditions", this time relating to action Musharraf was supposed to have taken against anti-Indian terrorist groups that are based in Pakistan.

Functional considerations will likely dominate the conduct of U.S. foreign policy during crises, as has happened again and again in the case of South Asia, unless there is a major restructuring in the foreign policy process that involves a strengthening of the State Department and the regional perspective that is the hallmark of the foreign service. The aftermath of the Iraq military action is perhaps the most dramatic example of what can happen when "functionalists" dominate the post-war reconstruction. Strobe Talbott successfully sought to get around the problem at the time of India's nuclear tests in 1998 and the subsequent fighting at the line of control separating the two parts of Kashmir by creating a specialized bureaucratic mechanism providing regionalists a prominent presence at the high table of decision-making. But the arrangement was temporary and highly dependent on a very creative policymaker. It has not been replicated. What is needed are structural changes that put in place the bureaucratic mechanism established by Strobe Talbott in the late 1990s. At least on this issue, the State Department was not the proverbial "fudge factory" that often made it an ineffective and slow-moving agent in Washington's bureaucratic battles.

The Rudolphs, based on their study of the conduct of U.S. foreign policy before and during the 1971 Indo-Pakistani war, came out for a restructured State Department that brought regionalists and functionalists together. Hart-Rudman some twenty-five years later, looking at the conduct of U.S. foreign policy on a much broader international context, came to the same conclusion. The global war on terror risks a major setback in South Asia unless the core recommendations of both studies—an enhanced role for regionalists—are addressed seriously. The formulation of policy on other important issues, like instability in Iraq, nuclear weapons in Iran and North Korea, suffer from a similar bureaucratic problem and weakens the State Department's role as the preeminent agency in the formulation of foreign policy.

NOTES AND REFERENCES

1. Lloyd I. Rudolph, Susanne Hoeber Rudolph, "*The Regional Imperative: The Administration of U.S. Foreign Policy Towards South Asian States Under Presidents Johnson and Nixon*", (Atlantic Highlands, New Jersey: Humanities Press, 1980).
2. The Commission, originally set up by the Secretary of Defense, was chartered as a Federal Advisory Committee to conduct what it calls "the most comprehensive review of American Security since the National Security Act of 1947." (Quoted in the Hart-Rudman Commission website, http://www.nssg.gov/About_US/Charter/Charter.htm, February 2001). The first report, *New World Coming; American Security in the 21st Century*, focused on the emerging global security environment for the first 25 years of the new century. The second, *Seeking a National Strategy: A Concert for Preserving Security and Promoting Freedom*, outlines a new national security strategy that reflects emerging challenges. The third and final report, *Roadmap for National Security: Imperative for Change*, offers a prescription for a significant overhaul of the structures and processes of U.S. national security. I will focus on the third report in this series. The Government Printing Office released the three documents in September 1999, April 2000, and February 2001, respectively.
3. Henry Kissinger, "The Tilt: The India-Pakistan Crisis of 1971" in his *White House Years* (Boston: Little, Brown and Company, 1979), pp. 842-918.
4. Christopher Van Hollen, "The Tilt Policy Revisited: Nixon-Kissinger Geopolitics in South Asia", *Asian Survey* (1980), Vol. 20, No. 4, pp. 339-61.
5. An especially good analysis of the lack of influence of State Department South Asian experts during this period is the contribution of Gerald A. Heeger to the Rudolph volume, *After the 'Tilt': The Making of U.S. Foreign Policy Pakistan, 1972-74*, op. cit., pp. 125-42.
6. Most prominent among them are the Lashkar-e-Toiba and the Jaish-e-Mohammed, both which are based in Pakistan and recruit mainly in Pakistan. Both have an anti-India program as part of their pan-Islamic agenda. Unlike many other anti-Indian groups in Kashmir, their major goal is not political (the political future of Kashmir), but the larger goal of disrupting the Indian state. Both have changed names since their designation as terrorist organizations after 9/11 and continue to function in Pakistan.
7. For a particularly good press report on this, see David Sanger, "Bush Offers Pakistan Aid, but No F-16's", *New York Times*, (June 25, 2003),

Section A, pp. 10. Sanger writes that, "Administration officials said today that it [the assistance] would require Congressional approval, and that General Musharraf understands that failure to democratize, curb terrorism and stop proliferation would halt aid. 'I'm not calling those conditions,' a senior administration official told reporters, 'but let's be realistic. Three years down the road, if things are going badly in those areas, it's not going to happen'."

8. For an account of the support extended to Musharraf see "Betting on the General", *Washington Post* (June 30, 2003), editorial, pp. A14.
9. The lopsided vote in favor of this amendment is partly a reflection of the growing political clout of the Indian American community and the 155 member-strong India caucus in the House of Representatives (the largest country caucus in the House). The Indian American community engaged in a major effort to get a favorable vote on this amendment, with the lobby effort led by the US-India Political Action Committee (USINPAC).
10. For a full text of the bill with amendments, see http://www.house.gov/rules/H1950ALL_RH.PDF on the House of Representatives website.
11. A very good summary of both sides in this debate is Dan Morgan, "A Debate over U.S. 'Empire' Builds in Unexpected Circles", *Washington Post* (August 10, 2003), pp. A3.
12. See a discussion of Kiesling's views in his "Preemptive Strike", *Washington Post Magazine* (July 27, 2003), pp. 12-16; 26-27.
13. See Gingrich's April 22, 2003 speech to the American Enterprise Institute for Public Policy Research, "Transforming the State Department: The Next Challenge for the Bush Administration," *AEI Online* (Washington, April 22, 2003); he spells out his argument in greater detail in "The Failure of US Diplomacy", *Foreign Policy Magazine* (July/August 2003) pp. 42-49. Much of the Gingrich attack on the State Department may be prompted by bureaucratic battles in Washington, more specifically the effort to undermine the role of Secretary of State Colin Powell, who many neo-conservatives viewed as a dangerous dove.
14. Frank J. Gaffney Jr., "Speaking Truth to Power", (http://www.natinalreview.copm/gaffney/gaffney042302.asp, April 23, 2003).
15. Many of these new functional bureaus fulfill mandates handed to the State Department by Congress to produce annual "reports" on a growing number of subjects.
16. *Roadmap for National Security: Imperative for Change* (Washington, D.C.: U.S. Government Printing Office, 2001), p. 53.
17. *Regional Security, op. cit.*, pp. 92.
18. When discussions of an expanded South Asia Bureau had come up for discussion, the usual candidates for inclusion had been the Central Asian republics, which in fact happened.
19. I have personal knowledge of these meetings since I was one of the invitees to the meetings chaired by Talbott. My office in the State Department's Bureau of Intelligence and Research was, among other

things, asked to provide to the participants "Red Team" papers which analyzed the likely responses of regional states to proposed U.S. policy.

20. In the likely case the reforms suggested by the Rudolphs and Hart-Rudman are not implemented, the next best recommendation would be a more common use of the sort of team effort set up by Talbott to handle South Asia. However, it was my experience that this bureaucratic strategy is a rare occurrence.
21. One of the projects that emerged from Talbott's meetings with Jaswant Singh was a very imaginative bilateral official project to review lessons learned from the mid-summer 1999 Indo-Pakistani confrontation. This was a unique bilateral endeavor that required inventing a process. I led the American team and Arun Singh, a confidante of then Indian External Affairs Minister Jaswant Singh, the Indian side; this Indo-American joint group held several meetings during 2000. These meetings, characterized by lively and frank discussions, turned out to be a confidence building exercise that reflected a greatly enhanced level of trust between the U.S. and India.
22. See my analysis of the terrorist issue in South Asia, "South Asia: A Selective War on Terrorism", in Ashley J. Tellis and Michael Wills (editors), *Confronting Terrorism in the Pursuit of Power* (National Bureau of Asian Research: Seattle, 2004), pp. 227-60.
23. This decision to deepen significantly the U.S. relationship with India was revealed on July 2005 on the occasion of Prime Minister Manmohan Singh's visit to the U.S. and then on March 2, 2006, on President Bush's visit to India.
24. The US Congress must again consider the negotiated US-India nuclear agreement, which was reached in September 2007, after India works out an India-specific agreement with the International Atomic Energy Agency and after the 45-country Nuclear Suppliers Group adds it support to the exception for India, a country that has not signed the 1970 Nonproliferation Treaty and would thus otherwise be denied access to nuclear fuel and nuclear related technology. The coalition government of Prime Minister Manmohan Singh has delayed taking the issue to the International Atomic Energy Agency because the communist members of parliament that support his minority government from the outside have warned him that they might withdraw support if he goes ahead of this project which they argue sacrifices Indian strategic autonomy.
25. Musharraf continues to function as both president and chief of army staff and this broad array of power is one of key issues in dispute with the elected members of the National Assembly.
26. For a deeper explanation, see my *South Asia: A Selective War on Terrorism*, *op. cit.*
27. Given the increasing disapproval in Pakistan regarding the fight against terrorism, there is some validity to the assumption that Musharraf plays a critical role in keeping Pakistan committed to it. Polls conducted by the

Office of Research at the State Department in 2003 indicate that "the public's support for Musharraf's decision to back the U.S. in the war on terrorism is becoming somewhat tenuous", with 70 per cent believing that the U.S. is giving little or no support to Pakistan on regional issues such as Kashmir; *South Asia Opinion Alert; Most Pakistanis Say Military Action in Iraq Unjustified* (May 1, 2003), pp. 1. Seventy two per cent also believe that "the country is going in the wrong direction"; *South Asia Opinion Alert: Musharraf Still Commands Public Confidence, But Dissatisfaction Mounts* (May 6, 2003), p. 1.

28. American Ambassador to Pakistan, Nancy Powell, in a January 23, 2003 speech to businessmen in Karachi, called on the Musharraf government to "end the use of Pakistan as a platform for terrorism". But a few weeks later, press reports from Pakistan report that the leaders of banned terrorist groups were released and their organizations continued to recruit and train cadre. See John Lancaster and Kamran Khan, "Extremist Groups Renew Activity in Pakistan: Support of Kashmir Militants is at Odds with the War on Terrorism", *Washington Post* (February 8, 2003), p. A1.
29. See John Lancaster, "Mulling Action, India Equates Iraq, Pakistan: Pre-emption cited in Kashmir Conflict", *Washington Post* (April 11, 2003), p. A20.
30. The U.S. has designated these two groups as Foreign Terrorist Organizations; both have links to al-Qaeda and the Taliban rooted in their common experience in the terrorist training camps of pre 9/11 Afghanistan. Under U.S. pressure, President Musharraf also ostensibly banned these two groups, though they continue to function inside Pakistan, as reported by John Lancaster and Kamran Khan, "Extremists Groups Renew Activity in Pakistan", *op. cit.*
31. In that interview, Musharraf said that there was "no movement across the Line of Control" in Kashmir; moreover, he asserted that he did not think of anti-Indian activities in Kashmir as terrorism, but as part of a "freedom struggle". Commenting on any commitment the press was saying he had made to the U.S. Deputy Secretary, Musharraf stated that he did not talk about closing training camps in Kashmir. In that printed interview, he does not say whether he had made a commitment to stop cross border infiltration of terrorists. See full text in Lally Weymouth, "Voices from a Hot Zone", *Newsweek* (July 1, 2002), p. 30.
32. On June 20, 2002, Defence Minister George Fernandes, for example, told reporters in Srinagar that infiltration had declined significantly, though the ground situation in Kashmir remained essentially unaltered; *Doordarshan Channel 1*, New Delhi (June 20, 2002).
33. For a discussion of this, see John Lancaster, "Mulling Action, India Equates Iraq, Pakistan; Pre-Emption Cited in Kashmir Conflict", *Washington Post* (April 11, 2003), p. A20.
34. In a strongly worded address to the Confederation of Indian Industry (CII) on July 16, 2003, the outgoing U.S. Ambassador to New Delhi,

Robert D. Blackwill stated that: "These murderers are not misunderstood idealists. They are not disadvantaged dissidents. They are not religious perfectionists. And they are not freedom fighters. They are terrorists, and we should never fail to call them exactly that . ..the United States and India must have zero tolerance for terrorism. . . .our joint US-India mantra in the war against terrorism [should be]: "the first and most important reply to evil is to stop it." For a copy of the speech, visit the website of the Confederation of Indian Industry; www.ciionline.org/Common/164/Images/Robert/20D./20Blackwill/20-/20Speech170703. pdf

35. For a report of such backsliding regarding terrorist groups, see John Lancaster and Kamran Khan, *op. cit.* They report that groups ostensibly banned by Musharraf following his much publicized January 12, 2002 speech to the nation, continued to function a year after the speech and many of their leaders had been released.
36. Musharraf walks a fine line as he seeks to satisfy conflicting demands of Islamic groups, his military and the United States. But Musharraf, a secular person who seems genuinely to want to make Pakistan a modern secular state, would more likely succeed in his goal if he were to crack down hard on the radical pan-Islamic forces that threaten his vision of a modern Pakistan and his own person.
37. Delivery of contracted F-16s was stopped in 1990 when Pressler Amendment sanctions were applied to Pakistan because the U.S. had evidence that Pakistan was developing nuclear weapons. At the time, Pakistanis viewed the termination as a signal of the end of any kind of special security relationship with the U.S. Indians came to the same conclusion.
38. Following the devastating October 2005 earthquake, President Musharraf decided to delay purchase.

2

THE REASONS WHY
America's Half-Century Struggle to Control the Political Agenda in South Asia[1]

— *Harold A. Gould*

Our purpose here will be to examine why American foreign policy failed to achieve its stated ends in South Asia, a region where initially at least the United States invested major political, military and economic capital in the hope that outcomes would prove favorable to its perceived strategic interests.

My thesis is that, regrettably, US South Asia Policy was a failure according to its own stated premises. Let us recall here that the policies pursued from the Eisenhower/Dulles administration onward had three such premises. They were: (1) The exclusion, or at least minimization, of Communist Bloc power and influence from South Asia; (2) the deterrence of internecine war in South Asia; (3) the promotion of democratic institutions and economic development in South Asia on a scale that would immunize the region from becoming a breeding ground for political radicalization.

In my view, these policies failed in all three respects due to cultural ignorance, historical naiveté and political obsessions which from the end of World War II increasingly impelled the United States to incorporate South Asia into a militarized grand strategy which, however appropriate it might have seemed for the global challenges it faced, was in fact inappropriate and destined to become counterproductive for South Asia. In the end, as we shall see, this scenario had the opposite effect from what was intended: (1) It did not prevent the penetration of Soviet and Communist Bloc influence into the region: it in fact facilitated it. (2) It did not deter war in South Asia; it in fact made intra-regional war inevitable. (3) It had limited success in promoting representative government and economic progress because in the main it obstructed the evolution of democratic institutions in Pakistan, had little to do with their promulgation in India (India did it on its own), and retarded economic progress in both states by whatever degree each found it necessary to divert scarce capital resources toward an intraregional arms race that plagues the region to this day.

To achieve a deeper understanding of where these matters stand today we must review the phases through which US relations with India and Pakistan have coursed over the past half-century. They now can be seen as prologue to the nuclear tests conducted at Pokhran and Chagai Hills on May 11 and 13, 1998, respectively, to the skirmishing at Kargil in 1999, and in South Asia generally since 9/11.

It is worth noting that as early as World War II the United States government showed an interest in evolving nationalism in the Indian subcontinent. This in part was because it seemed evident to many members of the Roosevelt administration that some form of political autonomy would inevitably occur there once the war ended. In part it was because during the war itself, and particularly as the Japanese war machine drove relentlessly through Southeast Asia until its forces were lapping against India's eastern frontier, there was a desire to encourage maximum Indian support for the Allied cause. In this latter connection the United States government was actively employing its good offices to try and persuade its British ally to make concessions to the leadership of the Indian National Congress (most particularly Gandhi and Nehru) that would elicit their cooperation in the struggle against the Axis powers. Sir Stafford Cripps's mission to India in early 1942 was an explicit concession to American concerns about the failure to involve the nationalists in the war effort. Leading up to this initiative, the Roosevelt administration engaged in persistent remonstrances that the British adopt a more conciliatory line toward its colonials in general and India in particular. These urgings were promulgated in the form of private diplomacy, however, because Roosevelt did not want open disagreements between the United States and Britain to jeopardize the public posture of unity which he regarded as vital to the preservation of the complex coalition that comprised the Western Alliance.[2]

As is well known, the Cripps initiative failed, primarily because Prime Minister Winston Churchill, an old imperialist curmudgeon, had no intention of allowing it to succeed. He basically went through the motions in order to placate his American ally. When the deliberations failed, Churchill was able to blame it on Indian intransigence and say, "I told you so!".[3]

American concerns about the alienation of the Indian nationalists did not wane with the failure of the Cripps Mission, however. In its wake the US government prevailed upon the British to appoint a senior native Indian to the sub-ambassadorial position of Agent General in Washington. The post was allotted to a very elite and "safe" Indian aristocrat, who was nevertheless nominally pro-nationalist, named Sir Girja Shankar Bajpai. Reciprocally, Roosevelt appointed a very senior and talented professional diplomat, William Phillips, as his next "personal representative" to India (after Col. Louis Johnson) with the mission of trying to find some other formula for softening British intransigence and reconciling the differences between the colonial regime, the Indian National Congress and the Muslim League. Phillips, a Boston Brahman and somewhat of an Anglophile, to the dismay of the British, proved to be highly skeptical of their political tactics in India and strongly sympathetic toward the nationalists. He sent many memoranda back to Washington in this vein, including a final one a copy of which fell into the hands of *Washington Post* investigative reporter, Drew Pearson. When he published excerpts from it in his column, *Washington Merry-Go-Round*, it generated a major eruption in US-British relations that included a demand that Roosevelt personally repudiate its contents. When this did not happen, recriminations festered for a long time. In the end, however, they faded away, because there remained a war to fight.[4]

What was important about the deputation of high-level American representatives to India during World War II was not the substantive effect they had on British imperial policy toward Indian nationalism. For they really had none. What was important was the impact they had on the perceptions of Indian nationalists, especially adherents to the Indian National Congress, toward the United States. These perceptions were uniformly positive, because they engendered a belief that the quest for political independence had found sympathetic and understanding witnesses in high places in America. It set the stage for the first phase of US-Indian relations that encompassed the early postwar years when India and Pakistan achieved independence. This phase lasted until the early 1950s when the Cold War came to entirely dominate America's global strategic orientation

Political independence in South Asia was achieved at a high cost. The partition of the Subcontinent in 1947 into two separate states, one demographically predominantly (and doctrinally) Muslim and the other demographically predominantly (although not doctrinally) Hindu[5], which were from the outset politically antagonistic toward one another, clearly got the region off on the wrong foot in the postwar era. The exchange of populations between the two new states took on the characteristics of what these days is referred to as "ethnic cleansing" and resulted in the deaths of no less than half a million, perhaps as many as a million, people, and to the uprooting of several million more.[6] Within a matter of months following partition the two new nations were at war with each other over Kashmir which led ironically to another partition as India and Pakistan assumed *de facto* sovereignty over those portions of the province (now referred to as Line of Control or LOC) which each country's armed forces were occupying at the time of the armistice in 1948.

For the five years that followed partition, despite the state of belligerency existing between India and Pakistan, the United States's relationship with the two subcontinental powers got off to a reasonably positive start. Especially with regard to India this was the case for two important reasons. First, India had opted to become a secular state governed on the Westminster model, and had been led to this choice by Jawaharlal Nehru, one of the century's most articulate Asian proponents of genuinely popular government. The fact that this made India the first major non-Western nation to wholeheartedly and unambiguously adopt fully representative government caught the imagination of many Americans. Second, the Truman administration appointed Chester Bowles as the United States' third, but first long-term, ambassador to India.[7]

Pakistan, by contrast, hesitated to go as far as India along this path, in part because of the attraction of its leaders to Islamic theocratic predilections and in part because the dominant elites who inherited power in the new state were predominantly landed aristocracy, traditional bureaucrats, and professional soldiers steeped in the old colonial culture who saw mass politics as a threat to their sense of public order and their special privileges. The result was the failure to carry constitutional development beyond the limited franchise structure which the British and the nationalists had negotiated in 1935 but which India had begun to supercede as soon as freedom had been won.[8] Th is process consummated in the 1950 Constitution of India, one of the most comprehensive democratic constitutions ever written. In Pakistan, by contrast, the retention of a limited franchise constitution which preserved the dominance of the propertied classes resulted in an autocratic/paternalistic pattern of government, sometimes referred to as the "viceregal model," which by 1959 had culminated in military dictatorship under General Ayub Khan, and was followed in subsequent years by three more such episodes of military dictatorship—in 1971 (Yahya Khan), 1988 (Zia-al-Haq) and 1999 (Pervez Musharraf). This difference between the type of government that each state chose was destined to be a crucial factor in determining America's differential orientation to them over the ensuing years, as we shall see.

Even though the Cold War had begun to take form in earnest by the commencement of Harry S. Truman's second (although first elected) term as President, initially its focus was primarily on Europe and somewhat secondarily on the Middle East, because at this point in time that is where the greatest threats to American security were perceived to be. However, the triumph of the Maoists in China in 1949 followed by the Korean war in 1950 rapidly drew American attention to the political situation in Asia. Strategic doctrines were being developed at this time in the context of the National Security Council, the State Department, and the newly created Department of Defense. But thinking on the European dimensions of international security was much more advanced and sophisticated than was the case for Asia for the simple reason that there were less people in high places who were experienced Asia-hands, particularly after many such experts whose insights might have been helpful had been discredited and purged by McCarthyism. In the context of such threadbare expertise on Asia, it is not surprising that conceptualizations concerning the nature of threat structures and the manner of dealing with them were in large measure projections onto the Asian situation of America's reading of European history and most particularly the perceptions of political cause and effect that were drawn from the recently concluded struggle against the Axis alliance.[9]

Undoubtedly the most important step the United States government took at this time which reinforced its positive image in the region was the appointment in 1951of Chester Bowles as the American ambassador to India. Ironically, the reason why Bowles was given this assignment had little to do with any kind of cultural or historical insight into South Asia on the part of the Truman administration. Basically, it was the first of two occasions (the next would occur after John F. Kennedy became president) when consigning Bowles to an Asian ambassadorship was a ploy by his political enemies to move him as far as possible from Washington!

The reasons for this were indicative of a dramatic change that took place in the Democratic party following Franklin Roosevelt's death in April 1945. The passing of Roosevelt and the emergence of Harry Truman was more than a presidential succession. It was a *de facto regime change* that reflected both domestic and international developments associated with the end of World

War II. Internationally they were associated with emerging tensions between the United States and the Soviet Union. Domestically, it represented the swing toward the political right in the country writ large which resulted in a displacement within the Democratic Party of the radical New Deal reformers who had advised Roosevelt during the Great Depression and the War by a far more conservative, hard-line coterie of advisors and policy-makers who viewed the international environment in much less idealistic, more hard-line Realpolitik terms than had their predecessors. This new coterie was determined to politically neutralize the left-leaning idealists, symbolized by Vice-President Henry Agard Wallace, whom Roosevelt had gathered under his political wing.

While Bowles's assignment to the Indian ambassadorship might have been a tactical device to politically isolate him, once he arrived in South Asia, Chester Bowles found the perfect venue for the articulation, indeed the amplification, of his political values. Because of this he was able to do his country a lot of good in the emerging Third World until the stridency of the Cold War finally overwhelmed the last vestiges of Rooseveltian liberalism.

Bowles actually professed anti-Communism as stridently as did any of his Washington peers. His differences with the hard-liners were over methods and style. From the moment he reached South Asia, his liberal proclivities enabled him to instinctively understand that a militarized grand strategy was an unworkable means of garnering support for America's diplomatic objectives in the post-colonial, non-Western world. He believed the answer was economic assistance, plus any and all measures that encouraged the development and perpetuation of secular democratic institutions. From the outset of his arrival in New Delhi he blended his "New Deal" orientation toward India's postwar social and economic requirements with a shrewd (for the times) realization that nationalism was the dominant ideological preoccupation of Asian leaders like Nehru rather than the ideological categories that were relevant to recent Western political experience. He repeatedly emphasized these perspectives in reports to his superiors at State, in a steady stream of public statements, and in numerous articles and interviews published in the press. In the words of Howard Schaffer, who published a definitive political biography of Chester Bowles:

> Bowles's clear preference for aid to popularly based Third World governments over help to authoritarian ones, especially right wing regimes, reflected his strong democratic values. He was convinced that only governments enjoying strong public support would be able to create the climate of popular enthusiasm required for successful economic development.[10]

As Bowles himself stated it:

> How silly we must sometimes seem reducing every question to the Communist equation. *Some of the questions are bigger than communism*. . . . If all the Communists on earth disappeared overnight, the need for foreign aid to assist new struggling peoples to achieve stable democratic societies would still be there. [11]

Chester Bowles's activist style of diplomacy, along with his opposition to the rapidly crystallizing conventional wisdom about how best to checkmate Soviet expansionism, made him a highly controversial emissary. One might say that in Indian eyes he made US South Asian foreign policy appear more progressive than it actually was. Neither the Truman administration nor the US Congress were particularly enthusiastic about Nehru's Fabian approach to Indian economic development or his reluctance to decisively commit his nation to the Western camp. The so-called "non-alignment doctrine" was interpreted as being equivalent in the international arena to what the term "fellow traveler" had come to connote in the McCarthyist atmosphere that prevailed in the domestic American political environment. It was mainly Bowles who insisted that India's maverick foreign policy was driven not by sympathy for Communism but by a genre of nationalism that was an endemic, Third World reaction to the long night of colonialism, and therefore constituted no threat to American strategic interests as long as she remained democratic.

Bowles's achievement was quite remarkable in the face of the strategic mentality that already pervaded the State Department and the defense establishment. With the gathering clouds of the Cold War, even this New Deal administration was by no means a monolith respecting foreign policy. Bowles was for a time able almost single-handedly to save America from itself, as it were. Secretary of State Dean Acheson, passionately believed that old fashioned Realpolitik alone could successfully contain Communist expansionism. Men like Forestall, Henry L. Stimson, James Byrnes and Clark Clifford in the defense establishment were if anything even more hawkish than Acheson. The mounting Republican opposition in the country was even more shrill. In 1949, the *Subcommittee for the Near and Middle East of the State-Army-Navy-Air Forces Coordinating Committee (SANACC)*[12] prepared a document which stated that "our national interests require . .. the orientation of South Asia toward the U.S. and other Western democracies, and away from the USSR." The "basic strategic objectives of the U.S." require, the report said, "that Soviet encroachment or domination must be prevented; that the Soviets must be prevented from obtaining military support from these nations or given access to any of their facilities; that our side must endeavor to obtain the support and access to facilities denied to the other side; and *that Pakistan should be cultivated with a view to gaining access "in emergency"' to "base facilities in the Karachi-Lahore area."* (*Emphasis added.*)

Even though such formulations at this point remained far from being crystalized into a coherent policy, they clearly presaged what eventually would become the dominant American strategic orientation to South Asia. Doubts about which course of action was appropriate for South Asia persisted throughout the Truman administration, due mainly to Bowles's admonitions, but also because others in that administration as well, even some of the nascent hawks, harbored doubts about the soundness of a military relationship with Pakistan. As late as 1951, following talks with Pakistani officials in Washington, Acheson himself was uneasy enough about this to observe that "what Pakistan could do would be very much affected by its relations with India."[13] Kux (2001) concludes: "The Truman administration's reaction to Pakistan's willingness to help in the defense of the Middle East remained one of wariness, *lest arming Pakistan ensnare the United States in India-Pakistan disputes*."[14]

Ambivalence arose from the fact that deciding what to do about Pakistan was not seen as being solely dependant upon the implications that the militarization of Pakistan would have for relations with India. This ambivalence was destined to impose painful choices on Washington policy-makers. It was also, indeed primarily, being viewed from the standpoint of Pakistan's potential value to America's evolving global strategy for inhibiting Moscow's expansionist inclinations.

Poised on the eastern flank of the Middle East, with her northern border facing Inner Asia, and ultimately the Soviet Union, there were strong voices that inevitably favored treating Pakistan as the strategic anchor of a grand alliance for assuring control of the world's principal source of petroleum resources, on the one hand, and maintaining Afghanistan as a buffer against Soviet southern expansionism, on the other. As the rising tide of ethno-religious Separatism in South Asia was tumultuously careening toward Partition, these divergent perspectives on how to achieve a stable postwar security structure for the Subcontinent were in dynamic interplay with the antipathies and factionalism that beset the two nationalist organizations—the Indian National Congress of Gandhi, Nehru and Patel, and the Muslim League of Muhammad Ali Jinnah and Liaqat Ali Khan—that were contending with one another as each struggled toward the establishment of an independent postcolonial state that fulfilled their particular vision of political autonomy and cultural authenticity.

British officials identified with the outgoing colonial administration favored the establishment of a militarized Pakistani state that would secure Western strategic interests in the southern Asian region. Their perspective was in essence an analogical perpetuation of the geopolitical Great Game which had driven imperial perspectives on Inner Asia and the Middle East for more than a century. They fretted over the Nehruvian and Gandhian "pacificism" and "neutralism" which seemed destined to dominate the new Indian state. Their concerns and biases put them at odds with Mountbatten and other members of the Atlee government who desired a quick exodus from India even if that meant the installation of an Indian National Congress in India which entertained a contrapositive view of the subcontinent's strategic destiny.[15] It also inspired them to reach out to the foreign policy hawks in America who were rapidly replacing the Rooseveltian New Dealers in the Truman administration whom they knew were groping for a postwar, anti-Soviet grand strategy.

Sir Olaf Caroe (1892 to 1981) was a leading player in the effort of the 'Greater Pakistan' faction in White Hall and in the soon-to-be extinguished British-dominated Government of India who wished as much as possible to sustain the old balance-of-power model for the Subcontinent, Southwest and Inner Asia. Caroe had been Minister of External Affairs in the colonial government throughout World War II, and in 1946-47, as Partition was taking place, Governor of the Northwest Frontier Province (NWFP). He was totally identified with the Pathans and their Islamic heritage, fluent in the languages and dialects of that region, which, of course, is the main reason why he was designated as governor of this strategically vital province at this point in time.[16] In Caroe's own words, "during my times (1919-1947) the Pathans were protected from exterior buffets by able British and other diplomats on the Frontier and in Kabul who could win and sustain Afghan—and Pathan—confidence." (p. 523) Applying the purported lessons of the imperial past to the contemplated challenges of the postwar future, Caroe declared: "Surely the main British contribution to the stability of South Asia lay in our success in unifying the entire region for defense, from the Hindu Kush to the Himalaya in the north to the shores of the Indian Ocean." (p. 524). His lament was that this "unity of concept was shattered to be succeeded by mutual enmity, suspicion and hatred, leading to war. ..." In the wake of Partition, in other words, "no common purpose remains." (*Idem*). For Caroe the remedy was an Anglo-American *de facto* imperium that incorporated Pakistan within its strategic embrace.

Caroe's hope seemingly began to materialize in 1952 following Dwight D. Eisenhower's defeat of Adlai Stevenson. This led the

Republican Party back to the White House after a twenty year hiatus. By then, the die had been cast in favor of Containment. The Cold War was on! This heralded the demise of the Roosevelt/New Deal political consensus that envisioned a world free of colonialism and nourished by leftist-tinged social reform and economic development. With the change of administrations, and most importantly, *administration philosophy*, Chester Bowles was shunted into political oblivion for the time being. He would have to wait eight years before surfacing once again as a significant player in the field of South Asian diplomacy.

As is well known, John Foster Dulles emerged as the country's new foreign policy apostle. The word apostle is highly apt. It was not so much that Dulles represented a radical departure from the global perspectives of the bulk of his immediate Democratic predecessors. His achievement was, as Gould and Ganguly (1992) put it, his ability to infuse American foreign policy with an ideological intensity that was the equal of and opposite to the edge that Marxist-Leninist ideology had imparted to Soviet (and later Chinese) foreign policy. Extremism had bred counter extremism."[17]

Dulles harbored a loathing for the "neutralist" or "non-aligned" position espoused by Jawaharlal Nehru, which Bowles tacitly endorsed. This antipathy blended well with Caroe's and White Hall's misgivings about the strategic implications of Indian political developments, and the need for a countervailing 'Pakistan policy'. As early as January 17, 1947, while Nehru headed a caretaker regime that was overseeing the transition from British rule to formal Independence, Dulles had made his position clear. In a speech before the *National Publishers Association*, he heaped disdain on India's new government. "In India," he declared, "Soviet Communism exercises a strong influence through its interim government." Nehru issued an angry rejoinder to this assertion the very next day. "I have read with surprise and regret a report of a speech made by Mr. John Foster Dulles in New York in which he criticizes [the] policy of [the] interim government. I can hardly believe that report is a correct one. Mr. Dulles was one of [the] representatives of [the] US Govt. in [the] UN general assembly and his words therefore carry weight."[18] The atmosphere of rancor and distrust between India and the United States intensified when Dulles followed up these remarks with his famous declaration that neutralism is "immoral."

Predictably and understandably, and to the delight of the imperialist faction in Britain, once John Foster Dulles became Secretary of State, US policy toward South Asia turned decisively away from an emphasis on the patient nurturance of democratic institutions and economic development for which Chester Bowles and the liberal establishment had stood. In its place came a militarized grand strategy that denied legitimacy to India's non-alignment doctrine and conscientiously recruited Pakistan into the mosaic of mutual security structures that were forming along the perimeter of Soviet and Chinese power. Pakistan was designated by the emergent generation of Cold Warriors to become America's strategic partner in South Asia—against Soviet expansionism, in opposition to the rising Red Star over China, and implicitly (though never publicly acknowledged) against India's growing influence in the emerging Third World.

Recently available archival material, and Dennis Kux's masterful treatise on US-Pakistan relations[19] make it clear that from the outset the attempt to forge a strategic relationship between the United States and Pakistan was beset with the contradictions which Ambassador Phillips and even Acheson had sensed. From the American standpoint a Pakistan alliance was intended to exclude Soviet power and influence from the Subcontinent, prevent intra-regional conflicts (primarily over Kashmir), and promote economic growth through the market economy. From the Pakistani standpoint, however, it was perceived as a way to strengthen Pakistan's military hand *vis-a-vis* India, enhance international diplomatic support for its claims on Kashmir (over which it had already unsuccessfully fought a war with India in 1948), and, not inconsequentially, to strengthen and stabilize the authoritarian political system which the feudal landlords/British-trained officer corps/ bureaucratic elite were busily attempting to establish by systematically undermining the initial attempts made by the country's founders to create some form of broadly representative democracy.

Especially after Jinnah's death (September 11, 1949) and Liaqat Ali Khan's assassination at Rawalpindi (October 16, 1951), the emergent Pakistani leadership's principal motivations for associating itself with an American global containment treaty system had nothing to do with any perceived Communist threat emanating either from domestic or international sources. It was driven by Pakistani expectations that "double-dipping" on American military and economic largesse would enable them to strengthen the country's economy in a manner that enhanced the capacity of its army to successfully win a future military showdown with India. However, the fact that bringing Pakistan into these alliance systems laid the foundation for a prolonged pattern of intra-regional conflict, not over Communism but over a modern manifestation of centuries-old ethnoreligious antipathies, was at the time entirely beyond the comprehension to Eurocentric, anti-Communist ideologues like John Foster Dulles and his coterie of domestic hawks who saw the world almost entirely in one-dimensional terms.[20]

The Pakistan policy was set in motion during the first year of Eisenhower's presidency. It's impact in India is well known. The new ambassador who arrived with it in New Delhi was a career diplomat named George V. Allen. By all accounts, Allen was an able professional who found himself burdened with a profoundly unpalatable assignment. His burdens were probably increased by virtue of the fact that unlike Bowles he had no background or constituencies in the political arena. He was a career diplomat unable to build public support for, or to modify, his designated role, as Chester Bowles had been. Given the policy's great unpopularity in India, however, it is doubtful in any event whether a more politically viable person would have made very much difference. Despite the vilification to which the United States was subjected by the Indian government and press, and the personal pressures that Allen experienced, it is clear that his enthusiasm for a policy that would disturb the political and military balance in South Asia was not great. In testimony before the Senate Foreign Relations Committee in May 1954, Ambassador Allen sounded more like Chester Bowles than John Foster Dulles. "I do not see a better alternative [than Nehru] on the horizon at the present moment," he declared. "If the democratic processes were to fail in India, an extremist movement, either to the left or to the right would occur, either one of which would be bad for us." Allen ruefully declared, "You may be sure that our decision to give military aid to Pakistan has not made my life in New Delhi any easier." However, like any good soldier with a job to do, Allen concluded that "if the United States is going to carry out a policy of collective security, it seems to me we have got to go through with it rather stubbornly in spite of certain difficulties it is going to cause us in our relations with other countries." And finally, "I have impressed on my staff that no matter how our relations with India may be affected by this decision, we must show that we are entirely ready to continue to be friendly with India."[21]

As the new policy toward South Asia unfolded, it rapidly became clear that the rewards to be garnered from incorporating Pakistan into America's global treaty system were destined to be meager. On the Indian side, the reaction of both the press and the political establishment far exceeded American expectations. Nehru was bitterly upset over the turn of events. In Robert J. McMahon's (1994) words, "He blasted the United States repeatedly for its militaristic approach to world affairs, a charge repeated and embellished in the increasingly venomous Indian press." (p. 214)

In one sense, the Indian reaction reinforced the already growing tendency by the Cold War hawks in the new administration and on Capitol Hill to view the Pakistani leadership as more congenial than the Indian. Washington officialdom, says Kux, "found Pakistani leaders—Liaqat Ali Khan, Ghulam Mohammed, and Zafrullah Khan—more agreeable and easier to deal with than their Indian counterparts." Nehru was seen as "prickly" and Krishnan Menon as "obnoxious and procommunist."[22] This affinity for affable, seemingly compliant political leaders who were "firmly in command" of their states and could therefore make quick decisions favorable to US interests, because they were not answerable to democratically structured political constituencies, by contrast with politicians like Jawaharlal Nehru, was already proving to be the Achilles Heel of American foreign policy that until very recently it still was.

But this was not the worst consequence of the decision to convert Pakistan into a Cold War bastion. It must be remembered that the whole point of the policy was to prevent Soviet penetration of South Asia. Yet this turned out to be precisely the result. It didn't come through any conversion of Nehru to Communism, or by the kind of civil disintegration and grassroots revolutionary upheavals that the United States, by projecting perceptions that had grown out of the orgy of witch-hunting which had consumed its own body politic for almost a decade, imagined would be the case unless India could be persuaded or coerced into joining the Western alliance. It came as a strategic reflex to the US decision to inject the Cold War into South Asia.

Nehru, believed (rightly) that India would eventually become the target of increased Pakistani militarization. Despite his reputation for being a vacillating peacenik, disdained by macho American hardliners for this reason, he revealed an unanticipated willingness to forthrightly engage in Realpolitik when India's security was at stake. He turned to the Soviet Union in search of countervailing military and diplomatic support. This did not happen all at once, to be sure, but ultimately Russia responded positively once it had wisely abandoned the old Stalinist position that the ruling classes of Third World countries like India were nothing more than brown-skinned lackeys of Western imperialism. This altered the balance of power in South Asia to the detriment of US long range interests.

After having committed itself to an alliance with Pakistan, the United States discovered that it had stumbled into a political quagmire. To paraphrase McMahon, ambivalence, misunderstandings, tensions and unfulfilled expectations plagued the relationship from the beginning. (p. 190) Documentary evidence amassed both by McMahon and Kux vividly show that a major disconnect existed between what Pakistan expected from the United States and what the United States wanted from Pakistan. What seems to have shocked the Eisenhower administration most was their belated discovery that the country they had selected as the keystone of their Southern Asian strategy was so politically unstable and such an economic basket-case that it had little chance of becoming the robust bulwark against Communist bloc expansionism that Dulles had envisioned. It was a political liability instead of a strategic asset!

As these realizations painfully dawned, a subtle shift took place in America's assessment of Pakistan's strategic value. This is a good example of how grassroots realities intervene to compel modifications in grand strategy. Instead of seeing Pakistan as a pro-active partner in the great crusade (as Dulles in his naiveté originally imagined), many members of the administration began to view Pakistan as an anguishingly difficult client state that constantly needed to be nurtured and mollified in order to keep the wolf of political collapse and social chaos from her door. The more realistic Eisenhower soon realized this. United States policy-makers grew increasingly skeptical about what sort of relationship with Pakistan would best serve American long-range interests. Factions emerged that were less inclined to support the kind of *carte blanche* toward building up the Pakistani military machine which that country's leaders had anticipated, and Dulles's circle of policy-makers hoped, would be the outcome of an alliance with the American superpower. Key US officials, although reluctant to publicly admit it, were finally coming to comprehend the dimensions of the closet agenda that drove the Pakistani leadership. Pakistan was a rumbling volcano whose eruption could be triggered by a critical mass of US arms. The archives reveal an almost desperate attempt on America's part to formulate a mix of military and economic sustenance that would keep Pakistan from "going Communist" and "going under" without at the same time enabling her to attack India. This disparity of perceptions and expectations between the two states laid the foundation for the perpetual tension that dominated the relationship almost from the start and continues to do so to this day.

What was most regrettable about taking on the Pakistan burden is that it sacrificed for years to come any chance of achieving a constructive and enduring accommodation with democratic India. The failure to go this route bespeaks of a common American tendency, as evidenced as much today in Iraq as it was then in relation Pakistan, to pursue simplistic solutions to foreign policy challenges. Bowles and the liberals were prepared to pursue the more difficult course of subtle diplomacy. Rightly, in my view, they believed that a strong, stable and prosperous India, its non-alignment policy to the contrary notwithstanding, offered the best chance for the success of America's long-range interests in South Asia, *viz*., intraregional political stability, and imperviousness to the inroads either of domestic subversion or external aggression.

One salient fact that emerged from the early stages of the US-Pakistan relationship that has persisted to this day is the futility of trying have one's cake and eat it in relations with the two major South Asian states. This was inherent in the US's determination to try and build up the Pakistani military machine, on the one hand, while simultaneously trying to avoid being perceived either as a *de jure* or *de facto* ally of Pakistan should an eruption of intraregional war with India occur. This dilemma was compounded by the fact that the Cold Warriors, in the course of the first Eisenhower administration, tried to nuance the Pakistani relationship in such a way as to exert 'containment pressure' on India without explicitly stating that this was their purpose. They wanted the Indians to "read" the strategic implications that way in the hope that this would inhibit any hegemonic predispositions the Indians might harbor within the region.

Kux contends that the "contain India" aspect of the policy did not exist at the official level. He seems to be right as far as Eisenhower and the more moderate players in his administration were concerned. The documents show Eisenhower directing that "every possible public and private means at our disposal be used to ease the effects of our action on India."[23] This clearly indicates that policy considerations concerning South Asia were by no means a monolith—that awareness of intra-regional factors were feeding into the deliberative mix. It appears to be indisputable that the President's own sense of caution played a role. He seemed genuinely concerned about Indian sensibilities, more so than were many other key administration officials, and many members of the US Congress. Dulles and then-Vice-President Nixon both obviously saw the Pakistan alliance as part of a scenario for checkmating India on the non-alignment front. Dulles expressed his resentment "testily" to Anthony Eden by remarking that "India did not have the right (*sic!*) not only to remain neutral herself *but to prevent other countries from lining up with the West*"[24] Nixon was blatantly pro-Pakistani and anti-Indian, something that became totally obvious during the Bangladesh war a decade-and-a-half later. He had described Nehru "as the least friendly leader" he had encountered during an Asian tour he had undertaken in 1953. "Pakistan," by contrast, "is a country I would like to do everything for. The people have less complexes (*sic!*) than the Indians. ..." [25] Coming from a man with as many complexes as Nixon had, this was a remarkable miscarriage of analytical insight!

The point is that whatever may have been the officially stated intent of the Pakistan alliance (*viz.*, to anchor the Middle East security system and inhibit Soviet expansionism), the known views of some of the administration's ranking officials certainly made it easy for Nehru and India's Ministry of External Affairs to conclude that the regional containment of India was one of its implicit purposes. Under these circumstances, it is not surprising that Nehru gave a cold shoulder to both Nixon and Dulles when they showed up in New Delhi, and why, to their annoyance, he relentlessly denounced US foreign policy!

With respect to the US-Pakistani relationship, apart from the practical difficulties already alluded to, tensions and pique inevitably flowed from the never resolved fact that, as Kux observes, "the United States and Pakistan entered the alliance for different and ultimately conflicting reasons." While anti-Communist in ideological orientation, "Pakistan remained at heart concerned about the threat from India rather than any menace from the communists." (p. 84) Both parties were grounded in fatally flawed constructions of political and historical reality. Particularly in the sense that both exaggerated the proportions of the threat they respectively imagined that they faced. This in turn drove them both to want and expect more from each other than was realistically warranted. The residues of this "disenchantment" persist to the present day.

The comments by Dulles and Nixon alluded to above typify another element in the difficulties that the United States made for itself in South Asia. This is the role that cultural ignorance, historical *naiveté* and unadulterated bigotry played in setting the United States up for the foreign policy disasters that it experienced.

Negotiations between the two countries had reached such an impasse by the end of Eisenhower's first term that the General himself had come to realize that the Pakistan alliance had been a mistake. This is a remarkable latter day revelation yielded by the archives! As McMahon relates it: The president said he felt that "our tendency to rush out and seek allies was not very sensible." He voiced concern that "we were doing practically nothing for Pakistan except in the form of military aid." The military commitment to Pakistan was "perhaps the worst kind of a plan and decision we could have made," Eisenhower lamented. "It was a terrible error, but we now seem hopelessly involved in it." (p. 207) The dimensions of the problem are clearly revealed in the rich detail that Kux unearthed in his recent work on Pakistani-American relations, which he calls, "Disenchanted Allies." We are also indebted to the seminal scholarship of Robert J. McMahon for illuminating these stunning developments. We know now that Eisenhower must be credited not only with seeing the futility of expecting anything very constructive to come from the Pakistan alliance, but realizing that its effects on America's grand strategy for South Asia was proving to be counter-productive. Says McMahon: "U.S. officials, who monitored closely India's relations with China and the Soviet Union, found ample evidence to support the view that ... *a shift was indeed underway*. Throughout 1954 and 1955 they expressed grave concern with what seemed to be unmistakable signs that India was forging closer ties with both communist states." (p. 216. *Emphasis added.*)

The tragedy is that in the end Eisenhower was himself too much the traditional 'real-politician' to abandon the policy. The compulsions and intellectual conventions of the Cold War had become so deeply entrenched in Washington that Eisenhower found himself imprisoned in the intellectual shackles which McCarthyism, his own secretary of state, his vice-president, and indeed opportunistic aspersions he himself had cast upon the loyalty and integrity of his predecessors during his first presidential campaign, had forged. Once you were in, you could not get out! "Not even the program's most severe critics in the CIA and the State Department," declares McMahon, "considered an aid cutback either practical or prudent." (p. 207) Unquestionably Pakistan's strategic status in the US's and Britain's Middle East policy was a major factor in establishing the limits to how far Eisenhower was willing to go to correct this mistake. Pakistan had become America's tar baby!

However, Eisenhower did attempt to ameliorate the effects of the policy. His weakness was excessively relying on face-to-face contact and personal charm as means of turning things around. Eisenhower repeatedly employed personal diplomacy to try and achieve some kind of compensatory *modus vivendi* with India. Nehru was invited to Washington in 1956 for face-to-face talks with Eisenhower which, McMahon asserts, "stemmed from the president's great faith in his own ability to overcome misunderstandings through the sheer force of his personality" (p. 224). Eisenhower reciprocated and visited India in 1959. This interaction did indeed improve the political atmosphere somewhat, in part because Nehru and Eisenhower really did hit it off, but more importantly because the failure of America's militarized grand strategy for South Asia was drawing both the Soviet Union and China into the equation, forcing the United States to rethink its strategic orientation. The Third World was becoming an arena where the two superpowers would fight proxy wars both for economic and military advantage. By the Kennedy years this would become the dominant motif of competition between the United States and the Soviet Union outside the European arena.

The specter of Soviet penetration of the region drew others into the breach. Eugene Rostow voiced his fear that the United States might be facing "a diplomatic Pearl Harbor" in India.[26] Dulles himself started to back away from an exclusively militarized grand strategy and moved toward the view that economic assistance and serious efforts at political rapprochement were measures that might keep India from gradually slipping behind the Iron Curtain.

Dulles himself finally traveled to India in March 1956 in an attempt to try and mend diplomatic fences. The hostile reaction he got there made it clear that major policy changes were needed if significant improvement in US-Indian relations were to be effectuated. "Public opinion had become so aroused," says McMahon, "that the government needed to take special steps just to insure Dulles's safety." (p. 225) The Secretary of State confessed, "while I knew they did not like our alliance with, and armament program for, Pakistan.. . . I never appreciated before the full depth of their feeling." As McMahon aptly puts it, "Dulles's admission that he never really understood the reasons for the Indian furor over U.S. aid to Pakistan *almost defies comprehension*."[27] It reflects, of course, the vast quantum of cultural and historical ignorance about South Asia from which not only John Foster Dulles suffered, but so many other Washington officials of that era did as well.

Despite these ameliorative efforts, however, it was clear to the Indians that the fundamental source of peril to their country remained in place. Consequently, Nehru pressed on with his quest for countervailing security. India and China signed a treaty of friendship in April 1954. Chou Enlai visited India in June of that year, and Nehru reciprocally visited China in November 1954. Nehru was in Moscow on an official visit in June of 1955. In November and December of 1955, Communist Party General Secretary Nikita Khrushchev and Soviet Premier Nikolai Bulganin traveled to India on a three-week state visit, touring the country and drawing large and enthusiastic crowds wherever they went. Not only did the Soviets pledge all manor of military and economic assistance to India, they offered her diplomatic support as well by taking India's side in the Kashmir dispute and on Goa and promising to use their UN veto to generally protect India's interests in the international arena.[28] "At a time, when the West was trying to contain the Soviets—vigorously trying to limit Moscow's contacts with the newly emergent nations—the chance to expand relations with the largest nonaligned country was an opportunity the Russians eagerly seized." The whole point was, as Kux (1993) observes: "*Nehru was now prepared to edge closer to the Soviet Union to offset US support for Pakistan.*"[29]

With the benefit of perspective distance, it is now possible to understand the structural and historical reasons why the US's Pakistan policy proved to be counterproductive. It was not entirely the result of militarized grand strategy *per se.* After all, American mutual security pacts with a number of nations around the perimeter of Communist bloc power proved to be fairly effective. Japan, South Korea and Taiwan come to mind with regard to East Asia. Turkey and Israel proved to be eminently workable in the Middle East, as was the case with Greece in southeastern Europe. NATO in Western Europe was certainly a success story. In these instances, militarization admittedly was coupled with massive economic assistance, even though the military aspect was the major component. What prevented American policy-makers from grasping the ruinous implications of projecting their Cold War anti-Communist phobias into South Asia was their misreading of the special regional imperatives that were in play *there* and most crucially the historical forces that had established their contours over the past century. As suggested earlier, this pertained especially to the roots of the contemporary ethnoreligious antipathies existing between Hindus and Muslims that ultimately led to the establishment of separate multivocal states and the perpetual state of war that followed in their wake. Historians refer to this as the *Separatist Movement*.

The exception in high places to these imperfect perceptions, as we have seen, was Chester Bowles. He too was a creature of his time, however, in the sense that he framed his advocacy of non-militarized policies toward South Asia in terms of the belief that it would be the most effective way to stem the rise of Communism. He believed that Nehru was much too sanguine about the Communist threat primarily because at this point in time he seemed to be handling it so effectively. Said he: "Because of his very success in checking the Communists, he underestimates, in my view, not only the problems of world communism, but also the real dimensions of the Communist threat in India over the coming years." Also, and prophetically: "It is in the broader area of communism in world politics and the Cold War that the differences between Nehru and his American critics become sharpest." This, of course, because Nehru "has not yet drawn the conclusion . . . that the whole world must finally choose up sides."[30] In retrospect, however, one may conclude that Nehru was more correct than Bowles, at least as far as the South Asia region is concerned. Communism as an indigenous revolutionary movement, with or without external stimuli, never was and never has been a major threat either in India or Pakistan. Perhaps this is another illustration of how lack of regional depth impinges on strategic clarity.

I think it is now possible to conclude, however, that had Chester Bowles's vision carried the day during the early years of the Cold War, the panoply of war, arrested development, public disenchantment, and strained relations with the United States that has plagued American foreign policy in the region for almost a half century might well have been avoided, or at least minimized. Separatism would have remained the region's principal 'internal" problem and the Cold War would have remained primarily peripheral to the region. There is an abundant literature on this crucial phenomenon which should be read in order to properly gage the significance.[31]

There were painful consequences for failing to comprehend where the security threat to South Asia genuinely lay. By getting it wrong, the United States denied itself many opportunities to play the impartial, mediatory role which as a great power it readily could have played by remaining above the region's "internal" conflicts. In fact, this was precisely the role which, by contrast, the Soviet Union successfully played at Tashkent. Critics like Bowles and Nehru had been right. Neither the Cold War nor intraregional war were kept out of the region through the militarized grand strategy pursued by the United States. The Kashmir dispute was internationalized and rendered insoluble instead of containing it to a bilateral dispute between the two South Asian states which they should have been encouraged to resolve on their own without manipulation. American arms supplied under the terms of the mutual-security pacts enabled the Pakistani officer corps to increase the army's military capabilities and, as well, to enhance their political influence by infiltrating most of the country's key economic sinecures. Unlike India, where viable popular government was achieved very early, effective civilian political institutions in Pakistan needed all the help they could get. And they derived little from US foreign policy.

The main reason for the difference between the two states arose from the fact that Pakistan's constitutional evolution retained what Waseem calls the "viceregal system." While the 1947 Indian Independence Act established a fully responsible government at the center, he declares, "it also conferred emergency powers on the governor-general" which Jinnah employed "to control the deliberations of the Constituent Assembly and the functioning of federal and provincial governments from outside Parliament."[32] Jinnah, in other words, set a precedent at the outset for a "dyarchical" pattern of government that retained the logic of the *1935 Government of India Act*. He failed to put his trust in a free electorate, as Nehru had done in India. After his death from natural causes in 1948, and Liaqat Ali's death by assassination in 1951, the way was opened for the reactionary civil and military establishments to seize power by coopting the office of Governor-General along with its decisive extraparliamentary powers. When the transition from Governor-General to President occurred as an aspect of the Republican Constitution adopted on March 5, 1953, the first military cooptee of that office, Major-General Iskander Mirza, was elected Provisional President of the Islamic Republic of Pakistan and was sworn-in as President on March 23rd.

The militarized grand strategy that was promulgated for South Asia during these critical years when democratic processes in Pakistan were being strangled by the military-bureaucratic-landlord nexus, made the United States an enabler in the process of political perversion that was taking place. Practically every measure that American officials took, or failed to take, from 1951 through 1969, strengthened and legitimized the anti-democratic machinations of these classes. It is striking, in retrospect, to see how little regard or sympathy US officials manifested toward substantial segments of Pakistani society that were struggling against the totalitarians in their midst. Driven by their obsessive preoccupation with anti-communism, American decision-makers consistently sided with the Sandhurst-style military officers, anglicised bureaucrats, and wealthy, tribalized landlords and entrepreneurs, and winked at the methods they employed to establish their political dominance at the expense of parliamentary government. They were anathema to everything that the United States claimed it stood for. These elitist proponents of extraparliamentary government played the American card to the hilt once they realized how vulnerable US leaders were to anticommunist rhetoric. In Kux's words, "the Pakistanis, unlike the Indians, said the things that Dulles wanted to hear about the dangers of Communism." Whenever, Pakistani officials journeyed to the United States, they always "stressed their allegiance to the anticommunist cause and emphasized Pakistan's desire to join the free world."[33]

Even within the official family, misgivings about the Pakistan relationship eventually surfaced and affected President Eisenhower himself, as we have already seen. When Governor General Ghulam Mohammed sacked Prime Minister Nizamuddin in 1951and arbitrarily dissolved the Constituent Assembly the following year it set off alarm bells. The US voiced objections to these measures. In the end, however, the compulsion to treat the emerging US-Pakistan alliance as a crown jewel in its "southern tier strategy" for protecting the Middle East and South Asia from Soviet encroachment overrode all considerations of political morality and common sense. For example, while US diplomats regarded Ghulam Mohammed's autocratic behavior as "constitutionally questionable", they nevertheless ultimately endorsed it because it brought a political strongman to power, which in their eyes represented a "*welcome gain as far as U.S. interests are concerned.*" When President Mirza wrote to Eisenhower and Dulles explaining the "necessity" for abrogating representative government, the two "*responded with understanding.*" While Dulles, says Kux, emphasized the American interest in a return to constitutional government, he nevertheless asserted that, "'*The changes which have occurred do not alter in any respect the close ties which exist between our two countries*'." But as Kux himself declares, "What the embassy failed to note was that Nizamuddin's dismissal marked an important step toward the demise of popular government and the control of the government by the predominantly Pakistani civil service and military leadership."[34] The documents reveal countless such instances over subsequent years when the course of Pakistani domestic politics raised doubts in the minds of American officials about how efficacious the alliance would ultimately prove to be. But nothing significant was ever done to use American clout to try and turn the tide in favor of the proponents of genuine representative government. In the end, there always was acquiescence to the *status quo*, which by definition inevitably reinforced antidemocratic processes in the country.

The documents also reveal a *persistent* disconnect between American and Pakistani perceptions of how much military wherewithal was really necessary to guarantee Pakistan's security and strategic value to the grand alliance. American estimates of Pakistani military requirements always fell far short of Pakistani demands. This perceptual difference invariably ran through military-assistance negotiations: In American eyes, the amount necessarily had to reflect congressional budgetary realities, on the one hand, and perceived global (not intra-regional) strategic realities, on the other. In Pakistani eyes, there could never be enough arms to satisfy what was in essence their obsessive quest for "parity" with "Hindu India." This "pathology" was an obvious byproduct of the Separatist Movement, not fear of *Communism* and the Soviet Union. This is the distinction that American officialdom seems never to have comprehended, or simply refused to acknowledge.

President Iskander Mirza's and Defense Minister Ayub Khan's *coup d'etat* in 1958 brought to power the man who embodied all of the illusions that dogged and eventually doomed the US-Pakistani alliance. Within three months after the *coup* took place, Ayub had forced Mirza out of office and assumed complete control of the country. The subtitle of Chapter 4 in Kux's book (2001) is, "Ike Likes Ayub." More than anything, this summarizes the fatal dilemma that eventually led to the collapse of America's

South Asia policy. As noted earlier, Ayub Khan was adored by the hawks. To them he was the incarnate, stereotypical, British-style, 'bully' military man who might have stepped out of the movie, "*The Lives of a Bengal Lancer.*" There was no recognition of the fact that at the very time when India was creating Asia's most vibrant democracy, Ayub's ascent to power had been achieved by scheming and intriguing with his fellow generals and civilian authoritarians to shatter any chances for the democratic process to successfully take root in Pakistan.

McMahon contends that Ayub Khan's use of American military equipment in 1965 to attack India dealt a death blow to whatever chances were left to the United States to play an impartial, constructive role in South Asian affairs. This event demonstrated America's failure to control the forces it had unleashed in the Subcontinent. It was, he says, "a watershed in the history of American relations with the Indian *Subcontinent.*" The US condemnation of the Pakistani attack and the corresponding embargo of arms shipments shocked Pakistan's leaders into a realization that the purposes for which they had entered the alliance with the United States had essentially failed to fulfill their expectations. Despite all of the substantive benefits Pakistan had received from the relationship, they commenced looking elsewhere for political succor. The attack itself convinced India's leaders that they had been right all along about the United States. What there was of trust of American *bona fides* faded. It did not disappear completely, of course, because one cannot ignore super-powers no matter how recalcitrant they may be! The outcome of this event so badly shook United States policy-makers, however, that essentially they capitulated to it, stepped aside and gave the Russians free reign to broker a peace agreement at Tashkent. In McMahon's words:

> Pakistan's alignment with the United States combined with subsequent U.S. efforts to balance its South Asia priorities by pumping massive amounts of economic assistance into India .. .had been predicated on the belief that the United States could cultivate friendly, productive relations with both

> countries. Four presidential administrations had formulated policies for South Asia that sprouted from and were nourished by that same fallacious assumption. ... Now those illusions were shattered.[35]

Kux's (1994) research reinforces these conclusions. He calls Operation Gibraltar (the code name for the Pakistani operation) "a gamble to seize Kashmir" that was supported by most factions in the Pakistani political establishment. The attack on India came on Lyndon Johnson's watch. It revealed what had all along been the contention of the policy's critics—that Pakistan's obsession with India and not anti-Communism was the primary driving force behind its quest for inclusion in the Cold War alliance system. This was the point where for all practical purposes the United States gave up on its original South Asian agenda—of course, without officially acknowledging that it had done so. Hopes for democracy had been extinguished in Pakistan for the foreseeable future. A major share of America's regional influence had been surrendered to the Soviet Union, *the very outcome that twenty years of US foreign policy had been designed to prevent*. President Johnson was fed up, and in any event was increasingly turning his attention toward Vietnam. Sadly, Secretary of State Dean Rusk declared, "We encouraged the Russians to go ahead with the Tashkent idea, because we felt we had nothing to lose." The confession that the US no longer had anything to offer after two decades of trying is truly amazing![36]

Following Tashkent, a new dimension was added to the rivalry between the US and the Soviet Union for the hearts and minds of Third World countries. Economic assistance increasingly was being viewed as a supplement to, if not a substitute for, guns and bullets. Ironically, the Eisenhower administration which had been responsible for perfecting the US's ill-fated militarized grand strategy during its first term had planted the seeds for an alternative strategy of systematized economic assistance during its second. This, of course, is a backhanded testimony to the power of the regional imperative.

Even the *NSC* had come full cycle by 1959, as McMahon notes: "Paper 5701 declared*: A strong India would be a successful* *example of an alternative to Communism in an Asian context*."[37] This theme was picked up in several quarters of the American press and political establishment. It was heavily stressed when Nehru came to the United States in 1956. Significantly, "The President kept India's *bete noire*, John Foster Dulles, in the background. The Indian leader, in turn, saw to it that Krishna Menon, the US's *bete noire*, stayed away from Washington." Despite the frankness of their talks, the outcome was that, "Eisenhower liked Nehru even though he found him 'a personality of unusual contradictions'."[38] Eisenhower's reciprocal visit to India in 1959 also went very well from a public relations standpoint. While none of this led to full rapprochement, it did pave the way for changes that were in the winds.

The policy modifications that impelled the United States to try to have its cake and eat it too in South Asia created a situation within the confines of the Subcontinent where there would occur an interplay between two competing strategic models. That is, military pacts where they proved possible, on the one hand, and, on the other hand, subtler strategies featuring economic assistance combined with support for democratization where this was adjudged to be the most feasible way to influence political outcomes. Inevitably, of course, there was overlap between them, but the differences in degree were strategically significant.

This was the door which the failure of Dulles's hardline policy opened, not so much out of conviction as of necessity if anything was to be salvaged from US South Asian diplomacy. It would be the unanticipated legacy that Eisenhower passed on to his Democratic successor, John F. Kennedy.

The Kennedy administration brought this new policy orientation to fruition. It also brought Chester Bowles back into the arena for a second stint as ambassador to India (1963-1969). This in itself was a measure of how essential the readjustment of grand strategy to regional realities had become. Kennedy clearly manifested a strong preference for the economic aid model, particularly for India, given its superior infrastructural capacity to assimilate large infusions of capital and expertise and given its spectacular progress toward building a viable democratic polity.

For a brief time, however, the military model also achieved an unanticipated saliency for India when in 1962, during John K. Galbraith's tenure as ambassador, the Chinese attacked and routed Indian troops in the Northeast Frontier and Ladakh regions. Under these circumstances, India literally pleaded for increased American military assistance, including air support to protect its cities in case the Chinese kept coming into the North Indian heartland. Once the threat ended, however, Nehru, to the consternation of Washington, returned India to its non-aligned posture and resumed his criticism of the military model from which he had just so richly benefited. This sudden intrusion of Cold War violence into South Asia had temporarily disturbed the delicate equilibrium that Nehru had for so long attempted to maintain. It had severely shaken his confidence. The result had been a pragmatically driven 'model-shift' which many believe contributed to the rapid decline in his political viability and personal vigor that followed.[39]

Lyndon Johnson's ascendancy under the tragic circumstances of John F. Kennedy's assassination, like the transition from Roosevelt to Truman, represented another 'regime change' as opposed to a simple succession. Like Truman, Johnson had come from a less socially and intellectually sophisticated background than his predecessor. This carried with it the well documented LBJ "inferiority complex" *vis-a-vis* 'the Kennedys' that generated his animus toward purported 'East Coast liberals' in general. His predilection for a macho-style of politics clearly enhanced his rapport with the proponents of militarized grand strategy. This progressively drew him so deeply into the Vietnam quagmire that it eventually destroyed his presidency. It also drew him toward adopting a harder line toward India regarding economic and fiscal policy, especially after Indira Gandhi publicly adopted a critical stance toward US Vietnam policies. By the end of the Johnson presidency, US relations with and concerns about both South Asian states had essentially sunk into a state of limbo. Nixon's presidency, commencing in 1969, for a time revitalized the militarized grand strategy and with this produced a dramatic upturn in the traditional US-Pakistan relationship, at the cost, however, of a precipitous decline in relations with India. These juxtapositions dramatized once again the fallacious American belief that two disparate and indeed incompatible models for managing events in South Asia could long endure.

The Bangladesh War in 1971 was a further testament to the futility of the US's competing-models approach to the region. It marked the point where India, under Indira Gandhi, decided to definitively craft a strategic relationship with the Soviet Union, and assert her determination to make India the hegemonic power in South Asia. From the American standpoint, Bangladesh was more than another outgrowth of the flawed policies of the past. It was a shallow, amateurish attempt to pursue a pattern of power politics that virtually destroyed what was left of American prestige there. So shallow and crude, as a matter of fact, as to cast considerable doubt on the reputation for shrewdness and strategic perspicacity that mainstream foreign policy commentators often attributed, and even now attribute, to Richard Nixon and Henry Kissinger.

When Pakistan's next military dictator, general Yahya Khan, turned his country's American equipped army against his own people, on March 26th, in a brutal but unsuccessful attempt to suppress rebellion in East Pakistan, the United States government acted as it had in the past—as an enabler of political repression when the choice was between democracy and dictatorship.[40] The record clearly shows that the principal motivations for the famous "tilt" toward Pakistan after war broke out between India and Pakistan over Bangladesh were (1) Nixon's irrational animosity toward India, and (2) his and Kissinger's determination to let nothing, even genocide, stand in the way of facilitating the President's impending "opening" to China. As is well known, Kissinger had made his secret journey to Beijing on July 10, 1971, via Pakistan. Now, he and Nixon were fearful that war between India and Pakistan would somehow disrupt the scenario for the President's trip. When war broke out, there was pique and exasperation, almost an attitude of, 'How could they do this to us at such a propitious moment?' While Nixon paid lip-service to the "intrinsic tragedy" that was unfolding, he privately lamented that it "could disrupt ...o ur policy toward China."[41] Wanting to placate Yahya in order to keep him in the China game, Hitchens says: "In late April 1971, at the very height of the mass murder, Kissinger sent a message to General Yahya Khan, *thanking him for his 'delicacy and tact'*." (Emphasis added) He also declares that, "The Kissinger policy towards Bangladesh may well have been largely conducted for its own sake as a means of gratifying his boss's animus against India." Personal animus obviously played a role in fanning Nixon's hysterical assertions that India intended to use the Bangladesh war as an excuse to dismember Pakistan. However, the saber-rattling to which he resorted, particularly the touch of gunboat diplomacy when a carrier task force sailed up the Bay of Bengal, also had a larger purpose. As Kissinger puts it in his memoirs: while indeed the "unstated mission of the Enterprise, never spelled out to the US navy, was to send a signal to the Indians and the Soviets to give emphasis to our warnings about West Pakistan," it was also undertaken as a ploy to impress the Chinese that "if they entered into a relationship with the United States they could count on US steadfastness in times of trouble."[42]

This sophomoric diplomacy, however, must not be seen simply in terms of the venality and pettiness of an individual American President and his macho Secretary of State. It must as well be seen as one more manifestation of a bankrupt foreign policy that repeatedly defeated its own declared premises.

The ascent of Zulfikar Ali Bhutto in 1975 provided further confirmation of how much things had changed. While paying lip service to American support in the recently concluded Bangladesh war, Bhutto in fact, set out to severely attenuate Pakistan's participation in the American global security system. Before he was finally done-in by the combination of his personal political pathologies and the machinations of the country's disgruntled anti-democratic elites, Bhutto, on the positive side, had moved Pakistan closer to the achievement of genuine popular government than at any time in its history. On the negative side, from the standpoint of American interests, Bhutto had proceeded to abandon *SEATO* and *CENTO*, had established links to the non-aligned movement, had developed a relationship with China that was structurally equivalent to India's counterfoil relationship with the Soviet Union, had opened up a relationship with North Korea (thereby laying the foundations for the eventual development of a Pakistani nuclear bomb, and *A.Q. Khan*), had established lucrative economic ties with the Gulf states which reduced Pakistani dependence on American aid, and made Pakistan an active player in the Organization of Islamic Countries (OIC).

On the other side of the border, Prime Minister Indira Gandhi initiated a similar course of action. Stung by the "tilt" and its accompanying saber-rattling, by President Johnson's sanctimonious "short-tether" policy at a time when severe drought was ravaging large portions of North India,[43] angered further by the terms and conditions that were imposed by the US administration (including an unwanted devaluation of the Rupee) as the price for restarting food aid and other economic assistance, Mrs. Gandhi undertook three countermeasures which, all rhetoric to the contrary notwithstanding, essentially downgraded the American relationship: (1) By visiting Moscow in September 1971, and signing a friendship treaty between India and the Soviet Union on August 9, 1971, she turned decisively to the Soviet Union as India's strategic partner. Although not a formal alliance, nevertheless, "the accord provided for bilateral consultations in the event of crises and pledged that neither country would support a third party against the other." Most important, the new relationship provided "*the full support and additional military supplies for which the Indians had been pressing.*"[44] (2) She exploded a nuclear device on May 8, 1974, signaling thereby an intensification of India's determination to become a major regional power and see to her own security. (3) She retaliated against 'short tether' diplomacy by renouncing further dependence on American economic assistance. The timing of the latter was apt because the so-called 'Green Revolution' was beginning to reduce India's food deficits by means of indigenous agricultural technologies.

The Vietnam and Bangladesh wars, the opening to China, and the crude resort to economic coercion and political blackmail had thus administered the *coup de grace* to what remained of the original American strategic scenario for South Asia. The policies subsequently pursued by the Carter (1977-81), Reagan-Bush (1981-93) and Clinton (1993-2001) administrations all reflected this structural change in one way or another. The catch-phrase became "bilateral relations'—that is, implicitly acknowledging the primacy of the regional imperative over grand strategy by backing away in whole or in past from most of the policies which for almost half a century had sought to bend indigenous history and cultural norms to the purposes of America's and the West's strategic and ideological predilections.[45]

Jimmy Carter was the first to attempt an adaptive orientation to newly emergent regional realities. He initiated a genre of moral politics which until the Soviet invasion of Afghanistan focused almost exclusively on nuclear proliferation, that is, trying to manage the consequences of Pakistan's and India's newly asserted determination to enhance their nuclear sinews and chart their own political course independent of American tutelage. Economic aid, once conceived to be the magic key for enticing India into the American camp, was downgraded to a policy of "meeting basic needs." In Tahir-Kheli's words, "The Carter administration elevated nonproliferation to the forefront of American foreign policy concerns."[46] This initiative was given a self-serving spin by conceptualizing it as an aspect of what was called the "Carter-Brzezinski policy." According to Robert Goheen, who was Carter's ambassador to India, its stated purpose was to "cultivate regionally influential countries as a means of devolving some of the excessive responsibilities (*sic*) that the United States had assumed in the post-War decades." Goheen saw this early phase of the Carter administration in an essentially positive light, despite tensions over the supply of enriched uranium for the Tarapur nuclear reactor. He felt that the Simla agreement negotiated between Zulfikar Ali Bhutto and Mrs. Gandhi had resolved many perplexing issues and markedly reduced tensions between India and Pakistan. He felt that a balance had been struck in the US's relations with the two South Asian states which embodied the kind of limited-interventionist, two-track bilateralism, that the administration henceforth wished to follow. When Morarji Desai assumed office as Prime Minister under Janata Party rule (1977-79), the US found they had an Indian politician who was ideally suited to the new dispensation. Desai was far more centrist and pledged to pursue a more even-handed Non-alignment policy than his predecessors. When Ambassador Goheen was dispatched to New Delhi in early May 1977, he carried a very conciliatory message from the American President. He was to tell Prime Minister Desai that: "If India would (1) pledge not to develop nuclear weapons and (2) enter into discussions with the United States to try and bring the two countries' nuclear policies into alignment, then the president would assure India of the receipt of the shipment of the nuclear fuel ... that it was awaiting." Desai agreed to this and the two leaders exchanged state visits.[47]

Unfortunately, the Soviet invasion of Afghanistan on December 19, 1979, Mrs. Gandhi's return to power that same year, plus the US Senate's refusal to approve the second shipment of enriched uranium for Tarapur all intruded and once again muddied the diplomatic waters. As Goheen puts it, "Mrs. Gandhi had shown no great love for the United States, and her agents were talking a tough line on the Tarapur issue."[48] The Afghanistan crisis elicited an immediate knee-jerk reaction in the White House and on Capitol Hill. "Pakistan almost at once regained her image as a "frontline state" in the struggle to block any further southerly extensions of Soviet influence and power."[49]

Representatives of the Carter administration fanned out in South Asia to sell their contemplated policy. National Security Advisor Zbigniew Brzezinski and Secretary of State Warren Christopher visited Pakistan, whose President was the country's latest military dictator, Zia-al-Haq, to try and reinstate some semblance of the old Cold War alliance. Simultaneously, another team headed for New Delhi to seek Indian acquiescence in their plan to once again reinvigorate the Pakistani military machine as a counterfoil to Soviet aggression. In Islamabad, National Security Advisor Zbigniew Brzezinski and Secretary of State Warren Christopher offered Pakistan $400 million worth of "immediate assistance" as an inducement to strengthen their frontier forces. General Zia sniffed at this, calling it "peanuts", because he knew the United States was over a barrel and rightly saw it as an opportunity to resuscitate the old policy model from which the Pakistani elite had so handsomely profited throughout the Cold War. Presidential advisor Clark Clifford and State Department Representative Howard Schaffer arrived in New Delhi on the same day that their counterparts reached Islamabad to try and convince the newly installed Indira Gandhi government that the Soviet invasion of Afghanistan represented as much a threat to India as to Pakistan. While External Affairs Minister, P.V. Narasimha Rao, agreed that the Soviet action constituted a serious problem for the region, he rejected the proposed US solution. Remembering the result of past attempts to arm Pakistan as a buffer against external threats, he retorted that India's preference was for measures that prevented any further introduction of arms into the Subcontinent by all parties. It was in some ways the equal and opposite reaction to Pakistan's when, during the China War, India sought American military assistance.[50]

For a time, therefore, the invasion of Afghanistan had reawakened the 'Pakistan lobby' in Washington, and had correspondingly aroused expectations in Pakistan itself that a renewed militarized grand strategy would, as had been the case at the height of the Cold War, prove to be a boon to the country's anti-democratic elites. Haqqani has characterized Pakistan under its military rulers and their civilian cohorts as a "rent-seeking state, living off the rents of its strategic location," a state of affairs that has existed "since its involvement in US-sponsored treaties of the cold war era." The Carter administration was in effect endeavoring to "rent" the services and resources of the Pakistani state once more![51]

While Ronald Reagan's ascendancy to the American presidency in 1980 intensified American involvement in Afghanistan and the aggressive utilization of Pakistan as a base for promoting the Afghan insurgency against the Soviet occupation, it did not impel a complete return to the levels of piquish politics which had characterized past US-Indian relations. This is because perspective changes had occurred on both sides. The Reagan administration, in a new spirit of measured bilateralism, succeeded, as Stephen P. Cohen notes, in forging a "limited strategic relationship" with Pakistan which did not at the same time, despite Narasimharao's prior reservations, "commit the United States against India but did stiffen Pakistani resistance against the Soviets."[52]

Probably Indira Gandhi's assassination in 1984 and the succession of her son, Rajiv Gandhi, played a greater role than many realize in sustaining the trend toward less invasive and strident diplomacy. The Rajiv Gandhi regime ignited optimism not only about the prospects for an improved security environment but for crucial economic changes as well which if implemented augured well for greater long-term compatibility in the Indo-American relationship. Rajiv's visit to the United States in 1985 intensified these expectations because at this point he had established a reputation as a modern, "can-do", new-generation Indian politician who functioned in a 'chairman of the board' style.[53] In India, says Pranay Gupte, "There was wide euphoria, particularly among young Indians, that Rajiv Gandhi would inaugurate a new era of domestic prosperity."[54] Reagan was "impressed" with Rajiv. "Personal chemistry between Reagan and Rajiv Gandhi was exceptional," declares Tahir-Kheli. He interpreted Rajiv's emphasis on high-tech as a "pragmatic desire to go to the best source" and "as reflecting a change in the international environment."[55] Even before Rajiv's visit there had been signs of a new mood in Indo-US relations which had reverberated all the way to Capitol Hill. Conservative Senator Orin Hatch had sung India's praises on the floor of the United States Senate. "I believe a historic shift is underway," he had intoned.[56]

Although Rajiv Gandhi, due to his political inexperience, had pretty much lost control of both his agenda and the Congress Party by the time of his assassination (May 21, 1991), his successor, P.V. Narasimha Rao (1984-1989) got things back on track, no doubt because the forces driving change were proving to be irresistible. Although far less comprehensive than many critics thought to be feasible, the economic liberalization policies begun during his prime minstership must be seen retrospectively as a watershed which marks the point where significant structural differences between India and Pakistan became immanent. Coupled with the continued success of democratic government in India, and its failure in Pakistan, the changes underway once and for all undermined the American rationale for treating India and Pakistan simply as two equally culpable rivals enmeshed in a symbiotic political *danse macabre*. The two states were now gravitating in very different directions—India toward increasing economic prosperity, political stability and international respectability; Pakistan toward economic stagnation, political instability, enmeshment in the world of international terrorism, and the institutionalization of its status as a 'strategic landlord'.

The mounting intensity of the Afghan war must be seen as the principle catalyst of the growing post-Cold War differentiation occurring between India and Pakistan. The eventual defeat of the Soviet invasion was a 'stinger-missile victory' achieved by Muslim radicals ideologically driven by Wahabism, bankrolled by the United States and the oil rich Gulf States (particularly Saudi Arabia), whose base of operations was Pakistan. In the end, this force would replace Bolshevism as the pervasive doctrinal challenge to Western secularism, and transform Pakistan into a nuclear armed, conspiratorial state tacitly, where not overtly, held hostage to, if indeed not in overt collusion with, the new Islamic radicalism. Its unsupervised *madrassas* would churn out the human raw material for the *Taliban* fundamentalists and the growing legions of international terrorists. The Separatist-rooted obsession of its military-bureaucratic-feudal establishment with reclaiming Kashmir would provide its legitimizing *raison d'etre*.

In an important sense, India's ability to remain on the sidelines of the Afghan struggle turned out to be a long-range blessing. This left its capital and infrastructural resources free to be invested in the country's further industrialization, to connect with the global economy, and to establish itself as a dominant regional power. These developments have made it increasingly less easy for the lingering residues of the US's past failed diplomacy to exert the retrograde influence they once did in Washington.

The nuclear issue persists as the greatest threat to the survival of South Asian society. Since the Carter administration identified it as such, there has been scant progress, if any, in resolving it. The full proportions of this peril came home to roost when India and Pakistan only two weeks apart in May of 1998 tested atomic bombs. By the time the Cold War ended and nonproliferation became an overriding security issue in South Asia, the United States discovered its capacity to influence events either by persuasion or coercion, or any combination of the two, had enormously eroded. This outcome was presaged by America's long and unsuccessful attempts to persuade India and Pakistan to sign the Comprehensive Test Ban Treaty (CTBT) which, ironically, it proved impossible for the Clinton administration to induce even the United States Senate to do. Both states had reached the conclusion that American coercion could be endured while American assurances were unreliable. Not only had US military power proven to be incapable of preventing war in South Asia. The ill-conceived use of its power in the region had actually, albeit unintentionally, enabled Pakistan to wage war there. US economic power failed to achieve the results it should have because at critical points in the relationship between both states, but especially India, it came to be seen as dependent upon willingness to conform to American doctrinal predilections.

The remaining challenge before the United States following the non-proliferation imbroglio was how to employ what influence it had left in South Asia to help create a wholly new structure for peace and stability in the region. Kargil and the recent coup in Pakistan showed that the perils are many, especially now that India and Pakistan have nuclear weapons and have indicated a willingness to employ them as a last-resort means of staving off military defeat. What has thus far prevented escalation to the ultimate level is an emergent regional "balance-of-terror" not unlike that which prevailed between the US and the Soviet Union throughout the Cold War and even today remains in place on an implicit basis. More obviously needs to be done in order to reduce the risks of accidents and improve the chances for genuine peace in South Asia. This has proved to be more difficult than ever in the face of 9/11, the War on Terrorism, the persistence of double standards on such key issues as Kashmir (the continued winking at cross-border terrorism there while condemning it elsewhere), the rising tide of anti-Americanism throughout the Islamic world, and the seeming unwillingness or inability of the Bush adminis-tration to invest the resources and support the nation-building efforts needed to pacify and rehabilitate post-Taliban Afghanistan.

The talks that occurred between Assistant Secretary of State Strobe Talbott and External Affairs Minister Jaswant Singh, on the one hand, and his Pakistani counterparts, on the other, at the end of the 1990s were a positive development and a measure of how difficult the task of making fundamental changes in US foreign policy remains. It is clear that the United States will have to get over its pique at having been unable to prevent the Indian and Pakistani nuclear tests. Recovery will be signaled when the United States acknowledges that India and Pakistan, whether America likes it or not, are now regional nuclear powers much as China became by 1964. Petulantly keeping them out of the Club, or at least refusing to acknowledge their changed status, merely reinforces the paternalistic atmosphere which, first, incorrectly assumed that American threats and arm-twisting could make them conform to our behavioral specifications, and second, that their concerns as "mere Third World states" about their own security in the post-Cold War nuclear environment are not as cogent and legitimately vital to their well-being as those concerns were and are for the world's Big Boys.

It has by now been almost forgotten that the American reaction to China's first nuclear detonation in 1964 was identical to that which followed Pokhran and Chagai Hills 34 years later. When news of the detonation reached the White House, Lyndon Johnson cried doom in much the same manner as Bill Clinton did in 1998. In Gould's words: "yet 35 years later, China, today possessing 400 warheads and missiles capable of delivering them anywhere in the world, is now an accepted member of the Club of Five, a signatory to the ...C TBT, and a 'responsible voice' piously deploring India's (but less so Pakistan's) decision to use the same tactics she herself used to gain big power status."[57]

The operative phrase for dealing with a nuclear armed China became "constructive engagement." It proceeded on the assumption that China's status as a nuclear power is an accomplished fact, whether the US likes it or not. This is another illustration of the power of regional imperatives to limit global-power universalism. In the end, the US was no more successful in controlling the nuclear agenda in East Asia than it has been in South Asia. Once the reality of American limitations was recognized and accepted, Washington was able to pursue policies designed to draw China into the community of responsible nuclear powers. Trade was a major impetus for this. The allure of the old "China market" still lives! Incorporating them as much as possible into the international structures designed to promote feelings of equal participation in nonproliferation processes has served to reduce Chinese xenophobia. Sanctions and other punitive measures directed against India and Pakistan for following the same course as China failed for one simple reason. Sanctions have never worked anywhere except in the most limited and arcane circumstances. National states will see to their own security needs according to their own light as long as they perceive no constructive alternatives to doing so. It was recently pointed out by Dan Poneman, a former NSC member, that states facing real threats of nuclear attack, such as India and Pakistan, can hardly be expected to surrender their nuclear option without receiving credible "security assurances" in return.[58] Both Indian and Pakistani resistance to signing the *NPT* and the *CTBT* have centered upon this very point. Tahir-Kheli points out that in spite of American "encouragement", India and Pakistan continued to resist signing the NPT [and by extension the CTBT, of course]" for very obvious reasons. The Pakistanis "would do so only if India signed." India wouldn't because she felt the treaty [and also the CTBT] "was inherently discriminatory in favor of the nuclear-have states," and because "subscribers to the treaty [and by extension the CTBT] violated it through tests and explosions."[59] Finally, from the Indian standpoint, there was additionally the ever-present specter of a less than reliable nuclear-armed China poised on her northern border.

How to achieve the security guarantees that might encourage middle-range states to place their trust in internationally structured nonproliferation mechanisms? Apart from Poneman's suggestion, and in the light of the US Senate's rejection of the CTBT, it seems clear that fresh thinking and renewed negotiation are called for. Perhaps, with respect to South Asia, a "peace process" on the Middle-East model might constitute a first step. Within such a framework, all parties would in principal at least have an equal voice and an equal stake in a constructive outcome. Such a process, if it could be undertaken, would augment the dualistic bilateralism that has been furtively evolving in the wake of the failure of militarized grand strategy. It would acknowledge the relevance of the regional imperative to the achievement of lasting solutions anchored in the "grassroots."

In sum, the contradictions inherent in America's original South Asia policy were no more successful in preventing nuclear proliferation than they were in preventing intraregional war and Communist bloc penetration during the Cold War. This, of course, is because the quest for nuclear capability was not an impulse of the moment; it had been an ongoing quest at the basic-research level dating almost as far back as Independence. When the weaponization urge arose, in response to intraregional tensions, it merely got factored into the rollercoaster relationship between Pakistan, India and the United States in the same manner as had the prior pursuit of conventional weapons.[60]

"It was thought (and as of 1991 correctly so)," declares Cohen, "that as long as Pakistan received American military equipment it would halt or restrain its nuclear program, slowing the pace of regional proliferation."[61] It was, in other words, a continuation of the same basic logic of 'balanced dualism' that had always characterized US strategic thinking. This was, however, a point in time where interests on all sides did happen to converge in such a way that the dualistic model proved to be moderately effective. As a result, the constrictions on American power and influence in the region lessened somewhat. But this had little to do with strategic erudition. Once the Afghan invasion was repelled and the Soviet Union collapsed, the conditions favoring its workability ended. India drifted to the right politically, as the *Bharatiya Janata Party* (*BJP*) rose to political prominence. Pakistan once again fell off the American gravy train. Tensions between India and Pakistan escalated, now with the ethnoreligious bogeyman back on center stage as the *Sangh Parivar* aggressively pushed its Hindu chauvinist agenda. Lal Kishan Advani's *Rath Yatra* in the late 1980s, the prolonged telecasting in soap opera fashion around the same time of the traditional Hindu classics, the *Mahabharata* and the *Ramayana*, and the destruction of the *Babri Masjid* at Ayodhya in December 1991[62] were events that intensified communal tensions once more in India, both with the country's Muslims and across the border in Pakistan. Implicitly, of course, this enhanced the saliency of the regional imperative, as had Separatism in the pre-independence era. Critical, as always, were the repercussions of ethnoreligiously inspired political unrest in Kashmir. Although at the outset essentially an attempt on the part of the indigenous, overwhelmingly predominant Muslim population of the province to acquire a greater voice in their own governance, it progressively spilled into the international arena when Pakistan fished more directly than ever before in those troubled waters, using 'unemployed' *mujahideen* from the waning Afghan war to function as what India's ambassador to the United States referred to as "guest terrorists".[63] These were intra-regional developments concerning which the United States could do little except counsel restraint. Yet as had repeatedly been the case in the past they were essentially manifestations of the same 'domestic' cleavages which always had confounded American attempts to control the political agenda in South Asia. Now, however, the nuclear factor had become an ominous additional aspect of the equation.

In the unipolar world order that emerged at the dawn of the 1990s, the US was compelled to deal with three interconnected issues in South Asia: (1) the escalation of ethnoreligious tensions in India, (2) insurgency and cross-border terrorism in Kashmir, and (3) the determined pursuit of nuclear weapons by both India and Pakistan.

From the standpoint of America's strategic orientation to South Asia in this new environment, policy formulation was profoundly affected by intra-institutional divisions between the White House, Congress and many groups inside the Beltway with strong motivations to side either with India or Pakistan, depending on where their material interests and ideological predilections were thought to lie. While Congressional attitudes had always, inevitably affected US policy toward the region, these attitudes intensified once the existence of nuclear arsenals on both sides of the border entered the picture. It brought out not only understandable alarm, but also aroused a great deal of the latent paternalism which has always haunted official America's perceptions of South Asia.

Proliferation concerns commenced in earnest, of course, after India exploded its original nuclear device in May of 1974. This event "created shock and consternation in the West," declares Ambassador Robert Goheen, "particularly among India's principal nuclear suppliers, Canada and the United States."[64] At the time of the Indian explosion, the US had no major nuclear constraints in place. The Glenn and Symington initiatives over the ensuing four years were very much a response to what was obviously an accelerating pace of weapons-specific nuclear development in both countries. The fact that Pokhran had happened at all (in 1991), and that in general neither India nor Pakistan had shown any inclination to respond to American pressures against pursuing the nuclear option, necessitated in the eyes of many legislators on both sides of the aisle the promulgation of measures designed to arrest this trend.

The ensuing nuclear proliferation debate brought to the forefront the well known, but often insufficiently appreciated, fact that policy outcomes are the byproduct of many competing interests and are never resolved to anyone's complete satisfaction. This, of course, is one respect in which *carte blanche* indictments of American diplomacy are unfair. In the United States, controversies cut across administrations, reflecting strong ideological differences within the White House and the Congress, between Congress and the White House, from lobbying groups representing the military-industrial complex, from the scholarly community, and from the growing number of Indians and Pakistanis resident in the United States who now have sufficient resources to influence the domestic political agenda. Between Congress and the White House the principal differences revolved around the efficacy of rigidly imposed sanctions and other coercive measures as the appropriate means for dissuading India and Pakistan from pursuing further the nuclear option. Such differences between the two branches were never absolute, of course. The attraction to rigidly apply sanctions and other legislatively derived coercive measures was strongest in the US Congress, however. This is because the executive branch, regardless of political complexion, always felt it needed flexibility to deal with exigencies arising on the ground that are not easily resolved by moral absolutes. Events were constantly arising in South Asia where, regardless of party, it was believed that regional imperatives demanded adaptive policies, even respecting nonproliferation, that did not lend themselves to pat solutions. Thus, while Pakistan in the 1980s, despite all entreaties to desist from doing so, was obviously surreptitiously pursuing the bomb, thus making them especially a target of Congressional wrath, it had also been designated at one time or another by every White House administration as a "frontline state" in the campaign first against Soviet aggression in Afghanistan and subsequently against Al Qaeda and the Taliban. The Carter, Reagan and Bush administrations all wanted to bend the rules in order to keep a militarized Pakistan in the game. Although things never went that far, it was a situation containing many of the temptations that earlier had led to the Iran-Contra scandal.[65]

Over ensuing years, therefore, the battles between Congress, the White House, and the Beltway lobbies ultimately revolved around which strictures to enforce and which to circumvent. The pro-Pakistan faction in Congress, consisting mainly of conservatives with lingering residues of the Cold War culture, and substantial links to the defense industry, who had profited from the Pakistan alliance when it was in full flower, tended to support circumvention of the rules (in the name of the Afghan war and what was left of 'anti-Communism') where Pakistan was concerned, but enforcement of them (out of resentment over Indian refusal to outwardly condemn Soviet aggression, and its non-alignment policies generally) where India was concerned. When the administration was proactive on utilizing the military model, as it understandably was during the Afghan conflict, it turned to this faction. When the administration was tilting toward India, usually in the name of "balancing" its relations with the two South Asian states, it turned to the "India caucus" on Capitol Hill which was usually willing to go along with conciliatory gestures to the Indians in matters where their need for loans and their desire for high-end technology imports could have been blocked because of their unwillingness to accept controls on reprocessing nuclear fuels and other restrictions designed to deter the achievement of weapons capability.[66]

Rubinoff offers some excellent insights into how erratically the balance could swing from one side to the other. Just when during the 1980s the bilateral structure that the Reagan administration had been trying to establish between India and Pakistan appeared to be on track, a scandal broke which created a legislative furor.

As Rubinoff expresses it, "developments outside Congress reversed the fortunes of India and Pakistan in Washington." He continues:

> In mid-July [1985], a Pakistani-born Canadian citizen, Arshad Parvez, was arrested for allegedly trying to purchase and export to Pakistan 25 tons of a special steel alloy used in the manufacture of nuclear weapons. Following a June 1984 incident in which another Pakistani citizen, Nazir Vaid, was arrested in Houston trying to smuggle krytons. . .. Congress passed a measure in 1985 jointly introduced by Representative [Stephen] Solarz and Senator Larry Pressler stipulating that American assistance should immediately be cut off if the president found that a country had tried to illegally acquire American material for making nuclear weapons.[67]

In the face of Pakistan's strategic importance to current US South Asian policy, the Congressional outrage that had turned to harshly punitive legislation created additional obstacles to the pragmatic requirements of the moment. With the Reagan administration pleading for a way out of its dilemma, the compromise solution was for Congress to backtrack *de facto* while *de jure* adhering to "principle." The solution that finally emerged was what might be called "waivers diplomacy" which kept all punitive legislation on the books while nevertheless empowering both Congress and the President under various circumstances to suspend enforcement of instruments like the Pressler Amendment for specific periods of time as long as the White House could certify that a target country, viz., Pakistan, had not actually produced atomic weapons. Basically, the only way to resolve differences between Cold War hardliners and nonproliferation true-believers was to maintain such an atmosphere of policy ambiguity.[68]

The "result of the multiplicity of plans and the failure of anyone on the authorization committees to coordinate an approach to the matter," says Rubinoff, was to essentially reify the ambiguity. This occurred when the Senate Appropriations Committee came up with a provision "denying assistance to any South Asian country that produced weapons-grade nuclear material."[69] India's gains early in the debate were eradicated by this "final solution" because it equated India with Pakistan as proliferation miscreants, something which India has perennially deemed to be unfair. The much more sophisticated Pakistani lobbying campaign which led to this outcome, in Rubinoff's words, "succeeded in changing the venue from the authorization committees to the appropriations committees and the issue from non-proliferation to aid to Afghanistan." (p. 171) In this arena, the Pakistanis held the best cards. To save as much of the situation as possible, "a compromise at eleven O'clock at night on December 31[1987]" initiated by Senators Inouye, Kasten, Moynihan and Pell, was adopted by the Senate. This was a revised amendment to *Continuing Resolution H.J. Res. 395* which "dropped all references to India and effectively gave Pakistan a six-year waiver of the Symington and Glenn amendments on the condition that the President certify annually that termination of assistance to that country would damage the national security interests of the United States." (p. 172)

After the Clinton administration came to power, Washington experienced for a while a revival of the pro-Pakistan lobby. It was driven by a combination of Realpolitik and fall-out from the non-proliferation wars on Capitol Hill. In this context,, the opposition assumed a somewhat different character from past incarnations. Instead of being dominated by Chester Bowles-style, pro-India liberals, they were dominated by John-Glenn-style non-proliferation theologists. This is because the main concern was no longer which strategies would prevent the spread of Communism or keep the Soviet Union at bay, but the feared spread of nuclear weapons, on the one hand, and the radicalization process that was crystallizing in Afghanistan and already impacting on Kashmir, on the other. Both camps professed deep concern over these matters but differed with regard to the best methods for preventing the proliferation of both nuclear weapons and Mujahideen terrorism. In the Realpolitik domain, the pro-Pakistan lobby, with whom the White House initially sided, took the position that resuming the arms relationship was a 'confidence building measure' that reverted to the old saw that by reassuring Pakistan they had a "friend" in America, this would encourage them to pursue the democratization process that was allegedly underway and, most of all, persuade them to desist from further pursuit of the nuclear option. The opposition contended that any form of assistance to either South Asian state unless they abandoned their pursuit of the nuclear option would merely encourage them to go on doing so. On the radicalism issue, the belief on both sides of the political spectrum was that "de-nuclearizing" the Subcontinent and stimulating free-market economics would gradually quiet the storm that was brewing.

The 'denuclearization-of-Pakistan campaign' commenced in 1995 by focusing on two pieces of legislation. One was an amendment to the Foreign Operations Appropriations Bill that was passed by the House of Representatives on October 24, 1995.

The other was a "new section" inserted into the *Foreign Assistance Act of 1961[22 U.S.C. 2199]*.[70] The political maneuvering that took place well illustrates the dilemmas posed by trying to adapt grand strategy to regional imperatives, and particularly the interactive dimensions of the process. For this reason I shall deal somewhat extensively with the details.

Initiated on the Senate side of the aisle at the behest of Senator Hank Brown of Colorado, and passed first by the Senate on September 21st, the former piece of legislation mandated a one-year suspension of the Pressler amendment so that a "modest" quantum of 'confidence building' armaments could be sold to Pakistan. Because it was widely believed both in the White House and among Realpoliticians on the Hill that the Pressler amendment excessively impeded necessary diplomatic and strategic flexibility, the obvious long-term goal was to make the assault on this act a tactical first step toward its eventual nullification. In the South Asian context, the rationale behind such a maneuver, as noted above, was a reiteration of the time-worn logic of the old militararized model, *viz.*, that strengthening Pakistan's conventional weapons capability would diminish her security anxieties, which, in turn, along with the tranquilizing effects of knowing that America still "appreciated" Pakistan's "loyalty" and "friendship", would persuade them to abandon the pursuit of nuclear weapons. The argument on Pakistan's behalf thus was unchanged since the height of the Cold War. In this1990s manifestation, the expectation was that $400 million worth of military supplies was somehow going to rescue Pakistan's teetering democratic institutions, put the country on the road to economic prosperity, and transform her military into a dependable component of America's global security system. It was depicted also as some kind of sentimental payback for Pakistan's alleged loyalty and fidelity during the great anti-Communist crusade throughout the Cold War.

During the debate, which at times bordered on trite melodrama and outright disingenuousness, Senator Brown recited a litany of services that Pakistan supposedly had rendered on America's behalf during that period.[71]

Senator John Glenn led the now-outnumbered non-proliferation stalwarts. They included Senators Paul Simon, Diane Feinstein, and John Kerry. Glenn stated that: "What this is all about is whether the United States has a nuclear non-proliferation policy and whether we are truly willing to stick to it or are we not." If not, then "it sends all the wrong signals to the 178 non-proliferation members around the world who are doing what we want them to." The hawk and dove positions had to a certain extent traded ideological content. Strong supportive statements favoring disarmament were coming from persons (viz., Glenn and his allies) who in the past were logically more inclined toward policies that favored imparting enough military capability to Pakistan to encourage "balance" between the two regional powers and sustain Pakistan as a deterrent force in the region *vis a vis* both India and Inner Asia. Now they were claiming that any arms for Pakistan would be a *destabilizing* not a *stabilizing* factor in South Asia both because it would encourage Pakistan's quest for nuclear capability as well as impel India toward further compensatory weaponization. "The supporters of this amendment," said Senator John Kerry, "want to lavish Pakistan with destabilizing conventional weapons while that country proceeds full throttle with its nuclear program." The opponents of the Glenn position, on the other hand, were now those who in the past had held that supporting Pakistani militarization was a strategic error, even in the name of Realpolitik, because it subsidized the country's anti-democratic elites and risked war with India.

This was clearly a battle over whether universalistic moral politics or regionally-targeted Realpolitik should dominate American diplomacy. However, the cross-currents in the debate, driven by Cold War residues combined with the search for new policy formulations had severely muddled the policy-making waters both on the Hill and in the White House. No one was quite sure what course would follow in its wake.

The House hearings exemplified this pattern, where the contestants, including the Government of India's lobbying resources, were unable to muster sufficient support to stem the stampede back to the past. The Clinton administration weighed in with emphatic endorsements from Defense and State Department notables, and a clear indication that President Clinton accorded a high priority to some degree of Pakistani remilitarization. Numerous "arms control experts" were summoned from Washington think tanks and university campuses to testify that the contemplated military infusions for Pakistan were insufficient in magnitude to "upset" the strategic balance in South Asia.[72] The irony is that in this instance of juxtaposing universalistic and regional imperatives, the two positions had once again become contextually reversed.

Thus, as a legislative initiative, the passage of the Brown amendment was quite successful. As a piece of legislation indicative of a decisive turn in South Asia policy toward the better, it was not. In some ways, the best outcome in the end was that very little of substance followed from it. It had all been more a symbolic exercise than a serious policy undertaking. Pakistan did indeed receive a trickle of military supplies, but never obtained the F-16s it so desperately wanted and for which it had already paid. The Pakistani economy continued to sink toward bankruptcy. The country's already fragile democratic institutions continued to erode. And most important, Pakistan continued her overseas quest for nuclear weapons technology, including closet support from North Korea and China in this enterprise.[73]

But the determination of the White House and the pro-Pakistan caucus on Capitol Hill had for the time being gained considerable political, if not substantive, momentum from the Brown Amendment victory. This was evident when in 1997 a further step was undertaken on the road to by-passing Pressler and partially restoring the old mutual security relationship with Pakistan. In this case, the coalition's approach to reopening the door was through an attempt to meld the military and economic models into a single package which made the purely military aspects appear to be an almost incidental part of the whole. This occurred through restoration of Pakistan to the list of eligibles for the International Military Education and Training program (IMET) (under the rubric of an amendment to the Foreign Assistance Act of 1961). It would authorize *IMET*, and the Overseas Private

Investment Corporation (*OPIC*) and Trade and Development (*TDA*) programs. Her removal from eligibility had, of course, been the consequence of having run afoul of Pressler and other non-proliferation sanctions.

While in substantive terms these two struggles may have had no more than symbolic value, they were nevertheless important from the standpoint of what they revealed about the condition of American South Asia policy almost fifty years after its inception. Namely, its failure to evolve a culturally sensitized and doctrinally consistent strategic vision. The fact that this rather tiresome and irrelevant drama could rear its head so late in the day attests to the dimensions of this failure of imagination. Time and circumstances had rendered this style of Cold War diplomacy obsolete and irrelevant to the evolutionary processes that were currently underway in South Asia. Important segments of the American political establishment were still living in the past, demonstrably misreading the most fundamental source of cleavage and potential strife in South Asia, *viz*., the deep-seated intra-regional ethno-religious antipathies that drove their mutual enmity, and America's Cold War driven militarized grand strategy which had exacerbated rather than ameliorated this cleavage.

Things took one more ironical twist leading up to and following 9/11. There occurred another implicit 'regime change' in the US affecting US South Asian diplomacy. Without specifically saying so, the Clinton administration switched positions on Pakistan midway through their term in office. The regional imperative once more asserted itself in a manner that reversed the policy positions which had earlier been adopted. This occurred when Pakistan engaged in a series of actions which convinced the US government that neither the so-called 'even handed' policy nor the policy of open-endedly treating Pakistan as a 'front-line state' was any longer working. Pakistan was bordering on political and economic chaos. Yet it had conducted nuclear tests at Pokhran, weaponized its nuclear arsenal, and escalated its proxy war against India over Kashmir. The effects were twofold. Domestically it ignited a political crisis that ultimately led to another coup in which the civilian regime of Prime Minister Nawaz Sharif was replaced by still another military dictator, General Pervez Musharraf, who had been the chief instigator of the Kargil misadventure. Internationally, it provoked a powerful but carefully orchestrated counterattack by Indian armed forces that successfully eliminated the 'Kargil salient' and, when Kargil was followed by a terrorist attack on the Indian parliament (Dec. 3, 2001), provoked a massive mobilization of Indian troops (and a counter-mobilization of Pakistani forces) which for a time made it appear that a nuclear war in South Asia was only one more provocative incident away.

It was in the face of these circumstances that the Clinton administration felt constrained to undertake another shift in the country's South Asia policy. It was not as total shift, to be sure, but enough to recognize and cope with the fact that the qualitative gap was now widening more than it ever had before—Pakistan toward ambivalent entwinement in the Islamic revolution, and a growing atmosphere of political instability and economic decay; India toward immersion in the global economy, impressive domestic economic progress, and increasing status as a major regional power. In retrospect, it is clear that these regional realities had ultimately afforded the US no alternative but to alter its past policies if it was to salvage any credibility in the current South Asian political environment. 'Even-handedness' could no longer be justified if that meant treating India and Pakistan as though they had equal political weight, economic equivalence, and equal culpability for the prevalent regional instability. President Clinton's visit to South Asia (March 19-25, 2000) not long after the Pakistan coup, and following unsuccessful American efforts to pressure the Pakistanis into terminating cross-border terrorism, dramatized this differentiation. It marked a real turning point in US policy toward the region. His warm embrace of India, on the one hand, and his pointed decision to make only a perfunctory stopover in Islamabad (March 25-26, 2000) en route home, on the other, dramatically symbolized this change. After this, Indo-American relations began to more and more resemble the "constructive engagement" mode which President Clinton had adopted toward Mainland China. Now, under the current Bush administration, joint-military training ventures have been undertaken, talks have been taking place concerning regional military collaboration, business enterprise between the two countries' nationals is taking on the hues that once were only spoken of in relation to China.

Perhaps the strongest testimony supporting this widening differentiation between India and Pakistan comes from the Pakistanis themselves. An article written by Masood Hasan, a Lahore-based Pakistani journalist, speaks eloquently about the contrast between India's rapid economic progress and his own country's lack of it.[74] An Indian-American journalist, Kaushik Kapisthalam, augments these perceptions with a depiction of Pakistan's descent into what he terms the "Islamist swamp" where General Musharraf flirts with Islamic extremists in the Urdu medium while in the English medium reassuring the Americans of his dedication to the War on Terror.[75] Masood reminisces about a journey he recently took toward Sialkot on the Wazirabad-Sialkot road. The "potholes and bumps on that narrow ribbon [of a] road began to revive memories of long forgotten journeys made on that same road." It was the same as when he was in Kindergarten, he moans: "Nothing seemed to have changed except the dust was thicker." In the past, he continues, the knowledge that things were not that different in India "might have given us years of self-induced smugness, *but things across the divide are changing at a speed that baffles the mind.*"[76]

Masood recites statistics showing the dimensions of the increasing contrast between his country and her neighbor. He calls this the fruit of India's "IT revolution." This is a reference to the high-tech payoffs emanating from and symbolized by the Indian Institutes of Technology which were established in the 1950s at Jawaharlal Nehru's behest. They established the intellectual and technological milieu and accompanying industrialization from which India's current surge into the global economy ultimately evolved. While Pakistan languishes in the social and political quagmire created by its long career as a "rent-seeking-state" available for a price to satiate America's strategic preoccupations, quench Islamist *jihadis'* thirst for true-believing foot soldiers, to fill the technological gaps in North Korean,

Iranian, Libyan, and other marginal states' nuclear arms programs, India invests its burgeoning fiscal, productive and intellectual resources in creating a modern economy, a vibrant democracy, and an increasingly prosperous middle-class. Citing the innumerable major companies churning out every conceivable product both for the domestic and inter-national markets, from Honda motorcycles, Maruti automobiles, to pharmaceuticals, and CD-recorders, Masood declares, "India's success can no longer be denied and the gap between us and them grows wide .. .by leaps and bounds."

These, then, are transformations within the South Asian regional system that United States foreign policy can no longer take lightly nor fail to factor into its strategic formulations. The 'equal culpability' thesis has become obsolete, indeed defunct.

Conclusions

The United States got off on the wrong foot in South Asia following the establishment of India and Pakistan in the wake of World War II. The failure to realize that the principal threats admixed with subtle coercion to the region emanated from the cauldron of ethno-religious antipathies spawned by Separatism rather than international Communism, was the reason why. In almost *karmic* fashion, this led to a series of disastrous policy failures that ultimately destroyed US credibility both in India and Pakistan. This failure of strategic imagination resulted in the very consequences that these policies were designed to avert, *viz.*, intra-regional war, the erosion of democratic institutions, the persistence of poverty, and the serious penetration of Soviet bloc influence.

For two generations, US diplomacy tried, as the saying goes, to work both sides of the street—using the military aid model to try and keep Pakistan in the anti-Communist orbit; using the economic aid model and pro-democratic rhetoric admixed with the subtle coercion to try and prevent an alienated India from slipping too deeply into the Communist camp. The strategy failed because these models, as well as the bilateralism that followed in their wake, were mutually exclusive, and rooted in faulty historical premises concerning South Asian regional realities.

The bottom line is that the Cold War need not, indeed should not, have been introduced into South Asia on the scale that it was. There was never a threat either of indigenous Communism or Soviet aggression sufficient in magnitude to warrant the abject militarization of American grand strategy for the region. This is what liberals and moderates like Chester Bowles contended, and right wing ideologues like John Foster Dulles failed to understand. Each milestone in the subsequent history of US relations with India and Pakistan reveals the regrettable consequences of this initial error in strategic judgment. Once initiated, it was inevitable that whatever the US tried to do to placate Pakistan negatively reverberated in India and vice versa. It was the inevitable fruit of a 'one-size-fits-all' diplomacy. It created contradictions rather than resolve them and actually nullified any basis for executing a structurally consistent foreign policy. Thus, in the end, war was not kept out of South Asia. Instead it became an endemic aspect of the region's internal affairs. Nor was Soviet influence kept out of the Subcontinent. Instead, Indian alienation plus American inability to prevent periodical eruptions of intraregional war enabled the Soviets to become major strategic players and political arbiters in the region. From Tashkent onward, one can say the Soviets became the predominant players as far as brokering Indo-Pakistani relations were concerned. The United States by contrast saw its capacity to influence events in the region progressively decline despite the investment of billions of dollars and untold man-hours of diplomacy. The 1998 nuclear explosions and the Musharraf coup placed the final stamp of failure on the US's half-century effort to conform South Asia to its strategic vision.

This outcome is the more regrettable because America's South Asia policy arose from good intentions and a genuine desire to get things right, for the people of the region as well as for its own strategic interests. The inability to find a formula which could reconcile and satisfy the felt needs and aspirations of both India and Pakistan, towards whom there was no surfeit of good will, proved to be a perpetual source of frustration and despair. The anguish rose to especially painful heights once the nuclear factor entered the picture. But in the end no resolution satisfactory to all parties could be found. This is the case not because the desire was ever lacking but because from the outset the premises were fundamentally wrong.

Recent developments both within and outside the region confirm almost by default the accuracy of this assessment. In the second Clinton administration, course adjustments finally were made. The Bush administration has transformed Clinton's early initiatives into a systematized policy which decisively applies the merit system to each South Asian state. India emerges as a winner and Pakistan a loser in this new dispensation. Prior to President Clinton's trip to the region in the Spring of 2000, I stated: "Mr. Clinton has now placed his administration in a position where he can put an end to double-standards diplomacy if only he will seize upon the opportunity presented by his impending *yatra* to do so." He clearly did. Kargil, the sacking of Nawaz Sharif, and the emergence of General Pervez Musharraf as another in the long succession of Pakistani military dictators at a time when conciliatory gestures by Indian Prime Minister Atal Behari Vajpayee had brought about the Lahore Agreement, was the straw that broke the camel's back. Kargil "was a turning point in US-Indian relations precisely because for the first time in memory the doctrine of equal culpability was not resorted to. Instead, the United States removed its moral blinders and called spades spades."[77]

The Bush administration has provided the *piece de resistance*. A broadly structured strategic agreement which includes relaxing the sanctions on Indian nuclear development has now been fashioned and awaits Congressional ratification. The latter will not be an easy sell due to the resistance being offered by non-proliferation purists, and unreconstructed Cold Warriors who still have not forgiven India for her Non-Alignment apostacy. Nevertheless, this is "the final breakthrough promising a new era of common sense diplomacy toward South Asia" in which concedes, "at least on a *de facto* basis, that India is a responsible nuclear weapons state entitled to the rights and privileges attendant upon occupying this status."[78]

NOTES AND REFERENCES

1. This chapter is a comprehensively revised version of a chapter entitled "The Reasons Why: The US Failure to Control the Nuclear Agenda in South Asia," that appeared in Ashok Kapur, Y.K Malik, Harold A. Gould and Arthur G. Rubinoff, eds., *India and the United States in a Changing World* (New Delhi: Sage Publications, 2002). The original inspiration for this study was a paper presented at the Panel, "India: Nuclear Weapons and World Order," at the 1999 American Political Science Association Annual Meeting in Atlanta, GA, September 2-5, 1999.
2. Cordell Hull, *The Memoirs of Cordell Hull, Vol. 2* (New York: Macmillan, 1948).

   > ... we kept our public statements general ..b ut in private ... the president talked very bluntly about India with.. .. . Churchill just as I was talking with Ambassador Halifax. . .. While for the sake of good relations with Britain we could not tell the country what we were saying privately, we were saying everything the most enthusiastic supporter of India's freedom could have expected. ... (p. 1483)

3. For a valuable account of America's early diplomatic contacts with India, see Gary Hess, *America Encounters India, 1941 to 1947* (Baltimore: Johns Hopkins Press, 1971).
4. Essentially Phillips excoriated the British for their imperious attitudes toward their Indian colony. In his memoirs, Phillips relates his impressions of an encounter with Churchill in London prior to his departure for India. "I realized," he says, "that once Churchill in London had made up his mind, nothing could change it. Later I was to discover the same uncompromising attitude about India." (p. 346) Not long after commencing his tenure in India, Phillips observed: "The British insisted that the Indians show a willingness and ability to get together, yet they were holding incommunicado the Indian leaders, Gandhi and Nehru. .. ." (p. 352) In one part of the memo which Pearson featured, the Ambassador declares: There would seem to be only one remedy to this highly unsatisfactory situation ...an d that is to change the attitude of the people of India towards the war, make them see and feel that we want them to assume responsibilities to the United Nations and are prepared to give them facilities for doing so, and that the voice of India will play an important part in the reconstruction of the world. The present political conditions do not permit of any improvement in this respect. (p. 388)

Phillips's great sensitivity to the South Asian situation extended even to a prophetic speculation concerning what might be the implications of the Muslim League's demand for a separate nation, to be called Pakistan. In his words, "the more I studied [Mohammed Ali] Jinnah's Pakistan, the less it appealed to me as the answer to India's communal problem, since *to break India into two separate nations would weaken both and open Pakistan, at least, to the designs of ambitious neighbors.*" (p. 359. *Emphasis added.*) The ambitious neighbors, unfortunately, turned out to be the United States of America and the Union of Soviet Socialist Republics!

William Phillips, *Ventures in Diplomacy* (Boston: Beacon Hill Press, 1952).

5. Pakistan explicitly declared itself to be an Islamic state. India, however, declared itself a secular democratic state in which no religion, even Hinduism, would receive endorsement by the state.
6. See Larry Collins and Dominique LaPierre, *Freedom at Midnight* (New York: Simon and Schuster, 1975).
7. His two predecessors were Henry Byroade and Loy Henderson respectively, both career diplomats.
8. For an excellent treatment of constitutional development in India, see, M.V. Pylee, *Constitutional Government in India* (Bombay: Asia Publishing House, 1960). Also, Granville Austin, *Working a Democratic Constitution: The Indian Experience* (New Delhi: Oxford University Press, 1999).
9. Moreover, among the major Asian regions, South Asia and Southeast Asia ranked lowest in terms either of available expertise or policy concerns at this juncture in time. With regard to reportage on South Asia, the journalist Phillips Talbott, then a reporter for the *New York Times* (subsequently a senior diplomat and eventually Assistant Secretary of State for the Near East and South Asia) was almost alone in providing anything resembling regular coverage of the region. There were no language and area studies programs in those days and the closest one came to scholarly treatment of South Asia were the Foreign Service Institute (that from 1947 taught Hindi and Urdu) and departments of Oriental Languages and Religion in a few of the Ivy League schools plus a handful of others around the country, most notably Harvard, Yale, Columbia, the University of Pennsylvania, the University of Chicago, and the University of California (Berkeley), where Sanskrit, Hindi and perhaps one or two other Indian languages were offered. The first South Asian area studies program in the United States was established at the University of Pennsylvania in the early 1950s by Professor W. Norman Brown, a Sanskritist, and an experienced "India hand" who had served with the OSS in World War II.
10. Howard Schaffer, *New Dealer in the Cold War* (Cambridge, MA: Harvard University Press, 1993). p. 76.

11. *Ambassador's Report* (London: Victor Gollancz Ltd., 1954), p. 343. (*Emphasis added*).
12. There was as yet no Department of Defense.
13. *The Foreign Relations of the United States, 1947, Vol. 3.* (Washington, DC: U.S. Government Printing Office), p. 138.
14. Dennis Kux, *The United States and Pakistan: 1947-2000* (Washington, DC: The Woodrow Wilson Center, 2001), p. 47. (*Emphasis added*).
15. See R.J. Moore, *Escape from Empire: The Atlee Government and the Indian Problem* (Oxford: Clarendon Press, 1983). Maulana Abdul Kalam Azad, *India Wins Freedom: The Complete Version* (Hyderabad, India: Orient Longman, 1988). Prem Shankar Jha, *Kashmir, 1947* (Delhi: Oxford University Press, 1999).
16. Olaf Caroe, *The Pathans* (Karachi: Oxford University Press, 1958).
17. Harold A. Gould and Sumit Ganguly, co-eds., *The Hope and the Reality: U.S.-Indian Relations from Roosevelt to Reagan* (Boulder, CO: Westview Press: 1992).
18. *FRUS-1947*, Vol. 3 (Washington, DC: US Government Printing Office), p. 138.
19. *Op. cit.,* 2001.
20. This was vividly reflected in a conversation that Walter Lippmann reported with John Foster Dulles at a Washington dinner party shortly after the 1954 Geneva Accords. "Look Walter," Dulles said, blinking behind his thick glasses, "I've got some real fighting men into the south of Asia. The only Asians who can really fight are the Pakistanis. That's why we need them in the alliance. We could never get along without the Gurkhas." When Lippmann reminded him that the Gurkhas are Indian, not Pakistani, Dulles replied, "Well, they may not be Pakistanis, but they're Moslems." Lippmann once more corrected Dulles, saying, "No, I'm afraid they're not Moslems either, they're Hindus." Dulles merely replied, "No matter," and proceeded to lecture Lippmann for half an hour on how SEATO would plug the dike against communism in Asia.

    This conversation was originally reported by Richard J. Barnet, *The Alliance: America, Europe, Japan, Makers of the Postwar World* (New York: Simon and Schuster, 1983), p. 34.
21. *Thought* (Delhi, India), Vol. 6, No. 45 (November 6, 1954), p. 7.
22. These passages are taken from Kux (*Ibid*, pp. 60 & 61) who obtained them respectively from (a) Memorandum of conversation between Vice-President Nixon, Ghulam Mohammed, and Ambassador Horace Hildreth, December 7, 1953 *FRUS*, 1952-54, pt. 2, 1831-32." and (b) "Minutes of December 24, 1953, *NSC* meeting, *NSC* Series, *WF, DDEL.*
23. p. 61. Memorandum of January 14, 1954, meeting with the President, *FRUS*, 1952-54, Vol. 9, 453-54.
24. Robert J. McMahon, *The Cold War on the Periphery: The United States, India and Pakistan* (New York: Columbia University Press, 1994), p. 170.

25. *Ibid*, p. 171.
26. *Ibid*, 220.
27. p. 226. *Emphasis added.*
28. Dulles shocked India when in the course of his public statements on Goa he characterized it as the "last outpost of Christian civilization in South Asia"!
29. Kux, 1993, p. 118.
30. *Ambassador's Report*, Victor Gollancz, Ltd., 1954, pp. 108-09. See also Howard Schaffer, *Chester Bowles: New Dealer in the Cold War* (Cambridge: Harvard University Press, 1993).
31. There is a vast literature on this subject with which anyone wishing to comprehend the basis for the establishment of India and Pakistan as separate states must become familiar. See Paul R. Brass, *Religion and Politics in North India* (Cambridge: Cambridge University Press, 1974); C.A. Bayly, *The Local Roots of Indian Politics* (Allahabad: Oxford University Press, 1975); Francis Robinson, *Separatism Among Indian Muslims* (Cambridge: Cambridge University Press, 1974); Anil Seal, *The Emergence of Indian Nationalism: Competition and Collaboration in the Later Nineteenth Century* (Cambridge: Cambridge University Press, 1968); John Gallagher, Gordon Johnson and Anil Seal, *Locality, Province and Nation: Essays on Indian Politics, 1870-1940* (Cambridge: Cambridge University Press, 1973); Harold A Gould, *Grass-Roots Politics in India: A Century of Political Evolution in Faizabad District* (New Delhi: Oxford & IBH, 1994).
32. Mohammad Waseem, "Pakistan's Lingering Crisis of Dyarchy: Prime Minister-President Relationship," *Asian Survey*, July, 1992, Vol. 32, No. 7, p. 623.
33. *Ibid*, 2000, p. 55.
34. Kux, 2001, pp. 53-54. *Emphasis added.*
35. McMahon, *Ibid*, p. 333.
36. Dean Rusk oral history, *LBJL*. Cited by Kux, 2001, p. 165.
37. McMahon, *Ibid*, p. 260. *Emphasis added.*
38. Kux, *Ibid*, pp. 140-43.
39. See John W. Galbraith, *Ambassador's Journal* (Boston: Houghton Miflin, 1969).
40. Detailed accounts of the Bangladesh War are available in Kux (1993 and 2001), and in Christopher Hitchens, *The Trial of Henry Kissinger* (London/New York: 2001).
41. Kux, *Ibid*, 2001, p. 194.
42. Kux, *Ibid*, p. 305. Dennis Kux, the author of the two books on South Asian diplomacy, was a personal witness to the intrigues revolving around this arcane undertaking. He was at the time an "acting embassy political counselor, to replace [Deputy Chief of Mission Sidney] Sober as the control officer for the [Kissinger] visit. I had fewer high-level Pakistani contacts," Kux says, "and was less likely to become aware of

Kissinger's true mission." The ruse which preserved the secrecy of Kissinger's mission began when Kissinger supposedly had contracted "stomach trouble". Around midnight "[Ambassador] Farland and [NSC aid Harold] Saunders showed up at my home. Kissinger's stomach trouble had [allegedly] become much worse and he could not carry on with the planned schedule, they said." Yahya had suggested that he "rest for a day or two in the nearby 8000 foot mountain resort of Nathiagli. ... This meant that he had to depart at 4 a.m. ... I said that I would be at the state guest house, where Kissinger was staying, at 3:30 a.m. to make sure everyone left in good order. Saunders and Farland insisted that this was not necessary. I disagreed, saying this was part of a control officer's responsibility. After Farland still insisted, I acquiesced, frankly happy to get a full night's sleep." While all this maneuvering was taking place, Kissinger and his party left the government guest house and headed for Islamabad airport where they boarded a PIA flight for Beijing. Kux had remained in the dark about the actual events that were unfolding, purportedly under his control. So much so, in fact, that at an evening party, "Associated Press correspondent Arnold Zeitlin, the sole resident American journalist, asked me about the rumors [that Kissinger was holding secret talks]. I replied fliply, 'You're right, Kissinger is off to China for secret talks with Chou Enlai.' Zeitlin's eyes lit up, but they dimmed when I said it was only a joke. .. . On July 15, 1971, President Nixon announced Kissinger's trip to China and his own planned visit there." (*Ibid*, 2001, pp. 191-92).

43. For an understanding of the "short tether" policy. See, James Warner Bjorkman, "Public Law 480 and the Policies of Self-Help and Short-Tether: Indo-American Relations, 1965-68," in Lloyd and Suzanne Rudolph, *The Regional Imperative: US Foreign Policy Towards South Asian States* (Atlantic Highlands, New Jersey: Humanities Press, 1980), pp. 201-62. The "short tether" policy was initiated following the report of a joint congressional committee that was sent out to India for the purpose of undercutting Ambassador Bowles's objections to using food as a cudgel at the very time when drought and famine were afflicting the eastern portion of the gangetic plain, India's bread basket. The rationale for pressuring India was a belief that "the availability of US food—at little or no cost—removed the incentive for New Delhi to adopt policies encouraging farmers to produce more." This allegedly ensured low priced grain for Indian consumers which in turn was "a political boon to the Government of India. ..." (Kux, *Ibid*, 1993, p. 242) Why this would have been bothersome to the White House has never been explained, since one would have thought that economic conditions that contributed to political stability and governmental continuity were devoutly to be wished for. There are hints that pique over Indian criticism of American involvement in Vietnam, however muted at the time, had much to do with it. Kux mentions that a conversation between Under Secretary of

State Thomas Mann and Ambassador B.K. Nehru over the short tether policy "became somewhat heated, especially the Indian attitude toward Vietnam. ..." (p. 241) One suspects that a degree of 'Protestant Ethic-style paternalism' may also have been a subliminal factor. Research that I undertook in the LBJ library at the University of Taxas at Austin in 1991 indicate this. But this must await a subsequent study.

44. Kux, *Ibid*, 2001, p. 195. *Emphasis added.*
45. See Stephen P. Cohen, Chapter 8: "The Reagan Administration and India" (pp. 139-1540) in Gould & Ganguly, *op. cit.*, 1992.
46. Shirin R. Tahir-Kheli, India, *Pakistan and the United States: Breaking with the Past* (New York: Council on Foreign Relations), p. 73.
47. Gould & Ganguly, *Ibid*, Robert F. Goheen, "U.S. Policy During the Carter Presidency," pp. 122-27.
48. *Ibid*, p. 130.
49. *Ibid*, p. 149.
50. There are some differences between the American and Indian perceptions of what actually took place in New Delhi. By contrast with the American version, P.V. Narasimha Rao, the incumbent external affairs minister, told this author, in the Fall of 1981, that Clifford responded to Indian objections over providing $400 million in military assistance to Pakistan by saying, "If you are uneasy about our sending $400 million to the Pakistanis, we would be willing to give you $400 million as well!" Rao claims that he replied by saying, "We would prefer it if you refrained from giving $400 million to either side, because it means introducing more weapons into South Asia." Ambassador Schaffer denies Rao's assertion that $400 million was offered to India on a *quid pro quo* basis. He contends that the New Delhi mission had no specific figures on what was to be offered to Pakistan and that, in fact, Brzezinski, had made this offer on the spot. Clifford, on the other hand, says Schaffer, that Clifford had no authorization to offer India anything and was known as a scrupulous public servant who would never exceed his authority in such a fashion. (*Interview with Ambassador Howard Schaffer*, July 12, 1999.)

    On the effect of the Clifford mission from the standpoint of its stated objective, there is this to add. It is known that Mrs. Gandhi pulled her punches and failed to emphatically condemn the Soviet action. This, of course, angered the Carter administration. Given the complex relationship with the Soviets following Tashkent, and as a testament to how much the Soviets had profited from American policy defaults in South Asia, the Indian government did not wish to unduly offend its Soviet patrons and decided to pursue quiet diplomacy in an effort to persuade Brezhnev to amicably settle the Afghan situation. Narasimha Rao spoke of a meeting in Moscow during this period where he expressed Indian displeasure with the invasion and told Andre Gromyko, "You are making it difficult for your friends to help you." (*Interview with Minister of External Affairs, P.V. Narasimha Rao*, South Block, New Delhi, January 1982.)

51. Husain Haqqani, "Pakistan's Perennial political Crisis," in *The State of Pakistan*, a publication of papers presented on April 2, 2003, at a colloquium organized by the South Asia Studies Program of the Paul H. Nitze School of Advanced International Studies, The Johns Hopkins University, Washington, DC, pp. 3-7.
52. Stephen Phillip Cohen, *Ibid*, p. 148.
53. In a personal conversation with me, shortly after the commencement of the Rajiv Gandhi's regime, External Affairs Minister P.V. Narasimha Rao spoke in very positive terms of the new Prime Minister's 'business-like', 'chairman of the board' style of performance in cabinet meetings. He saw this as a contrast with Mrs. Gandhi more peremptory style of dialogue.
54. *Mother India: A Political Biography of Indira Gandhi* (New York: Charles Scribner's Sons, 1992), p. 542.
55. *Ibid*, p. 43.
56. Hatch went on to say, "Ten years from now scholars will look back on this past year as an end to the Ice Age, or to shift the metaphor, the slow death of certain dinosaurs which have symbolized the cool relations between the United States and India for many years." Speech in the US Senate, May 19, 1983.
57. Harold A. Gould, "China model is suggested for US-South Asia ties," *India Abroad*, May 14, 1999.
58. Presentation at the Center for Strategic and International Studies *(CSIS)*, Washington, September, 1999.
59. *Ibid*, p. 87.
60. Determined under Jawaharlal Nehru to plunge headlong into the modern era, the Indian parliament passed an Atomic Energy Act in April 1948. The Bhabha Atomic Research Center (*BARC*) opened in 1954. A uranium heavy water research reactor went "critical" in 1969. A "peaceful nuclear explosion" took place at Pokhran in 1974, a decade after China's first detonation, signifying India's arrival at the threshold of before nuclear powerdom. Being a poorer country, and constrained somewhat by its client status *vis a vis* the United States, Pakistan got into the game a little later. It established an Atomic Energy Commission in 1956, and with Canadian assistance had its first nuclear power plant on line in 1965. Pakistan did not move to nuclear testing until May of 1998. But, as Tahir-Kheli (1994) states: "The U.S. arms-cutoff in the midst of the 1965 Indo-Pakistani war and the loss of East Pakistan .. .in 1971 left Pakistanis feeling vulnerable, which fostered thoughts of a stronger nuclear program." (*Ibid*, p. 71) To her way of thinking, and probably rightly, "National prestige was less weighty a factor in Pakistani thinking than in Indian." For them, the nuclear weapons option was more an act of desperation to build a weapon of 'last resort'." (*Ibid*, p. 72) Ambassador Teresita Schaffer agrees with this assessment. In her words: "Pakistan's defeat in the 1965 and 1971 wars, and *especially the Indian military role*

in assisting the former East Pakistan to secede and became the newly independent Bangladesh, precipitated then Prime Minister Bhutto's decision to establish a nuclear program. India's 1974 'Peaceful Nuclear Explosion' spurred it on." [Teresita Schaffer, *Sanctions and Security: The Case of Pakistan* (Sanctions Paper Document, Washington, DC: Center for Strategic and International Studies. Nd.]

61. Cohen, *Ibid*, p. 147.
62. See Harold A. Gould, "The Babri Masjid and the Secular Contract," *Contributions to Indian Sociology (n.s.),* 32, (1998); pp. 507-26.
63. Ambassador Naresh Chandra, July 1999 in *India Abroad.*
64. *Ibid*, p. 145.
65. The road blocks began to accumulate in earnest in the immediate aftermath of India's 1974 nuclear test. Representative Clarence Long, chairman of the foreign aid appropriations committee got a bill passed directing the United States to vote against all loans that India requested from the World Bank. This legislation had no teeth in it because the United States didn't command a majority of votes in that body. As Kux observes, "It was, however, a symbolic slap that made clear the force of congressional annoyance about the nuclear test." (*Ibid,* p. 316) Worse was to come from the nuclear nonproliferation lobby, "far stronger among Democrats than Republicans" (*Idem.*), on Capitol Hill. In 1978, the Nuclear Non-proliferation Act became law. It mandated that all nuclear cooperation be terminated with any country (specifically India in South Asia with reference to Tarapur) which failed to institute "full scope safeguards" against the use of its facilities to manufacture atomic weapons, or reprocess nuclear fuels supplied by the United States to that end. Amendments (sections 669 and 670) to the *Foreign Assistance Act of 1978*, known as the *Symington and Glenn amendments*, "Prohibited aid or arms sales to countries that deliver or receive nuclear enrichment equipment or technology and do not accept *IAEA* [International Atomic Energy Agency] safeguards"
66. During the interim between these two periods, however, the India caucus was a less reliable source of support for the Indian cause. As Ambassador Teresita Schaffer notes (in a personal communication, November 8, 1999), "In the 70s and especially in the 80s, the India caucus had just about disappeared. The old liberal group no longer cared about India; Afghanistan had become the 'bleeding heart' cause in the region. Indeed [Rep.] Wally Herger and [Rep.] Dan Burton were routinely able to get large majorities in the House to vote for an aid cutoff for India. The revival of the 'India caucus' in the 1990s reflected (1) the Pak nuclear aid cutoff; (2) India's economic liberalization and resulting increase in trade with the US, and most recently; (3) the increasing importance of the Indian-American community for Congressional fundraising." Another source of division and oscillation in the India caucus's fervor was the emotional state at any given time of

the many nonproliferation purists in its ranks whose appetite for the universalization of sanctions regimens could impel them to diminish their support for India whenever India appeared to be straying too far off the nonproliferation reservation.

67. Arthur Rubinoff, "Congressional Attitudes Toward India", in Gould and Ganguly, *Ibid*, pp. 127-29.
68. The need for political ambiguity had another facet as well. Most members of Congress, on both sides of the aisle, actually believed that India either had the bomb or something close to it after 1974. However, it was concluded that India's nuclear program, like Israel's, had been achieved through largely indigenous development whereas Pakistan's program relied primarily on imported components and technology, as the Vaid and Houston cases dramatized. Under these circumstances, in Ambassador Terresita Schaffer's words, "Congressional figures writing sanctions legislation didn't want to make Israel subject to the sanctions, so the triggering mechanism was *imports* of 'equipment, materials and technology.' That effectively let India off the hook." Moreover, since Pakistan had been receiving significant quanta of aid from the US, whereas India was not, "the US felt it was entitled to impose terms on Pakistan and that Pakistan was likely to listen to." Finally, talk of an "Islamic bomb" made Pakistan appear to constitute a greater threat to broader US interests than did India's "peaceful" nuclear arsenal. (*Ibid*, November 8, 1999).
69. *Ibid*, p. 170.
70. *Congressional Record*, Vol. 141, September 21, 1995, pp. S13997-14003.
71. "In 1950, we asked them to condemn the invasion of Korea and they gave us unqualified support," including a condemnation of North Korea as well. In 1954, we asked them to be an initial member of the Central Treaty Organization and help contain communism. ... In 1955, Pakistan joined the Southeast Asia Treaty Organization, SEATO. ..." In 1966 (pointedly) they condemned the Hungarian invasion. "In 1959, we asked Pakistan to sign a mutual defense treaty with the United States at a tough time, and they did." Brown, of course, cited Pakistan's role "in fighting the Soviet invasion of Afghanistan." He even mentioned the fact that Pakistan helped us with troops sent to Haiti! What he did not mention, of course, was Pakistan's thoroughly parochial reasons for rendering these various services to the "cause of freedom!"
72. Typical was the testimony which Professor Stephen P. Cohen, then an arms control specialist at the University of Illinois, currently Senior Fellow at the Brookings Institution, gave on the Senate side that was designed to disarm fears that resuming the arms relationship with Pakistan would have a destabilizing impact on the region: "In terms of the regional military balance, I don't think that the release of this military equipment ...wi ll have ...s ignificant impact on the balance one way

or the other." The late George Tanham, then a retired military analyst from Rand Corporation, chimed in with a tacit endorsement of this view: "In fact, there is no balance now. India dominates so strongly. They have twice as large an army as Pakistan. Twice as large an air force, twice as large a navy, twice as many tanks, twice as many airplanes. India has overwhelming strength."(*Ibid*, p. S14001).

73. See Harold A. Gould, "Indian and Pakistani Lobbies seen as Irrelevant," *India Abroad*, July 14, 1997.
74. Masood Hasan, "Beyond the Edge," *The News International* (Pakistani Newspaper), December 14, 2003.
75. Kaushik Kapisthalam. "Pakistan: Nuclear Trader, Islamist Swamp," *Front Page Magazine*, December 15, 2003.
76. Masood Hasan, *Ibid, Emphasis added.*
77. *India Abroad*, March 3, 2000, "Visit may Serve to Undo Damage of Cold War Years."
78. *India Abroad*, Feb. 17, 2006, "Non-Proliferation Blues: Cold War Songs in a Flat World."

3

FROM INDIFFERENCE TO ENGAGEMENT
The Role of the U.S. Congress in Making Foreign Policy for South Asia*

— *Arthur G. Rubinoff*

This essay analyzes the role Congress has played in the Indo-American bilateral relationship. Consistent with what Stephen Weissman calls "a culture of deference" to the executive branch,[1] there has been a basic congruence of policy between the executive and legislative branches towards India. Even so, congressional hostility has sometimes exceeded that of the executive branch. Whether it is conscious or not, members of Congress have often damaged bilateral relations with outspoken criticisms of India's leaders, policies, and ways of life.[2] If ignorance of South Asia has typified American attitudes, neglect has characterized American policies. As the opening essay in this volume argues, the United States often conducted relations with India in a global geopolitical context that downplayed bilateral and regional considerations. In both the executive and legislative branches, South Asia was attached to the Middle East or the Asia Pacific regions. As a result, issues concerning South Asia were often addressed in a subsidiary way, e.g., by amendment to foreign operations bills, instead of by

* An earlier version of this article appeared as "Changing Perceptions of India in the U.S. Congress," *Asian Affairs*, 28, No. 1 (March 2001). The author would like to thank William L. Richter for his comments and suggestions on an earlier draft.

specific legislation directed towards the region. Washington's bilateral ties with New Delhi were further subordinated by pre-occupation with Anglo-American concerns, U.S.-Soviet competition, and Indo-Pakistani rivalry.

The winding down of the Russian occupation of Afghanistan and the end of the cold war freed Indo-U.S. relations from their subordination to global geo-political calculations. In order to recognize a regional imperative, Representative Stephen Solarz (D-NY), the chairman of the Asia Pacific Subcommittee of the House Committee on Foreign Affairs, succeeded in establishing a separate South Asian Bureau in the Department of State. Yet, most legislators were slow to adjust to changing international circumstances. Suspicion of India lingered on Capitol Hill as late as the passage of the Brown Amendment, which weakened sanctions against Pakistan in 1995. Some legislators remained wary of India's relationship with Russia—despite the fact that Moscow was no longer regarded as a threat to the United States. Despite the controversy created by India's nuclear tests in 1998, the growing importance of Indian-Americans to the political process in the United States led to a fundamental change in congressional attitudes and public policy towards New Delhi. The 1998 Brownback Amendment, which waived sanctions against the South Asian nuclear states, demonstrates that legislators now play a more active role in the formulation of bilateral relations. Many members of the U.S. House of Representatives who formed a Caucus of India and Indian Americans—a development replicated in the Senate—came to believe that increased attention to the Indian subcontinent can benefit U.S. interests. This newfound realization had two immediate results. First, it prompted greater congressional interest in South Asia. Second, it led to a dramatic shift in congressional sympathies.[3] However, since September 11, 2001, ethnic politics and New Delhi's standing on Capitol Hill have been diminished by Washington's prosecution of the war on terrorism in Afghanistan. By again making Pakistan a frontline state in a global campaign, the United States has once more conducted its relations with India in the context of broader issues.

Ironically, the attempt by President George W. Bush in March 2006 to make nuclear cooperation with India the centerpiece of improved bilateral relations—negotiated without congressional input—has placed Capitol Hill in the position of endorsing the administration's initiative while repudiating over thirty years of nonproliferation legislation. For the first time good relations with Indian overrode global concerns. Many friends of India in the U.S. Congress now have to choose between upholding their nonproliferation principles and a desire for better relations with New Delhi.

The Residual Nature of Relations

Despite India's growing economic, political and strategic importance, the United States has neglected that country, relative to other areas of the world. Within both the executive and legislative branches, South Asia has structurally been accorded a low priority. As a region it has been more associated with problems rather than opportunities. Until 1991 the state department included South Asia with the Near East and resisted the creation of a separate bureau for the region. As a result, relations with India were handled by a deputy assistant secretary four levels removed from the secretary of state. Under this arrangement, the "Near East received the lion's share of attention, holding six country directorates compared to two for South Asia, although the three to one population ratio was the inverse."[4] South Asia is also attached to the Near East in the National Security Council and in the Central Intelligence Agency. Sometimes regional issues were handled intermittently by functional experts.[5] Only with the creation of the National Intelligence Agency in 2005 was a separate South Asia Bureau, that reported directly to a director of intelligence, established.

Congressional Structures

The legislative scene is even more diffuse. The post-Viet Nam revolt against the imperial presidency and the breakdown of the congressional seniority system produced an atomization of power on Capitol Hill. By 1983 there were twenty-six standing and select committees in the House of Representatives. Most of them had at least one subcommittee active in the foreign policy field. The proliferation of congressional committees has created problems of coordination and jurisdiction. On the one hand, this proliferation of authority has made it easier to find allies on the Hill. On the other hand, the growth in the number of committees and subcommittees meant that key players found it more difficult to establish a legislative consensus or to reliably interpret congressional views to the executive branch.[6] Of particular note was the decline of the Senate Foreign Relations Committee which had historically managed the process. Although at one time presidential contenders had vied for a seat on the committee,[7] by 1981 it had become the preserve of freshman senators.[8] Under the leadership of its longtime chairman (1959-1975), J. William Fulbright (D-AK), who was estranged from Presidents Lyndon Johnson and Richard Nixon over the conduct of South East Asian policy, the committee concerned itself primarily with U.S.-Soviet issues and the Vietnam conflict. South Asia was marginalized at best; ignored at worst.[9] Subcommittee chairmen who showed an interest and desired a platform sometimes paid attention to South Asia. During the Bangladesh crisis of 1971-1972, the Subcommittee on Refugees of the Judiciary Committee, chaired by Edward Kennedy (D-MA), held more hearings in the Senate than did the Foreign Relations Committee.

The interest and expertise of staff also plays a role in what issues congressional committees consider. Because of staff input, the Senate Foreign Relations Committee was more concerned with South Asia under the chairmanship of Senators Frank Church (D-ID, 1977-1981), Richard Lugar (R-IN, 1985-87) and Claiborne Pell (D-RI, 1987-95) than it had been under Senators J. William Fulbright and John Sparkman (D-AL, 1975-1977). However, interest has not always translated into influence.[10]

As the importance of the Foreign Relations Committee declined, the partisanship of its members increased. In the 1990s the result was stalemate. Diplomatic appointments were delayed and negotiations on arms control and the international criminal court were stymied. Those who have not prevailed at the subcommittee or committee levels have complicated matters by proposing amendments from the floor. These developments contributed to legislative authority passing to the House Foreign Affairs Committee.

A major reorganization of House subcommittees in 1970 further marginalized South Asia.[11] Continuity and expertise in that chamber were reduced. At times South Asia, in the manner of the state department, has been paired with the Near East in a subcommittee of the House Foreign Affairs Committee. As a result, the region was overshadowed by Arab-Israeli and Iraqi matters. At other times it has been coupled with the Asia and the Pacific region where it was dwarfed by concerns, such as the Vietnam War and bilateral relations with China and Japan. Under the chairmanship of Stephen Solarz (1981-1993), there was a reversal of fortune. Committee interest in South Asian issues reached an all-time high, as the New York Democrat gave region a particularly high profile that it did not have on the full Foreign Affairs Committee. However, rivalry between the Asia-Pacific subcommittee chaired by Solarz and the full Foreign Affairs Committee chaired by Dante Fascell (D-FL) often contributed to legislative gridlock.

As recently as the mid-1980s, only about five per cent of the members of Congress had an interest in South Asia.[12] Given this situation, congressional attention to India has not been constant. Legislative activity tends to cluster around related issues such as human rights and nuclear proliferation. When issues are peripheral to interest groups, political parties, and the congressional leadership, members have more discretion regarding their activities.[13] However, this also enables marginals to become involved in the foreign policy process as it relates to regional and bilateral areas peripheral to the national interest. Hence "India Bashers", such as Dan Burton (R-IN), Dana Rohrabacher (R-CA), and Robert Dornan (R-CA) have used the Foreign Affairs and Intelligence Committees as platforms to criticize New Delhi with impunity.[14] To counter their activities, improve bilateral relations, and fill the vacuum left by Stephen Solarz's departure from Congress, a bipartisan "Caucus of India and Indian-Americans" that included future speaker Newt

Gingrich (R-GA) was formed in February 1993 by nearly fifty members of the House.[15] One of the few congressional organizations dedicated to promoting relations with a single country, it was co-chaired by Frank Pallone (D-NJ), who had a district with a significant Indian population, and Bill McCollum (R-FL), who was critical of Pakistan's record on narcotics and terrorism. Pallone was deposed by Gary Ackerman (D-NY) in October 1998, after being accused of using the organization for personal aggrandizement.[16] Jim McDermott (D-WA) succeeded Ackerman two years later. James Crowley (D-NY), whose district has the second largest population of Indian-Americans, replaced McDermott in 2002. Ackerman again headed the grouping in 2004. McDermott replaced him at the helm in 2006.

As Richard Fenno suggests, and examples concerning South Asia confirm, Congress shapes foreign policy in committee during the foreign aid appropriations process.[17] Because of the pressures of the budgetary process, the appropriations committees (which allocate funds) have usurped the influence of the authorization committees (which make policy) in both the House and the Senate. In the 1980s foreign assistance bills were replaced by continuing resolutions and supplemental appropriations as the principal legislative foreign policy mechanisms. Under such circumstances, policy gets made without structural or long-term direction.[18] As a rule more liberal internationalist members of Congress gravitate towards the foreign-policy authorization committees, and conservatives concerned about limiting expenditures gravitate towards the appropriations committees. Appropriations Committee chairmen can engage in countless tradeoffs on various issues to gain support, but authorization chairmen have less to offer their members.[19] Legislators on the two committees do not work with each other individually or along party lines.[20] In general, the authorization committees have shown a more favorable disposition toward India than have the appropriation committees. The shift of policy control to the appropriations committees placed legislative power in the hands of legislators unsympathetic to New Delhi.

Congressional Perceptions and Policies

Congress, like the United States in general, was late in discovering India. Prior to World War II, American contact, except for missionary activity with India, was nominal, and political and economic relations between the two countries were sporadic. As late as 1940, there were only 4,000 persons of Indian descent in the United States. Consequently, relations with their country of origin were of little domestic importance to either the general public or to Congress. As Harold Isaacs stated in a classic study, American interaction with India occurred "less dramatically, along a narrower arc, in a smaller compass of awareness and interest" because the United States had much less shared history with that country than with China or Japan.[21]

The relative lack of contact was responsible for uniformed perceptions transmitted by Christian missionaries.[22] As anthropologist Milton Singer suggests, these subjective images often reflect more about the psychology of the holder than about reality.[23] This was certainly true in the case of Mahatma Gandhi, who was alternatively depicted in the United States as a saint or a fraud.[24] Images of India in the United States projected by Katherine Mayo in 1927 were highly negative—picturing the country as characterized by fabulous opulence or pervasive poverty.[25] As a consequence, public opinion surveys have consistently documented that most Americans have had misconceptions and negative feelings about India and Indians.[26] A 1928 poll found immigrants from India were regarded "as the most undesirable" of all newcomers living in the United States.[27]

These unflattering sentiments were developed and reinforced by a "self-indoctrinating" and circular information system,[28] including school textbooks, the media, and academic writings, which depicted India as a backward society. A 1979 academic survey indicated that scholars continued to perceive South Asian countries as exclusively backward societies, neglecting the foreign trade and industrial economies of the region.[29] The Asia Society, in a review of some 300 school textbooks, found that the presentation of India was the most negative of all Asian countries.[30]

According to a state department analysis, American attitudes concerning India focus on disease, death, and illiteracy more than for any other place.[31]

Most American legislators and decision-makers are subject to the same impressions as the general public. The late John Mellor argued that U.S. policy is the product of similar stereotypes that portray India "as poverty-stricken and helpless."[32] During the 1971 Bangladesh crisis, it seems apparent that President Richard Nixon's policy of tilting toward Pakistan "was influenced by his long-standing dislike for India and the Indians."[33] A similar sentiment is attributed to President Lyndon Johnson, who "regarded Indians as weak and indecisive."[34] John Lewis, a former high AID official, who had been posted in New Delhi in the mid-1960s, described "a majority" of key players in the White House, the state department and Congress to be *ab initio*, anti-Indian.[35]

Robert Dahl has argued that the American Congress is more likely to be representative of public attitudes than is the executive branch. He found that legislative attitudes tend to be "persistent, consistent and shared."[36] Like other Americans, most congressmen get their news and impressions from the media.[37] The information they get about India is neither adequate nor accurate.[38] Even service as Ambassador to New Delhi did not prevent Senator Daniel Patrick Moynihan (D-NY), perhaps the most knowledgeable legislator of his time on the subject, from stating, "What does [India] export but communicable diseases?"[39] One of the most informed and thoughtful Congressmen, Lee Hamilton (D-IN), for many years a chairman of a House Foreign Affairs subcommittee that dealt with South Asia and the Near East and later chairman of the full committee, responded in 1973 to testimony describing India's circumstances, "I don't know that I have ever heard such a long list of difficulties, ills and problems and so little hope.. . ."[40]

The complaint was raised that although India has one of the largest populations, most powerful military establishments and dynamic economies in the world, it has not been taken seriously by the United States.[41] Myron Weiner cogently explained the reasons why South Asia was accorded such a low priority in American thinking in the late 1970s:

> Unlike the Middle East, Indonesia or Nigeria, it has no resources vital to the American economy. Unlike Latin America it is not a region with substantial American private investment. Its geo-political position raises no fundamental problems for American security.... .Unlike China ...I ndia has no deep cultural or historic ties with the United States, and unlike the countries of Western Europe, Israel and Greece, no significant segment of the American population originates from India nor had an enduring association with the region. In short, none of the elements exist that attract the daily concerns of the president, Congress, the press, or the foreign policy publics.[42]

The tendency toward neglect of India and South Asia has implications for U.S. policy. Sulochana Raghavan Glazer and Nathan Glazer discovered that perceptions—including indifference, hostility, resentment and disdain—had until recently been more important than security interests in shaping U.S. policy towards South Asia.[43] The most compelling factor in Washington's bilateral relations with New Delhi was the belief that India was on the wrong side of the two most important conflicts of the past century: World War II and the cold war. Although millions of Indian soldiers served in the British Army, the Indian National Congress refused to support the war against the Axis powers so long as London would not promise independence. During the cold war Prime Minister Jawaharlal Nehru was viewed as "clearly pro-Russian," and Indian nonalignment was seen as "a major obstacle to US efforts to rally and unite the free nations of Asia in the struggle against Soviet world domination."[44] While there is little institutional memory in Washington, these perceptions persisted in the state department and on Capitol Hill.[45]

Despite the perceived democratic systems of both countries, Indo-American relations until the end of the cold war were rarely on an even keel—oscillating between high and low points.[46] The high points were U.S. support during India's 1962 border war with China—which coincided with the Cuban missile crisis—and Washington's economic development programs that began in the early 1950s and extended into the next decade. The low points are more numerous and included differences that emerged during the Korean War, India's failure to sign the Japanese Peace Treaty in 1952, Pakistan's inclusion in the American CENTO and SEATO alliance systems in 1954-55, the attempt to prevent India's use of force in Goa in 1961, the sending of the battle-group and carrier *Enterprise* into the Bay of Bengal during India's intervention to liberate Bangladesh in 1971, and resentment over the accrual of rupee currencies in payment for food assistance by the United States. Economic and nuclear issues have been more recent irritants. The situation of the Sikhs in the Punjab and the ensuing civil war in Kashmir added a human rights dimension to bilateral relations in the 1980s.

In what follows, I examine the attitude of Congress towards India on the issues of immigration in the mid-nineteenth century, foreign aid, and the development of nuclear weapons. James A. Robinson's contention that the function of Congress is primarily to legitimate or amend executive foreign policy decisions in situations identified by the president applied to the pre-independence period of U.S.-Indian relations.[47] Hence, "In the nine years which preceded Swaraj," the legislature in the United States "followed the President and the State Department in leaving to the British and the Indians the details of their arrangements for the liquidation of colonial rule."[48]

Immigration

The first issue to attract the attention of Congress in U.S.-Indian relations was immigration. The first South Asian immigrants in the mid-nineteenth century were Punjabi males who gained agricultural employment in California.[49] Early congressional activities, directed by Representative Emanuel Celler (D-NY), the chairman of the House Judiciary Committee, were directed at redressing the civil rights grievances of Indians in the United States. No matter what their religious persuasion, all Indians were deemed "Hindus" and subjected to the widespread prejudice against Asians that prevailed in the United States during the first half of the twentieth century. Immigration from India for purposes of employment was completely barred under a 1917 statute. In 1923 the Supreme Court ruled that

Indian nationals were ineligible for citizenship on grounds that as "Hindus" they were not "white persons."[50] The barring of Indians and the denial of citizenship to them on grounds of race scarred America's relations with India.[51] After further restrictions banning Asians were applied by Congress in 1924, the Indian legislature retaliated in 1926 by passing the Indian Naturalization Act, which denied Indian citizenship to nationals of any country that denied the same privilege to Indians. Proposals for reform of the quota and naturalization provisions introduced by Claire Booth Luce (R-CN) and Celler in 1945 were stalled by an anti-civil rights coalition of southern Democrats and Republicans. It required the active intervention of President Truman to secure passage of the immigration reform measure on July 2, 1946.[52] It would take the 1965 U.S. Immigration and Naturalization Act to reverse decades of discrimination and initiate preferential admission of skilled Asian professionals such as physicians.[53] However, its impact on immigration from South Asia would not be felt until the 1980s.[54] As will be discussed later in this essay, it would take another decade after that for Indian-Americans to become a factor in bilateral relations.

Foreign Assistance

The annual debates on foreign assistance—which involve a plethora of committees, including agriculture, foreign affairs, and most importantly appropriations—have provided venues for criticism of a country whose policies were seen as not in accordance with American interests. Although a wheat loan agreement was signed in 1951 and was followed by a $53 million package of direct assistance, the bitter comments that were made in the course of acrimonious debates[55] "largely counteracted the goodwill toward America that aid in time of crisis would have otherwise produced."[56] Many legislators were infuriated by India's opposition to a February 1, 1951 General Assembly resolution that branded China as the aggressor in Korea. Among those who expressed reservations about providing aid to a country that was perceived as voting against American interests was Senator Tom Connolly (D-

TX), the chairman of the Foreign Relations Committee.[57] In response to a special message from President Truman recommending emergency assistance for India, a bipartisan group of forty senators and representatives introduced legislation calling for the immediate dispatch of one million tons of American surplus wheat to India and authorizing the eventual shipment of another million tons. Although the House Committee on Foreign Affairs reported the bill favorably, conservatives on the Rules Committee blocked the measure until it was rewritten in the form of a loan. Finally, the Senate Foreign Relations Committee reported a bill that was partly a loan and partly a grant.[58] India's ties to China during the Korean War led many on Capitol Hill to deem it unworthy of American economic assistance. William Knowland (R-CA), who later became majority leader, accused India of "giving aid and comfort to the enemy."[59] The Battle Act of 1953, which barred American aid to any country that traded in strategic goods with Communist China, targeted India, and became a source of acrimony in bilateral relations.[60]

Bilateral rancor resurfaced during the stewardship of Secretary of State John Foster Dulles (1953-1959). His bringing Pakistan into the American alliance system was vehemently opposed by Senator J.W. Fulbright, who declared the decision to supply arms to Pakistan to be "an unfortunate mistake" that could cause the loss of an alienated India to communism.[61] Even supporters of Pakistan, such as H. Alexander Smith (R-NJ), feared that arming that country would cause an insurmountable rupture of relations with New Delhi. Indian skepticism about American anti-imperialism resurfaced after Washington's critical reaction to the Indian invasion of Goa in December 1961. To express its displeasure, the Senate Foreign Relations Committee attempted over the objections of President Kennedy to cut foreign aid appropriations to India in 1962 by twenty-five per cent.[62]

In 1963 congressional conservatives, who had been hostile toward India, reneged on a $500 million public sector steel plant at Bokaro in the state of Bihar that was to be a showcase of Western aid. A seven volume report—produced at a cost of $686,000 by a United States Steel team for the Agency for International

Development—had the effect of providing an opportunity for members of Congress opposed to funding the Bokaro endeavor to embarrass the Kennedy administration. In August 1963 the House attached a provision to its foreign aid authorization bill forbidding any allocation of more than $100 million to a public sector project without specific congressional authorization.[63] The reluctance of the U.S. Congress to build a 'socialist' steel mill with capitalist dollars enabled the Soviet Union—as was the case with the construction of the Aswan Dam in Egypt—to fill the breach. The American denouement over Bokaro led India to cancel an agreement to share radio transmitters with the Voice of America.

Despite setbacks like these, bilateral relations with India improved throughout the late 1950s and 1960s as Sino-Indian relations deteriorated. This was the period of the greatest U.S. involvement and interest in South Asia. Both humanitarian and security concerns worked to India's advantage, with Congress giving more emphasis to the former than the administration.[64] In the view of the state department, "South Asia became a testing ground for the free world. In this area will be determined whether nations can surmount tremendous economic and social problems, can achieve far-reaching changes in their entire pattern of life without resorting to the totalitarian system of communism."[65] In the period 1954-1964 American aid totaled $10 billion. Relations between New Delhi and Washington approached the point of alliance during the 1962 Sino-Indian border war. A bipartisan coalition supporting enhanced relations, including presidential aspirants John F. Kennedy (D-MA)[66] and Hubert Humphrey (D-MN)[67] was forged by Senator John Sherman Cooper (R-KY), a former ambassador to India.

The improvement in U.S.-Indian relations was accompanied by a corresponding deterioration of the U.S.-Pakistani connection, even though the United States continued to arm both South Asian rivals as part of its policy of containment of communism. That policy ended when the United States imposed its first arms embargo during the 1965 Indo-Pakistani war—a development that hurt Pakistan more than India.[68] The 1965 Indo-Pakistani war was a turning point in Washington's dealings with the subcontinent. For the first time, regional considerations began to prevail over a cold war calculus as the United States attempted to remove South Asia from cold war competition.

As it turned out, this regional calculation was short lived and worked against India, as a result of the U.S. thaw in relations with China. The American tilt toward Pakistan that followed India's intervention in the 1971 Bangladesh war of independence demonstrated the dichotomy of executive-legislative views. According to Henry Kissinger, "...Ind ia basked in Congressional warmth and was subject to Presidential indifference [while] Pakistan's situation was exactly the reverse."[69] Washington's tilt toward Rawalpindi was pronounced by the administration as an effort to preserve the territorial integrity of Pakistan, but was seen in congressional eyes as a tilt toward China.[70] Legislators, such as Cornelius Gallagher (D-NY), the chairman of the House Foreign Affairs Subcommittee on the Near East and South Asia and Senator Stuart Symington (D-MO), deplored Pakistan's oppression in East Bengal and praised India's restraint while absorbing millions of refugees. However, a divided Nixon administration[71] ultimately viewed the conflict in geo-strategic terms, even if it meant that relations with New Delhi were a casualty. According to Henry Kissinger, the United States sent a naval force to protect Pakistan and threaten India because Rawalpindi had been a conduit to the opening of relations with China, while New Delhi's recent friendship treaty with Moscow extended Soviet influence in the region.[72] Under congressional pressure[73] Washington imposed its second arms embargo to the region, but the Nixon administration's intervention on the side of Pakistan and revelations that military supplies continued to be shipped to that country caused lasting resentment in India.

In the 1960s and 1970s, legislators such as Otto Passman (D-LA) and Clarence Long (D-MD) ensured that the foreign operations appropriations subcommittees they chaired only grudgingly provided aid to a country that seldom agreed with American positions on global issues.[74] Even though Presidents Johnson and Nixon kept aid to India on a short tether in protest to

New Delhi's criticism of its policies in South East Asia,[75] India, nevertheless, received $4.2 billion in assistance between 1965 and 1971. However, after the protracted and costly Vietnam debacle, Congress suffered from "foreign aid fatigue."[76] Liberals, such as Representative Jonathan Bingham (D-NY), began to make arguments that had formerly been advanced by conservatives, such as Senator Owen Brewster (R-ME). They perceived that billions of dollars in American assistance to India came at the expense of domestic programs and produced resentment rather than improved relations with New Delhi. Every appropriation for the Agency for International Development became an occasion to demonstrate Congress's displeasure with New Delhi's ingratitude for American assistance.

During the 1970s, American interests were seen as limited in South Asia,[77] a region that in 1973 attracted less than one per cent of U.S. overseas investment and contained "seemingly unsolvable problems."[78] Ambassador Daniel Patrick Moynihan described the American attitude as "benign neglect." Moynihan, as ambassador in the mid-1970s, reduced the size of the U.S. diplomatic establishment in India, negotiated an agreement to forgive the significant rupee sums India owed the United States in payment for PL480 food shipments and generally presided over American disengagement in the region.[79] India incurred the wrath of members of Congress over such issues as the detonation of a nuclear device in May 1974 and the suppression of human rights during Mrs. Gandhi's Emergency, which ran from June 1975 through March 1977.[80] Clement Zablocki (D-WI), the chairman of the House Foreign Affairs Committee, expressed apprehension that India would give the Soviet Union a naval base, but oppose the construction of the U.S. installation at Diego Garcia.[81] Moreover, India had alienated many of its most ardent supporters, like Emanuel Celler and Jacob Javits (R-NY) who were Jewish, by its overt antipathy towards Israel. New Delhi's West Asian policies were designed to neutralize Arab support for Pakistan over the Kashmir issue, but they had adverse consequences for bilateral relations with the United States.

Because of its cold war alliances with the United States, Pakistan had been exempt from the same impediments that marked

U.S.-Indian relations, such as unhappiness over nuclear proliferation, abuse of human rights, and hostility towards Israel. Influential Senators such as J.W. Fulbright, the longtime chairman of the Foreign Relations Committee, and Richard Russell (D-GA) regarded Pakistan as a reliable ally that deserved special consideration.[82] As a result, the Indian government felt that the United States applied a double standard towards the subcontinent.

In the 1980s, during the Soviet war of occupation in Afghanistan, Pakistan was portrayed by Congressman Charles Wilson (D-TX)[83] and other lawmakers on the appropriations committee as a frontline state sheltering 2.5 million Afghan refugees. India, by contrast, was depicted as being one of the "persistently anti-United States members" in the United Nations, endorsing Soviet positions on Cuba, Kampuchea, Nicaragua, and, especially Afghanistan. Some Democrats, who had voted to cut off funding for the Nicaraguan contras, demonstrated their anticommunist credentials by joining Republicans to punish India over the Afghan issue. In 1987 an Amendment by Representative William Broomfield (R-MI), ranking member of the Foreign Affairs Committee and a critic of India for a generation, succeeded by a vote of 18-14 in cutting developmental assistance to New Delhi from $50 million to $35 million. Following Broomfield's retirement in 1993, Congressman William Goodling (R-PA) annually introduced legislation that would deny assistance to countries that do not support American positions in the United Nations General Assembly. In 1992 Representative Dan Burton, succeeded in having the House eliminate aid to India, but the legislation never became law.

Human Rights

In the 1980s, New Delhi's suppression of Sikh extremists, who were trying to achieve an independent Khalistan, added a human rights dimension to bilateral relations with Washington. In the next decade that concern was extended to New Delhi's campaign to put down the rebellion by Muslim separatists in Kashmir. Both liberals and conservatives, for different reasons, have been critical of the way India has dealt with secessionist movements. In 1998 Congress passed the Religious Freedom Act, whereby the United

States Commission on International Religious Freedom reports on violations that could lead to congressional sanctions against any government that violates religious freedom. Their reports, which are based on annual state department submissions, have provided ammunition to opponents of India. Accusations that Christians are persecuted after the Bharatiya Janata Party came to power in 1998 have concerned many in Congress—especially some members of the Black Caucus.[84] In recent years Representative Edolphus Towns (D-NY), even though he is a member of the India Caucus, has become the leading critic of New Delhi on Capitol Hill.

The return of the Congress Party to government with a Sikh as prime minister in 2004 has reduced criticism of India with respect to human rights.

Nuclear Issues

In the 1980s many of India's friends in Congress felt compelled to advance the cause of nuclear nonproliferation at the expense of bilateral ties with New Delhi. After India's 1974 detonation, that country's possession of nuclear weapons was the dominant issue in bilateral relations with the United States. South Asia has been "a testing ground" of the global aspects of nonproliferation.[85] The United States threatened to cut off foreign aid and reliable supplies of nuclear materials if international safeguards were violated. India felt it had been subjected to standards that have not been applied to China and Israel. Successive administrations offered India incentives, while Congress provided the sanctions.[86] In 1974 the Ford administration withheld nuclear fuel shipments to the Tarapur installation until it could determine that American materials were not used in the Indian detonation. In a move that embarrassed the administration, in July 1974 Congress instructed the U.S. representative to the International Development Association not to vote for loans to countries that had exploded nuclear weapons but had not signed the nuclear nonproliferation treaty—a provision that applied exclusively to India. When Prime Minister Morarji Desai, of the short-lived Janata government, promised that India would not develop nuclear weapons or conduct further tests,

Congress in April 1977 repealed the prohibition, and aid to India resumed.

In the early years of the Carter presidency, concern about nuclear proliferation peaked in both the executive branch and on Capitol Hill. Congress passed legislation in 1976 stipulating that countries that do not have nuclear weapons but that import material to develop bombs and refuse to put their nuclear installations under international safeguards are not entitled to American assistance. The administration refused to sell 110 A-7 attack aircraft to Islamabad, and it encouraged the French to cancel the sale of a reprocessing system to Pakistan. Congress passed the Symington and Glenn Amendments, sections 669 and 670 to the Foreign Assistance Acts of 1976 and 1977, which prohibited aid or arms sales to countries that deliver or receive nuclear enrichment equipment or technology and do not accept International Atomic Energy Agency (IAEA) safeguards. As a result of evidence that Pakistan—which had just had a military coup—was engaged in such activities, U.S. assistance to that country was terminated for the third time in April 1979.

The climate in Washington changed later that year with the Iran hostage episode and the Soviet invasion of Afghanistan. Global security issues once more overrode regional considerations. Washington turned a blind eye to Islamabad's clandestine development of nuclear weapons because it needed Pakistan's assistance to supply the Afghan guerillas. A decision to sell F-16 planes to Pakistan was viewed by New Delhi as providing its rival with a potential nuclear delivery system. In the meantime, President Carter, believing that a 1963 American commitment was at stake, approved export licenses for two fuel shipments and spare parts for India's Tarapur reactor. He did so even though the Nuclear Regulatory Commission claimed that India did not meet the criteria set forth by the 1978 Nuclear Nonproliferation Act. The decision pitted the commitment that members of Congress had to nonproliferation against the importance they attached to relations with India. At the time opponents of proliferation were stronger in the House, which rejected Carter's decision. The Senate, the most important venue, sustained the president's decision by the narrow vote of 48 to 46. In 1982, the Reagan administration helped negotiate an end to the Tarapur dispute by getting the French to assume the obligation to supply fuel. A year later, Secretary of State George Shultz promised that the United States would be the supplier of last resort. A Senate effort to overturn Shultz's commitment was thwarted in conference by Representative Solarz. The New York Democrat also weakened an amendment by Senator Rudolph Boschwitz (R-MN), chairman of the Senate Foreign Relations Subcommittee on Near Eastern and South Asian Affairs, that would have prohibited the sale of nuclear material to India and South Africa.

Since 1981, Pakistan has been the target of a dwindling number of opponents to nuclear proliferation, as the Indian program was described as "dormant." That year the Reagan administration proposed weakening the 1976 Symington Amendment (which gave Congress the authority to suspend foreign aid or arms sales to countries which receive nuclear enrichment equipment or technology and do not accept International Atomic Energy Agency safeguards) in order to permit the approval of a $3.2 billion aid package for Islamabad. The proposal was described as a way of enabling Pakistan to meet its security requirements with conventional weapons and thus obviate the need for it to embark on a nuclear weapons program. Congress declined to weaken the Symington Amendment at that time, but instead granted Pakistan a six-year exemption in the interest of national security.[87] In 1984 Senators Alan Cranston (D-CA) and John Glenn (D-OH) persuaded the Senate Foreign Relations Committee to adopt an amendment to the foreign aid bill making assistance conditional on "Presidential certification that Pakistan does not possess a nuclear explosive device, and is not acquiring, overtly or covertly, technology, material or equipment for a nuclear explosive device." Although President Reagan succeeded in having the decision reversed by a 9-8 vote, the committee put a warning to Pakistan in the bill. Reagan used his authority under Public Law 97-113 signed in December 1981 to waive the application of the Symington Amendment in the case of Pakistan as long as Soviet forces were stationed in Afghanistan.

After an incident in which a Pakistani citizen was arrested in Houston trying to smuggle electronic switches that trigger nuclear bombs, Congress in 1985 passed the Pressler Amendment (section 620E of the Foreign Assistance Act of 1961), requiring annual presidential certification that Pakistan did not possess a nuclear device. The amendment stipulated that American assistance to Pakistan would immediately be cut off if the president found that Islamabad had attempted to acquire American material for making nuclear weapons illegally. When press reports, including claims from Pakistani scientists and officials, and independent evidence indicated that Islamabad's bomb was near completion, some in Congress like John Glenn, the Chairman of the Senate Government Operations Committee, attempted to terminate the administration's six year $4.02 billion Pakistani aid package. Working through a Senate Appropriations Subcommittee that was dominated by Chair Robert Kasten (R-WI) and his predecessor, Daniel Inouye (D-HI), lobbyists for the Pakistani Embassy succeeded in cutting off all aid to India until foreign assistance to Islamabad was restored. The ability of Pakistan to induce Congress to temporarily cut off aid to India in 1987, when its own funding was in jeopardy for embarking on a nuclear weapons program, was testimony to the strength Islamabad had on Capitol Hill and the lack of influence New Delhi had at the time in Washington.[88] Hence, although New Delhi's economic and strategic importance had increased, knowledge and concern about India in the U.S. Congress had declined. The episode demonstrated that Pakistani assistance to the Afghan rebels overrode congressional concern about that country's clandestine nuclear activities. It also revealed that there was a latent hostility towards India that could be tapped by New Delhi's opponents and supporters of Pakistan.

However, the end of the cold war and the winding down of the conflict in Afghanistan resulted in a dramatic deterioration of U.S.-Pakistani ties and a corresponding improvement in U.S.-Indian relations, which made possible the transfer of previously embargoed technologies. After President George H.W. Bush refused to certify that Pakistan did "not possess a nuclear explosive device" in October 1990, aid to that country was suspended for a fourth time, and arms transfers or transfers of technology to Pakistan were prohibited if it developed a nuclear weapons capability. Upon restoration, future assistance to Islamabad was to be cut by more than half from $564 to $208 million a year. As a stern warning to Pakistan, Congress at the behest of Senator Glenn inserted the Nuclear Proliferation Act of 1994 into the Foreign Relations Authorization Act (Public Law 103-236), which called for mandatory presidential sanctions against any country that conducted nuclear tests.[89] Incredibly, the Clinton administration did not attempt to prevent passage of this legislation that denied it discretion.

The Campaign to Repeal the Pressler Amendment

In the face of a foreign exchange crisis that followed the Gulf War, the Congress Party government headed by Prime Minister Narashima Rao, which assumed office in June 1991, abandoned that party's reliance on the discredited Nehruvian economic model and a foreign policy that reflected hostility towards the United States. Finance Minister Manmohan Singh recognized that substantial American investment and massive assistance from aid consortiums, like the International Monetary Fund, were critical to the success of its new economic policy. Indian politicians from all non-communist parties felt that a consensus for a positive relationship with the United States had been established. For the first time a strong pro-U.S. lobby had emerged in the Indian parliament. A joint US-India interparliamentary working group was established by Mumbai Congress MP, Muril Deora, and Washington Democrat Jim McDermott.[90] However, the policies of the new Clinton administration disappointed and bewildered Washington's supporters in India.

It was anticipated that the Clinton administration, which was pledged to support democratic regimes and encourage American investment abroad, would build on the foundation established by its predecessor and further improve bilateral ties. India, as one of the few established democracies in Asia and the second most populous country in the world, felt it was a candidate for positive attention from Washington. However, other global tenets of the Clinton agenda—such as stopping the spread of nuclear weapons and promoting human rights in regions affected by civil wars—worked against better relations. The United States reduced its foreign aid appropriations by twenty percent, reneged on the delivery of promised cryogenic rocket engines to India and began renewing certain types of commercial sales to Pakistan that Congress had found to be prohibited by the Pressler Amendment.[91]

The contradictory agenda of the Clinton administration[92] was reflected by confusing messages. The administration praised the Rao government's economic and foreign policies, and at the same time criticized its violation of human rights in suppressing the ongoing Sikh rebellion in the Punjab and especially in Kashmir, where half a million troops were fighting a civil war waged by Muslim militants. Washington's failure to name an ambassador to Delhi for sixteen months after the departure of Thomas Pickering in March 1993 created a diplomatic vacuum.[93] In January 1994, to compensate for its lack of official contacts, the Indian government belatedly hired former presidential aide Michael Deaver's firm of McAuliffe, Kelly and Rafaelli to be its first professional lobbyist in Washington.

Ironically, it was an achievement by Congressman Solarz that further muddied the waters. In the belief that the state department had long ignored India because it was attached to the Near East, he had secured passage of a bill establishing a separate South Asia Bureau. However, in the absence of an ambassador in New Delhi or attention by the secretary of state or the president, the Assistant Secretary of State for South Asia, Robin Raphael, assumed the most prominent role in the United States' relations with India. (She was a friend of Bill Clinton from Oxford who had been married to the late American Ambassador to Pakistan). When the administration was claiming that the disputed territory of Kashmir was the most dangerous place on earth, Ms. Raphael was suggesting the United States had reconsidered its position on the Muslim-majority state's partition. While her less than diplomatic statements drew little attention in Washington,[94] they created the illogical impression in the highest levels in New Delhi that the

Clinton Administration was out to destabilize India, even as the U.S. was trying to promote American investment there.

The return of Pakistani Prime Minister Benazir Bhutto to power in late 1993 complicated the effort to improve bilateral relations between the United States and India. Well-connected in Washington, she was perceived in the U.S. capital as pro-American. The Clinton administration announced its determination to do something that would bolster her fragile domestic position which was jeopardized by the unprecedented violence that was transpiring in Karachi. Unable to promote Pakistan as a front-line state, Washington began advancing Islamabad as a moderate Islamic influence and a linchpin to the new Soviet Central Asian countries.

In November 1993 Senator Larry Pressler (R-SD) revealed that the Clinton Administration was considering rescinding the legislation which had cut off assistance to Pakistan in 1990.[95] The mechanism was to be the repeal of any country-specific language in a major revision of the 1961 Foreign Assistance Act. The Pressler Amendment was depicted as an "obstacle" to improved ties with Pakistan. Because of the legislation, Congress could not authorize delivery of 71 F-16 aircraft even though Pakistan had already paid the American aircraft manufacturer $658 million for the first 28. Given its budgetary situation, the U.S. was unable to return the money. It was costing the Government of Pakistan $50,000 a year to store and maintain each aircraft in the United States. In the guise of fairness, the Clinton administration, led by the Defense Department, set out to find a compromise.[96] It attempted to convince Congress to enact a one-time waiver of the Pressler Amendment because there was no more non-proliferation mileage to be gained from it. While Prime Minister Benazir Bhutto was in Washington, Mr. Clinton pledged "to ask Congress to show some flexibility in the Pressler Amendment so that we can have some economic and military cooperation."[97]

Even though Senator Pressler and John Glenn, the Chairman of the Government Operations Committee, documented hundreds of violations of the original legislation by Pakistan, which was covertly proceeding with its nuclear program, the Clinton administration's campaign to improve relations with Pakistan received important congressional backing. Significant changes which took place in committee membership after the 1992 elections made Clinton's task easier. Because of Solarz's defeat after redistricting, Gary Ackerman became chairman of the Asia-Pacific Subcommittee of the House of Representatives. While this assured continuity in staff and policy outlook, Solarz's departure diminished the panel's influence. More importantly, with the retirement of Dante Fascell, Lee Hamilton—perhaps the most respected figure in the field of foreign policy in the entire House of Representatives—assumed the chairmanship of the Foreign Affairs Committee and greatly enhanced its stature. Hamilton, who had previously chaired the subcommittee that dealt with South Asia when it was attached to the Middle East, was receptive to improving ties with Pakistan because of its geo-strategic importance in the Muslim world. He also felt that the Pressler amendment had "outlived its usefulness," because it "threatens to drive Pakistan into an unholy partnership with Iran, Iraq, or other would-be proliferators." Hamilton claimed it was "time to modify this amendment, or even to lift it altogether."[98]

The Senate, however, was the important congressional actor regarding South Asian relations in the 1990s. Because the leadership of the Foreign Relations Committee was lackluster under the ailing Claiborne Pell, the Subcommittee for the Middle East and South Asia assumed uncharacteristic significance under the chairmanship of Daniel Patrick Moynihan. As a former Ambassador to India, Moynihan was well positioned to become the principal congressional player on South Asian issues, but unlike John Sherman Cooper a generation earlier, he had been reluctant to do so. Although Democrats, in an attempt to enhance the stature of the Foreign Relations Committee, waived a rule so that he could serve on two major committees, Moynihan concentrated on Banking Committee matters.

Further changes in committee assignments followed after the Democrats lost control of both houses of Congress in 1995. Senator Glenn yielded the chairmanship of the Government Operations Committee, which had been monitoring Pakistan's compliance with the Pressler Amendment, to William Roth (R-DE), who showed no interest in the subject. Benjamin Gilman (R-NY), a twelve term representative who was primarily interested in Arab-Israeli affairs, took over the chairmanship of the renamed House International Relations Committee, and Doug Bereuter (R-NB), a nine term legislator, assumed the leadership of the Asia and the Pacific subcommittee. On the Senate side, Jesse Helms (R-NC) became chair of the Foreign Relations Committee.[99] Under his stewardship the full committee became particularly interested in human rights violations in Kashmir. Significantly, Hank Brown, who had recently demonstrated interest in Near East and South Asian Affairs, was elevated to head that subcommittee while Moynihan was "ousted" from it as well as the Foreign Relations Committee.[100]

The Brown Amendment

Senator Brown, as chairman of the Foreign Relations Subcommittee dealing with South Asia, became the Clinton administration's point person for diluting Pressler on Capitol Hill. Brown replicated the administration's contradictory approach toward India. He held a series of hearings where State and Defense Department officials were given a platform urging the re-examination of the Pressler amendment. In testimony remarkable for a lack of balance and perspicacity, experts were repeatedly paraded before the Brown and Bereuter committees where they branded India "as the greatest source of instability in South Asia."[101] They resurrected anachronistic cold war logic to portray India as tied to Russia, and described Pakistan as linked to the American security system through Saudi Arabia. They suggested that the Pressler cutoff was not even-handed, but had produced a conventional balance of forces favoring New Delhi, and that a one time exception to the arms embargo would not materially influence proliferation in the region. All of these arguments were repeated on the Senate floor when the Brown Amendment (No. 2708) to the Foreign Operations Bill (HR1868) was taken up on September 20, 1995.[102] Tom Harkin (D-IA) depicted Pakistan as a loyal partner of the United States on every cold war issue from Korea to Afghanistan and portrayed India as a Soviet stooge always taking positions contrary to American interests. Brown objected to the Pressler amendment as being "Pakistan-specific," and contended that a one-time waiver of the Pressler amendment to sell Pakistan $368 million in "obsolete" equipment would not upset the military balance on the subcontinent. He described Washington's failure to deliver aircraft or return money to Pakistan as a breach of contract.

In rebuttal, critics of the Brown Amendment, such as Larry Pressler, pointed out that over $4 billion in American military and economic assistance during the 1980s had failed to give the United States leverage over Pakistan's nuclear program. John Glenn referred to the building of a nuclear weapon with American tax dollars as "an extraordinary act of deception" which had been compounded by clandestine collaboration with Iran and China. He found the argument that the Pressler Amendment was unfair because it applied only to Pakistan "completely disingenuous." In his words, "If we had not had the waiver, we would not have needed Pressler," which was passed as a "unique special exemption" to the earlier Glenn-Symington bill. Other opponents of the Brown Amendment such as Jim Exon (D-DE), Diane Feinstein (D-CA), Joseph Biden and John Kerry (D-MA) were particularly concerned that Pakistan was being rewarded for noncompliance by legislation that required no nuclear guarantees or concessions from Islamabad.

Significantly, one of the most respected Senators on international issues, Richard Lugar, who as Chairman of the Committee on Foreign Relations had steered the Pressler Amendment through Congress in 1985, did not participate in the debate. Like a majority of others, he voted in favor of the Brown Amendment, which passed by a margin of 55-45. The dissenters included 34 Democrats and 11 Republicans. On November 1 the House, over objections raised by the India Caucus, followed suit by a vote of 348-69. Very few congressmen were willing to defeat the entire foreign operations bill in order to uphold nuclear nonproliferation. The passage of the Brown Amendment was symbolic of the way the United States has conducted policy with India. Because South Asia is considered a residual matter, the region was once again dealt with in a "compromise" amendment to a foreign operations bill, and not as an independent issue area.

Predictably the passage of the Brown Amendment, signed into law by President Clinton on January 27, 1996, caused outrage in India, worsened its relations with the United States, and embarrassed Washington's friends in New Delhi.[103] Politicians from across the political spectrum urged renewed acceleration of India's short range Prithvi and medium range Agni missile delivery systems, and the militant Hindu Bharatiya Janata Party, then the principal opposition party, renewed its call for a nuclear option. The passage of the Brown Amendment and the Indian Parliament's reaction to it, showed the delicate nature of the Indo-American rapprochement. By resurrecting cold war slogans, American congress-men and Indian parliamentarians demonstrated their inability to adjust to the realities of the new unipolar international system.

Ethnic Politics: The Transformation of the Perception of India in Washington

Despite predictions that bilateral ties would worsen when the Bharatiya Janata Party—on record as opposing the Comprehensive Test Ban Treaty—came to power in March 1998, there were indications that a sea change has taken place in Indo-American relations. The end of the cold war has enhanced the importance of ethnic politics in the U.S. Congress. For the first time American domestic considerations have worked to New Delhi's advantage in Washington's formulation of foreign policy.

Ironically, when India ended its self-imposed 24-year moratorium and embarked on a series of nuclear tests in May 1998, most of the criticism directed at New Delhi came from friends of that country who were also opponents of proliferation. Many members of Congress seemed outraged at New Delhi for not honoring assurances, supposedly made to Energy Secretary Bill Richardson in April, that it would not test nuclear weapons. Congress seemed more willing to excuse Pakistan for following India's example and conducting its own explosions. Edward Markey (D-MA), one of the few remaining nonproliferators in the House, denounced New Delhi's actions as "reckless, shameful and irresponsible," while Dan Burton, predictably, urged his colleagues to "stop subsidizing" India's nuclear program by cutting foreign assistance. In particular, John Glenn, who had announced his retirement from the Senate, felt betrayed.[104] Most pro-India congressmen were conspicuously silent; Frank Pallone, India's principal defender on Capitol Hill, expressed regret about the tests, as well as hope that they would "not derail" the improving U.S.-India relationship.[105] He urged his colleagues to delay the imposition of sanctions if India pledged to refrain from further testing. Nevertheless, the minority leader, Richard Gephardt (D-MO) felt that in light of the tests there could no longer be "business as usual" with India.[106] He and several other lawmakers cancelled plans to visit India and scaled back appearances before the Indian-American community, whose overly enthusiastic support of the tests was viewed as repugnant by Americans. In the Senate, Tom Harkin repeated President Franklin Roosevelt's remarks on the bombing of Pearl Harbor by condemning the Indian tests as a day of "infamy." He and Sam Brownback (R-KS), who had succeeded Hank Brown as the chairman of the Foreign Relations Subcommittee on Near Eastern and South Asian Affairs in January 1997, promised Pakistan they would attempt to repeal the Pressler Amendment if Islamabad refrained from testing. Other legislators offered inducements if either country agreed to sign the Comprehensive Test Ban Treaty.

Pro-Pakistani legislators in Congress were forced to defuse their criticism of India when Islamabad conducted its own tests seventeen days after the Pokharan detonations. Yet, there was a widespread feeling on the Hill that Pakistan was much less culpable than its neighbor, because New Delhi had tested first and historically espoused nonviolence. In a widely shared sentiment, Richard Lugar, the leading Senate Republican authority on foreign affairs, claimed the administration shared the blame for India's tests because it had not seriously engaged New Delhi. Senators Daniel Patrick Moynihan and Joseph Biden, the ranking Democrat on the Foreign Relations Committee, called for an end to America's benign neglect of South Asia.[107] Connie Mack (R-FL) expressed a similar view, pointing out that India—unlike China—was not a nuclear proliferator and had broken no American laws.[108] Senate opponents of the Comprehensive Test Ban Treaty, such as Jesse Helms, the chairman of the Foreign Relations Committee, and the Majority Leader Trent Lott (R-MS), blamed the South Asian tests on administration pressure to get India and Pakistan to sign the CTBT.

Senator Glenn's 1994 Amendment, the Nuclear Proliferation Prevention Act, called for sanctions against states that engaged in nuclear tests—legislation that automatically applied to India. President Clinton imposed sanctions against New Delhi on May 13 two days after the Pokharan tests. Similar penalties followed the Pakistani explosions on May 28 and 30—the fifth such American arms embargo in the region. Because Pakistan's fragile economy was viewed as being dependent on international assistance, Islamabad was treated more leniently than India with respect to the curbing of multilateral assistance by international granting agencies so that sanctions would not destabilize its weak government. Pakistan was also the third-largest foreign purchaser of U.S. wheat at a time when the U.S. farm economy was in a desperate crisis. Almost immediately legislation that called for exemptions was introduced. An 18-member Senate task force headed by Senators Mitch McConnell and Joseph Biden recommended that agricultural credits be exempt, in order not to penalize the American farmer. Senator Sam Brownback, who came from the agriculturally depressed farm belt, introduced an amendment to an appropriations bill to waive non-military sanctions against India and Pakistan for a year. The legislation (The India-Pakistan Relief Act of 1998) passed the Senate without hearings 98-0. It granted the president authority for one year to waive all sanctions except those pertaining to military assistance, dual-use exports and military sales. Only a threatened filibuster by Senator Glenn, who conveniently had left for a NASA training exercise in Houston, forced the dropping of provisions that applied to other categories.

The Clinton administration had misgivings about the original Brownback Amendment because it gave Congress rather than the president the power to determine sanctions. At the same time it viewed the legislation as a further opportunity to water down the Pressler Amendment and resume arms sales to Pakistan. The president immediately restored military training programs and government-backed financing credit guarantees to both countries. The Indian government, while welcoming the lifting of sanctions, benefited less than its rival, since it purchases weapons systems and spare parts from Russia. In December the president eliminated a longstanding irritant in U.S.-Pakistani bilateral relations by paying Islamabad $325 million in cash and $140 million in goods as compensation for the undelivered 28 F-16 aircraft that had been purchased but whose delivery had been precluded by the Pressler Amendment.

In "a stunning retreat from Capitol Hill's decades-long reliance on punitive measures to block the spread of weapons of mass destruction,"[109] Congress passed a second Brownback Amendment in October 1999. It gave the president the authority to waive permanently (an earlier version was limited to five years) all provisions of the Glenn Amendment for India and Pakistan, as well as all sections of the Symington Amendment which had prohibited most U.S. economic and military assistance to Pakistan. Ironically, seventeen months after its nuclear tests, Pakistan—through the efforts of its principal lobbyist, former Texas congressman Charles Wilson—was restored to pre-October 1990 status under American nonproliferation law.[110] India, which does not purchase American wheat, was piggybacked on the waiver through the efforts of Senator Pat Roberts (R-KS) whose state had Boeing contracts in India that were affected by the sanctions legislation. Roberts, a former House Agriculture Committee chairman, played a key role in getting his colleagues in both houses to accept the package in a Defense Authorization Bill.

Nevertheless, developments in 1999 worked in New Delhi's favor. India's restraint in repelling Pakistan's unprovoked-armed incursion in the Kargil area of Kashmir in April through June was appreciated in Washington. The military coup in Islamabad, which occurred coterminous with India's thirteenth democratic national elections in October, led Congress to reauthorize the Clinton administration to lift indefinitely most remaining sanctions against New Delhi, while retaining the Glenn Amendment prohibitions that were directed against Islamabad. For the first time, according to Congressman Gary Ackerman, India and Pakistan were viewed as distinctive entities in the congressional mindset.[111] Representative Benjamin Gilman, the chairman of the House International Relations Committee, led a congressional effort to oppose the resumption of military aid to Islamabad. By a vote of 21-4 his committee passed a resolution introduced by Congressmen Sam Gejdneson (D-CT) and Sherrod Brown (D-OH) that "condemned" the military coup in Pakistan and went on record as opposing the resumption of military assistance and training programs to Islamabad until a civilian government was restored.[112] A conference committee on the Defense Department Authorization Act (H.R.2561) determined that any further waiver of the Pressler provisions by the president would be dependent on his certification that democracy had returned to Pakistan (P.L.106-79).

Ironically, India's nuclear tests led to an ongoing dialogue between Deputy Secretary of State Strobe Talbott and Indian Foreign Minister Jaswant Singh. Initially condemned by the Clinton administration, the tests precipitated the longest series of high level bilateral talks in the history of the Indo-American relationship. For the first time there was an attempt to structure the Indo-American relationship independent of Indo-Pakistani or Indo-Russian concerns. A new bilateral relationship was proclaimed in a vision statement signed by President Clinton and Prime Minister A.B. Vajpayee during the president's March 2000 visit to the subcontinent, and in the Indian leader's remarks before a joint session of Congress in Washington the following September. Moreover, the failure of the BJP government to sign the Comprehensive Test Ban Treaty faded as an issue when the Republican-controlled Senate also rejected U.S. ratification. These developments led to the warmest bilateral relations since the military cooperation that occurred during the Sino-Indian Border War of 1962. A Congressional panel urged President Clinton to "broaden our special relationship into a strategic partnership,"[113] and the entire House by a margin of 396 to 4 lauded India as "a shining example of democracy for all of Asia to follow."[114]

There are many reasons for this increased sensitivity to India's concerns on Capitol Hill. According to Representative Benjamin Gilman, Congress (especially the Republican majority) appreciated that India, because it is surrounded by Islamic terrorist threats and has conflicts with China and Pakistan, "is living in a tough neighborhood."[115] Ironically, India has benefited from the defeat and retirement of non-proliferators who were its friends, like Larry Pressler and John Glenn, and a loss of appetite for sanctions by Republicans sensitive to the business community. In a Republican-controlled Congress, agricultural exports have a higher priority than nuclear issues. Moreover, American legislators have finally realized that India's 1991 economic liberalization can yield domestic dividends. Its hundreds of millions of consumers have "attracted the attention of both Wall Street and Main Street."[116] Economic opportunity has for the first time figured in congressional thinking about India. Legislators, who once avoided the region,[117] now regularly visit the commercial centers of Mumbai (Bombay), and India's silicone valley in Bangalore, as well as the capital of Delhi.[118] Pepsico and General Electric, which have major investments in India, have become important lobbyists for that country in Washington. Their input assures that the region can no longer be ignored.[119] As American investment in India increases, so too has New Delhi's influence in Washington, thanks to the activity of the U.S.-India Business Council and the India Interest Group lobby. Indian lobby groups have replicated the tactics of the Israeli lobbies in Washington,[120] and in recent years have held a number of joint functions with them on Capitol Hill.

New Delhi's position on Capitol Hill has especially been bolstered by the political activity of the over 2.3 million Indian-Americans—up from 387,000 in 1980—who reside in the United States.[121] They, as Myron Weiner speculated two decades ago, serve as a bridge between their country of origin and their country of residence.[122] While their influence is countered by Khalistani and Kashmiri separatists and Pakistani-Americans,[123] it is nonetheless growing. The Pakistani-American community—which is one tenth the size of the Indian-American community—had been very active in working for the passage of the 1995 Brown Amendment and the defeat of Senator Larry Pressler by Representative Tim Johnson in the congressional elections a year later.[124] Its success in these two endeavors stimulated the Indian-American community to become much more involved in American politics.

The educational achievement and economic status of this upwardly mobile community, publicized by the India Abroad Center for Political Awareness, has succeeded in changing the perception of Indians in the United States Congress.[125] In 2003 Indian-Americans had a median income nearly fifty per cent higher than the average American—$60,000 compared to the national average of $38,885.[126] The community, which included 200,000 millionaires,[127] had a higher per capita income and a larger percentage of its workforce holds a managerial or professional position than any other group except Japanese-Americans.[128] The community has an especially high represen-tation of doctors, engineers, scientists, architects and computer technologists. Moreover, these highly paid professionals, derisively characterized by their opponents as the "chapati lobby," are politically active—especially in high tech California and the major urban-industrial states of northeast and midwest. Their outreach through such groups as the Indian American Forum for Political Education (IAPE), which has twenty-eight chapters across the United States, and the Indian American Political Advocacy Council (IAPAC) translates into political and financial clout.[129] Members of Congress see little downside, and have many reasons to be attentive to the community's concerns.[130] The Indian American Friendship Council attracted nearly 40 law makers to a July 1999 function in Washington which featured speeches by House Minority Leader Richard Gephardt, House International Relations Committee chair, Benjamin Gilman, and Doug Bereuter, the chairman of the House subcommittee that dealt with Asia.

This growing influence of the Indian-American community is reflected in the strength of the Caucus of India and Indian Americans, which claimed 173 House members (105 Democrats and 68 Republicans), making it the largest country caucus on the Hill in the 109th Congress (2005-07). The positions of the caucus on South Asian and related matters, such as immigration, family reunification, and civil rights issues, have to be taken into account by any administration. However, the executive—as the Clinton administration demonstrated—regards the caucus as a potential threat to its control of foreign policy. Even though a half dozen often-competitive lawmakers control its activities, by enlisting floor speakers, lining up votes, and placing material in the *Congressional Record*, the India Caucus has for the first time provided India "with an institutional base support on Capitol Hill."[131] Whereas a generation of ago supporters of India such as Stephen Solarz and Charles Percy, had difficulty in finding colleagues and community activists to advance India's interests, the Caucus has been instrumental in negating the influence of Pakistan and defeating Dan Burton's annual amendments to slash assistance to India.

Although my research indicates that the caucus' strength and accomplishments are exaggerated[132] and limited to "congratulatory" resolutions and not substantive legislation, its existence in the House reinforced the administration's preference to deal with the Senate which can pass amendments that are not germane to legislation under consideration. Senator Brownback, in particular, used his chairmanship of the Senate Foreign Relations Committee Subcommittee on Near East and South Asian Affairs as a platform to advance a wider agenda, such as religious freedom, at a time when the comparable House committees were involved in jurisdictional and personal disputes that prevented the institution from being effective.[133] The Clinton administration was forced to react to Brownback's promise to introduce legislation removing all remaining nonmilitary sanctions toward India.

The example of the House caucus was not lost on the Senate. In March 2004 a thirty-five member "Friends of India" grouping was formed in the Senate in conjunction with the Indian Embassy, the first such country-focused grouping in the history of that body—a development made easier by the retirement of legislators with a broader agenda than ethnic politics, such as John Glenn and Daniel Patrick Moynihan. Co-chaired by John Cornyn (R-TX) and

Hillary Rodham Clinton (D-NY), its members included Senate Majority Leader Bill Frist (R-TN), Senate Minority Leader Tom Daschle, Judiciary Committee Chair Orrin Hatch (R-UT), Finance Committee Chair Charles Grassley (R-IA), Appropriations Chair Thad Cochran (R-MS), and other influential senators such as Kay Bailey Hutchison (R-TX), Paul Sarbanes (D-MD), Joe Lieberman (D-CN), and Edward Kennedy (D-MA).[134]

At the same time, India's critics, judged by an unsuccessful attempt to involve the U.S. directly in the Kashmir dispute, have been reduced to forty-six members in the House, and a very important fifteen, including former minority leader Tom Daschle who was defeated in 2004, in the Senate. With the retirement of such stalwarts as minority whip David Bonior (D-MI), who represented a district with a large Muslim population, Gerald Solomon (R-NY) the Chairman of the Rules Committee and Robert Livingston (R-LA) the Chairman of the Appropriations Committee, most of Pakistan's supporters outside the Black Caucus and the Armed Services Committee[135] in the House of Representatives and their financial supporters have been marginalized and discredited.[136] Other legislators, like Tom Harkin and Dana Rohrabacher (R-CA), were temporarily silenced by the coup in Islamabad. Dan Burton's annual amendments to slash assistance to India have found little support in recent years. The net result of these diverse developments has been a remarkable turnaround in congressional attitudes toward India and U.S.-Indian ties. The transformation of congressional attitudes from indifference or deep-seated hostility to their current positive state on Capitol Hill confirms the necessity for a foreign country to have a strong domestic base of support in the American political system if it intends to be influential in Washington.

Congress and Post 9-11-2001 Developments

However, after the terrorist attacks on New York and Washington, D.C., ethnic politics now take a back seat to security issues. Secretary of State Colin Powell initially was spending as much time in South Asia as he did in the Middle East. While the region only gets noticed if there is a crisis, South Asia had been a focus of the Bush administration even before the United States launched its campaign against the Taliban in Afghanistan a month later. In a reversal of historical practice, South Asia was one of the few regions where the new administration had policy and personnel in place soon after assuming office. Senator Sam Brownback's aide Christina Rocca was appointed assistant secretary of state for the region, and deputy secretary of state Richard Armitage assumed the role of principal actor that Strobe Talbott had played in the previous administration.

Hence, South Asia was virtually the only place where the Clinton administration's policies were not abandoned. The normalization of relations with India continued unabated, and there was talk of partnership and a natural alliance with New Delhi by Secretary of State Colin Powell.[137] The segment of the Republican Party typified by Benjamin Gilman wanted to use India to contain China. Perhaps for this reason, Robert Blackwill, a China expert, had been named ambassador to New Delhi. The need for a grand coalition against terrorism which included China changed Washington's calculation. The war on terrorism caused the United States to again consider relations with India and Pakistan in a broader context—instead of the promised bilateral basis—as Washington has attempted to expand cooperation with both India and Pakistan simultaneously.

As a consequence, the major area where bilateral relations between the United States and India has been enhanced is in the realm of military cooperation.[138] The Defense Department, formerly an ally of Pakistan, is a principal advocate of improved ties with India. Economic and political ties have been less smooth than cooperation in the space and nuclear sectors. Foreign investment from the United States, which peaked at $737 million in 1997, fell below $250 million in 2001 before rising to around $400 million in 2004. Bilateral trade with India has also failed to live up to expectations, reaching only $14 billion in 2001 compared to over $116 billion with China. India's sales to the United States rose to $10 billion, while U.S. exports to India remained flat at $4 billion until reaching $19 billion and $8 billion in 2005.[139] The principal economic impediment to improved relations has been the practice of outsourcing of white-collar jobs to India by American corporations.[140] While economists such as Catherine Mann of the Institute for International Economics and Jagdish Bhagwati promote the long run benefits of outsourcing to the United States,[141] legislators from districts suffering from rising unemployment are sensitive to their constituents' concerns about the practice in an election year.[142] Interestingly, some of the most vocal critics of the practice, including Frank Pallone and Tom Lantos (D-CA), the ranking member of the House International Relations Committee, have been prominent supporters of improved Indo-American relations.[143] Another pro-Indian legislator, Senator George Voinovich (R-OH), attached an amendment to the Omnibus Appropriations Bill to ban federal funds to agencies that subcontracted overseas.[144] Congressman Gary Ackerman bemoaned what he called "India bashing," arguing that "for years we told the Indians they were too aligned with the Soviet Union, they were too socialist; they had to free their economy and be entrepreneurial. Now that India is free and entrepreneurial, we are telling them you are coming on too strong."[145]

Political ties were damaged by the February-March 2002 communal violence against Muslims in Gujarat, but the United States Congress was strangely uncritical of the financial support of non-resident Indians in the United States to the campaign that targeted Muslims for persecution.[146] However, both Congress and the executive branch were offended by the insistence of the government of India that the United States officially recognize permanent resident Bhishmar K. Agnihotri as a representative appointed by New Delhi to the Indian community.[147] This unprecedented request to give official status to a BJP political operative violated established diplomatic protocol and undermined the Indian Embassy's effectiveness in Washington. By the same token, Washington's attempt to involve New Delhi in a dangerous and unpopular occupation of Iraq reveals a lack of understanding of India's domestic politics. That New Delhi would even consider the proposition is evidence of how much relations have improved.

New Delhi has been repeatedly restrained by Washington from striking Pakistani-based terrorists who attacked the Kashmiri assembly in Srinigar in September 2001 and the parliament in New Delhi in December of that year because such actions divert Islamabad's resources from the Afghan border and undermine the campaign in Afghanistan. The attacks against democratic institutions have bonded India and the United States against terrorism,[148] but not against Pakistan. For this reason the Indians—who hoped to settle regional scores—see a double standard in the war against terrorism. As a result, Indians—particularly former Defence Minister George Fernandes—were "unhappy" that Washington has overlooked Pakistan's connection with terrorism directed at them.[149]

Pakistan—once again a frontline state—is taking full advantage of what could be a temporary opportunity for leverage. President Pervez Musharraf has become so indispensable to Washington's war effort "that you can't say anything bad about him in Washington" even though he reneged on his promise to relinquish power after three years.[150] By March 2003 all remaining sanctions imposed against Islamabad after the October 1999 coup were waived by executive order, even though it has been established that Pakistan connived with Iran, Libya, and North Korea on their missile and nuclear programs. Ironically, some of the very legislators who charged the administration with a "cover up" were aware through intelligence briefings of Pakistan's clandestine activities and had voted for the Brown Amendment that legitimated them.[151] Nor did Pakistan's proliferation activities cause Washington to reconsider its aid to Islamabad. After receiving confirmation of Pakistan's marketing of weapons of mass destruction, Congress approved a $390 million assistance package for 2003-04 and a further $701 million for 2004-05.[152] By comparison India was to receive $85 million out of a total assistance package of $1.9 billion for South Asia—a disparity that left some lawmakers incredulous.[153] The Bush administration justified its lack of even-handedness by maintaining that the appropriation "supports our number one policy goal—combating terror and the conditions that breed terror" since Pakistan was a frontline country in the war against terror, while

India is "a growing world power."[154] To this end—in a move that embarrassed New Delhi—Secretary of State Colin Powell designated Pakistan a "major non-NATO ally" only two days after a visit to the Indian capitol.[155]

For its part, the Bush administration knows that it can no longer avoid confronting the Kashmir problem, which it considers a nuclear flash point. Since it is mired in two quagmires in the Middle East—the Arab-Israeli dispute and the conflict with Iraq—it has no desire to take on another conundrum in South Asia. The mobilization of a million troops on the frontier in Kashmir in 2002 underscored the urgency for a political settlement in a nuclearized South Asia. For this reason the state department has encouraged the Indian and Pakistani roadmap to settle their differences on all contentious bilateral issues.[156]

Meanwhile, the U.S. Congress has acted as though it were no longer interested in South Asia. Henry Hyde(R-IL) (who after being term-limited as Chair of the Judiciary Committee in the House, took over the International Relations Committee), showed almost no interest in the region. The ranking Democrat, Sam Gjedenson of Connecticut, a protégé of two-time ambassador Chester Bowles, who had a deep interest in India, was defeated in the 2000 elections. When the Democrats reorganized the Senate after Jim Jefford's (R-VT) defection from the Republican caucus in 2001, Joe Biden became Chairman of the Foreign Relations Committee in place of an ailing Jesse Helms, and Paul Wellstone (D-MN) replaced Brownback as chairman of the Near East and South Asia Subcommittee. Biden was distracted by Afghanistan, while Wellstone, whose energies were consumed by a tough re-election campaign, had little time for committee activities before a plane crash took his life just before the 2002 election. After the Republicans regained control of the Senate, the respected Richard Lugar—who has a demonstrated interest in South Asia—reassumed the chairmanship of the Committee on Foreign Relations, while Lincoln Chafee (R-RI)—and not as expected Sam Brownback—became head of its Subcommittee on Near Eastern and South Asian Affairs. Chafee was not the active player on South Asian issues that the Kansas senator was. In the House, where district of eighty year old Benjamin Gilman was reapportioned out of existence, South Asia was once again attached to the Asia and the Pacific Subcommittee of House International Relations Committee under the chairmanship of Jim Leach (R-IA) and not Dan Burton.[157] Moreover, in a move that reduces the area's, Afghanistan was detached from the South Asian region and placed under the jurisdiction a new Subcommittee on the Middle East and Central Asia. This turnover has impeded the ability of Congress to define its policies on South Asia.

The Indian government has also de-emphasized its contacts with Congress, even though the legislative underpinnings of Indo-American relations are only "half-built."[158] With the administration directly engaging the Government of India, its embassy in Washington neglected the legislative branch which had opened the door to better relations with New Delhi. New Delhi's friends in Congress, upset by being ignored by its Embassy in Washington, feel that India will have to start re-cultivating relations with Capitol Hill or repeat the problems of an earlier era.[159] The longer it takes the process to begin, the more difficult will be the task of rebuilding India's ties to American legislators. This need to take the legislative branch into consideration became apparent when the Bush administration negotiated an agreement to assist India's civilian nuclear program without congressional input, even though New Delhi remained outside the non-proliferation regime constructed by Congress.

Congress and the Nuclear Deal

In September 2004 the United States agreed to expand cooperation with India on civilian nuclear activities, space programs and technology transfers.[160] During her visit to the subcontinent in March 2005, Secretary of State Condoleezza Rice went further, expressing a willingness to discuss such highly contentious issues as alternative energy resources, the proposed Indo-Pakistani-Iranian gas pipeline, and the stimulation of moribund bilateral trade. This was followed by a ten year "new framework for the U.S.-India defense relationship for the next 10 years" signed by Defence Minister Pranab Mukerjee and Secretary of Defense

Donald Rumsfeld in June. It provided for increased technology transfers, as well as collaboration in research and development and co-production of weapons systems.[161] The momentum in Indo-American relations culminated in an agreement on nuclear cooperation reached during Prime Minister Manmohan Singh's July 2005 visit to Washington. The accord was an attempt to accommodate the great power ambitions of a country that had developed nuclear weapons completely outside of the non-proliferation regime. Despite the fact that the agreement required permission from the 45 member nuclear supplier's group, as well as amending the Nuclear Non-Proliferation Act of 1978—which had been directed at India—and the Atomic Energy Act of 1954, no members of Congress were briefed in advance.[162] Even though the pact engendered opposition from the long dormant non-proliferation lobby,[163] the Bush administration—disregarding the displeasure registered on Capitol Hill—proceeded to negotiate additional nuclear arrangements with India without consulting any members of Congress.[164] Embroiled in failures over the military occupation of Iraq, his inadequate response to Hurricane Katrina, and the Dubai ports management fiasco, the American president was determined to achieve a diplomatic success during his March 2006 trip to India. Unlike the case of Bill Clinton in 2000, Bush took no members of Congress with him six years later. Even though Joe Wilson (R-SC), the past co-chair of the India Caucus in the House, and John Cornyn, the founder of the Senate Caucus, asked to accompany the president, the White House refused to include them.[165] Bush used the occasion to announce that Washington would provide assistance to India's civilian nuclear program and allow India to expand its military arsenal of fissile material.[166] The fact that India agreed to place 14 of its existing 22 nuclear reactors under international inspection enraged opponents at home, but its ability to build new facilities outside the IAEA regime outraged critics of the deal on the left and the right in the United States. Among others, Congressman Edward Markey and Robert Einhorn, former Assistant Secretary of State for Non-proliferation, were incredulous that the United States would abandon over three decades of a common after that Non-proliferation policy at a time that it was attempting to sanction North Korea and Iran.[167]

As a result of its lack of consultation, the Bush administration unnecessarily complicated an already lengthy process involving a myriad of committees on Capitol Hill. Although it was expected that most resistance would be encountered in the House of Representatives where Henry Hyde, the chairman, initially threatened to scuttle the measure,[168] and Tom Lantos the ranking member, tied approval to India's support of the American position against Iran in the International Atomic Energy Agency,[169] the International Relations Committee passed the United States and India Nuclear Cooperation Promotion Act of 2006 (H.R. 5682) by a 16-2 vote and the full House endorsed it by a majority of 359 to 68. 219 Republicans and 140 Democrats voted in favor of the bill, while nine Republicans and 58 Democrats opposed it. In an effort to placate its American critics, India supported the American initiative in the IAEA to have the Iranian nuclear program referred to the United Nations for possible sanctions at considerable domestic cost.[170] Although it was thought that the legislation would have an easier time in the Senate—even though Richard Lugar, the Chairman of the Foreign Relations Committee, raised 80 reservations—it ran into difficulties in that chamber. While the committee endorsed the measured (S.3709) by a margin of 16-2, it failed to pass before the election campaign recess. The House passed the so-called "Henry J. Hyde United States and India Cooperation Act of 2006" by a vote of 359 to 68 on December 8 and the Senate followed on December 9. President Bush signed the measure into to law (P.L. 109-401) on December 18, 2006.

The reaction of Congress is the result of a White House that in the words of Senator Lindsay Graham (R-SC) is perceived as "non-responsive and arrogant," even by Republican legislators.[171] This pattern of neglect by an administration that prefers to act unilaterally abroad and ignore separation of powers at home has required members of the executive branch to engage in back filling in order to sell the deal with India as a measure that expands the domestic civilian nuclear capacity of a growing energy competitor.[172]

The Congruency of Executive-Legislative Policy towards South Asia

Most observers agree that the legislative process functions best if Congress and the President operate in a consultative and coordinated fashion, rather than struggle for supremacy. As this survey of relations indicates, presidents have generally attained their objectives toward the South Asian region. In doing so, they have seldom been without allies on the Hill. John Sherman Cooper collaborated with John Kennedy to enhance relations with India, while Hank Brown worked with Bill Clinton to dilute the Pressler Amendment's sanctions against Pakistan. Congress, for institutional, political, and personality reasons has usually abdicated its oversight responsibilities and characteristically deferred to the executive branch in the context of a broader agenda.

However, a congruent legislative process does not necessarily produce policies that are in the national interest. Washington's conduct of bilateral relations with India has been less than exemplary. For fifty years the government of the United States, including the legislative branch, dealt with India in a residual fashion, even though New Delhi's economic and strategic importance to the United States increased. Regional matters have consistently been dealt with in amendments to foreign operations or defense authorization bills produced by conference committees, instead of as discrete issue areas by informed authorizing committees. U.S. bilateral relations with India were treated as a subsidiary, first of Anglo-American and then of Soviet-American concerns. Despite lack of institutional memory and its turnover of personnel, Congress—even more than the executive branch—historically viewed New Delhi's international positions as being contrary to American interests. India was perceived on Capitol Hill as needy, but unworthy of assistance. The cold war enabled India's principal rival Pakistan to exploit New Delhi's negative image in Washington and deflect attention from its own clandestine nuclear program. Pakistan's position as a frontline state resisting the Soviet invasion of Afghanistan enabled the executive and legislative branches of the American government to overlook Islamabad's proliferation of nuclear weapons and punish India, even though New Delhi has never been engaged in such activities. This was true even during the Carter administration when Congress and the president both supposedly had a nonproliferation agenda and an emphasis on regional concerns.

The end of the cold war and the growing influence of the sizable and affluent Indo-American community,[173] as well as the opening up of India to foreign investment, led to speculation that for the first time New Delhi would be dealt with by the United States on a purely bilateral basis. When Washington and New Delhi engaged in their longest dialogue in history, it was in reaction to the nuclearization of the region and an ongoing brinkmanship between India and Pakistan that had to constantly be defused by the United States. Such factors as ethnic politics and lobbying by business interests appear to merely assure that India be given consideration, rather than ignored or punished by Washington. When Congress, by means of the Glenn and Brownback Amendments, asserted itself during a period of executive inattention during the Clinton administration, relations with Pakistan, rather than India, were given priority. It is important to remember that the removal of sanctions against New Delhi after India's 1998 Pokharan tests were piggybacked on a waiver that applied to Pakistan.

Paradoxically, Islamabad has benefited more than New Delhi in Washington from the war on terrorism, even though its intelligence service created the Taliban that made Afghanistan a sanctuary for Al Qaeda, and its operatives in Kashmir have made India a target of violence. As the *New York Times* observed, Iraq, which did not proliferate nuclear weapons has been invaded by the United States, while Pakistan, the biggest proliferator in history, has been excused for its actions and congratulated for pardoning Abdul Qadeer Khan, the country's chief atomic scientist, after he admitted selling weapons of mass destruction to rogue states such as Iran, Libya, and North Korea.[174] Despite a military coup, Pakistan once more remains exempt from meaningful American punishment because of Washington's global priorities. Moreover, Islamabad, like India, did not support the American war in Iraq, and the United States remains extremely unpopular in Pakistan. Under the circumstances, New Delhi naturally resents Washington's contradictory policies.

While Washington and New Delhi have increased their military and political cooperation, their national interests, which are by no means identical, are likely to come into increasing conflict given India's great power aspirations.[175] Ironically, now that the United States recognizes a regional imperative in a nuclearized South Asia, India considers itself a global rather than a regional power. The United States remains a status quo nation, while India, which has never been comfortable with a unipolar world, is in many ways a revisionist state. The test of the Indo-American relationship will be how the U.S. accommodates India's ambitions.[176]

The Bush administration has determined that assisting India's civilian nuclear technology is the way to engage India as a major power. It has done so without consulting Congress, whose co-operation is needed to achieve its objectives. If Congress—even in recognizing the importance of good relations with India—goes along, it will have repeated its pattern of deferring to the executive branch.

NOTES AND REFERENCES

1. Stephen R. Weissman, *A Culture of Deference* (New York: Basic Books, 1995).
2. Norman D. Palmer, *South Asia and United States Policy* (Boston: Houghton Mifflin, 1966), p. 10.
3. Robert M. Hathaway, "Unfinished Passage: India, Indian Americans, and the U.S. Congress," *The Washington Quarterly*, 24 (March 2001), 23.
4. Lloyd I. and Susanne Hoeber Rudolph, "The Coordination of Complexity," in *The Regional Imperative, U.S. Foreign Policy towards the South Asian States* (Atlantic Highlands, N.J: Humanities Press, 1983), p. 95.
5. Report of an Independent Task Force, *A New Foreign Policy toward India and Pakistan* (New York: Council on Foreign Relations, 1997), p. 45.
6. See Lee H. Hamilton and Jordan Tama, *A Creative Tension, The Foreign Policy Roles of the President and Congress* (Washington: The Johns Hopkins University Press for the Woodrow Wilson Center Press, 2002). Incredibly, the state department did not open its first liaison office on Capitol Hill until 2001. http://www.Rollcall.com/pages/news/00/2001/1022.html.

7. As Majority Leader Lyndon Johnson rewarded his supporters with seats on the Foreign Relations Committee and denied them to his opponents. See Robert A. Caro, *The Years of Lyndon Johnson, Master of the Senate* (New York: Vintage Books, 2002), pp. 487-99.
8. *New York Times*, November 11, 1984, p. 10.
9. Revealingly, Francis R. Valeo, chief aide to Senate Majority Leader and longtime Foreign Relations Committee member Mike Mansfield (D-MT), makes no mention of India or South Asia in his biography, *Mike Mansfield Majority Leader* (Armonk, N.Y.: M.E. Sharpe, 1999).
10. One of Senator Church's chief aides was Tom Dine, who had been a top assistant to Ambassador Chester Bowles in New Delhi. Peter Galbraith, the son of former Ambassador John Kenneth Galbraith, was a senior committee aide to Senator Pell. Jonah Blank, a recognized scholar of South Asian affairs, is on the staff of Senator Joseph Biden (D-DE) the ranking member. Over thirty staffers of Indian-American descent are now employed on Capitol Hill.
11. See John F. Stack, Jr. and Colton C. Campbell, "Congress: How Silent a Partner," in Colton C. Campbell, Nicol C. Rae, and John F. Stack, Jr., eds., *Congress and the Politics of Foreign Policy* (Upper Saddle River, N. J.: Pearson Education, Inc., 2003), pp. 29-31, for details.
12. According to a senior analyst at the Congressional Research Service. Interview, Washington, D. C., April 15, 1986.
13. See Arthur Maass, *Congress and the Common Good* (New York: Basic Books, 1983), p. 5.
14. See *India Today*, November 15, 1993.
15. Given the overwhelmingly Democratic character of the Indo-American community a concerted effort was made to recruit Republican members in order that the caucus not appear partisan. According to a 1996 study, 42% of Indian-Americans identified themselves as Democrats, and 13% as Republicans. *Washington Post*, internet edition, October 25, 2003. In the 1988 presidential election 56.3% of Indian-Americans voted for Michael Dukakis, the Democratic candidate for president, and 23.8% voted for George Bush, the Republican nominee. Tanmay Kanjil, "The Indian-Americans in the United States: Participation in the U.S. Political Process," *International Studies*, 32 (October-December 1996), 90.
16. See *India Abroad*, October 16, 1998, p. 18 and October 23, 1998, p. 12 for details.
17. Richard Fenno, *The Power of the Purse* (Boston: Little, Brown, 1966).
18. Alvin Peter Drischler, "Foreign Policy Making on the Hill," *Washington Quarterly*, 8 (Summer 1985), 171.
19. Small wonder that Mitch McConnell (R-KY), who became the chairman of a powerful Senate subcommittee responsible for assistance, abandoned the Foreign Relations Committee for the Appropriations Committee. As he put it, "The difference between us and them is we're shooting with real bullets. .. .We spend real money." New *York Times*, January 1, 1995.

20. Peter Tomsen, *U.S. Congressional Perspective of India: A Case Study* (Washington, D.C.: Department of State, n.d.), p. 5.
21. Harold Isaacs, *Scratches on Our Minds* (Armonk, N.Y.: M.E. Sharpe, 1980 edition), p. xxxiii.
22. For an elaboration see Selig Harrison, "Dialogue of the Deaf: Mutual Perceptions in Indo-American Relations," in Sulochana Raghavan Glazer and Nathan Glazer eds., *Conflicting Images, India and the United States* (Glenn Dale, MD.: Riverdale Publishers, 1990), p. 58.
23. Milton Singer, *When a Great Tradition Modernizes* (New York: Praeger, 1972), p. 12.
24. See Lloyd I. Rudolph, "Gandhi in the Mind of America," in Glazer and Glazer eds, *Conflicting Images*, pp. 143-77.
25. W. Norman Brown, *The United States, India, Pakistan and Bangladesh* (Cambridge: MA: Harvard University Press, 1972), p. 392.
26. See William Watts, *The United States and Asia: Changing Attitudes and Policies* (Lexington, MA: Lexington Books, 1982).
27. Gary R. Hess, *America Encounters India, 1941-47* (Baltimore: Johns Hopkins University Press, 1971), p. 7.
28. Charles H. Heimsath, "The American Images of India as Factors in U.S. Foreign Policy Making," in Michael L. Krenn ed., *Race and U.S. Foreign Policy During the Cold War* (New York and London: Garland Publishing Inc., 1998), p. 99.
29. "National Target for South Asia Specialists," A Report to the National Council for Foreign Languages and International Studies, p. 18.
30. *Asia and American Textbooks* (New York, 1976).
31. U.S. Department of State, *United States-Indian Cultural Relations* (Washington: Bureau of Educational and Cultural Affairs, 1982).
32. John W. Mellor, *India as a Rising Middle Power* (Boulder, CO.: Westview Press, 1979), p. 359.
33. Christopher Van Hoellen, "The Tilt Policy Revisited: Nixon-Kissinger Geopolitics and South Asia," *Asian Survey*, XX (April 1980), 341.
34. James Warner Bjorkman, "Public Law 480 and the Policies of Self-Help and Short-Tether: Indo-American Relations, 1965-68," in Lloyd I. Rudolph and Susanne Hoeber Rudolph, *The Regional Imperative, U.S. Foreign Policy towards South Asian States*, p. 234.
35. John P. Lewis, *India's Political Economy, Governance and Reform* (Delhi: Oxford University Press, 1995), p. 87.
36. Robert Dahl, *Congress and Foreign Policy* (New York: Harcourt, Brace, 1950), p. 15.
37. Norman Ornstein, "The Open Congress Meets the President," in Anthony King ed., *Both Sides of the Avenue* (Washington, D.C.: American Enterprise Institute, 1983), p. 208.
38. Pramod Vas, *Dawning on the Capitol, U.S. Congress and India* (Calcutta: Mascot, 1966), p. 1.

39. Quoted from *Playboy*, March 1977, p. 78, by John W. Mellor and Philip Oldenburg, "India and the United States." in Mellor, ed., *India: A Rising Middle Power*, p. 4.
40. U.S. Congress, House Committee on Foreign Affairs, Subcommittee on the Near East and South Asia, *Hearings, Political Trends in India and Bangladesh*, 93rd Congress, 1st session, October 31, 1973, p. 18.
41. Baldev Raj Nayar, "Treat India Seriously," *Foreign Policy*, No. 18 (Spring 1975), pp. 133-54.
42. Myron Weiner, "Critical Choices for India and America," in Donald C. Hellmann ed., *Southern Asia: The Politics of Poverty and Peace* (Lexington. MA.: Lexington Books, 1976), p. 65.
43. Glazer and Glazer, *Conflicting Images*, p. 4. On this point also see Andrew J. Rotter, *Comrades at Odds: The United States and India, 1947-1964* (Ithaca: Cornell University Press, 2000).
44. U.S. Department of State, Office of Intelligence Research, "India's Political and Economic Position in the East-West Conflict," *OIR Report No. 5526*, May 15, 1951, p. 1.
45. For an elaboration see my "U.S. Attitudes towards India" in Arthur G. Rubinoff ed., *Canada and South Asia: Political and Strategic Relations* (Toronto: South Asia Centre of the University of Toronto, 1992), pp. 63-73.
46. Norman D. Palmer, "Indo-American Relations: The Politics of Encounter," *Orbis XXIII* (Summer 1979), 403-19.
47. James A. Robinson, *Congress and Foreign Policy-Making* (Homewood. IL: Dorsey Press, 1967), p. vii.
48. A. Guy Hope, *America and Swaraj* (Washington, D.C.: Public Affairs Press, 1968), p. 49.
49. Karen Isaksen Leonard, *The South Asian Americans* (Westport, CT: Greenwood Press, 1997), p. 39. Sixty per cent of more recent immigrants come from Gujarat.
50. *United States* v. *Thind 261 U.S. 204 (1923)*.
51. See Frenise A. Logan, "Racism and Indian-U.S. Relations, 1947-1953: Views in the Indian Press," in Krenn ed., *Race and U.S. Foreign Policy in the Cold War*, pp. 89-97.
52. See D: S. Saund, *Congressman from India* (New York: E.P. Dutton, 1960) for a discussion of efforts to redress these matters. Saund, the first legislator of Indian descent to serve in Congress, entered the United States in 1920 and earned a Ph.D from the University of California at Berkeley. Elected to the House of Representatives as the first Democrat from the Imperial Valley of California in 1956, he served on the Foreign Affairs Committee. In 2004 Bobby Jindal (R-LA) became the second Representative to be elected.
53. See Binod Khadria, The *Migration of Knowledge Workers* (New Delhi: Sage Publications, 1999), chapter 2.
54. Leonard, *The South Asian Americans*, p. 70.

55. For a summary see H.W. Brands, *India and the United States, the Cold Peace* (Boston: Twayne Publishers, 1990), pp. 56-58.
56. Palmer, *South Asia and United States Policy*, p. 10.
57. Robert J. McMahon, *The Cold War on the Periphery: The United States, India, and Pakistan* (New York: Columbia University Press, 1994), p. 93.
58. *Ibid.*, p. 15.
59. *Ibid.*, p. 63.
60. Prime Minister Nehru explicitly states that New Delhi could not allow "the United States to tell India with whom it could trade as a price of aid." Dennis Kux, *Estranged Democracies: India and the United States, 1941-1991* (New Delhi: Sage, 1993), p. 124.
61. Quoted by McMahon, *The Cold War at the Periphery*, p. 173.
62. Arthur G. Rubinoff, *India's Use of Force in Goa* (Bombay: Popular Prakashan, 1971), p. 103.
63. Palmer, *South Asia and United States Policy*, p. 150.
64. See Joanne F. Loomba, "U.S. Aid to India 1957-67: A Study in Decision-Making," *India Quarterly*, 28 (October-December 1972), 310.
65. U.S. Department of State, *The Subcontinent of South Asia*, Near and Middle East Series, No. 41, 1959, p. 6.
66. For a statement of Kennedy's support of India, see Selig S. Harrison ed., *India and the United States* (New York: The Macmillan Company, 1961), pp. 63-64.
67. Humphrey was quoted by Brands, *India and the United States, the Cold Peace*, p. 49, as saying he wanted "to be for India what Walter Judd is for China." Judd, a Republican representative from Minnesota, was head of what was known as "the China Lobby."
68. See Stephen P. Cohen's essay in this volume for details.
69. Henry A. Kissinger, *White House Years* (Boston: Little, Brown and Company, 1979, p. 848.
70. U.S. Congress, House Committee on Foreign Affairs, Subcommittee on the Near East and South Asia, *The United States and South Asia*, 93rd Congress, 1st session, May 25, 1973, p. 20.
71. See Philip Oldenburg's essay in this volume for details.
72. Kissinger, *White House Years*, chapter 21.
73. The Senate Foreign Relations Committee voted unanimously for a complete and immediate cutoff of all arms transfers. Dennis Kux, *The United States and Pakistan, 1947-2000* (Baltimore: The Johns Hopkins University Press for the Woodrow Wilson Center Press, 2001), p. 189.
74. For a representative sample of Passman's views, see U.S. Congress, House Subcommittee on Appropriations, *Hearings, Foreign Operations Appropriations for 1963*, Vol. 55, Part 3, *Economic Assistance Program*, 87th Congress, 2nd session, p. 233. Long, in particular, viewed himself as an expert on India. In testimony, U.S. Congress, House Committee on International Relations, *Hearings and Markup, Export of Nuclear Fuel to India*, 95th Congress, 2nd Session May 23, June 1 and 14, 1978, p. 20, he

stated, "I have been through India. I know a great deal about it. I have written on it, and I would have to say that ...I ndia is a country that is run for the benefit of about twenty per cent ...an d the rest of the people get almost nothing out of our foreign aid or out of their own economic progress." It was Long's opinion that, although the United States provided assistance to help India's poor, the Indian government spent millions on its military establishment, using scarce resources to purchase Soviet arms and develop nuclear weapons. U.S. Congress, House Subcommittee on Appropriations, *Hearings: Foreign Assistance and Related Agencies*, 95th Congress, 2nd session, vol. 25, part 1, 1978, p. 830.

75. See James Warner Bjorkman's essay in this volume for details.
76. *The United States and South Asia*, p. 20.
77. Francis R. Valeo, *South Asia: Report on Bangladesh, India, and Pakistan to the Majority Leader*, Senate Committee on Foreign Relations, 94th Congress, 2nd session, 1976, p. 13.
78. U.S. Congress, House Committee on Foreign Affairs, Subcommittee on the Near East and South Asia, *Hearings, United States Interests in and Policies Toward South Asia*, 93d Congress, 1st session, March 12, 15, 20, and 27, 1973, p. vi.
79. Congressman Lester Wolf (D-NY) pronounced these actions "Moynihan's 'fait accompli.'" U.S. Congress, House Committee on International Relations, Subcommittee on the Near East and South Asia, *Hearings, The Persian Gulf, 1974: Money, Politics, Arms and Power*, 93rd Congress, 2nd session, July 30, August 5, 7, and 12, 1974, p. 138.
80. U.S. Congress, House Committee on International Relations, Subcommittee on International Organizations, *Hearings, Human Rights in India*, 94th Congress, 2nd session, June 23, 28, 29, September 16, 23, 1976.
81. US Congress, House Committee on Foreign Affairs, Subcommittee on National Security Policy and Scientific Development, *Hearings, The Indian Ocean: Political and Strategic Future*, 92 Congress, 1st session, July 20, 22, 27, 28, 1971, p. 13.
82. McMahon, *The Cold War at the Periphery*, p. 165 and p. 212.
83. See George Crile, *Charlie Wilson's War* (New York: Atlantic Monthly Press, 2003). Wilson is now a lobbyist for Pakistan.
84. Legislators with a significant number of Pakistani-Americans and other Muslim constituents have been targeted for financial support by the pro-Pakistan lobby.
85. Norman D. Palmer, *The United States and India* (New York: Praeger Publishers, 1984), p. 216.
86. Peter Galbraith, "Nuclear Proliferation in South Asia," in Glazer and Glazer, *Conflicting Images*, p. 72.
87. See Richard P. Cronin, "Congress and Arms Sales and Security Assistance to Pakistan," in U.S. Congress, House Committee on Foreign Affairs, *Congress and Foreign Policy 1981* (Washington, D.C.: Government Printing Office, 1982), pp. 103-14.

88. See my case study in "Congressional Attitudes towards India" in Harold Gould and Sumit Ganguly eds., *The Hope and the Reality: Indo-American Relations from Roosevelt to Reagan* (Boulder Co.: Westview Press, 1992), pp. 167-73.
89. Randy J. Rydell, "Giving Nonproliferation Norms Teeth: Sanctions and the NPPA," *The Nonproliferation Review*, 6 (Winter 1999), 1-19.
90. See Arthur G. Rubinoff, "Legislative Perceptions of Indo-American Relations," in Ashok Kapur, Y.K. Malik, Harold A. Gould, and Arthur G. Rubinoff eds., *India and the United States in a Changing World* (New Delhi: Sage Publications, 2002), pp. 412-57, for a comparison of the views of Indian members of parliament and American congressmen.
91. On the latter point see James M. Lindsay, *Congress and the Politics of U.S. Foreign Policy* (Baltimore and London: The Johns Hopkins University Press, 1994), p. 92.
92. See Arthur G. Rubinoff, "Missed Opportunities and Contradictory Policies: Indo-American Relations in the Clinton-Rao Years," *Pacific Affairs* 69 (Winter 1996-97), 499-517.
93. While it was believed that Stephen Solarz, a long-time supporter of India and the former chairman of the House Foreign Affairs Subcommittee on Asia and the Pacific, who had been defeated in 1992 after his involvement in the House Bank check-kiting scandal, would be the new envoy, he was never officially nominated. Halfway through the process, the administration became reluctant to subject Solarz to a Senate Foreign Relations Committee hearing until the prospective ambassador could be exonerated on charges of influence peddling. The Indians, who did not understand the American confirmation process, were indignant at what they regarded as an ongoing diplomatic slight. Eventually the Clinton administration nominated a career diplomat Frank Wisner, who took up his post in July of 1994.
94. However, Senator Daniel Patrick Moynihan, the Chair of the Senate Foreign Relations Subcommittee on the Near East and South Asia, stated he held subcommittee hearings in February 4, 1994 because, "I do not believe in the history of our diplomatic relations with the Republic of India we have ever had such a interregnum." He was particularly disturbed that Robin Raphael's statements questioning the legitimacy of the accession of Kashmir to the Government of India had caused Indians to perceive "a shift in U.S. policy." At the same session Senator Hank Brown (R-CO), who had just returned from the subcontinent, reported that he had found the Indians "outraged." He advised Raphael that her job as a diplomat was to keep her "mouth shut," not to inflame bilateral relations. Stenographic Transcript of Hearings of the Subcommittee on Near Eastern and South Asian Affairs, Committee on Foreign Relations, U.S. Senate, February 4, 1994.
95. *Hindustan Times* (New Delhi), November 29, 1993, p. 14.

96. In a speech to the Foreign Policy Association in New York on January 31, 1995 Secretary William Perry called the Pressler Amendment "a blunt instrument that undermined U.S. influence with Pakistan."
97. *New York Times*, April 12, 1995, p. 1.
98. "Statement by Rep. Lee H. Hamilton submitted to the Subcommittee on Near Eastern & South Asian Affairs, Senate Committee on Foreign Relations", March 9, 1995.
99. Helms claimed he had first developed an interest in South Asia when he was an administrative assistant to a senator in the 1950s. "Stenographic Transcript of Hearings of the Subcommittee on Near Eastern and South Asian Affairs," Committee on Foreign Relations, U.S. Senate, February 4, 1994.
100. *New York Times*, January 6, 1995. In interviews with the author, congressional staffers attributed Moynihan's ouster as punishment for backing Christopher Dodd (D-CN), rather than the victorious Tom Daschle (D-SD), to be party leader in the Senate.
101. Testimony of Bruce Fein Regarding South Asian Foreign Policy Before the Senate Foreign Relations Subcommittee On The Near East and South Asia, September 14, 1995.
102. *Congressional Record*, Vol. 141, No. 147, September 20, 1995, pp. S13909-13971 and Vol. 141, No. 147, September 21, 1995, pp. S13995-14005.
103. Parliamentarians from the left parties ridiculed the Rao government for pursuing what they regarded as a misguided policy of cooperation with the United States. *Indian Express*, September 25, 1995. The setback to American-Indian relations was signaled by a speech Home Minister S.B. Chavan made to the Rajya Sabha on November 29, 1995. According to him, the selling of arms to Pakistan was indicative of the "evil designs" the United States had on the subcontinent. The BJP opposition leader endorsed his unfounded assertion that the United States was interested in acquiring a "foot hold" in Kashmir. *The Hindu* (International Edition), December 16, 1995, p. 5. Foreign Minister Pranab Mukherjee decried that by selling arms to Pakistan, the United States was once again forcing India to divert scarce resources to the military sector. Commerce Minster P. Chidambaram claimed that the Brown Amendment "cast a shadow over commercial ties" because higher military spending undermined the free enterprise economy the United States desired to see established in India, *Indian Express* (New Delhi, December 8, 1995), p. 1.
104. Robert M. Hathaway, "Confrontation and Retreat: The U.S. Congress and the South Asian Nuclear Tests," *Arms Control Today*, Vol. 30 (January/February 2000), 7.
105. *Congressional Record*, Vol. 144, No. 59, May 12, 1998, p. H3080.
106. Quoted by Hathaway, "Confrontation and Retreat," p. 7.
107. *Congressional Record*, Vol. 144, No. 98, July 23, 1998, pp. S8685-87.
108. *Ibid*, Vol. 144, No. 78, June 16, 1998, pp. S6357-58.

109. Hathaway, "Confrontation and Retreat," p. 9.
110. *New York Times*, February 12, 2000, p. 8.
111. Remarks spoken at the Center for Strategic and International Studies, Washington, D.C., February 24, 2000.
112. *Indian Express* (Internet Edition), November 11, 1999.
113. *Indian Express* (Internet Edition), October 28, 1999.
114. *The Times of India* (Internet Edition), November 18, 1999.
115. *India Today* (Online Daily Edition), August 3, 1999.
116. Hathaway, "Unfinished Passage: India, Indian Americans, and the U.S. Congress," p. 26.
117. On this point see Godfrey Hodgson, *The Gentleman from New York, Daniel Patrick Moynihan a Biography* (Boston: Houghton Mifflin Company, 2000), p. 206.
118. In January 2004 Joseph Crowley, the Co-Chair of the Caucus on India and Indian Americans, and Steny Hoyer (D-MD), the Democratic Whip, headed a 15 member congressional delegation—the largest American legislative contingent ever to visit India. *India Abroad*, December 12, 2003, p. 8.
119. See Thomas L. Friedman, "India, Pakistan and G.E.," *The New York Times*, August 4, 2002, p. 13.
120. In this connection see Ralph Nurnberger, *Lobbying in America: A Primer for Citizen Participation* (Washington: India Abroad Center for Political Awareness, 2000). Nurnberger spent eight years as a senior lobbyist for the American Israel Public Affairs Committee before becoming a Washington associate of the India Abroad Center for Political Awareness.
121. See Arthur G. Rubinoff, "The Diaspora as a Factor in U.S.-India Relations," *Asian Affairs*, Vol. 32, No. 3 (Fall 2005), 169-87.
122. Myron Weiner, "The Indian Presence in America: What Difference Will It Make?" In Glazer and Glazer, *Conflicting Images*, pp. 241-56.
123. Although they deny it, there appears to be coordination in the activities and overlap in the congressional support of the pro-Pakistani and Khalistani organizations. There also appears to be a division of labor: the Pakistanis take the high road in promoting their policies and leave the attacks on New Delhi to supporters of the Indian separatist organizations.
124. A Pakistani-American managed the 2002 re-election campaign of Johnson, who had been a member of the India Caucus in the House. The career of Robert Torricelli (D-NJ) evolved in the opposite direction. As a member of the House of Representatives, Torricelli had been a leader of a nascent Pakistani caucus. In the Senate, he was identified as a supporter of India.
125. Arthur G. Rubinoff, "Changing Perceptions of India in the U.S. Congress," *Asian Affairs*, Vol. 28, No. 1 (Spring 2001), 37-60.
126. *New York Times*, January 12, 2003, p. 4.
127. "U.S. is largest wealth market for Indians," *Yahoo! India News*, May 15, 2003, http//in.news.yahoo.com/030515/43/24aog.html.
128. See Leonard, *The South Asian Americans*, pp. 77ff.

129. Sadad Dhume, "From Bangalore to Silicon Valley and Back: How the Indian Diaspora in the United States is Changing India" in Alyssa Ayres and Philip Oldenburg eds., *India Briefing, Quickening the Pace of Change* (Armonk, N.Y.: M.E. Sharpe, 2002), pp. 117-19. According to *Fortune*, July 19, 1999, p. 85, 20 per cent of Congressman Frank Pallone's donors have Indian surnames and 68 per cent of those live outside of New Jersey.
130. Miles A. Pomper and Sumana Chatterjee, "Congress Embraces India as Pakistan's Influence Fades," *Congressional Quarterly Weekly*, 58, No. 12 (March 18, 2000), 57883.
131. Hathaway, "Unfinished Passage," p. 27.
132. When Gary Ackerman first chaired the caucus's his office would not provide a list of its members—perhaps because it would not be accurate. As Robert M. Hathaway, "The U.S.-India Courtship: From Clinton to Bush," *The Journal of Strategic Studies*, 25 (December 2002), 27 notes, "Several members of the US Congress ...w ho at the time of the Gujarat earthquake early in 2001 loudly advertised their support for a generous American response to the disaster, subsequently voted against a US aid package."
133. Benjamin Gilman unsuccessfully attempted to retain the chairmanship of the House International Relations Committee beyond the Republican caucus's three-term limit at a time when several other legislators, including Asia Pacific Subcommittee Chair Doug Bereuter, sought the post. *Roll Call*, March 27, 2000, p. 1.
134. Aziz Haniffa, "Friends of India Formed in the U.S. Senate," http://rediff.com/news/2004/mar/31aziz.htm, and Katharine Goodloe, "Senators Urge Closer India Ties .. .to Address Trade, Job Growth [and] Terrorism Issues, *The Dallas Morning News*, internet edition, April 14, 2004.
135. The Defense Department remains an important supporter of Pakistan on the Hill. See the "Statement of General Anthony C. Zinni, Commander in Chief U.S. Central Command Before the U.S. Senate Committee on Armed Services," February 29, 2000, p. 6, which called the country "the key to stability in Afghanistan and Central Asia."
136. These include Gary Condit (D-CA). Dan Burton has been accused of demanding and obtaining illegal contributions from Sikh and Pakistani lobbyists, *The Hill*, April 16, 1997. Dr. Gurmit Singh Aulakh, president of the Council of Khalistan, was found to have sent out unauthorized letters supporting his positions in the name of members of Congress on official congressional stationary. Michael S. Gerber, "Sikh Lobbyist Riles Lawmakers," *The Hill*, May 1, 2002.
137. *Hindustan Times*, online edition, October 21, 2001.
138. On this point see Hathaway, "The U.S.-India Courtship: From Clinton to Bush," pp. 6-31.
139. Dennis Kux, "India's Fine Balance," *Foreign Affairs*, 81 (June 2002), 104 and http://www.indianembassy.org/newsite/indoustrade.asp
140. Outsourcing has replaced the importation of skilled workers from India

on temporary H1B visas. These fell from 195,000 in 2000 to 65,000 in 2003. *Los Angles Times*, internet edition, October 20, 2003.

141. See Eduardo Porter, "The Bright Side of Sending Jobs Overseas," and Jagdish Bhagwati, "Why Your Job Isn't Moving to Bangalore." *New York Times*, February 15, 2004, p. WK3 and WK11.
142. The House International Relations Committee, concerned with the misuse of temporary visas by skilled foreign workers, held a hearing titled "L1 Visas: Losing Jobs through Laissez-Faire Policies" on February 4, 2004. See *India Abroad*, February 13, 2004, p. 1 and p. 8.
143. The New Jersey congressman called outsourcing "indefensible." *India Abroad*, January 9, 2004, p. 20.
144. *India Abroad*, February 6, 2004, p. 1.
145. *India Abroad*, February 13, 2004, p. 8.
146. Robert M. Hathaway, "Charity or Terrorism?" *The Hindu*, August 8, 2002, internet edition.
147. *India Abroad*, August 9, 2002, p. 6.
148. "Brownback Condemns Attack on India's Parliament," press release, December 14, 2001.
149. Rediff.com, January 9, 2002.
150. Interview, U.S. Department of State, Washington, D.C., April 2, 2002.
151. See Aziz Haniffa, "US support for Musharraf angers Senate panels," *India Abroad*, February 13, 2004, p. 9, and U.S. Congress, Senate Committee on Foreign Relations, *Steps toward Rapprochement*, 108th Congress, 2d Session, 28 January 2004; and Pauline Jelinek, "Senators [on the Senate Budget Committee] Complain about Pakistan Scientist," http://seattlepi.newsource.com/nationalapasia_story.asp?category=1104&slug=US%Pakistan 2/29/04.
152. http://in.news.yahoo.com/040225/139/2bo24.html
153. http://headlines.sify.com/3123news3.html, March 4, 2004.
154. "The FY2005 Foreign Assistance Budget Request for South Asia Statement Before the United States Senate Committee on Foreign Relations by Christina Rocca Assistant Secretary of State South Asian Affairs," U.S. Congress, Senate Committee on Foreign Relations, *Foreign Assistance Oversight*, 108th Congress, 2d Session, 2 March 2004. http://www.foreign.senate.gov/testimony/2004/RoccaTestimony 040302.
155. Pranay Sharma, "Delhi red-faced over US tilt to Pakistan," *The Telegraph* (Calcutta), http://www.telegraphindia.com/1040321.
156. *India Abroad*, January 16, 2004, p. 1.
157. See *The Hill*, on line edition, www.hillnews.com, January 29, 2003.
158. Robert M. Hathaway, "Coming of Age: Indian-Americans and the US Congress," in Kapur, Malik, Gould, and Rubinoff eds., *India and the United States in a Changing World*, p. 389.
159. This assessment is based on interviews with legislative staffers conducted in Washington, D.C. in April, 2002.
160. U.S. Department of State, "United States-India Joint Statement on Next Steps in Strategic Partnership," 17 September 2004.

161. http://www.dailypioneer.com/30/06/05
162. Teresita Schaffer, "India and the United States: Turning a Corner," *CSIS South Asia Monitor*, No. 85 (August 1, 2005).
163. See in particular Henry Sokolski, "The India Syndrome: U.S. nuclear nonproliferation policy melts down," *The Weekly Standard*, August 1, 2005.
164. See Aziz Haniffa, "Nuclear debate rages on," *India Abroad*, January 6, 2006, p. 6.
165. Aziz Haniffa, "Bush team to India big on heft, but small in number," *India Abroad*, March 3, 2006, p. 10.
166. *New York Times*, March 3, 2006, p. 1.
167. *Ibid.*, p. A10.
168. Aziz Haniffa, "US Senate likely to favor N-deal, Congress uncertain," *India Abroad*, March 31, 2006, p. 1.
169. Aziz Haniffa, "India-Iran ties a drag on nuclear deal," *India Abroad*, April 14, 2006, p. 1.
170. Ramandada Sen Gupta, "India's Iran vote ruffles political feathers," *India Abroad*, February 17, 2006, p. 16.
171. Jim Vandehei, "GOP Irritation at Bush Was Long Brewing," *Washington Post*, March 17, 2006, p. A1.
172. Glenn Kessler, "India Nuclear Deal May Face Hard Sell, Rice Set to Defend Landmark Accord She Orchestrated without Congress," *Washington Post*, April 3, 2006, p. A1.
173. Mike McIntyre, "Indian Americans Test Their Clout on Atom Pact," *New York Times*, June 5, 2006, p. 1.
174. *New York Times*, February 7, 2004, p. A30.
175. For discussions of India's ambitions see Stephen P. Cohen, *India, Emerging Power* (Washington: The Brookings Institution, 2001), and George Perkovich, "Is India a Major Power," *Washington Quarterly*, 27 (Winter 2003-04), 129-44.
176. On this point see Baldev Raj Nayar & T.V. Paul, *India and the World Order, Searching for Major-Power Status* (Cambridge: Cambridge University Press, 2003).

PART II

COORDINATION

4

THE COORDINATION OF COMPLEXITY IN SOUTH ASIA

— *Lloyd I. Rudolph* and *Susanne Hoeber Rudolph*

I. WHAT WAS DONE, AND WHY

This report is based on an analysis of the conduct of foreign policy in South Asia during the decade that encompassed the Johnson and Nixon administrations, 1965-1975. Its methodology deploys inductive and deductive modes of analysis, drawing upon case studies on the one hand and reasoning from concepts, assumptions and findings from the literature on organization and foreign policy on the other. The cases* were chosen with an eye to illuminating three broad policy areas in the conduct of foreign policy: diplomatic, economic and people to people. They were also selected with an eye to representing "normal" and crisis activity. Finally, our interviews were in part designed to provide an ethnography of bureaucratic sub-cultures.

Prescriptions for organizational reform seem to have a cyclical quality; yesterday's pathologies become today's cures only to

* In addition to the case studies printed here, the project benefited from a number of background papers, not printed:
United States Foreign Aid to India: An Overview, by Stephen J. Blake.
Impact of U.S. Military and Economic Aid to Pakistan 1954-1969, by Muzammel Huq.
The Power of Information in the Conduct of U.S. Foreign Policy: Examples from South Asia, by Robert Rich.
United States Military Aid to the Ayub Khan Regime, by Roger E. Sack.
The Devaluation of the Indian Rupee in 1966: A Case Study of the World Bank and the United States in India, by Harinder Shourie.

become, again, tomorrow's pathologies. But the recurrence in organizational change of various principles and strategies should not be dismissed as mere re-inventions of the wheel by those who never got the word. Organizational principles change with historical context. The cyclical nature of organizational reform reflects applications to changed circumstances of a limited repertoire of organizational possibilities. We find, for example, that excessive centralization and isolation of power and the layering of control mechanisms associated with it call for a return to a decentralization more finely tuned to the diversities of complex and differentiated circumstances and capable of protecting long-term goals from depredation; that excessive presidential domination of the direction of foreign policy generates good reasons to restore a modified State Department centred system; that policy planning and management dominated by staffs encapsulated in the meta-realities of global strategy and the balance of power engenders justifications for increasing the participation and influence of line officials whose operating responsibilities bring them in contact with events and people on the ground; that the imperium of non-career policy intellectuals deploying strategic and generalist knowledge on behalf of the President enhances an appreciation for the experience and expert knowledge of departmental professionals; and that the costs of hierarchically patterned relationships highlight the benefits of collegiality. Most, if not all, of these "new" directions have been tried before in one form or another and, under different circumstances and for a variety of reasons, found wanting. But as circumstances and leading personalities change and as organizational medicines administered to cure pathologies come to generate new ailments, reformers return again to older remedies from the organizational repertoire.

The principal investigators and contributors, all of whom have had extensive research experience in South Asia, met in Chicago early in June, 1974, to discuss and coordinate the research designs of case studies jointly selected in the light of the principal investigators' proposal to the Commission and of ongoing discussions designed to relate the knowledge and interests of the contributors to the requirements of a regionally based study of the conduct of foreign policy. Background material designed to provide a common conceptual language for the meeting included some of the Commission's early papers on organizational reform, three books on the organizational dimensions of the conduct of foreign policy,[1] and a book on the substance of US policy towards South Asia in the post-war era.[2]

From June to September, the principal investigators and contributors pursued their research, interviewing extensively in Washington and South Asia. Preliminary drafts were presented and criticized at the second conference in early September and the case studies were revised throughout September and October in the light of written and oral criticism by the principal investigators. On November 20, the report was discussed at the Commission headquarters in Washington by Commission staff and senior officials and scholars with South Asia experience. These scholars and officials, and several others that did not attend the conference, provided general and specific comments on the report. On the basis of the conference discussion and the comments, the introductory essay was again revised, culminating in the present report.[3]

II. THE PRESENT CONTEXT OF ORGANIZATIONAL CHANGE

A. Administrative Reform and Presidential Aggrandizement

The conduct of foreign policy in South Asia and elsewhere during the decade encompassed by the Johnson and Nixon administrations did not occur in historical isolation. The presidency as an institution and executive organization for the conduct of foreign policy were shaped by the political contexts and administrative reforms that preceded and followed World War II. The reforms of the 1947-1949 period creating the National Security Council, the Department of Defense, the Central Intelligence Agency, etc. are frequently cited and commented upon in studies of administrative reform dealing with the conduct of foreign policy; but these arise out of the earlier reforms of 1939 proposed by the President's Committee on Administrative Management. Both periods are important in promoting and accelerating a process of presidential aggrandizement that peaked at the beginning of President Nixon's second term. It is this historical experience, particularly its administrative origins in the recommendations of the President's Committee on Administrative Management (the Brownlow Committee), that orients our argument.

Clark Clifford has observed that the executive branch is like a chameleon, taking its color from the character and personality of the President.[4] The "color" of the presidency makes a difference to some some of the time but it is the nature of the institution, whatever its color, that matters to everybody all of the time. When the Brownlow Committee adopted as its slogan and strategy, "The President needs help," and provided help in the form of presidential assistants and a White House office, it prepared the way for fundamental change in the presidency. The Brownlow Committee believed itself to be making the President a more efficient executive. But its reform proposals, once implemented, also made him more powerful within the executive branch and in relation to the Congress. President Roosevelt, transmitting his version of the Brownlow Committee recommendations to the Congress, depicted them as providing "the tools of management and authority to distribute work" and insisted that they were "not a request for more power."[5] What began in 1939 as an effort to promote administrative reform was continued and enhanced by the legislation of 1947-1949, particularly the legislation creating the National Security Council. The intention, again, was to help the President with the formulation and execution of policy by giving him more and better access to advice and information. The practice and precedents of the "cold" and Vietnamese wars accelerated and deepened the process by further "liberating" the President from executive branch and Congressional constraints.

The ambiguities buried in the technocratic populism of Louis Brownlow, Charles E. Merriam and Luther Gulick were not evident in 1937 when Brownlow said of his committee's recommendations: "There is but one grand purpose, namely, to make democracy work today in our National Government; that is, to make our

Government up-to-date, an efficient, effective instrument for carrying out the will of the Nation."[6] But the latent thrust of these ambiguities became more manifest in the post-war period and in the policy literature, notably of the bureaucratic politics school, it produced.[7] Writers in this post-war tradition continue to found their hopes for greater efficiency, coherence and "rationality" in the President. As one writer puts it after rehearsing the personal and partisan limitations and biases that flawed the motives and actions of actual incumbents, "There is no other choice."[8]

Presidential expansion was not solely or merely a product of administrative reform; it was more fundamentally a product of hopes and aspirations for the presidency on the part of those seeking in the pre-war period social justice at home and after World War II national security abroad. From the Brownlow Committee onward, intellectuals and professionals in the neutral garb of management or policy science have collaborated with Presidents in the essentially political task of expanding and strengthening the presidency. Doing so seemed wholly justified; who else could represent the national constituency and purpose? What other institution or office could create and lead a welfare state to social justice at home and insure national security and international order abroad? The Congress, the states and, later, the cities were seen as representing narrow constituencies and interests and, in any case, lacked the capacity and will to secure needed change.

Proposals since Brownlow have argued that the President must be strengthened, not only because he must efficiently manage a continuously increasing volume and range of responsibilities but also because he should be able to direct and control the vulnerable and amorphous executive branch of government and to protect it from Congressional and interest group rivalry for power and control over policies and bureaucracies. The President is the best hope for policy and administration directed to national goals and purposes; he was said to represent the people, particularly the weak and powerless, against vested and partial interests, and the nation, especially its national interest and security.

Richard Neustadt captured the mood and goals of this school of administrative reform when he invoked Harry Truman's bemused reflection on the surprise he believed was in store for the military man who was to follow: "He'll sit there, and he'll say, 'Do this, do that', and nothing will happen."[9] Neustadt elaborated on this image by contrasting a President in sneakers and a President in boots and spurs, the first the President as he was, the second a phantasy of what he was thought to be. The President in sneakers figuratively pads about the corridors of power in search of leverage, trying to persuade or cajole his putative administrative or political subordinates that what is in his interest is in theirs too.[10]

The organizational and procedural prescriptions that flow from an image of a President in sneakers seek to amplify his influence, enhance and tighten his control, improve the quality and quantity of advice and information and provide the means to counter resistance and sabotage. This model of the problems and needs of presidential power, no doubt, provided a more valid empirical account of the President in action than did conceptions which credited the idea that Presidents could automatically command the organizational behavior they required. This model of the presidency also directly countered conceptions that celebrated or tolerated a pluralism that left the public interest in the hands of Congressional committees, bureaucracies and private interests.

Writing at a different historical moment we take a less sanguine view of presidential power. We do not question that existence or the costs of bureaucratic politics, organizational dysfunctions or interest group liberalism, but we also recognize the limitations and costs of presidential power. Those limitations and costs are visible in the conduct of foreign policy towards South Asia and elsewhere, as well as in the conduct of domestic politics, and they have been with us for some time.

The problem is how to reconcile a Hamiltonian with a Madisonian presidency, i.e., how to reconcile a presidency of energy and initiative with a presidency that is constrained by forms of representation, debate and advice that are at once independent of presidential power but subject to its influence. Among the means to hand, given an understanding of their desirability and the will to act on that understanding, is the institutionalization in policy planning and management of the professional and expert knowledge available in the bureaucracy and the routine and systematic involvement of Congress in the foreign policy government. The deleterious effects of presidential power can be contained and turned in positive directions by recognizing and legitimizing an autonomous but coordinated role for the bureaucracy and the Congress in the foreign policy government. Giving knowledgeable professionals more autonomy and authority will generate, within the executive branch, more collegiality, multiple advocacy, dissent, insulation of policy arenas and, in relationship to Congress, fixed means to consult with and account to a Congress willing and equipped to maintain an independent but cooperative role in the making and conduct of foreign policy.

B. The Relevance of the South Asian Region for Administrative Reform

The focus of this study is the coordination of complexity in South Asia. We address ourselves, therefore, to the value of comparative inquiry by examining why and how the analysis of a particular region provides organizational lessons for the conduct of foreign policy generally.

We start with the assumption that each region can be profitably dealt with as a separate policy arena with a distinguishable "government," composed of United States Government bureaucratic actors concerned with that region. The range and type of USG, foreign governmental, international agency and "private" actors and the norms and patterns that govern their activity and relationship vary significantly by region. So too do the presenting problems and the proximate and distant "causes" of conditions, events and policies.

Among the more salient variables that affect the conduct of foreign policy towards regions are: (1) the level and continuity of

USG interest and attention; (2) the amount and quality of knowledge available at various levels of the USG; (3) constraints in the USG and in the region on USG intervention; and (4) the type, influence and number of private US actors with interest in the region. For example, US government for South Asia has been characterized by sporadic but forceful high level (presidential) attention; like Japan, by little knowledge of high quality at the presidential level and considerable knowledge of good quality at the bureau level; by relatively low levels of constraint within the USG and from the region on USG actions; and by few, relatively uninfluential private actors. (As Ambassador Saxbe put it, to the consternation of some Indians, America's interest in India was largely humanitarian and cultural.) The US government for Inter-American Affairs shares some of these characteristics, but not others. USG attention to Latin America has been similar but not precisely like that towards South Asia. There has been even less of it, but when it has come, it has been sporadic, high level, and sometimes violent. Again, like South Asia, knowledge at the presidential level has been low in quantity and quality. An important contrast between the two regions can be found in the constraints dimension. Constraints on action in Latin America arise not so much from powerful actors within the executive branch or in the region but from the existence of a plentiful supply of private actors and their Congressional allies. According to a recent study, the regional bureau is subject to pressure from a wide range of powerful private interests and has had to face them "alone, without the backing of a counter-constituency" or a President.[11]

The US government for Europe has very different characteristics from those associated with South Asia and Latin America. Relative to other regions, it attracts continuous high level attention. Goodly amounts of high quality knowledge about Western and Eastern Europe are available not only at the presidential and bureau levels but also, and this is distinctive for the European region, on the seventh floor of the State Department among deputy and under secretaries and policy planners. USG intervention in Europe is more constrained than in any other region by competition and conflict among governmental agencies, not least of which are the military and intelligence bureaucracies, and by the existence in Europe of powerful foreign governmental actors, including political personalities who are sufficiently familiar in their culture and style to matter to Presidents and other senior officials. Finally, the plethora of private actors concerned with European-US relations—a result of immigration, trade, investments, and culture—creates constituencies and publics that cannot, taken together, be equalled by any other region.

Differences and similarities among regions imply that certain organizational strategies may be relevant across regions, others not. Organizational proposals should be explicitly examined in this comparative light. Several of our organizational proposals which are designed to strengthen the articulation of policy planning at the regional level, such as the Assistant Secretary Policy Planning Council and the Regional Conference, speak to the problems of other areas as well.

III. DEFINING COORDINATION

A. Imperative and Deliberative Coordination of Complexity

Complexity generates the need for coordination. Scale and diversity compounded by continuous change in conditions and goals characterize the organizational life of governments. Coordination without complexity is easy; if all are alike, they can share the same questions and answers, the same ends and means. Alternatively, coordination is easy if all can be made to be or think alike, an induced form of simplicity captured by the German term *Gleichschaltung*, all on the same wavelength. But these are the conditions of simplicity, not complexity and they are not easily achieved in modern governments. The conduct of foreign policy engages a world of multifarious activities, domains and timeframes that do not ordinarily lend themselves to this kind of direction and control, nor should they.

We have organized the discussion of coordination around two terms, imperative and deliberative. Imperative coordination relies upon the mystique of high office, hierarchy in organizational and personal relationships, and will as the source of policy and of compliance. Deliberative coordination involves the knowledge and judgment of officials, collegiality in formal and informal relationships and reasoned argument and bargaining as the source of policy and compliance. Like all models, these models of two types of coordination simplify and exaggerate in order to generate questions for analysis.

Our argument is counter-cyclical; it tends to highlight the costs of imperative coordination and the benefits of deliberative coordination. Yet we are under no illusion that the world with which the conduct of foreign policy is engaged can do without the benefits of imperative coordination or can be made free from the costs associated with deliberative coordination. Indeed, during the period when this report was being researched and written, the presenting problems for the conduct of foreign policy in the United States may have begun to change in ways that will generate in the not too distant future a need to emphasize in doctrine and practice the virtues of imperative coordination. Even if this proves to be the case, it in no way lessens the importance of learning from the experience of the past decade in South Asia. That experience supports the need to develop the counter-cyclical position argued here.

We take as our text for exploring imperative coordination Henry Kissinger's statement to the Washington Special Action Group meeting of December 3, 1971: "The President is under the 'illusion' that he is giving instructions.. .."[12] The President is invoked. He has been elected by a national constituency, represents the national will and purpose, commands the largest, most comprehensive view of the national interest, has constitutional responsibility for the direction of foreign policy and command of the armed forces, and, as the head of state as well as the head of government, commands the authority, respect and reverence which a secular state in a secular age invests in the highest office of the land. He can generate the majesty associated with a sovereign power and the mystique associated with the attitudes that develop around such thoughts so as to possess the esoteric knowledge and skills associated with a unique calling.

When Henry Kissinger told the assembled WSAG members that the President was under the "illusion" that he was giving instructions he was, of course, mocking them. The implication was clear; some or all of them were not following the President's instructions. The presidential will was being thwarted. The man at the top had declared his policy but it was not being implemented. At best, there was a withdrawal of affect and efficiency, at worst subversion and sabotage.

The instruments of the President's will are the President's men organized in staffs in the White House, elsewhere in the Executive Office and, in the bureaucracies engaged in the conduct of foreign policy. In the imperative mode of coordi-nation, an essential component of effectiveness is to be close to the President and the most recent recipient of his views. President's men are, for the most part, "can-do" policy intellectuals, in-and-outers drawn from the academy, the law, investment houses, business firms, and journalism, whose knowledge of foreign affairs is usually of a general kind. Their appointment arises out of the President's confidence that they share his preferences and their continuance in service depends upon the president's pleasure.

Under imperative coordination, coherence is introduced by the President and the President's men who are depicted as the bearers of the public interest in domestic affairs and of the national interest in foreign affairs. This depiction made considerable sense in the days of Harry Truman, when a relatively weak President confronted great baronies which controlled large blocs of executive power. If presidential power and direction were to replace bargaining equilibriums with coherence, a relatively symmetrical distribution of power had to be replaced by a more asymmetrical one favoring the President, and this began to happen.

As Truman gave way to Eisenhower and Eisenhower gave way to Kennedy, Presidents became, relatively, more powerful and barons less. "Bargaining advantages" were, increasingly, held by the President and his men. In the policy arena of foreign affairs particularly, Congress and its leadership surrendered the bargaining advantages that lay at the roots of their power. In the federal bureaucracy, officials who offered non-presidential alternatives, or more commonly, suggested the costs and dangers associated with presidential decisions and strategies, became increasingly suspect.

Presidents came to live in a world of asymmetrical power relations, isolated from the kind of peership and collegiality that sustain argument and rational discourse and free from the restraints that competition and bargaining among actors in a political market provide.

Relying on the President for coherence made certain assumptions about him: his voice spoke for the people; his will expressed the national interest. But these assumptions proved at best only partially true. The President had his own political interests. The search for "immediate gains visible during the current term,"[13] the personal desire for honor and historical immortality, and the need to prove himself politically and personally too often lead to an activism divorced from the national purpose and interest.[14] Proponents of presidential power lament the fact that Presidents are deeply engaged in partisan and personal politics but see no alternative to imperative coordination by the President and the President's men in the conduct of foreign policy. "One may argue against enhancing presidential influence because of mistrust of a particular Oval Office occupant, or a more general belief that the potential dangers of executive power outweigh the benefits it can bring. But to do so would, for all practical purposes, be to renounce the aim of coherent policy altogether."[15] The argument for deliberative coordination below takes the dangers of executive power seriously but suggests a framework in which coherent policy is possible.

Deliberative coordination is the product of informed argument, rational persuasion and bargaining among knowledgeable professionals representing diverse interests in contexts mandated to consider common problems and recommend joint solutions. In invoking the word deliberative, we mean to invoke organizational arrangements and procedures that enable careful consideration for the matter at hand, a concern of consequences, and attention to the reasons offered for and against proposed measures. A necessary condition for deliberation is collegiality and the peership it generates. There is a direct relationship between the quality and effectiveness of deliberation and the degree of equality that characterizes those engaged in it. Governments are, of course, organized as hierarchies and appointed officials are and ought to be subordinate to elected officials. In the executive branch, the only elected official is the President. At the same time, we are concerned to mitigate the costs associated with administrative hierarchy and presidential power and to gain some of the benefits associated with deliberation among professionals. If Presidents are able to practise imperative coordination without any attention to the benefits of deliberative coordination, the conduct of foreign policy will be devoid of the kind of knowledge and accountability available to lawyers, legislators, politicians, academics, and, in some measure, to participants in formal organizations such as businesses, labor unions, churches, etc. While it may be true that there is no other office like the President of the United States and that this uniqueness is enhanced with respect to his responsibility for the national security, it is also true that the conduct of foreign policy involves the use of knowledge, skills, experience and judgment that are not the special or unique possession of presidents and presidents' men.

The benefits of deliberation in professional life are needed in the conduct of foreign policy. Lawyers are licensed professionals who carry on their work in the context of judicial processes that require adversary procedures. They must write briefs and make arguments that are disciplined by the precedents the law provides and the arguments of their opponents. It is a process that involves deliberation in the sense that we have described it. Legislators engage in the rational examination of proposals in committee, in reports and, to an extent, on the floor through debates and conference procedures. Politicians produce and debate platforms and defend their own record and attack their opponent's record. Legal, legislative and electoral processes require licensed or qualified practitioners to engage in deliberation. In academic life, the work of scholars is scrutinized by other scholars; scholars debate the validity of the arguments and findings of their colleagues and are held accountable by a deliberative process for the knowledge they produce or transmit. Doctors are held accountable by specialized medical boards and by malpractice suits brought by patients in courts. By contrast, Presidents in their conduct of foreign policy have been relatively unconstrained by deliberative processes found in professional and organizational life. Yet the conduct of foreign policy requires knowledge, experience, skills and judgment comparable to those found in professional and organizational life outside the foreign affairs government. Such knowledge and experience is available among foreign policy professionals organized in regional and finctional bureaus. Our arguments for deliberative coordination and our prescriptions for organizational and procedural means to realize it are designed to capitalize on its benefits.

There are family resemblances and differences between the "governmental pluralism" relevant for foreign policy and the interest group pluralism relevant for domestic politics. These comparisons have important implications for our discussion of deliberative coordination. Interest group pluralism in the domestic policy arena powerfully counteracts the hierarchical authority and asymmetrical power relations of the presidentially dominated executive branch. Our recommendations are designed to institutionalize in foreign policy the relative equality of bargaining that characterizes interest group pluralism in domestic politics. Interest group pluralism in the making of domestic policy involves an interaction of groups and their Congressional allies in the decision-making process that fosters outcomes favorable to group interests. Groups with more resources and effective leadership do better than groups with less; those without resources and leadership remain unrepresented. Groups bargain to produce compromise settlements. Losers, groups that find compromise settlements unsatisfactory, can attempt to expand the scope of conflict, bring other groups into the arena of those immediately concerned and establish a coalition with a better prospect of "winning."

But there are important differences that distinguish interest group pluralism characteristic of domestic policy formation and governmental pluralism characteristic of foreign policy formation. One is the nature of the groups constituting the pluralist universe.

Another is the nature of the process shaping policy outcomes. The groups active in interest group pluralism "represent" domestic producer and consumer interests capable of mobilizing electoral and other forms of support. The groups active in governmental pluralism are bureaucratic actors within the executive branch who "represent" expert knowledge and experience on the one hand and bureaucratic interest on the other. Organized interests outside the federal bureaucracy play some part in foreign policy formation but, relative to the domestic policy arena, their influence, with some notable exceptions, is marginal and their participation sporadic.

It is this difference that makes it possible to distinguish between interest group pluralism in domestic policy formation and governmental pluralism in the making of foreign policy. This difference profoundly affects the nature of bargaining. Whereas in domestic policy, bargaining occurs among relatively equal actors, in foreign policy formation the actors, insofar as they are affected by administrative hierarchy and operate in the shadow of presidential power, are relatively unequal. The kind of information, argument and rational persuasion that can be brought to bear under conditions of relative equality is more difficult to realize in the context of governmental pluralism where asymmetrical power and authority relationships inhibit or vitiate deliberative coordination.

A second difference that distinguishes interest group pluralism in domestic policy formation and governmental pluralism in foreign policy is the relatively greater importance of professional knowledge, judgment and accountability in foreign policy formulation, choice and management. This is not to say that professional knowledge and judgment are not important components in the formulation and implementation of domestic policy. The difference lies in the relative weight accorded in domestic policy to bargaining shaped by trade-offs, compromises and coalitions based on interests and the weight accorded in foreign policy to bargaining shaped by professional knowledge and experience. It is this difference that establishes the resemblance between the conduct of foreign affairs and the modes of deliberation characteristic of the professions and of scholarship.

If deliberative coordination is to occur within the context of the governmental pluralism that characterizes foreign policy conditions comparable to those that prevail in private professional domains are required. Institutional means and a psychological climate must be created that enable actors to "coordinate" on the basis of informed argument, rational persuasion and organizational accountability. Our prescriptions and recommendations are designed to strengthen such conditions. If governmental pluralism is to avoid the costs depicted in our discussion of imperative coordination and gain the benefits of deliberative coordination, organizational and procedural arrangements that allow relatively equal professional actors to deliberate are required.

It should be clear from the discussion so far that coordination, whatever its characteristics, is not an unmixed blessing. There are costs associated with coordination and these can be understood in terms of the relative success or failure of efforts to coordinate policy formulation and management. "Costs" is a neutral term that implies more or less and is associated with benefits. Costs can also be understood in terms of pathologies of administration, particularly those associated with coordination. For example, clearance, formally designed to foster coordination by informing or involving relevant actors, becomes a pathology when it fosters delays and excessive caution, takes the edge off good proposals, muddies priorities and blocks timely action. As pathology, clearance feeds the propensity of presidential actors to practice imperative coordination, to move the action up and out of the State Department to the Executive Office or White House level. In order to insure timely action and to block those with stakes in the issue from mounting counter-mobilizations and widening the conflict to gain added support, presidents and president's men practice counter pathologies such as non-consultation with informed officials close to the problem, the creation of "closely held" or "tightly held" decision contexts, and secrecy directed against other governmental actors. Other pathologies follow. Bypassing clearance and deliberative modes of coordination generates an underground form of clearance and deliberation in the form of leaks which introduce new or suppressed information and generate advocacy and argument.

Decision-making for the abortive Bay of Pigs operation in Cuba provides a striking example of the pathology associated with imperatively coordinated closely held decisions. Roger Hillsman, the then Director of Intelligence and Research at State knew nothing of the planned Cuban invasion. Overhearing a remark by the then Director of the CIA, Allen Dulles, he asked Secretary of State Dean Rusk about it. Rusk told him not to inquire further because "this is being too tightly held." State's Cuba Desk Officer, Robert Hurwitch, was equally in the dark. "There was, in my judgment," Hurwitch says, "a divorce between the people who daily or minute by minute had access to information, to what was going on, and the people who were making plans and policy decisions."[16]

The Bay of Pigs paradigm points to a more general pathology associated with secrecy and imperative coordination, the growth and operation of a "them and us" division of the world. President's men in the context of the bureaucratic struggle often regard actors in the non-presidential domain as "natural enemies" of the President,[17] identify the President's political interests with the national interest,[18] and believe that foreign policy officials, however expert, are cautious, *status quo* oriented and concerned to maintain good relations with clients of the moment.[19] The operating rule seems to be that the more we know and the less they know the better. In this context, information and advocacy, instead of promoting deliberative coordination, become weapons in a political struggle within the federal executive.[20]

B. An Evaluation of Operational Means for Coordination

Our discussion of coordination in terms of imperative *versus* deliberative has been at a fairly general level. There are operational means associated with particular forms of organization and procedure that require evaluation in the context of our typology.[21] Among the operational means advanced for insuring coordination is good management either in the form of a single high level official charged with "management" or a programming system designed to relate the allocation of resources to the realization of tasks and objectives, or both. The well documented history of the relative failure of management strategies to produce better coordination provides ample reason to doubt their efficacy. Among the lessons is the impossibility in the conduct of foreign policy of separating management from policy. Formal rationality, i.e., the effort to establish the most efficient relationship between means and ends, makes most sense when the goals of an organization are relatively clear and its tasks can be routinized. Put another way, the manipulation of organizational roles, tasks and resources with a view to maximizing output and minimizing input can be most efficiently accomplished when outputs are tangible, simple and predictable. The conduct of foreign policy is at the opposite extreme from the routine and repetitive production of a known product. It involves goals and actions that are, relatively, non-repetitive and, therefore, not easily subject to routine procedures and solutions and it is directed to an environment which is subject to frequent and often radical transformations, including those produced by the feedback effects of policies pursued and actions taken.

Another operating level procedure designed to foster coordination is comprehensive formal policy guidance. From the Eisenhower administration's BNSTs (Basic and National Security Policy Document) through the Nixon administration's NSSMs (National Security Memorandums) and, for a time, including foreign policy messages to Congress, formal policy guidance has constituted an important part of the effort to coordinate foreign policy. The record has not been encouraging. Such documents are too often overrun by events and cannot take account of or anticipate those particulars of a situation decisive for decision or action. Foreign policy messages in particular are often euphemistic, less than frank, or deliberately misleading in their effort to influence external or internal publics and actors. A great deal of effort has been invested over the past fifteen years in preparing such documents. More can be gained, we argue, from line officials close to operations directly and continuously exchanging views.

Standing interdepartmental committees constitute yet another attempt to coordinate foreign policy. Because they constitute an effort to capture the advantages of deliberative coordination by establishing collegial contexts for discussion and decision, we find the idea and the practice of the interdepartmental committee attractive. At the same time, the history of interdepartmental committees in the decade under review reveals problems and tendencies which require change in doctrine and practice. Unfortunately, the more serious the issue and the higher the level at which it is discussed, the less likely is it that appropriate interests and spokesmen capable of collegial interaction and deliberative coordination will be represented. When the fundamental purpose of an interdepartmental committee is to serve the president's will and preferences, then hierarchical behavior will govern discussion, procedure and outcomes, and membership will reflect presidential pleasure. If, on the other hand, committees are designed to foster deliberation among knowledgeable and interested actors, there is some prospect that collegiality will orient the norms governing discussion and decision.

The interdepartmental committee as a means to broadcast presidential preferences and to gain compliance with them is captured by Henry Kissinger's remark, previously cited, at the meeting of a leading interdepartmental committee, the WSAG of December 3, 1971: "The President is under the 'illusion' that he is giving instructions.. .." The record as far as it is known of decision-making in connection with the Cambodian invasion of 1970 suggests an even more dramatic conclusion, that interdepartmental committees can be fictional constructs that misleadingly imply consultation: The President sat with himself totting up pluses and minuses on yellow pads and preparing a speech for television without serious consultation with responsible advisors. He told the nation on April 30, 1970, that the Cambodian action was directed at "the headquarters for the entire Communist military operation in South Vietnam." No such communist headquarters was found by the attacking forces, an embarrassment the President might have been spared if he had consulted with almost any State Department official with Southeast Asia experience.

What is constructive about the interdepartmental committee is its potential for deliberative coordination. What is problematic about it is its susceptibility to exploitation by those willing and able to practice imperative coordination. So long as the interdepartmental committee system is dominated by the presidentially oriented National Security Council, it remains too susceptible to presidential influence and manipulation. Insofar as it does coordinate deliberatively as well as imperatively, it is often overweighted with representatives of the Department of Defense interests, particularly those of the services and the joint chiefs. If the conduct of foreign policy is to be political in the best and most comprehensive sense and to be coordinated by deliberative means, a high level committee dominated by State and drawing its membership mostly from within State is required. This leads us to the final practical means of coordination, organizational integration.

The proliferation of mini-state departments throughout the executive branch has created the most serious problem for the coordination of foreign policy. An observation of the Jackson Subcommittee captures what is at stake here: "The National Security Council was chiefly the inspiration of James Forrestal, who wanted to enhance the defense role in peace time policy making. .. ."[22] The domestic departments, Treasury, Agriculture, Commerce, and Labor, with major overseas operations also have succeeded in establishing organizational enclaves and procedural requirements to represent their interests in the conduct of foreign policy. The military services and the Department of Defense argue that because they have enormous stakes in the conduct of foreign policy their interests and outlooks should be represented organizationally and procedurally. Many domestic departments and agencies argue that their responsibilities and constituencies generate or involve major U.S. international objectives. These are clear instances of the tail wagging the dog. However elusive a term the national interest is and however contingent and problematic the relationship between domestic and foreign policy, the conduct of foreign policy should aim at something other and greater than the interests of particular federal bureaucracies.

The organization of the government for the conduct of foreign policy has proliferated in ways and to a degree that have, on the one hand, dwarfed the State Department and on the other created problems of scale and complexity of an unnecessary and counter-productive kind. State Department's primacy in the conduct of foreign policy and the radical reduction or elimination of non-State units now engaged in foreign policy activity can be achieved by a strategy of modified organizational integration. What is entailed by such a strategy includes making representation overseas a State Department function. The needs of other departments and agencies can be met by international travel and the deputation of State Department personnel; making routine gathering and evaluation of intelligence, a State Department function; eliminating non-mission connected intelligence activities by the military services and the Defense Intelligence Agency; dismantling of the USIA; furthering the movement of development assistance activities into multilateral agencies; dismantling the Office of the Assistant Secretary of Defense for International Security Affairs and providing the Secretary of Defense with a high level political advisor seconded from the State Department; cutting back the number of personnel serving in the Office of the Secretary of Defense, the Joint Chiefs of Staff and the headquarters staffs of the Army, Navy and Air Force departments; and dismantling the Bureau of Political Military Affairs in the Department of State. In these and other ways, the objective should be to reduce the scale and complexity of the foreign affairs government throughout the executive branch and to restore to a leaner State Department primacy for the formulation and the conduct of foreign policy. In such a context, an Assistant Secretary Policy Planning Council, which will be discussed further in the recommendations section, may be able to make deliberative coordination work.

Our preference for organizational integration as a practical means for furthering coordination is not unqualified. As we will make clear elsewhere in this report and in the recommendations, we recognize the need for insulation of policies with long-run timeframes and of programs dealing with activities that require autonomy. Specifically, certain economic policies and programs and activities associated with education and culture should be insulated from the usual pressures associated with the political struggle and the need for leverage.

IV. A CLOSER LOOK AT COMPLEXITY

Differences in the manifestation of complexity can be specified in terms of (1) organizational levels; (2) variations in timeframes; (3) functions expressed in policies and programs; and (4) regional contexts including variation within and among them. Each manifestation of complexity dynamically intersects with the others in continuously varying contexts. We conclude our discussion of complexity with an examination of variations in the types of diplomacy used by officials to manage complexity, i.e., normal diplomacy, crisis management and strategic diplomacy.

A. Levels

We categorize the complexity of levels in terms of global, regional and bilateral. The categories capture and organize discernable differences in organization, procedure and action in the conduct of foreign policy. Global perspectives and activity are associated with roles in presidential organizations (e.g., White House assistants and staffs, National Security Council, etc.) and with roles at the highest departmental levels, such as the "Seventh Floor" at State and the Office of the Secretary of Defense. Regional perspectives command fewer roles and organizational resources than global and bilateral. The regional bureaus in State and mini-regional units in other departments such as DOD's ISA capture the regional category but in a form diluted by the location of responsibilities at the bilateral level. The bilateral category is organized in the country director system in Washington and in embassies abroad.

The presenting problem for complexity manifested in levels is the parochialism associated with each level. How can each level be given its due in the face of differences of priorities, agendas and claims on resources?

Conventionally "parochialism" is a term of opprobrium that designates a narrow or exclusive attention to local concerns. Parochial officials are thought of as those who confine their attention to a country and have difficulty looking beyond bilateral relations and the needs of clientelism. They are thought of as parochial because they fail to relate their "client's" concerns to the broad framework of U.S. national interest.

Client parochialism is not the only form of parochialism. Global parochialism is another. The wide-angle vision of the global perspective loses particular information and detail. Its lens focus blurrs intra-regional linkages and country issues. This loss of information about proximate causes and presenting issues detracts from the adequacy with which foreign policy is conducted. The "mere" details seen by the bilateral and regionally oriented observer have critical implications for the global perspective even as the global vision indicates judgments and actions that regional or country perspectives may ignore or discount.

Parochialisms are theories about the world of foreign policy. As more or less articulated and systematized theories, they furnish the minds of key actors by identifying for them entities, processes and relationships and by shaping the way they know and explain what happens. Parochialisms as theories generate an observational language that establishes what counts as a fact and as a mistake and supply criteria for proof and validation. For example, when the "structure of peace" is defined in terms of "balance" among the superpowers and in terms of "linkage" that relates regional and lesser states to them in subordinate and reflexive relationships, those who conduct foreign policy are constrained to perceive and explain what they are doing and why they are doing it in these terms. As Gerald Heeger and Stephen Cohen suggest in their studies, such a definition of the structure of peace constitutes global parochialism. It creates a frame of mind among middle level actors in Washington and the field that lowers the salience and relevance of countries not essential to the hypothesized "global system," invites selectivity in reporting the facts and skews recommendations to fit the theory.

Too exclusive reliance on any one perspective, global, regional or client parochialism, is likely to jeopardize the conduct of foreign policy by divorcing it from "reality." As the Secretary of State, in an interview with James Reston, put it: "In the Bureaus—in the geographic bureaus—the relationship between a more conceptual approach and a more operational approach has not yet been fully balanced."[23] The cure for giving undue weight to any one parochialism is not to give undue weight to another. What is needed theoretically and institutionally are middle range concepts and organizational arrangements that mutually engage global, regional and country perspectives in the formulation of the national interest. Deliberative coordination, as we have defined it above and as we operationalize it below, provides a context and a process for involving the regional bureaus and the embassies in policy planning and management in ways intended to give each level its due.

B. Time

The time dimension of complexity is characterized by the critical contrast between simultaneous events and relationships, on the one hand, and sequential events and relationships, on the other. Simultaneous or synchronic time conceptualizes complex events and relationships in a limited timeframe and ignores historical antecedents. Diachronic or sequential time conceptualizes complex events and relationships as they occur or change over a period of time, i.e., historically. The fact that things happen all at once, that they happen together, is a very important and problematic condition for the conduct of foreign policy. Simultaneity creates opportunities, on the one hand, and difficulties, on the other. Opportunities have to do with positive forms of coordination such as creating complementary and reinforcing relationships within and among functional arenas and transferring or translating resources to provide leverage. Simultaneity creates difficulties because the finite nature of human and organizational capacities cannot respond to and process an infinite number of claims. Which claims should be given priority in the allocation of attention, resources and action? Simultaneity requires simplification. It is achieved by theories (world views) and concepts, on the one hand, and priorities, agendas and routines, on the other, that structure perception, organization and action.

Diachronic time or the sequential occurrence of events and relationships over a period of time poses equally difficult challenges for the conduct of foreign policy. The "half-life" (by analogy from a technical term in atomic physics that refers to the time required for half of the atoms of a radioactive substance present to become disintegrated) of the events and processes that constitute the substance of international politics varies enormously. The visitations of world statesmen, international kidnappings and border skirmishes have short half-lives, the development of weapon systems and the consumption of world resources have longer ones. The challenge here is how to order priorities among policies and programs with different half-lives, short term (one month to one year), medium term (one year to five years), and long term (five years and more). The great problem that diachronic time poses for the conduct of foreign policy is the propensity for high level actors to concentrate attention and resources on problems of the short term at the expense of policies and programs directed to the medium or long term. Known as leverage, it concentrates all available means on the solution of an immediate problem.

The durability of the half-life of presenting problems and the policies directed to meet them create an opposite kind of complexity. Long-run policies and programs such as those associated with global strategies, weapon systems and "facilities," because they are thought to entail particular commitments and arrangements with other states, inhibit or preclude short-run or medium-run responses sensitive to the facts and requirements of the moment.

Coordination of the complexity associated with diachronic time is most problematic in relationship to balancing the claims of the short run against the medium and long run. Because Presidents and Presidents' men are peculiarly sensitive to the timing of elections, the vagaries of poll support and the current state of the domestic political struggle, their sense of time gravitates to the short run with consequences that are often problematic for the generation or selection of information and the range of policy options actually considered. Presidents, of course, must be sensitive to elections, to polls and to maintaining their political ascendancy if their conduct of foreign policy is to be accountable to public opinion and the voter. At the same time, the coordination of complexity associated with variability in the nature and consequences of time can be strengthened by heightened consciousness of the risks and costs of sacrificing the medium and long term to the short term and by efforts to devise policies and construct programs that insulate medium and long term objectives from the political struggle at home and abroad.

C. Functional Complexity

Another dimension of complexity is to be found in the variety of activities pursued by the USG in a region. Complexity of governmental functions in a region is distinguished from regional complexity (discussed below) expressed in the variety of circumstances that characterize regions and the states that compose them and from the intra-organizational complexity that characterizes the missions and country teams in the region. Here we are concerned to explore within a regional framework the complexity that arises from the pursuit of a variety of functions and the programs and policies associated with them. The functional arenas to be considered here, primarily in a field context, are military, economic, intelligence, information and culture.

The U.S. foreign policy "government" for South Asia and its environment have undergone considerable change during the decade under review. The decade reveals major changes in players, motives and plot, such as the appearance of Bangladesh and changes of regime, leadership or governments in Pakistan, India and Sri Lanka. Even so, there have been some enduring and critically important characteristics. Among them are the relatively low level of U.S. private investment and commercial activity. Investment in South Asia represents a small fraction of total U.S. investment abroad and the states of South Asia are not among

America's major trading partners. Nor are there, with some important exceptions, major natural or scientific and technological resources located in South Asia that are vital to the U.S. economic or security interests. As a result of these circumstances, Treasury, commerce and labor have not had important stakes in the region, nor have firms, industries and organized economic interests and their allied Congressional committees played an active role in the regional government. In the heyday of bilateral and multilateral development assistance, particularly with respect to consortium and IDA loans managed by the World Bank, Treasury, was, of course, actively involved, but such activities have tapered off sharply in recent years. Such circumstances contrast markedly with, for example, the circumstances associated with the regional government for Latin America.

The major problems associated with the coordination of functional complexity in South Asia over the 1965-1975 decade have involved policies and programs related to security and economic relations. By the end of the decade, both types of programs had markedly declined. DOD, CIA, AID, and USDA, at the beginning of the decade, had important stakes in the region; by its end they no longer had stakes of the kind that existed in the 1960s. The Sino-Soviet split, followed by polycentrism and then detente with the major communist powers, led to the dissolution of the containment policy and, *de facto*, put an end to accompanying treaty arrangements that affected South Asia, CENTO and SEATO. At the opening of the decade, AID was engaged in administering large scale development assistance programs but by its end it had closed up shop in Delhi, for a time its largest recipient, and was doing business elsewhere in the region within the framework of a much reduced U.S. aid budget. USDA which, in the 1960s, in the context of agricultural surpluses served producer interests by sending billions of dollars and millions of tons of concessional food aid to the subcontinent, in the 1970s, in the context of scarcity, served the same interests through high price commercial sales. USDA's interest in sales for hard currency reduced its stakes in South Asia compared to those it held in the days of domestic and world surpluses.

With the closing of the U-2 base in Peshawar and other facilities in Pakistan, the CIA and DOD no longer had the kinds of vital stakes they once did. The conflict between the interests of the military and intelligence bureaucracies, which required good relations with Pakistan, and the aid and food bureaucracies which, while not indifferent to good relations with Pakistan, required good relations with their principal client, India, had subsided, fueled at best by the legacies and memories of the earlier era. For example, the resumption of military sales to Pakistan in 1975, while in part arising from the legacies of the earlier era, was argued and promoted by a rather different constellation of actors and done for a different reason (having to do primarily with domestic politics in Pakistan) than the large scale military aid programs of the period prior to 1965.

Changed world views, captured in strategies and slogans, have affected the content and structure of functional complexity in South Asia. The romance and promise of Third World development, the humanitarian concern to help the needy and the efforts to insure peace in the long run by a more equitable distribution of world resources, like the strategies of containment or counter insurgency to promote U.S. security, are now challenged by doctrines of "triage" and "life-boat," detente with Russia and China, and threats to counter "strangulation" with force. In South Asia, the presenting problems of the 1970s are defined by the geopolitics of the Indian Ocean, particularly its relation to Middle East oil, and by nuclear proliferation. Also present but of lesser concern is the fate of agricultural and industrial development in Third World countries faced with quadrupled oil prices. Under these new circumstances the DOD, particularly the Navy, and ACDA have developed major stakes in the region. The U.S. agencies active in formulating policy and funding for multilateral efforts to assist South Asian states to finance the import of critical resources, such as Treasury and State's Bureau of Economic and Business Affairs (EB), or those active in food policy, such as USDA, AID, and, not least, the Secretary of State and his staffs, also are among the actors that constitute the new dimensions of functional complexity in the South Asian government.

The process of decline and transformation is also apparent with respect to information and cultural functions. The USIA "presence" varies somewhat by country but its influence and impact are well below that which prevailed at the beginning of the decade. How much the decline in demand for library services, speakers and performing arts is related to the decline in supply and quality resulting from severe budget cuts and how much from indifference and hostility to American cultural products is hard to determine precisely. But there can be little doubt that the decline in the influence and impact of USIA programs is related to negative public responses to the U.S. policies and consequently to America's reputation and appeal. A similar fate has affected State Department programs such as those that deal with Fulbright and Visitor Exchange. The 1967 revelation concerning indirect CIA funding of labor, student, research and cultural organizations did considerable damage to them and, more serious, contributed to a climate of opinion which makes it possible to accuse with impunity any U.S. citizen or organization of CIA connections. The decline in America's reputation and appeal also affected the Peace Corps, whose program in India in the mid-60s was once its largest. Government of India policies, reflecting a growing tendency towards cultural nationalism, exacerbated the decline of U.S. people to people programs. They forced the closing of U.S. (and other) libraries-cum-cultural centres, and, for a time, cut the flow of U.S. (and other) visitors, academic programs, and scholars to a trickle. The nadir for U.S. cultural policy and programs was probably reached in 1971, when USG policies and actions alienated Indian, Pakistan and Bangladesh governments and public opinion. The Joint Commissions for trade and commerce, science and technology and education and culture established at the time of the Secretary of State, Henry Kissinger's, October, 1974 visit to India reflect an upturn in the prospects for people to people diplomacy and promise further reconstruction of cultural relations.

The record of functional complexity in South Asia makes clear the difficulty of reconciling the divergent interests of USG actors in the region. The "government" for South Asia in Washington as well as in the region lacks the means to coordinate functional complexity. Its reconstruction should include organizational integration focused on the State Department, particularly the scaling down or elimination of policies, programs, and operations outside State's direct control. The creation of contexts for deliberative coordination in the field and in Washington will also be helpful. Finally, insulation of medium and long-term interests in multilateral economic agencies and autonomous governmental units or quasi-private organizations for cultural and educational programs and for the Peace Corps can inhibit if not prevent the kind of precipitous declines in receptivity for such programs that occurred in South Asia over the past decade.

D. Regional Complexity

A presenting problem for the consideration of regional complexity is that regions as policy arenas are not adequately recognized nor organizationally articulated in the bureaucratic structure of the USG. Regions require organizational articulation because they are the most frequent source of international crisis. Present policy mechanisms are oriented to bilateral or global rather than regional policy formulation and management.

"Regional governments," particularly in their field dimension, are the least articulated and organized interests among those represented in governmental pluralism. By regional governments we mean the network of U.S. bureaucratic interests and actors that deal with the South Asia policy arena. Organizational actors are physically divided between those in the field and those in Washington, and each set is normatively "divided" by the claims of other orientations and roles. In Washington, the authority and bargaining advantages of bilateral and global actors and, in the field, the authority and bargaining advantages associated with ambassadors, country teams and specialist roles tend to be superior to the authority and bargaining advantages of actors concerned to articulate regional problems and policies. Among the states of the region, regional identities and institutions are, relative to national, also weakly articulated and organized.

Another presenting problem for regional complexity is the diversity of field environments within regions. The States of South Asia are complex in a variety of dimensions: regimes with different ideologies, governments with different policies, cultures with different ways of life, and economies with somewhat different needs and possibilities.

In Washington, South Asia is officially defined by two country directorates in a regional bureau of eight country directorates. One deals with Pakistan, Afghanistan, Bangladesh (NEA/PAB); another with Bhutan, Nepal, India, Maldives and Sri Lanka (NEA/INS). This composite regional bureau encompassed six additional Near East country directorates (including the North African Arab states); three deputy assistant secretaries, only one of whom, usually, is responsible for territorially defined South Asian affairs, and a regional affairs unit (NEA/RA) responsible for a variety of functional policy arenas.[24] A number of other actors can be located within the loosely defined boundary of South Asia regional government: actors at the under secretary level and other seventh floor units such as the Policy Planning Staff (in the Department of State); the Office of South Asian Affairs in AID's Bureau for Near East and South Asia (AA/NESA) and a variety of other AID functional units at various levels; and territorially defined South Asia units or functional units with South Asia concerns in the Executive Office of the President, including the White House, the National Security Council, the Central Intelligence Agency and the Office of Management and Budget; the Arms Control and Disarmament Agency; the United States Department of Agriculture; the Department of Commerce; the Treasury Department; and a variety of statutory, administrative and *ad hoc* interdepartmental committees.[25] Especially important in the environment of Washington USG actors dealing with South Asia policy are the ambassadors and embassy officials of South Asian states.[26]

These field, environmental and Washington characteristics of regional complexity are obstacles to the articulation of the regional idea and reality in organizational and policy terms. The coordination of regional complexity involves, in the first instance, improved institutionalization of the regional dimension. Several of our recommendations are designed to meet this necessary condition.

Most of the troubles with which the conduct of foreign policy has to deal arise in the relations among neighboring states. Distance under the technological conditions of modern warfare is a decisive deterrent to war among non-neighbors. Only the two superpowers can easily and readily fight wars against non-neighbors, or make it possible for others to do so. But the weak and amorphous nature of regional government limits its capacity to deal with crises that arise regionally from tensions and conflicts among neighboring states.

Policies and programs too are rarely formulated and implemented in regional frameworks yet policy needs and problems, like crises, are often region-specific. Variations among regions are greater for the most part than variations within regions; data that measure and organize regional characteristics and problems are often a better guide for policy formulation than aggregative world data designed to capture and define policy needs in arenas such as population, food, resources, trade, and science and technology. More important, regional needs and problems, unlike world needs and problems expressed in disembodied and abstract terms, can be connected to political forces and actors, to people on the ground with ideologies, policies and interests.

Our formulation of the nature of regional complexity and the problems for the conduct of foreign policy associated with it point to the need for conceptual, organizational and procedural reforms designed to strengthen regional government.

E. Complexity Management

Like policy, complexity has to be managed if it is to be coordinated. In this section, we distinguish, characterize and evaluate three types of complexity management—normal diplomacy, crisis management and strategic diplomacy.

By normal diplomacy we refer to those activities and tasks (e.g., political reporting; lateral clearance) which recur on a fairly regular and predictable basis even though their substantive content may be subject to rather large variations. By crisis management we refer to responses to events which threaten peace and security, particularly those that have a high saliency for U.S. interests. Unlike normal diplomacy, crises are unpredictable (although, of course, some can be anticipated). Strategic diplomacy deals with the relationships among the great powers including the rare but significant occasions when fundamental realignments occur. It is exemplified by the opening to China and the deepening of detente with the Soviet Union. Strategic diplomacy involves, then, the orientation and reorientation of great power relationships in the attempt to shape and manipulate the balance of power at the global level.

There are certain organizational implications that follow from these analytic distinctions. In the repertoire of organizational resources available for the conduct of foreign policy, some organizations are more suitable for one or several types of diplomacy and less suitable for others. Clearly, normal diplomacy is, in the first instance, the responsibility of the Department of State and U.S. embassies abroad. Strategic tends to be "presidential." The White House offices, including particularly the assistant to the President for national security affairs and the National Security Council (which, *inter alia* engages the attention of the secretaries of state and defense, the chairman of the Joint Chiefs of Staff, the director of the Central Intelligence Agency, etc.) have been the home of strategic diplomacy. In between normal diplomacy and strategic diplomacy lies crisis management. While we are not aware of any quantitative studies that use these or like terms to establish a distribution of activity or resources as among these three modes of conducting foreign policy, crisis management probably occupies the largest single proportion of time for higher level ("White House") personnel in organizations concerned with the conduct of foreign policy.

Because one of the characteristics of normal diplomacy is the relatively high degree to which activities recur, regularity and predictability make it possible to subject tasks and activities to organizational routines. On a scale bounded by predictability at one end and randomness at the other, crisis management is the least stable, normal diplomacy the most. Strategic diplomacy is ordinarily fairly stable although subject to occasional abrupt change. What concerns us here is the suitability of organizational capacity to the type of activity involved in the conduct of foreign policy. Crisis management involves the most difficult and problematic area. Yet it is precisely here that shifts in the location of action tend to occur, i.e., there is a certain instability in the organizational responsibility for crisis management. Conversely, there is a certain stability in the relationship between organizations and the management of normal and strategic diplomacy.

When crises occur there is a general tendency for the action to move up and out of those levels of the state department that are country and regionally informed. Action moves from roughly the embassy and country director level beyond the assistant secretary to the seventh floor policy planning levels and out to the White House and National Security Council. Efforts have been made to stabilize these relatively unstable organizational responses by creating such entities as senior review groups (SRGs) and Washington special action groups (WSAGs), arrangements designed to unite White House generalists with State Department professionals. But these have not been entirely satisfactory; they have not operated, in South Asia, to overcome several important undesirable effects which follow the movement of action up and out under crisis conditions.

One is the separation of professional from generalist knowledge, another the conflict between professional authority and presidential power. People who know most about the bilateral and regional relations involved in a crisis tend to lose control of the action; people who know most about strategic diplomacy and the global balance of power and least about bilateral and regional relations gain control. The result is not only that different organizational actors become dominant but also that they impose on the understanding and the analysis of the situation a different vocabulary and a different world view. It is in this sense that there is a separation of knowledge and power. Crisis management as it has been practiced also distorts or disrupts the coordination of time and functional complexity by subordinating longer term policies and programs to an often undiscriminating use of leverage directed toward "winning" in the short run and by subordinating political goals and means to military.

V. FINDINGS

A. Crisis Diplomacy and Imperative Coordination

The findings of the case studies in this report and our interviews in South Asia and Washington provide the bases for the organizational and procedural changes we recommend. Other often more detailed findings and additional recommendations can be found in the case studies. Here we present and analyze findings relevant for certain large issues in organizational change, drawing, where appropriate, on the cases for evidence and arguments.

Among our principal findings are: (1) Coordinating organizations and procedures of the Johnson and Nixon administrations failed to sustain compatible policies at the global, regional and bilateral levels. By unnecessarily subordinating regional and bilateral to global considerations, gratuitous losses were suffered in regional and bilateral relations. (2) The substantive failure of coordination among levels was related to the absence of organizational arrangements and of norms that adequately enlisted professional knowledge, experience and judgment. (3) Coordination under conditions of crisis diplomacy was effective but not successful because presidential initiatives, direction and control narrowed the scope of consultation and/or constrained deliberation in ways that blocked the appreciation of available information and options. The formulation and coordination of policy was relatively effective and successful under conditions of normal diplomacy because more collegial conditions supported deliberation and engaged bureaucratic interest and their professional knowledge. (4) Policies designed to further interests or achieve goals with longer run timeframes were less easily understood and justified than policies with short-run objectives and more immediate benefits. Because the need for leverage to solve crises in the short run was especially suited to presidential needs for political effectiveness and success, policies and programs directed to the longer term were sacrificed to the requirements of leverage.[27] (5) Presidential preferences for closely held decisions and/or personal control of plans and operations blocked non-presidential, line officials from knowledge of operative assumptions relevant for related policy arenas and, in turn, cut off presidential level actors from information, arguments and options relevant to the closely held decisions or operations.

We have categorized the studies of the conduct of foreign policy in South Asia over the past decade under two of the terms drawn from our discussion of the management of complexity: (1) crisis management, and (2) normal diplomacy. (The third term, strategic diplomacy, plays an important but indirect role in the crisis management cases.) Two cases fall under the first category, eight under the second. The crisis management cases, Johnson's food aid policy of 1965-66 and the formation of Bangladesh in 1971, exhibit two characteristics: (1) the strongest possible presidential level involvement, assertion of presidential preference and will, and use of imperative coordination, and (2) the absence of deliberative coordination in dealing with complexity (e.g. the absence of a balance between generalist and professional knowledge to promote the mutual appreciation of information, informed discussion and the representation of bureaucratic interests; between global, regional and bilateral levels of policy; and between longer- and shorter-run timeframes).

1. *Food Aid and the Primacy of the Presidential Will*

The first crisis management case (see James Bjorkman, "Public Law 480 and the Policies of Self-Help and Short-Tether: Indo-American Relations, 1965-1968") deals with President Johnson's food aid policy. In it, the President personally intervened to secure the aid and later, to control, in considerable detail, the amount and timing of its allocation. Johnson's food aid policy was a composite of many features. Partly in response to the efforts of the Ford and Rockefeller Foundations and to Chester

Bowles' conversations with Nehru, the Government of India (GoI) from about 1963 had begun to shift its development strategy from a heavy emphasis on industrialization to an increased attention to agriculture. Its interest in agricultural self-sufficiency was strengthened by the food aid cut-offs that followed the Indo-Pakistan war of 1965, and was accelerated by the severe food shortages that followed the monsoon failures of 1965 and 1966. In 1964, Ambassador Chester Bowles had begun a massive effort to relate U.S. aid to positive Indian initiatives in the agriculture sector.[28] This emphasis, in turn, was to be coordinated with policies and programs for industry, export promotion and population control. In the spring of 1965, these proposals under the direction of John Lewis, Director of AID, India, were translated into a detailed agenda for American aid over a five-year period. The strategy was predicted on Indian responses leading to food self-sufficiency in five years.[29] The World Bank, which was coordinating efforts and perspectives with those of the United States, joined these efforts in 1965 by coupling bank assistance with relaxation of licensing, devaluation and self-help in agriculture.

All of these efforts began to acquire urgency after the monsoon failure of 1965. In Fall, 1965, India requested and began to receive food aid. President Johnson ordered that the aid be put on stream on a short-term basis, in order, he said, to "judge requirements month by month," and assure that "India changed its farm policy."[30] Chester Bowles, citing American press commentaries, believed the reasons were different. "By this time a delay in granting economic assistance to India . . . was interpreted (often correctly) as an attempt by the administration to force the recipient nation to change its position on Vietnam," he wrote Bill Moyers on August 26, adding that such tactics would damage the good name of the President and of the United States.[31] In 1966, President Johnson promised additional food aid to Mrs. Gandhi during her March visit to the United States, and undertook a massive, successful effort to mobilize the House and Senate on behalf of food aid. This effort resulted in the joint Congressional resolution of April 19. Once again he proceeded to put food shipments on a short tether, and took personal charge of the dispatch of grain shipments. "I became an expert on the ton by ton movement of grain from the wheat fields of Kansas to ports like Calcutta. I described myself as 'a kind of country agricultural agent with intercontinental clients'."[32]

Ambassador Bowles saw the matter differently: "[President Johnson] embarked on a foot dragging performance that I still fail to understand. Assuming personal charge of a program, he adopted what was referred to in Washington as a 'short tether approach' holding up authorization for new shipments until the very last moment. ... This placed the Indian rationing system under almost impossible strain. India's needs could be met only by an uninterrupted stream of grain shipments. .. ."[33]

President Johnson's expressed motives for the strategy were to enlist other countries in the food effort, to shock India into a more expeditious approach to agricultural reforms, and to persuade Congress that he was hard-headed about food, not a rat-hole man, and would insist on self-help and early self-sufficiency. It is also true that the interruption of food aid, from August to December, followed Mrs. Gandhi's joint communique with the Soviet government condemning the Vietnam War, and accompanied repeated similar provocations—such as birthday greetings to Ho Chi Minh.

The August to December *de facto* food aid cut off followed by less than two months India's decision of June 6, 1966, to devalue the rupee in the face of enormous pressure by the USG and World Bank. Coinciding with a second massive failure of the monsoon, the cut off wrought havoc with an Indian food policy premised on American commitments. The anticipated food and development assistance aid needed to cushion the consequences on food prices of the devaluation was delayed for six months and anticipated large-scale consortium aid for subsequent years did not materialize.

The President believed the policy was a success. He related the self-help efforts of 1966-67 in India to it, as well as to the $200 [of $725] million contributed to food aid by other foreign donors. Again, Chester Bowles saw the matter differently: "It is a cruel performance. The Indians must conform; they must be made of fawn; their pride must be cracked. Pressure to improve India's performance was sensible, but . ..in this way ...d istrust and hatred are born among people who want to be our friends."[34] In retrospect, it seems evident that the August to December "delay" in food shipments played an important part in vitiating India's effort to keep its economy stable in the face of the consequences of the 1966 summer monsoon failure, the rupee devaluation, and the delay and subsequent unavailability of consortium aid. President Johnson's pressure operated to weaken the influence of those Indians who advocated a more liberal economic strategy, including devaluation and de-controls, by emphasizing the link among food and development assistance, adherence to American economic advice, and silence with respect to President Johnson's Southeast Asia policy.

From the point of view of organizational prescriptions, the notable features of the case are President Johnson's personal and direct involvement and his isolation from professional advisors on Asia. Bowles notes that here, as in other cases, Johnson frightened advisors out of their willingness to take initiatives: "Even the senior officials in our government dealing with India's food problem became so intimidated that they refused to make even those decisions which they could have made for themselves."[35]

The President explicitly saw himself as opposed in his actions by the professionals concerned with South Asia, and was confident he was right: "I stood almost alone, with only a few concurring advisors, in this fight to slow the pace of U.S. assistance, to persuade the Indians to do more for themselves, and to induce other nations to lend a helping hand. This was one of the most difficult and lonely struggles of my Presidency."[36]

The food aid case has in common with the Bangladesh case the element of unnecessary cost. If President Johnson hoped to exact silence from the GoI on Southeast Asia, which he does not acknowledge as a goal in *The Vantage Point*, but which observers of his administration assure us was his goal, Dulles' failure to influence Nehru under similar circumstances might have warned him off. Further, it seems unlikely that the self-help efforts of 1966-67 were speeded by the short tether policy. Such efforts were agreed upon and set in motion by 1965.[37] And it is unlikely that the Congress required the short tether as proof of hard-headedness. When Congress passed a supporting resolution in 1966 before the August hold up, the most significant factor in its doing so was the Congressional mission to India in late 1966, headed by Congressman Poage, chairman of the House Agriculture Committee. It seems unlikely too that short tether influenced U.S. allies to help with food aid. More influential were the mission of Under Secretary of State Engene D. Rostow and direct appeals to them by the GoI. If these goals were won by means other than the short tether and GoI could not be silence with respect to United States policy in Vietnam, it becomes apparent that the policy resulted in unnecessary costs—the discrediting of liberal economists and policy-makers in India; the loss of Indian goodwill and harm to America's reputation for disinterested humanitarian and development assistance.

However tenuous counter-factual arguments are, there is good reason to believe that a more routine handling of food aid policy for India, i.e., greater reliance on normal diplomacy, would have avoided such costs and secured the short-run and long-run benefits contemplated by key actors such as Ambassador Bowles.

2. *Bangladesh and the Dominance of the Global View*

The Bangladesh case of 1971 (see Philip Oldenburg, "The Breakup of Pakistan") illustrates how, despite organizational and procedural arrangements designed to engage generalists and professionals with each other in crisis management, a global policy orientation and imperative coordination exclude the regional and bilateral perspectives of professionals. As one former senior official put it, "Our policy [in 1971] ...s eems to me to have been a classic case of doing the wrong thing in a regional situation for the sake of wider relationships. .. ."[38]

The case depicts an extreme instance of the lack of engagement between global president's men and regionally oriented professionals. In judging the lessons of the case, it is important to recognize the difference between communication and engagement among administrative layers. Oldenburg's account establishes that information flows to the top were plentiful, continuous, informed and accurate. There is no question that those at the top were formally informed and presented with alternative evaluations and courses of action. When we say there was no engagement, we mean that there was no "appreciation" of the information supplied, no attempt to reason together, to jointly assess meaning or judge implications. The obverse of Henry Kissinger's remark at the WSAG meeting of December 3, 1971—"The President is under the 'illusion' that he is giving instructions ..." [39] was that officials of the South Asia establish-ment and other high-level officials outside the Department of State were under the illusion that they were providing information and policy guidance to the President. Much of the conflict took the form of Henry Kissinger and the President against everybody else. As one senior official observed, nobody saw it their way.

There were at least four areas in which actors with global roles and actors with regional roles "saw" different facts and made different judgments: (1) Was the crisis primarily global or regional? (2) What counts as the use of force in international politics? (3) What counts as a political settlement and were prospects for a political settlement promising? (4) Did India intend to "dismember" West Pakistan?

The main conflict of viewpoint, which governed all other differences, concerned whether the Bangladesh crisis should be regarded as global or regional. In part, this appeared to be beyond the reach of organizational arrangements to change but only in part. Whether only one policy level, global or regional, could be operative, or whether both might have been accommodated, was a matter of what was heard and appreciated.

The President's view of the crisis was stated after the fact in the State of the World Message of February 9, 1972:

> It was our view that the war in South Asia was bound to have serious implications for the evolution of our policy with the People's Republic of China. The country's attitude towards the global system was certain to be profoundly influenced by its assessment of the principles by which the system was governed. . ..

In WSAG discussions Henry Kissinger generally read events in South Asia to show that their primary significance was their effect on America's relations with the Soviet Union and China. He also read actions by states in South Asia as reflexive of global power strategies. In his 1972 State of the World Message, President Nixon interpreted the December 1971 War in South Asia in terms of the Soviet Union "projecting a political and military presence without precedence into many new regions of the globe;" warned that detente must not be "interpreted as an opportunity for the strategic expansion of Soviet power;" pictured America's stand as discouraging such Soviet aspirations and efforts; and deplored the Soviet Union's failure to prevent "the Pakistani conflict from being turned into an international war."

The questions that Mr. Kissinger's shop asked throughout the crisis turn on how China and the Soviet Union were involved with South Asia and how their involvement in turn affected the security of South Asia. South Asia was important to China, on this reading, because China feared Soviet penetration and influence in the subcontinent. Would the Soviet Union succeed in encircling China from that direction? Since the United States as a superpower was at that time concerned with establishing relationships with China, it needed to assure China that it was prepared to strengthen its ally Pakistan against Russia's ally India and thus limit or deter the encirclement. Furthermore, the United States was concerned to show its prospective ally, China, how it treated allies (such as Pakistan) generally. As one official familiar with the reasoning of the Kissinger group put it: "If the Chinese were looking to the United States as an ally, what kind of an ally would the United States be? They might learn something from how the United

States treated its ally Pakistan. . . . How we treated our ally Pakistan and how we stood up to India, the Soviet Union's ally, would indicate how we would act with respect to our allies generally. The United States did not go in for a pro-Pakistan tilt *per se* but rather engaged in behavior consistent with these kinds of concerns."

Officials close to Mr. Kissinger stressed the fact that the Soviet Union had decided to "back the Indians" in the Bangladesh crisis. "The Soviets dropped their earlier efforts to restrain India. They signalled the Indians that they could go ahead." Reports in October that the Soviet Union was willing to allow India to go ahead contrasted with reports on Soviet policy and intentions in July when it was thought that the Soviet Union wanted India to avoid war and wanted to preserve its influence and good relations with Pakistan. By this account, some time late in August it became apparent that the Soviets stopped urging India to avoid war. The global and reflexive interpretations reached their apogee when Henry Kissinger, returning on December 14, 1971 with President Nixon from the Azores where they had conferred with President Pompidou of France, signalled the Russians in a backgrounder that unless they restrained India "very soon" the "entire U.S.-Soviet relationship might well be reexamined" including the upcoming summit scheduled for May, 1972."[40]

This view is composed of two elements, one having to do with policy choices and the other having to do with perceptions of facts. The first element, the emphasis on a global conceptualization, selects global actors (China, Russia, United States) as the most significant element and the lever that effects action. The second element, related to the first, is a factual supposition about motives; non-global powers' actions are mainly reflexive of the needs and strategies of global powers, a supposition that influences perceptions of regional powers' behavior.

Regional officials read events in South Asia differently. India had interests and capabilities. Its decision about the use of force was a result, it thought, of the burdens that ten million refugees imposed and the progressively unlikely possibility that a political settlement would relieve them. There were gains for India; an independent Bangladesh meant a weakened and discredited Pakistan. Nor did they ignore Soviet interests and influence. It was, they held, one among a number of factors that shaped Indian action, not the overriding one. One official, noting that Mrs. Gandhi had gone to Moscow after her abortive November visit to the United States, characterized her conversation there more in terms of bargaining interdependence than reflexive subordination when he said: "She told the Russians she was going ahead and they said okay, if you must."

One can imagine another sort of report on Mrs. Gandhi's visit to Moscow that would interpret her conversations there in terms of them telling her what to do. Because the Kissinger shop was confident that Moscow was telling her, responding to India became much less important than signalling the Russians—as the *Enterprise* and backgrounder on the way back from the Azores did.

Does all of this mean that the China opening was, indeed, the real rationale for tilt? Many of our interviewees thought it was. Otherwise they found the tilt inexplicable. But some did not. One thought that the China factor made for good retrospective rationalization of American policy by providing a good reason as against bad reasons for the bad policies pursued. He argued that on balance the China factor was not the overriding reason for the U.S. policy. More important in his view were Mr. Nixon's prejudices and the need for striking initiatives in time for the elections.

Line officials concerned with the region entertained different assumptions about actors' motives than did global generalists on presidential staffs. Professionals credited the influence on regional actors of what they thought Russia's and China's and the U.S.' goals and actions might be but they were also deeply influenced by factors in the region: the economic and political problem of the refugees for India; the standing of the Awami League in the Pakistan political equation; the potential strategic gains for India of an independent Bangladesh. These judgments led to different conclusions about what signals and actions—the *Enterprise*, negotiations with Mujib—would generate desirable outcomes.

Global generalists and regional professionals differed on what counts as the use of force in international politics. In part, this question relates to the "facts" about who starts a war and they in turn relate to the kind of events that count for starting war.

For the secretary of state the facts that counted were, who bore the "major responsibility" for "broader hostilities" and what was meant by broader hostilities. Charles Bray III, the State Department spokesman, stated on December 4 that "India bears major responsibility for the broader hostilities." George Bush, over the next few days at the U.N. and on television, referred to India's action as aggression, and Henry Kissinger, in WSAG meetings, after wondering whether the facts of the Pakistan attack on India's airfields might have been misperceived (December 3: "Is it possible the Indians attacked first that day and the Paks simply did what they could before dark?") stated on December 6 that the President "is not inclined to let the Paks be defeated" and on December 8 that "the President believes that India is the attacker." Richard Helms, the Director of the CIA, at the WSAG of December 4, gives a different interpretation: "We do not know who started the current action (in East Pakistan), nor do we know why the Paks hit ...I ndian airfields yesterday." After the fact, CIA analysts wondered whether Pakistan escalated hostilities from the local to the international level to save a deteriorating situation by bringing in third powers or to win a decisive military victory from which to bargain.

By December 7, when Henry Kissinger held the backgrounder briefing that Senator Goldwater introduced into the *Congressional Record* of December 9, he had abandoned his question of December 3 about who had attacked first that day. Instead, he told the reporters that "On November 22nd, military action started in East Bengal." (The Indians acknowledge a "local" attack on the border town of Bovra on November 20 to end, as they put it, Pakistan shelling of Indian "villages.") He then went on to say that "international anarchy" would result if "the right of military attack is determined by arithmetic." India's population was 500 million and Pakistan's 100 million. The issue was, he said, should the United States "always be on the side of the numerically stronger?" and the answer was, of course, no.

Other kinds of facts were counted by professional middle-level officials as relevant to judgments about the use of force in international relations. For most of them, the Pakistan government's violent repressions, confirmed by AID, U.S. consular and World Bank reports, counted as the use of force. They saw it directed against the Awami League leadership, middle-class professionals and the civilian population in order to put down protests against the abrogation of the results of the general election that brought the Awami League to power in the center and in the East. They doubted whether a state's internal use of force properly extended to Islamabad's abrogation of the results of the recent (December, 1970) constitutionally conducted election. They also doubted whether killing and repression on a scale that generated 8 to 10 million refugees could be encompassed by the doctrine of a sovereign state's legitimate monopoly of force.

Another central question was what would count as a political solution to the Bangladesh crisis and what were the prospects for one? What was required and, in the light of what was required, what was being done with what effect when?

Before March 25, 1971, when Islamabad began its attempt to suppress the Awami League by force, some of those outside the President and National Security Advisor's immediate circle saw advantages for the United States in a Sheikh Mujib-led Pakistan government; it would be, they held, constitutional and would pursue a moderate foreign policy. Others cautioned against any suggestion of U.S. encouragement to Sheikh Mujib because it would feed West Pakistani fears about the steadfastness of U.S. support. After March, 1971, when Islamabad began what most professionals thought highly unlikely because of the improbability that it could succeed and because of the risk of Indian intervention—the use of violence to hold East Pakistan and to crush the Awami League and its supporters—many officials saw U.S. interests lying with measures designed to stop civil violence and restore peace even though such measures might displease the West Pakistanis.

Once Sheikh Mujib was arrested and imprisoned in West Pakistan, there was fundamental disagreement over what should be done to secure a political solution. Those outside the presidential circle held that some form of negotiation with the imprisoned Sheikh Mujib, the leader of the Awami League which had won a majority of assembly seats in the national election of 1970, spokesman for greater autonomy within a loose federal system, and prime minister-elect of Pakistan, was essential. Whether he was "released" by Pakistan or direct or indirect talks arranged were open and difficult questions, but to most of those outside the immediate presidential circle Sheikh Mujib was seen as the *sine qua non* of a political settlement.

To those who believed negotiations with Mujib were essential, the appropriate path was pressure by the U.S. government on President Yahya Khan of Pakistan, and other key actors, such as Z.A. Bhutto and leaders of army factions, to accept the possibility of autonomy and to negotiate with the majority party leaders. The Kissinger proposal of December 7, for civilian government and autonomy for East Pakistan, was not viable, they thought, because it assumed that even a loosely federated Pakistan could be governed without the participation of the Awami League, whose elected leaders, declared traitors by the Pakistan government, were dead, under arrest, or in exile. The President's approach to a peaceful solution was stated during the heat of the crisis in the Kissinger backgrounder of December 7 that appeared in the *Congressional Record* of December 9 and was repeated after the crisis, in the President's State of the World Message of February 9, 1972:

> Return to civilian rule was pledged for the end of December (1971) and could have increased the chances for a political settlement and the release of Sheikh Mujib. Meanwhile, in August, we established contact with Bengali representatives in Calcutta. By early November, President Yahya told us he was prepared to begin negotiation with any representative of this group not charged with high crimes in Pakistan. In mid-November, we informed India that we were prepared to promote discussion of an explicit timetable for East Pakistani autonomy.

The President and his advisors did not believe that Pakistan either could or should be pushed on release of Mujib. "We will go along," Henry Kissinger told the December 4 WSAG, with reference to political accommodation in East Pakistan, "but we will certainly not imply or suggest ... the release of Mujib." On only one issue were the President and his immediate advisors prepared to bring pressure on President Yahya Khan, sparing Sheikh Mujib's life. President Yahya Khan was advised that Sheikh Mujib was more dangerous dead than alive and the President obtained an assurance from President Yahya that Sheikh Mujibur Rahman would not be executed.

A fourth area where facts were in dispute and judgments differed markedly was India's intentions with respect to West Pakistan. Henry Kissinger warned at the December 8 WSAG that "what we may be witnessing is a situation where a country [India] equipped and supported by the Soviets may be turning half of Pakistan into an impotent state and the other half into a vassal." The theme of dismemberment, of the intolerability of the "complete disintegration by force" of Pakistan referred to by President Nixon in his February 1972, State of the World Message, was based on the "convincing evidence" received during the week of December 6, 1971, "that India was seriously contemplating the . . . destruction of Pakistan's military forces in the West." At the December 8, WSAG CIA Director Helms stated that Mrs. Gandhi "intends to attempt to straighten out the southern border of Azad Kashmir" and that "it is reported . .. [that] she intends to attempt to eliminate Pakistan's armor and air force capabilities." Mr. Kissinger commented that if the Indians do so, "we would have a deliberate Indian attempt to force the disintegration of Pakistan. ... It would turn Pakistan into a client state. ... Can we allow a U.S. ally to go down.. . Can we allow the Indians to scare us off .. .wit h a blockade?"

Later, in the context of the dispute over India's intentions in the West, an intelligence report was leaked to show that the Indian cabinet had discussed action in the West in ways that indicated an intention to dismember Pakistan. The publicly known hawkish proclivities of Defense Minister Jagjiwan Ram were reported in the leaked version, but Mrs. Gandhi's view that a major effort in the West was unwise and would not be attempted was not. The dispatch of the aircraft carrier *Enterprise*, the move which was probably most damaging to American relations with India and Bangladesh, was related to these estimates, as well as to the belief that the critical actor in the South Asian drama was the Soviet Union. In a move that some have characterized as gun-boat diplomacy and others as a dangerous bluff, the *Enterprise* was dispatched to the Bay of Bengal to signal the Soviet Union and India that America meant business on the sub-continent. "If we had not taken the stand against the war," the President argued in his 1972 State of the World Message "it would have been prolonged and a likely attack in the West greatly increased."

On the other hand, there is a trend in the WSAG discussions, coming mainly from the regional professionals but also from others, including the CIA, that India did not have aggressive intentions in the West. CIA Director Helms on December 6 reported that Indian activity in the West "is essentially limited to air attacks." Assistant Secretary Sisco and Deputy Assistant Secretary Van Hollen agreed that the Indians would pull their troops out of East Bengal once the Pakistan forces were disarmed, and AID Deputy Administrator Maurice Williams argued that the Indians, who may "have to give ground in Kashmir" were attacking from Rajasthan into Sind in the South to gain real estate to ward off parliamentary criticism. General John Ryan (representing the Office of the Joint Chiefs of Staff) "indicated that he did not see the Indians pushing too hard at this time [in the West], rather they seemed content with a holding action," and Joseph Sisco "doubted . ..tha t the Indians had the disintegration of Pakistan as their objective."[41]

The Bangladesh case represents a failure of understanding and judgment which improved organizational arrangements and procedures could reach if there were presidential appreciation of their value and the will to use them. Coordination did not succeed in harmonizing global, regional and bilateral interests; it did not harmonize the perspective of policy intellectuals at the presidential level with the professional knowledge of State Department officials in Washington and the field. It is not always possible to do so; not all goals are mutually compatible. But it is an essential element of the case that little effort was made to reason and bargain; to inquire whether China's reasons for agreeing to an opening were compatible with a regional formulation of U.S. interests in South Asia; to consider how much and what kind of support could be given to Bangladesh and to India without tearing relations with Pakistan; to explore realistically what was necessary to restore peace; in short, to establish to what extent and how global, regional and bilateral objectives could be simultaneously realized.

B. Normal Diplomacy and Deliberative Coordination

Normal diplomacy provides more fertile ground than does crisis management for deliberative coordination. However, less desirable attitudes and practices can and do grow in the same soil. The stereotype of the principal practitioners of normal diplomacy, the FSOs, depicts them as the prisoners of low risk routine, unwilling, even unable, to initiate; without imagination or breadth of vision; conventional conformists wedded to the safety and security of the *status quo*. Some of this image is an artifact of the conflict of interest and the struggle for influence between policy intellectuals oriented to presidential interests and favor and career officials oriented to professional knowledge and experience; some is the result of observable attitudes and behavior. Our research for this study and the normal diplomacy cases included in this report do not for the most part support the negative stereotype.

Five of the seven normal diplomacy cases, those by Moulton, Cohen, Kochanek, Hadden and Rubin, depict career officials responding to changed conditions and the need for policy with imagination, flexibility and skill. Lenth's study too, by showing how over time an organization can learn from failure and adapt its ideology and practice to organizational and environmental operating conditions, supports a positive view of normal diplomacy and its practitioners. The findings of Andersen's paper, to be discussed in the context of the need for insulation, are more problematic.

Stephen Cohen's paper on "South Asia and U.S. Military Policy" analyzes three policy contexts: the reformulation of weapons policy in 1966-67, the "one-time" exception to that policy in 1970, and the proposed expansion of the facility on Diego Garcia. The first is of primary interest here because it illustrates how and why deliberative coordination in the context of normal diplomacy works. The second and third, the result of *ad hoc* and isolated high level intervention, dramatize and illustrate the contrast between deliberative and imperative coordination.

Between 1954 and 1965, the USG supplied Pakistan with $750 million worth of arms and in 1962 it supplied India with $90 million worth. At the peak of the programs, American equipment amounted to over 80 percent of Pakistan's weapons. For years there was a "gigantic"[42] Military Assistance Advisory Group (MAAG) in Pakistan and, for a few years after 1962 a "huge" U.S. Military Supply Mission to India (USMMI) in India administering the flow of equipment for six mountain divisions, road building and air defense.

The 1965 war between India and Pakistan revealed the "dismal results" of American arms policy in South Asia to career officials in Washington and the field. Without U.S. equipment, "Pakistan would not have become a serious military power" but the consequences were not those intended. The 1965 war crystallized opinion. By 1965, Cohen finds, there was "remarkable agreement" among FSOs dealing with South Asia about the strategic and military situation in South Asia, an agreement that included the realization that Pakistan could not establish strategic superiority on the subcontinent and that a continuation of USG arms supply would continue to destabilize the regional balance. "This shared perception of local conditions and American interests" was a necessary condition for the reformulation of arms supply policy.

After fighting broke out in 1965, the USG began a policy of treating India and Pakistan identically, first by establishing an embargo on military shipments, then, in 1966, by allowing cash sales of "non-lethal" items. At the same time, the India and Pakistan desks were searching for an arms policy that "would maximize what they perceived to be American interests in the region," including recognition of China's new role as Pakistan's major arms supplier, of the Soviet Union's major role in supplying India's military needs, and of the findings of a major DOD study of military assistance, completed in 1965, that held that most current programs were obsolete.[43] The result, announced on September 23, 1967, was a "willingness to consider on a case-by-case basis the cash sale of spare parts for previously supplied lethal equipment." Grant assistance was terminated and the MAAG and U.S. Military Supply Mission were withdrawn. The policy, by removing the USG from its role as a major arms supplier in South Asia while maintaining limited military-to-military contact and some leverage over Pakistan via decisions over spare parts, reduced the USG's strategic involvement in South Asia.

The USG arms supply policy to South Asia did not, ostensibly, arise from an intention to affect the strategic balance in South Asia but it did effect it. Programs begun in the name of containment became self-justifying and self-perpetuating interests which involved the USG in fueling both sides of an arms race whose consequence, regional conflict, served neither the USG's nor India's or Pakistan's interest. Career officials in Washington and the field, recognizing that changed global conditions (polycentrism, detente and the Vietnam build-up) and unintended and counter-productive regional consequences required action, successfully initiated and coordinated a new policy.

The organizational and procedural characteristics of the "one time exception" of 1970 and the creeping commitment to a facility on Diego Garcia stand in marked contrast to those of the 1967 arms supply. The one time exception to the carefully prepared 1967 decisions foreshadowed some of the difficulties that surfaced in the decision-making and coordination associated with the break-up of Pakistan in 1971. Global (or at least extra-regional) objectives were pursued at the expense of U.S. regional interests in South Asia and imperative coordination practised in ways that isolated presidential level actors from the knowledge and goals of departmental professionals and cut off the professionals, in turn, from formulation of or knowledge about presidential objectives and plans. Earlier, isolated, *ad hoc* presidential intervention had almost upset the carefully orchestrated 1967 arms policy. President Johnson, on an around the world junket, conversed at the Karachi airport with Pakistan President Ayub Khan. Ayub made a statement on Vietnam and President Johnson, in contradiction to his recent support of the new arms policy, made conversational reference to the desirability of supplying tanks to Pakistan via USG pressure on Turkey.[44]

Richard Nixon too, soon after his election in 1968, took a trip around the world. With Henry Kissinger as "mentor and executor," he fashioned "a global foreign policy" that "relegated the Third World to a subservient position .. .important only as individual countries had a special relationship with one of the major power centers." Cohen surmises that Pakistan, "which had stubbornly pursued close ties with China," was one such country. When Nixon visited Pakistan in 1969, he probably "initiated discussions about future U.S.-Chinese relations" and as a *quid pro quo* undertook to modify the 1967 arms policy. Like the Johnson intervention, the commitment was made in an "off hand and casual" way; those in the President's party heard that he wanted to "do something for Pakistan" but no specific policy guidance was forthcoming until mid-1970 when President Nixon, after being reminded by the Pakistan Ambassador of his 1969 pledge and told that no action had followed, demanded immediate action from State Department officials who, in response to NSC requests, had for months been "blindly offering up suggestions without a clear understanding of the reasons for making an exception to the 1966-67 policy." The result was the one-time exception of 1970. More symbolic than substantive (no really offensive weapons were provided), the public justification (offsetting Pakistan's growing dependence on Chinese arms) in retrospect seems "almost comical" in view of Pakistan's intermediary role between the USG and the PRC. The Pakistanis were, at best, disappointed, but cooperated in the hope, no doubt, of better things to come. Whether the Chinese in any way indicated that a condition or price of an opening included sharing the burden of arming its ally Pakistan seems, particularly at this early stage, extraordinarily doubtful. We are left to conclude that the President and his national security advisor, in the face of a variety of other means to establish communication with the Chinese leadership, chose to disturb the South Asian regional balance in ways that, then and later, produced undesirable and unnecessary consequences.

Cohen concludes that, from a regional perspective, the one time exception was "calamitous." He also finds that "had a broader circle of participants been involved in the actual policy decisions during the 1970-71 period, it is quite probable that a way could have been found to minimize the harmful impact on U.S.-Indian relations and still bring off the China visit." Inadequacies in the form and quality of coordination, led to the unnecessary sacrifice of bilateral relations to extra-regional considerations, a result that can be mitigated by "periodic consultation between relevant Country Directors (most urgently, the India, China and Soviet CD's)" and by more frequent consultation among Assistant Secretaries "on issue that cut across their geographic boundaries."

The creeping commitment to a facility on Diego Garcia too is marked by isolated, *ad hoc* presidential-cum-secretarial level intervention. Although Diego Garcia had been an object of naval planning for over thirty years, deliberative coordination in the context of governmental pluralism had, until the mid-1960s, confined action to just that. Cohen reports that until 1973 "the Navy was the only agency which wanted to expand Diego Garcia, and they were successfully neutralized by civilian DOD officials in ISA working in collaboration with regional and functional bureaus (Political-Military Affairs) of the State Department."[45]

The Middle East war in 1973 gave the Navy case a new lease of life. Its ship movements in and around the Indian Ocean, it claimed, were "artificially constrained" for lack of a facility in the Indian Ocean. An alleged Soviet naval build-up in the Indian Ocean required a bigger balancing force. "Before these issues could be fully discussed within the bureaucracy," Cohen reports, secretaries Henry Kissinger and James Schlesinger "took Washington by surprise" when their decision, made "over breakfast," to raise Diego Garcia to the level of a significant support facility was made public. "Diego was to be expanded, and then the expansion would be properly justified in and out of the U.S. government." But by mid-1973, the Washington climate for the conduct of foreign policy had changed significantly; the constraints of governmental pluralism had revived and with them the strengths and weaknesses of deliberative coordination. A "full fledged political battle began to shape up" over Diego Garcia. On June 18, 1973, it became publicly known that the Navy had, on March 20, commissioned (i.e. put into operation) a communication station on Diego Garcia, making the U.S. the first major power to establish a base on foreign territory in the Indian Ocean area. But further expansion, despite President Ford's endorsement at his first news conference, will depend, in the new Washington climate, on something more closely approximating deliberative coordination.

Anthony Moulton's study of "The U.S., the International Development Association and South Asia" documents a dramatic though little known effort to extend the leverage and imperative coordination of the 1971 tilt towards Pakistan to the World Bank[46] affiliate, the IDA. Created in 1960 to make concessional development loans (termed credits) to countries whose per capita GNP is less than $375, the IDA is funded by periodic, non-reimbursable contributions from twenty donor countries. Its governing structure is identical with the World Bank's, which means that Robert McNamara, the President of the WB, is an important actor in the case, as is the U.S. Secretary of the Treasury (then John B. Connally) who, with nineteen other finance ministers, serves as one of the WB's Governors, and instructs the vote of the U.S. appointed Executive Director (simultaneously a paid WB employee and an unpaid special assistant to the Secretary of the Treasury) who, again, is one of twenty Executive Directors.[47] The key agencies dealing with multilateral economic aid, i.e. State, Treasury, the NSC and AID, Moulton finds, apply somewhat different perspectives. State is "enthusiastic,"[48] rarely objecting to IDA projects, concerned to use multilateral aid as a resource in promoting U.S. national interests. South Asia officials in particular "virtually always approve proposed projects."[49] Treasury emphasizes close financial monitoring, as do the Federal Reserve, Commerce and the Eximbank. "In normal times," the NSC staff shares State's view. AID consistently and strongly supports multilateral economic aid from a long-term economic and political perspective.

Moulton examines between December, 1971 and March, 1972 the adequacy of USG organizational and procedural arrangements to deal with two successive issues—IDA credits to India following suspension of bilateral aid to India on December 6, 1971, and an IDA credit to India in March, 1972 for purchase of four crude oil tankers. Policy formulation and implementation occurred in the context of "a pronounced antagonism" towards India that "not only exacerbated Indo-American relations but also seriously jeopardized the U.S.-IDA relationship."

One key factor that constrained U.S. policy in the face of rapidly changing circumstances between December 1971, and March 1972, was IDA's structure and decisional rules. The USG, with approximately 25 percent of total shares, holds the largest portion but by no means a majority of the votes required to decide questions brought before the twenty member Board of Executive Directors. (The minimal winning coalition needed, given the distribution of votes for the required simple majority, is six members.) Important conventions also constrained USG policy and action: Most important, "the WB president never has been defeated on a Board vote; if he were, it is understood he would resign;" IDA credits are usually approved by a consensus rather than by a formal vote of the Board; abstentions and votes against IDA credits are "extremely rare."

(The U.S. has never abstained and voted against only once, on the credit for Indian tankers in March, 1972.)

NSC studies and WSAG meetings in October and November on how to use economic aid as leverage in the context of the crisis in South Asia culminated, in late November, 1971, in a decision to request the WB management to defer action on two Indian credits scheduled for Board action on December 21. Henry Kissinger and John Connally "probably made direct contact with the Bank President [Robert McNamara] by early December." McNamara, after discussions with Bank management in early December, "decided against it [deferral] reportedly in order to avoid charges that the Bank was a tool of U.S. foreign policy. The outbreak of war on December 3 altered the situation by strengthening the USG's hand. On NSC directions, USG representatives successfully negotiated provisos, unprecedented in IDA history, requiring that the projects be unrelated to military operations and unimpaired by the war. Justification for "a non-routine stance on IDA credits to India were articulated to few of the participants" but most of them believed that it was meant to punish India in ways consistent with the December 6, 1971, cut-off of bilateral economic aid. The argument was phrased in terms of bilateral-multilateral "parallelism."

The issue in the USG, during the critical period when the war was in progress (December 3-16), was whether the provisos sufficed or whether the more severe options of abstention, deferral or opposition should be adopted or pursued. The White House and the NSC pressed for "an emphatic U.S. stance" while State (particularly NEA/INS and EB) and AID (NESA), in a joint memo to the Secretary of State, argued for treating the projects (now with the provisos) "routinely" at the upcoming December 21 Board meeting. The memo, which its drafters recommended be communicated to Henry Kissinger and John Connally, noted precedents for Bank lending to countries at war and pointed out that "U.S. opposition or abstention would neither 'penalize' India (since the credits would be approved anyway) nor further our longer run foreign policy interests, either in India or in the World Bank." Kissinger and Connally, who were in frequent contact about the USG stand at the December 21 Board meeting, found the memo orientation and recommendation unsatisfactory. The ensuing policy debate proceeded at two levels, the Secretarial (Kissinger, Connally and Rogers) and the Assistant Secretarial, but inter-level coordination lacked collegiality and an attendant appreciation of views. At the lower level, Assistant and Deputy Assistant Secretaries in State, Treasury and AID consulted with each other and with the NSC and WB staffs to ascertain agency and Bank positions and to attempt to find a mutually satisfactory policy. "Those daily consultations," Moulton observes, "involved contacts with friends and acquaintances and were conducted in informal but well-established channels, primarily by telephone. .. . Participants dealt with each other on equal or near-equal terms. . . ."

Somewhere between December 16 and 20, that is the day the war ended and three days after it ended, Kissinger and the NSC decided on an abstention policy; "... the end of the war undoubtedly being the most important consideration militating against a harder line."[49]

Between the January 11, 1972 and February 29, 1972 meetings of the IDA Board, at which additional credits for India were to be decided, Kissinger "presumably" decided to drop the abstention policy. Treasury had cooled in its support for provisos and for abstention, insisting that the NEA-drafted instructions to the USG Executive Director be appropriately revised at the NSC level, and Robert McNamara in a visit to South Asia in late January 1972, had made clear his strong support for IDA programs in that region by committing 40 percent of all IDA credits to India. As the crisis rapidly dissipated, so too did the bargaining advantages required for imperative coordination and the reasons for punishing India, an action that entailed jeopardizing USG relations with the WB and WB autonomy.

The USG's unprecedented decision on March 7, 1972 to vote against an Indian credit for the purchase of crude oil tankers to ply the Persian Gulf route stands in marked contrast to the earlier decisions, and provides a different and important lesson for the South Asia policy arena. The international crisis in South Asia was no longer an important consideration. The tanker credit was opposed by U.S. shipping and oil companies and within the USG, by Treasury, the Eximbank and the Federal Reserve. NAC, which advised the Secretary of the Treasury on how to instruct the U.S. Executive Director at IDA, rather than the NSC or WSAG, provided the context for coordination and decision. In the end, after support in NEA (but not EB) for the tanker credit collapsed only AID advocated supporting it. AID systematically rebutted arguments advanced for voting against, particularly the "major" argument that the tankers would hurt U.S. shipping, and recommended to NEA/INS that Robert McNamara should be urged to pre-empt negative USG action by making a USG vote against, much less a negative decision by the Board, a cause for his resignation. On March 3 or 4 "in an unknown forum", it was decided that the U.S. would vote against the tanker credit, an action that stands alone in the annals of USG-IDA relationships. The relationship survived, the credit was approved, and those responsible for the South Asia policy arena learned how vulnerable the arena was to powerful private interest.

The two decisions illustrate how the deliberative coordination of normal diplomacy, particularly when reinforced by the insulation that a multilateral agency can provide, may be able to give longer-run interests their due even when they are confronted with the short-run need for leverage or the powerful influence of vested interests.

Stanley Kochanek's study, "United States Expropriation Policy and South Asia," illustrates the capacity of deliberative coordination to make compatible seemingly incompatible objectives by delay, "slicing" and reconciliation. In 1972, the governments of India, Pakistan and Bangladesh nationalized the subsidiaries of two American insurance groups, the American Foreign Insurance Association (AFIA) and the American International Underwriters (AIU). U.S. policy towards commercial issues outside the communist bloc, Kochanek observes "tends to be global rather than oriented towards a particular region or country."[50] On January 19, 1972, President Nixon's statement on "Economic Assistance and Investment Security in Developing Nations" laid down that in future expropriation of U.S. assets, failure to pay prompt, adequate and effective compensation would result in withholding of new bilateral economic aid and a refusal to support loans from multilateral development banks unless over-riding considerations of national interest required the USG to act otherwise. "Within a few months this policy was being tested" in South Asia.

The vehicle established by the President to implement the policy declaration of January 19, 1972 was the Expro Group, a special sub-committee of the Council on International Economic Policy (CIEP). Chaired by the Assistant Secretary of State for Economic and Business Affairs (EB), its members included representatives from State, Treasury, Defense and Commerce.[51] Day to day monitoring, however, was the responsibility of the

India, Pakistan and Bangladesh country desks in the Bureau of Near East and South Asian Affairs (NEA) which prepared reports and recommendations for the Expro Group, advised the U.S. companies on strategy, coordinated inputs from the White House, other executive agencies, the companies and Congress, and drafted and cleared all major instructions to appropriate embassies.

The President's policy of January 19, 1972 allowed for flexibility in responding to expropriations in the light of national interest considerations, but this flexibility was constrained by the Hickenlooper[52] and Gonzalez[53] amendments. The first requires suspension of bilateral assistance if suitable steps, including arbitration, have not been initiated within a reasonable time (defined as six months) to provide adequate compensation. The second requires a negative vote by U.S. Executive Directors on multilateral agency loans unless prompt compensation has been paid, the dispute has been submitted to arbitration under the rules of the Convention for the Settlement of Investment Disputes, or good faith negotiations are in progress.

Responding to expropriation in three South Asia states with very different political conditions involved a variety of complex problems such as defining terms (e.g. what constitutes expropriation? how does a capital gains tax relate to expropriation? what about the exchange rate, "financial practices," and revaluation of assets?); the reliability of evidence (e.g. the value of property, the existence of good faith negotiations); and determining whether remedies, including internal remedies, have been exhausted. But "the most important problem .. .was conflicting U.S. interests." State and AID wanted good relations with countries of South Asia. Commerce, realizing that U.S. insurance interests totalled only $8 million, feared overreaction might jeopardize larger pharmaceutical and petroleum interests, both prime targets for nationalization. DOD, with minor stakes, supported the goal of good relations over support for private interests. Treasury, although the most active supporter of the insurance companies, did not challenge Expro Group decisions by taking them up to the CIEP. The basic strategy of State and the Expro Group was to secure negotiated settlements that freed the USG from a finding that expropriation without compensation had occurred. "Both Country Directorates and the Expro Group made special efforts to ward off triggering the Hickenlooper and Gonzalez Amendments. . .." They succeeded. Frequent efforts by the insurance companies "to force actions through repeated appeals to the White House, the Congress and other executive agencies considered to be more sympathetic" were marginally effective at best in the face of State's effort to avoid official action. Nor did they succeed in transforming the disputes between the insurance companies and particular host countries into direct confrontations with the USG on terms of settlement or as a result of sanctions associated with a finding of expropriation without compensation. Skillful maneuvering and negotiations by the companies, sometimes in collaboration with British firms and the British Government which were faced with parallel problems, led by the end of 1973 to settlements which, if less than the companies view of adequate, were, in the circumstances, acceptable. Kochanek concludes that because decisions within the USG did not go beyond the Expro Group and were based on consensus, "the case of insurance nationalization in South Asia ...re presents an excellent example of the type of significant foreign policy decisions which never reach the top levels of the United States Government decision-making system." The result succeeded in reconciling long-run U.S. bilateral and regional interests; the interests of the insurance firms, and the domestic policies of South Asian states by accommodating to a substantial measure the interests of the various actors.

Barnett Rubin's study of "The U.S. Response to the JVP Insurgency in Sri Lanka, 1971," portrays how a crisis of relatively minor proportions can be successfully handled by normal diplomacy. Confronted with an unanticipated emergency, the attack on the night of April 5-6, 1971, by the Janata Vimukti Peramuna (or People's Liberation Front) on administrative offices and police posts throughout Ceylon, and Prime Minister Bhandaranaike's appeal for military aid, the U.S. (along with India, Pakistan, Britain, the USSR, Yugoslavia and Egypt) responded with a timeliness and finesse that transformed poor into good relations, including the restoration of permission for U.S. naval ships to call, without a non-nuclear declaration on behalf of those ships. The successful handling of policy and action within the State Department, primarily at the regional bureau and country director level, supports the view not only that "the State Department be given a greater role as against the NSC in foreign policy planning, but that within State itself policy planning should more deeply involve the line officers."[54] Rubin recognizes that special circumstances, such as the spill-over effect of the parallel crisis in Pakistan, which attracted higher level attention than benefited those dealing with Sri Lanka, the fact that the JVP insurgency in effect failed, thereby obviating the possibility that foreign troops (e.g. Indian) might have intervened, and the lack of strong bureaucratic or national interest in Sri Lanka, contributed to the "normal" management of a crisis situation. Even so, the organizational and procedural means employed provide suitable prescriptions for comparable problems of policy formulation and management.

"The emergency was handled mainly in State," where the regional bureau had the action, and policy-making within it "was centered around the country director." NEA provided leadership and coordination for other actors such as Political Military Affairs (PM) and Intelligence and Research (INR) Bureaus in State, as well as for DOD's Office for International Security Affairs (ISA) and effectively utilized at the White House level the Senior Review Group (SRG) of the NSC to obtain, *inter alia*, a legally mandated presidential decision. Within NEA, the country director did almost all of the drafting of policy documents and hence most of the coordination of information and policy. Evaluation of options took place in the daily meetings in Secretary Rogers' office (an extraneous "benefit" of the Pakistan crisis) rather than in the NSC-presidential context. The NSC and its SRG provided "quick clearances and .. .com munications" of presidential decisions to NEA officials working on the problem. ISA and the military services were "content to act as support for State; they provided information on 'nuts and bolts' questions without pushing for greater authority or special military interests."

"It seems apparent," Rubin concludes, "that constant contact with high level officials and increased responsibility for policy lead working line officers to see issues in broader perspective. 'Clientelism' may not be built into their roles *per se*, but into the organizational structure which isolates line officers from decision-making and planning." In short, "this case gives an idea of the conditions under which a State Department, regional bureau centered foreign policy system can work, and what its limitations might be."

Charles Lenth's examination of "The Role of the Peace Corps in U.S. Relations with South Asia" also contributes insight into the strength of normal diplomacy, in part by offering a contrast to the model. The Peace Corps captured the 1960s optimistic interventionism so characteristic of the Kennedy administration. Its volunteers were suspicious of bureaucracy, whether in the U.S. State Department or among officials of South Asian governments, because such officials were crippled by routine and weighted down by conventional knowledge. The Peace Corps prided itself on its exclusion from normal diplomatic channels and activities, an exclusion expressed through its organizational detachment from State, both in Washington and the field. The excessive optimism of the mid-sixties, and its organizational and political innocence, led to rebuffs in Sri Lanka and Pakistan, and to an over expansion in India that exposed and discredited the Peace Corps' technical claims.

The Peace Corps learned from its setbacks, but in ways that did not lead Peace Corps volunteers and administrators to embrace careerism, bureaucratic caution or conventional thinking. The Corps assumed a more modest self-conception and developed a greater respect at home and abroad for coordination with other agencies. Its experience in South Asia illustrates how a people-to-people program with long-term interests cannot do without the sheltering framework of normal diplomacy, but at the same time requires sufficient autonomy to pursue its unconventional mission and preserve an identity separate from the USG.

Together, these normal diplomacy cases do not sustain the stereotype view of career officials. Using "routine" organizational and procedural means, the officials proved capable of imaginative, flexible and purposeful action in pursuit of the national interest. The positive features of normal diplomacy—the significance of professionalism and professionals in policy formulation and management; the integration of policy planning with operations; the importance of collegiality and deliberative coordination; the representation of multiple interests, levels and perspectives—can be promoted, we believe, by mechanisms suggested below, the assistant secretary policy planning council and the regional conference.

C. Coordination among Timeframes

1. *The Case for Insulation*

Several case studies highlight the conflict between long-run policy goals and the short-run requirements of crisis management. Organizational interests as well as public support are more frequently on the side of the short-run than the long-run. Operating officials in Washington and the field tend to focus on the most recent cable or on the need for leverage now. The President's need for immediate gains and the constraints of the next election push him too towards short-run solutions. Lyndon Johnson had to "solve" Vietnam in time for 1968, and Richard Nixon needed the opening to China in time for 1972. The media's concern for news leads them disproportionately to attend to today's crisis rather than to next year's solution; they are less likely to feature a President's or secretary's long range goals.

In our discussion of the time dimension of complexity, we argued that the half life of some programs required a medium or long-term framework because they addressed values and dimensions of the national interest incompatible with short-run competition for influence and power. Policies and programs designed to promote security and welfare through economic growth or the redistribution of wealth require time and autonomy from the vicissitudes of short-run political conflicts. Culture, knowledge and science stand apart from the ebb and flow of political relations; they cannot serve the national interest in the short or long-run unless they maintain their autonomy. There are no short-run solutions to the food, population, resource and pollution problems. Yet because they vitally affect security and welfare, they help define the national interest. In times of conflict, insulated programs not only sustain medium and long-term interests but also help to preserve those lines of communication and relationships without which the inevitable restoration of "normal" relations is much more difficult.

The principle of insulation has been recognized in the relative autonomy given to some agencies such as AID, the Peace Corps, and USIA and in the increasing use of multilateral agencies. Their (limited) autonomy recognizes that some programs profit by distance from the ordinary flow of policy. But organizational forms cannot, alone, assure insulation; a concept of insulation needs to be recognized and practised by policy-makers. Our cases suggest that AID, the Peace Corps, and multilateral agencies were drawn into the pervasive quest for leverage despite their organizational location.

Insulation makes it possible to pursue multiple interests or finely graduated strategies concurrently. The national interest is often complex and includes mutually conflicting goals. The insulation of programs and activities makes it possible when needed to speak with several voices and to pursue simultaneously different objectives.

2. *The Case against Insulation*

The notion of insulation made some of our respondents profoundly uneasy. (That a number of them understood us to be saying insulation is not quite accidental.) Essentially they saw insulation as a threat to political clout on the one hand, and to political protection on the other. It diminished, for example, their capacity to go to the ambassador for help or support. In Washington and the field officials feared being separated from the political definitions of national interest, particularly as it was being articulated and applied at high levels by persons whose estimate of them could affect their careers. Nor did the officials we interviewed feel comfortable with the notion that the instrumentalities and resources available for them or others when leverage was needed should be reduced or constrained by the doctrine or practice of insulation. They argued that insulation or autonomy would not be understood or, if understood, not accepted. In South Asia, political officials or public actors could not or would not, we were told, accept a distinction between the U.S. government and a U.S. government agency. India's unfriendly cultural policy in 1971-72, and Sri Lanka's hostility to the Peace Corps in the mid-sixties, confirm this estimate. (Charles Lenth's examples of continuing requests from Indian states for a Peace Corps presence during the difficult post-1971 period in U.S.-Indian relations suggest the opposite possibility.)

Officials in Washington and ambassadors in the region argued that they needed control over programs and resources to direct and manage policy. AID officials in Pakistan and Bangladesh, for example, argued that more insulation would deprive them of the means to tie aid to what they believed were demonstrated means of development and self-help. Insulation, in any case, would not protect you when the chips were down from the consequences of political conflict.

3. *Insulation in Practice: Multilateral Agencies*

Multilateral agencies in the last ten years have represented the most successful expression of insulation. Their specific political form has been a response to the belief in receiving countries that aid created less dependency when offered in internationalized form. In so far as the USG supports multilateral agencies, its formulation of national interest includes a commitment to trading off losses in the short-run context of crisis management for the gains attending growth and justice. The specific distance of multilateral agencies from American influence has varied over time. In the early and middle 1960s, many Indians alleged that the parallelism between U.S. and World Bank policies was too close to be accidental and that it arose more from American political influence than from objective economic reasons. More recently, the Bank has been accused by U.S. officials of being "too soft" on LDCs, a charge which may signify more distance between the Bank and the USG in the McNamara era. The World Bank's policies and programs do not bear out the fear that insulation obstructs the means to impose "conditions" on aid. Constraints imposed by multilateral agencies such as the World Bank are more likely to be perceived by recipients of aid as legitimate demands for performance than as objectionable political conditions.

The Bjorkman and Moulton studies cast light on the extent to which multilateral agencies have or have not acted independently of U.S. policies and interests, and on the reasons and mechanisms involved. James Bjorkman's study, Harinder Shourie's background paper, and our interviews in Washington suggest that in the 1966-67 period, when consortium aid under World Bank auspices was associated with devaluation and the liberalization of economic policy in India, World Bank and USG policies were at least parallel. On the other hand, the degree of agreement among American and some Indian economists concerning the nature of India's problems in 1964-67 and the steps needed to remedy them, lend some credence to the World Bank's claim that its policies and programs were independent of the USG's. Moulton's study of IDA suggests that multilateralism insulated IDA decisions on credits for India from USG efforts to use IDA programs to gain leverage for its "tilt" policy during the Indo-Pakistan war of 1971. The two examples suggest that, given the large U.S. contributions to multilateral agencies, those agencies are likely to be both responsive to but somewhat insulated from current U.S. political objectives and policies. It would, no doubt, be more difficult for a fairly autonomous USG economic aid agency to achieve a similar degree of insulation, but this may not be so for other functions and their policy arenas.

4. *Insulation in Practice: Cultural and Informational Agencies*

Walter Andersen's study of "United States Educational and Cultural Exchange Programs in India" reviews the severe difficulties that U.S. educational and cultural programs encountered in India in the years surrounding the 1971 tilt towards Pakistan, examines the policy and administrative relationships between informational and cultural (including educational) programs, and makes recommendations in the light of his evidence and findings. Our interest here is primarily those aspects of his analysis that illuminate the need for and the means to insulate educational and cultural programs.

In Washington, the principal agencies concerned with educational programs are State's Bureau of Educational and Cultural Affairs (CU) and the Institute of International Studies housed in HEW's Office of Education. In the field the United States Information Agency [whose parent agency in Washington is the semi-autonomous United States Information Service (USIS)] supervises educational and cultural programs through the Country Public Affairs Officer (CPAO). The Cultural Affairs Officer (CAO), appointed by USIA with the approval of CU, is responsible for CU's programs that involve scholars and books, including USIA libraries.

This is an unsatisfactory state of affairs. The USIA's principal goals are "to create support for U.S. foreign policy objectives and to develop a favorable image of American society."[55] The CAO, who reports back to the area desks of both CU and USIA's, is administratively subordinate to the CPAO and is "located within USIA's promotional system." "The major limitation on the CAO's ability to aggressively pursue educational goals," Andersen finds, "is the environment in which he must work." Not only is USIA's orientation "promotional" but also its means are informational with "emphasis on the 'fast' media such as radio, television and press releases." Under such circumstances, educational and cultural activities are subsumed to informational goals. The linkage of education to a propaganda agency creates the impression that U.S. scholarship and culture are related to propaganda.

Andersen proposes the creation of a single semiautonomous foundation analogous to the National Endowment for the Humanities to deal with the basic problems of insulating educational and cultural programs from the effects of USG and host country political leverage and separating them from promotional and information objectives and means. Like NEH, its governing board would include both public and private representatives and it would draw financial support from both public and private sources. It would have a full time staff whose members would periodically serve in the field. Like the British Council, which provides an effective example of an autonomous cultural agency, it should not, in the words of the Duncan Commission of 1969, "be regarded in any way as a mouthpiece of Government policy." Even though ninety percent of the British Council's funding is governmental, it has over the years succeeded in creating a reputation for recognizing in its programs and operations cultural and intellectual standards and competency rather than national political objectives of the moment. Its director, not a foreign service officer, distinguished his organization from the foreign service hierarchy and fought for his agency's independent standing and reputation. The considerable respect and success which the British Council, like the BBC, commands in many countries, including those in South Asia, are in large part related to successful insulation.

A semi-autonomous agency could deal more effectively with a number of other troublesome organizational and procedural problems that now plague educational and cultural administrative arrangements and programs. It could gather the presently dispersed and segmented organizations and programs into a common home. It could make possible longer term programming and budgeting. It could solve structural and operating problems in the field. It could provide, in the case of India, that single point of contact the GoI seeks (without, we are quick to add, jeopardizing the diversity and pluralism that characterize American cultural and educational life). It could mesh effectively with the newly constituted[56] Indo-U.S. Sub-Commission on Education and Culture by having its U.S. members appointed by and responsible to the foundation's governing board. It could give internationally oriented educational and cultural policy and programs visibility at home and abroad, including with the Congress and philanthropic-cum-internationally interested publics.

D. Coordination in South Asia

We identify four types of coordination in South Asia: (1) regional coordination involving relations among U.S. embassies in the region; (2) cross-sovereignty barrier coordination involving relations between U.S. government agencies and agencies of the host country; (3) South Asia-Washington coordination involving relations between U.S. government agencies and agencies of the host country; and (4) mission or in-country coordination among various embassy functions and goals. We shall focus mainly on regional and cross-sovereignty barrier coordination, where both our findings and our recommendations are more substantial.

1. *Regional Coordination*

One form of complexity associated with policy-making in South Asia arises from the need to devise policies appropriate to each country in the region even while dealing with their consequences for regional relations. It is in this context that we explore systematically the possibilities of regional coordination. Regional coordination relates to a number of processes, from sharing information, through systematic exchange and confrontation of perspectives on common problems and shared policies, to efforts to identify and to formulate policies suitable for the region. Both in the field and in Washington, we inquired into present actualities of regional coordination. How is it understood and how is it practiced? We have also considered means to improve coordination and their costs and benefits.

The region has traditions of conflictual relations between the ambassadors to India and Pakistan. One senior observer commented that ambassadors had sometimes fought more sharply than their respective clients and, at times, even egged them on. Such conflicts reflect more than the envoys' clientelist orientations. Different types of men are characteristically chosen for the two posts. The image of India as "the world's largest democracy" has contributed to ambassadorial appointments of men with public reputations and standing, executive and legislative connections, and an interest in communicating outside official channels. In

Pakistan, where strongmen have ruled in much of the post-independence period, a more conservative perspective was valued, leading to more appointments of envoys with military and business connections. That the selection process has produced ambassadors with different styles and views strengthened the propensities to conflict for which clientelism might have laid a base. Ambassadors Byroade and Moynihan, have talked about this legacy rather self-consciously as part of an effort to do better. Appointments to Sri Lanka and Bangladesh have not exhibited similar differences.

Good ambassadorial intentions may have difficulty overcoming conflictual traditions in situations where their clients are pitted against each other. On defense matters, where the interests of the regional clients have indeed been in conflict, there has not been very close coordination among embassies since the fifties; the consensus represented by the 1967 arms policy was more the product of State-Defense and desk officer and CD coordination in Washington than it was of coordination in the region. There has been some talk among embassies of sharing cables to the Department of Defense, but the Delhi embassy appears to learn after the fact and from the Department of State about Islamabad initiatives. Senior actors on both sides tend to believe that regional coordination is exceptionally difficult in situations where the ambassadors are fundamentally opposed. Then, instead of compromising, they attempt to win the contest at the next highest level—in Washington. One official thought that where ambassadors have had previous assistant secretarial experience, and thus recognize the appropriate higher constraints on clientelism, coordination even in crisis situations might be easier. The observation suggests a strategy of rotating ambassadors and assistant secretaries through each other's slots.

Ambassadors and their staffs at Islamabad, Delhi, Dacca and Kathmandu have encouraged some regional exchanges. In recent times, Ambassador Moynihan visited Islamabad. Ambassador Boster from Bangladesh has consulted at Delhi; Ambassador Byroade was scheduled to visit Delhi when we were interviewing in August, 1974. These visitations appear to promote some sense of common problems and habits of discourse concerning differences. We were told that there is rather brisk "back channel" traffic between the ambassadors to explore questions in a preliminary way, although reports differ concerning the frequency and importance of this communication link. While these efforts indicate some of the ways that coordination might be improved, their sporadic and irregular nature has not resulted in durable and significant coordination.

The South Asia specialists in Washington and in South Asia have a high degree of common consciousness with respect to the facts and judgments they command and the common experiences between them. This common cadre feeling has an important if hard to specify effect on regional coordination. The actors who are communicating are mutually known, as are their styles and previous roles. Officers who have served in Islamabad are posted to Delhi, Dacca or Kathmandu; those who have served on a country desk in Washington are sent to Delhi, Islamabad, and Colombo. A political officer who has served in Islamabad may become political officer in India or country director for INS. An excessive enthusiasm for GLOPping could well run counter to this infrastructure of regional coordination.

Throughout our interviews, whenever we pressed the possibilities of regional coordination, we encountered variations on a bilateral frame of mind. Actors see the lines of communications running to Washington, not across the subcontinent. The idea that a conflictual situation might be explored in the region instead of in Washington is generally not recognized and if recognized rejected. We discussed at length arms, food, the Indian Ocean and development assistance, and encountered resistance to the idea of a regional interest and strategy with respect to all of them. In fact, potentially difficult or conflictual issues are routinely referred to as issues that have to be handled in Washington. Washington actors in turn viewed the prospect of regional collaboration among embassies as a threat to their initiative and control over policy formulation, decision and management.

Embassy officers often believe that they do not have enough information to make recommendations, or even develop views, about matters that fall outside their own narrowly defined responsibilities. There is circularity in this reasoning: because there are no habits of regional coordination, country actors are not aware of information concerning other countries in the region that bears on their own situation. Often lack of information, in the areas of economic development or political costs, is a matter of not asking questions, or of choosing to collect information only on a country and bilateral basis. Since bilateral frames of mind follow from bilateral channels of communication, regional frames of mind would require more organizations and/or procedures emphasizing regional channels of communication.

Some of the policy areas where more and better regional coordination seems possible are food; economic aid and development assistance; cultural and scientific activity, relations and programs; arms supply; and crisis management, notably the settling of regional disputes. While officials on the whole resisted the notion of coordination in any of these areas, they considered the prospects better for the first two than for the last two. We investigated the possibilities for coordination in the areas of food, economic development and arms supplies in some depth.

The bilateral conception that subcontinental actors have of their roles militates against regional coordination with respect to food. People in the region felt, "We must trust those in Washington;" they believed that coordination was simply not their task. In only one of the three embassies was there any support for the idea by a high level official: "The embassies should be communicating with each other but they aren't. Everyone is going their own way. I assume that in Washington it will be put together and that some sort of strategy and set of priorities will be worked out."

One justification for regional coordination is to develop, at maximum, a reasonable and coordinated South Asia policy; at minimum, a clearer view of the costs and benefits of different allocations. It is obvious that the countries in this area (notably India, Pakistan and Bangladesh) have similar food needs and problems and that together they represent a substantial proportion of world food needs. The needs of the region are large enough to come in serious competition with food requirements in other nations, for example, Egypt, China and Russia. As this report is written, decisions about U.S. food shipments abroad are dominated by the Department of Agriculture's "market" orientation, an approach that leaves "policy" in buyers' hands as the Russian purchases in 1972 and 1974 make clear, and by the struggle over humanitarian as against political food aid, a struggle that, under current circumstances, pits Secretary of State Kissinger against key Congressional leaders and AID. Neither the states of South Asia nor the U.S. embassies have taken steps to shape the policy process, much less policy decisions, in a way that confronts and deals with the region's food needs. The international allocation of food involves political, developmental and humanitarian objectives as much as it does market forces. Formulating a regional interest and relating it to the world production and allocation of food would provide the Department of State with policy inputs that it could use to assess foreign relations impli-cations of economic development.

Food and guns do not appear on the same agenda in the South Asian region. The notion that food aid and arms supplies are subject to trade offs or that a shift to an emphasis on food (and economic development) could affect the salience or priority of security concerns in the region was not on anybody's mind or agenda. Clearly, a regional framework is required if South Asia is to shift its concerns and priorities from arms to food.

Development assistance too may be an appropriate area for regional coordination because certain problems, notably agricultural production, are common across the region, e.g. wheat in Pakistan and North India; rice in Bangladesh, Bengal, Madras, Sri Lanka. Regional coordination among U.S. officials concerned with common problems and challenges could help to promote sharing of resources and the development of common policies for development and regional cooperation and security. The use of subcontinental planning and coordination in the areas not only of food and development assistance but also trade and investment is likely to spill over in ways that affect the frame of mind and lines of connection between the countries of the region in ways that promote regional cooperation.

There may be obstacles to regional coordination. Officials in several of the embassies thought that regional coordination of food policy would unleash a struggle among them over relative proportions in the light of policy needs, political relations, etc. (should the ratio be 2 : 1 : 1, 4 : 2 : 1, etc.). In at least one case, a regional policy for food was opposed because the embassy could do better not coordinating than coordinating its country requirements with those of other countries in the region.

While such a struggle is not unlikely, it could also lead to the search for "objective" and political grounds to resolve it. To use an example drawn from the subcontinent, the fact that Bengal and Madras argued before the Sixth Finance Commission about the financial allocations that should go to each area has helped produce the principles by which the finance commission makes its allocation. Conflict may, and often does, contribute to coordination. Brokering the conflicting demands of different interests goes on in Washington in any case. Instituting a parallel process in the field would inaugurate the process earlier and, in the context of agreed criteria, shift it downward.

While we realize that regional coordination is no panacea, we do argue that it could produce better staffed options and a more comprehensive and comparative view than is now available of policy needs and choices. At a maximum, it would produce more thoughtful and weighty policy proposals and enhance the viability and autonomy of regions in the policy process.

Regional coordination of arms supply seemed exceptionally difficult to embassy officials because it approached the ground on which the two major countries and embassies in the area have been most deeply divided. Yet the possibilities for meaningful regional coordination seemed much better in 1974 than in 1964. As Stephen Cohen's paper emphasizes, the 1965 war brought home to U.S. officials serving in the region that the arms supply policy had led to regional military confrontation, not the result intended by the policy. The 1967 arms policy, which provided for a cash supply of non-lethal weapons on a relatively even-handed basis to both Pakistan and India, commanded substantial consensus in the Islamabad and Delhi embassies. Despite the 1970 "one time exception" to the general embargo on lethal weapons, and despite increased concern to respond favorably to Prime Minister Bhutto's request for arms, the consensual possibilities on arms policy remain viable.

Present trends in the region also conspire to make arms aid a more promising subject for regional coordination than it appears at first sight. To some extent since the 1965 war, and certainly since 1971, the notion that India is the dominant power in the area has been increasingly shared by all embassies in the region, although there are differences concerning the interpretation of that position. This relationship is generally accepted by the Pakistan government, although it emphasizes that in its view Indian "dominance" makes India that much more dangerous and Pakistan that much more insecure. But the sharp competition that existed when "balance" between India and Pakistan was sought by both the government of Pakistan and the U.S. ambassadors to Pakistan no longer exists. In so far as the Government of India preferred a Bhutto government to foreseeable alternatives, and insofar as the Bhutto government's viability depended on success in its effort to get arms from the U.S., the Government of India muted its opposition to limited arms supplies to Pakistan. Such a perspective could enable the Islamabad and Delhi embassies to see the issue through similar lenses.

With respect to Diego Garcia also, the sharp differences that characterized both the embassies and the clients on various arms issues a decade ago is no longer visible. The Dacca Government shares New Delhi's opposition to Diego Garcia, but lacks Delhi's sense of the facility's saliency to regional security. The Pakistan government, although not opposed to U.S. policies as articulated by the U.S. Navy, would like to avoid the issue. On the one hand, the Government of Pakistan finds it useful to oppose India and to side with the U.S. and the People's Republic of China. On the other hand, supporting Diego Garcia as a full fledged "base," because it puts the GoP on the side of American "militarism," "imperialism," or "capitalism," alienates many Third World nations from Pakistan or puts Pakistan in explicit opposition to their policies and concerns. Not least among them is Iran, which has its own ambitions (and capabilities) in the Indian Ocean area.

While the two embassies do not view the issue in the same light, their differences are not so sharp as they were when the USG military and intelligence interests in South Asia meant arming Pakistan and locating facilities there.

The preceding remarks suggest that the conventional view shared by officials in the region and in Washington, that regional coordination of military policy including arms is impossible, is, if not mistaken, at least less correct than is supposed. To what extent regional coordination on military matters appears impossible because habit linked to bilateral modes of thought blocks a regional perspective, and to what extent it appears impossible because of fundamental differences in the outlook and assumptions of the principal regional actors is a question that remains for the future.

Embassy personnel in the South Asia region see a number of problems attending regional coordination. They are apprehensive about the exacerbation of conflict among embassies where the problem is distributing limited resources among countries. More fundamental, if less articulated, is the fear of abandoning a known and rewarding orientation, that of representing a host country's views and interests, for an unknown and potentially costly orientation, that of representing a "regional" perspective. What if an ambassador or other official agreed to consider an issue from the perspective of "the other" country? The cost in Pakistan, for example, and thus the cost to the official and the embassy might be quite high. Critical Pakistani counterplayers might fear or suspect that "their agent" would help "the other side." To the extent that these attitudes depend upon the conflictual history of the two main actors on the subcontinent, India and Pakistan, these apprehensions may deserve less weight at a time when the level of tension appears to be abating. But to the extent that they are rooted in the relationship between foreign and host country counterplayers, they remain an impediment to regional perspectives and policy formulation.

Embassy spokesmen are also apprehensive, as was previously suggested, about a strategy of regional coordination because they do not believe they command the necessary expertise. Regional perspectives, policies or coordination, if they are to exist, are a job for Washington, not for bilaterally defined organizations and roles.

The assets of regional organization include the appearance, on a common agenda, of policy perspectives arising from country missions. At best, their confrontation might produce some consensus; at least it would promote clarification of costs and benefits, and the increased understanding comparison brings. How important is arms aid to Pakistan to the internal politics of India and Pakistan? How important is it to the structure of their respective foreign alliances? What are the comparative political implications of food shortfalls in Pakistan, Bangladesh and India? How should these implications affect policy if at all? Ambassadors can now formulate recommendations without substantial information and concern about the cost of their recommendation in the adjoining country, a condition which may create incompletely grounded recommendations and an incompletely argued case. Even where such confrontations do not produce consensus, they will produce a better understanding of trade-offs.

Strengthening regional coordination requires organizational means that can articulate and represent regional problems and priorities, i.e. organizations and procedures that can define a regional policy arena and regional interests. The purposes of regional coordination could be served by the periodic convening at rotating centres in the region, of regional conferences, organized on functional bases such as economic development, including aid; military policy, including arms; culture and science. Such conferences would include not only the relevant functional officers, who do not always (for example in the case of AID or USIS) command the required standing in their embassies, but also officers who, because of their rank, can speak authoritatively with other embassies. They should further include relevant actors from Washington, from desk officer and country director to deputy assistant secretary and assistant secretary. Conferences should be mandated to convene at times of regional crises; to generate and share information; and to recommend policies that bear on medium and long-term regional needs and problems. There are precedents for such assemblies in the regional meetings of the U.S. chiefs of mission with the assistant secretary and, of late, in the peripatetic activity of the secretary of state. But this proposal aims for a broader institutionalization of intra-regional and regional-Washington exchange.

2. *Coordination Across the Sovereignty Barrier*

State sovereignty expressed in terms of national jurisdictions and boundaries limits, in principle, the scope and degree of coordination in international relations. Coordination across the sovereignty barrier involves some form of influence or participation by one state in the affairs of another. Under asymmetrical conditions of dependence or coercion, such participation is likely to be seen as intervention. The limits on participation are set by legal and prudential considerations, legal in that states are called upon by law to recognize each other's sovereign autonomy, prudential in that the dependency or coercion associated with intervention generates political costs.

Legal prohibitions and political costs have not, however, eliminated the practice of intervention by means such as military force, covert operations or economic relationships. Here we are concerned with the more benign and "voluntary" forms of intervention that can accompany the dependency inherent in asymmetrical economic and political relationships. What special sensibilities or obligations does coordination across the sovereignty barrier entail?

Several cases reported in this study speak to this question. They emphasize an appreciation of the political and ideological environments in which counterplayers dwell. Bjorkman's study of President Johnson's short tether policy in supplying food to India in 1966-67 provides an example of flawed coordination, in which insensitivity to political consequences on the other side of the sovereignty barrier generated unnecessarily high political costs. President Johnson's grasp of the internal politics of his own nation was not paralleled by an understanding of the constraints that affect leaders of other countries. The policy was pursued when Mrs. Gandhi had only recently succeeded to office and when her parliamentary support was increasingly precarious.

Accepting foreign aid was problematic and politically dangerous. President Johnson's implicit conditions for food aid, muting criticism of the U.S. policy in Southeast Asia and publicizing India's dependence, did not make Mrs. Gandhi's efforts to establish her authority easier. These acts contributed to discrediting an economic policy that, at that time and subsequently, could have been mutually advantageous to America and India.

Sensitive coordination is especially important for economic programs that require political and administrative support in the host country and at home. They oblige foreign policy managers to respond to two environments simultaneously. The cooperative rural electrification program discussed by Susan Hadden required operating agencies to face in two directions at once. On the U.S. side of the sovereignty barrier, AID benefited from some very persuasive lobbyists, including John Lewis, AID Director in India, who appealed to the belief of Senators and Congressmen on the critical agricultural committees that cooperative rural electrification was an American invention suitable for export. On the Indian side, they found ways to adapt the program to satisfy Indian official notions of how cooperative rural electrification should be organized and administered. This kind of political bridging of the sovereignty barrier is essential if bilateral assistance programs are to be mutually fruitful.

Decentralization is a key to successful coordinations of development and cultural programs across the sovereignty barrier. Decentralization does not come naturally to embassies; a few senior officials are expected to deal with their counterparts at the host capital. Counterparts often expect embassies to deal only with them, and tend to suspect relations with organizationally inferior levels. But a more flexible and segmented structure is necessary, especially for economic and people-to-people programs. Charles Lenth shows that the Peace Corps was initially handicapped by an excessively centralized and federally insensitive liaison mechanism located in the Indian Planning Commission, and by its failure to recognize the requirements of states whose characteristics and needs differed markedly. In time, the Peace Corps in India improved its liaison relationship by shifting it to the Finance Ministry's Department of Economic Affairs, and improved its operations in the states by dealing directly with state governments in the context of central supervision. Such direct lines pre-supposed mutual confidence—especially confidence from the Indian end—that cannot always be achieved. The examples adduced in the Hadden paper reveal similar successful uses of decentralized arrangements (with state electricity authorities).

The comparative record in India and Pakistan of U.S. military personnel and missions provides important illustrations of the variations and possibilities in cross sovereignty barrier coordination, and the conditions of decentralization. The friendly relations between the U.S. and Pakistan before and during its military regimes arose in part out of the positive experience that U.S. military officers in World War II had with future Pakistan military personnel. American generals were among General Ayub Khan's earliest lobby in the U.S. supporting his requests for arms. Relations between U.S. and Pakistani military personnel were personal, direct, and based on their common military identities. They remained close up to 1971. In India, by comparison, where Prime Minister Nehru maintained civilian control over the military establishment, relations with foreign military missions were handled through intermediary civilian officials. A common community of military functionaries was discouraged. Even after the Sino-Indian war in 1962, when American military assistance reached its peak and U.S. military attaches and mission members came to know Indian military personnel, the GoI continued to interpose a civilian screen.

The contrast suggests that cross sovereignty barrier coordination has political consequences as well as conditions; bringing together functional experts on both sides can enhance communication and create a community of interests. If that community of interests is perceived as threatening by the host country, as was direct collaboration among military officers by the Government of India, such coordination may be resisted. Where it is regarded as benign, as was the case with rural electrification and other AID programs in India, or military collaboration in Pakistan, it can enhance communication and relations in ways that promote commonly intended goals.

The possibility that cross sovereignty barrier coordination can be criticized as undesirable sets limits on its use. Because direct channels to and collaborative arrangements with internal program agencies can become fair game for domestic politicians in the host country, they are peculiarly vulnerable. Thus if U.S. government officials in Bangladesh try to insist on better control of food (and other) smuggling into the Calcutta region and on an increase in food production as conditions for food aid, they may open the way to political costs that outweigh the hope for economic benefits. Susan Hadden reports in the case of rural electrification, that Indian officials were eager to have AID impose higher rates for electricity on Indian states unwilling on their own responsibility to do so. By shifting the responsibility to the U.S., raising rates might have become politically easier for the central and state governments. AID resisted the invitation (except in the most limited sense) in part because it believed the political consequences should be borne by the local governments.

U.S. officials also need to recognize that various local constituencies may respond differently to American programs, and calculate the consequences of local actions accordingly. Pleading political neutrality is no alternative for shrewd political judgment once cross sovereignty barrier relations are established. If Indian central government officials had succeeded in convincing AID to help them raise electricity rates, state governments, which were opposed, would have criticized and opposed the U.S. effort. A judgment concerning these responses had to be made. Similarly, when the Advanced Research Projects Agency, part of the Defense Department, financed research by American scholars on India's Himalayan borders, the project had the tacit support of high officials in New Delhi. This could not, however, protect the American scholars from the parliamentary criticism that followed the exposure of DOD sponsorship and support, exposure which spurred punitive measures against foreign cultural and educational institutions. Contradictory responses must be anticipated and weighed.

Cross sovereignty barrier coordination is less problematic for international or multilateral agencies than it is for U.S. sponsored bilateral programs. International agencies are less susceptible to charges that they are vehicles for imposing external national political interests. But they are far from immune, as the World Bank found in 1966 when, involved in the economic arrangements associated with the devaluation of the Indian rupee, it was accused of being the agent of disadvantageous U.S. intervention in the Indian economy. Generally, however, the supra-national standing and impartial expertise of multilateral institutions such as the World Bank and IDA, helped them to coordinate across the sovereignty barrier in ways and to a degree not normally available to national actors.

3. *South Asia-Washington Coordination*

Coordination between the South Asia embassies and Washington bureaus typically involves preliminary informal communication. The "official and informal" (not part of official records) letter is particularly significant, as are memos to the secretary which explore policy positions in a tentative way. They represent a step beyond the "official and informal" letter. Communication by inference, when embassy officials deduce or infer the department or USG position from statements by the national security advisor or the secretary of state, is especially important. Such forms of informal communication precede, for the most part, cable traffic that establishes "facts," takes positions and makes recommendations. Once a situation starts hardening, the telephone becomes particularly important because oral communication can "restore" the fluidity of preliminary informal exchanges. Embassy calls to Washington require special skills though, since it must be assumed that they may be subject to unfriendly monitoring and because talk is now in the context of interests, stakes, "effectiveness," etc. Such informal means are particularly important for effective intervention, manipulations or control of the decision-making process. Knowing, by phone or otherwise, on whose desk a piece of paper may be sitting, who is chairing a key committee or when a decision is to be made or a meeting held, can make all the difference in the choice of strategy and means and ultimately for success and failure.

Travel back and forth between the field and Washington is not a significant form of communication and coordination yet it may be the most promising underutilized means available. It allows the field officer to confront directly the bureaucratic stakes and Congressional interests vital to policy making. It allows Washington officials to experience the policy environment in which embassy officials dwell. A single act of peripatetic diplomacy, not uncharacteristic for the ambassadors accredited to India, who frequently are recruited from domestic politics, illustrates the importance of exchanging venues.

The PL-480 rupee settlement, achieved in 1973, reverses the usual center-periphery image of relations between Washington and the field. Ambassador Moynihan, like Chester Bowles and John Kenneth Galbraith before him, came to Washington where he successfully converted an infinite into a finite problem by disposing at a discount India's accumulated debt of three billion dollars in rupees. He deliberately selected the problem for special emphasis because of its promise for improving Indo-U.S. relations and became increasingly aware that success or failure here would make or break his embassy. Officials who worked with the ambassador in preparing the coalition of thirty U.S. rupee spending agencies to support the settlement before Congress, thought its successful conclusion depended heavily on the ambassador's political skills, strategy and connections, a view with which he concurs. Ambassador Moynihan was able to call upon Secretary Schultz's cooperation at Treasury; persuaded Secretary Butz at USDA to lend his support; mobilized the support of presidential assistant Kissinger and in turn gained President Nixon's consent at San Clemente. Having spoken to the President last, he made sure that he kept and used that strategic and psychological advantage. But above all, he participated in the Washington arena.

Ambassador Moynihan mobilized the appropriate Congressional support for the settlement by enlisting the aid of his friend, former speaker John McCormack, and talking personally with forty senators and Congressmen. His inadvertent failure to approach Senator Harry Byrd almost proved fatal to his purpose because, as a result of Byrd's initiative, the Senate on September 28, 1973, voted to prevent the administration from settling the three billion dollar debt at two-thirds discount without Congressional approval. Good State Department liaison and support from the highest levels of the administration led, eventually, to the defeat of the rider and a happy ending to a complex and perilous maneuver.

Ambassador Moynihan believes that the settlement could not have been made through the institutional apparatus of the Department of State. His leadership to the finale was, no doubt, central. But many elements of the agreement, including the concept of a substantial discount, were prepared through normal bureaucratic channels. He added two elements: (1) orchestrating legislative support for the measure by carefully attending to Congressional opinion; (2) assuring that the field and Washington pushed in the same direction by personally shuttling back and forth between locales. The personal influence he exercised was no doubt special; but the devices he used were amenable to more general application.

The PL-480 settlement suggests the utility of more frequent Washington-field movement, particularly opportunities for representatives from the field to inform and influence elected and appointed officials in Washington. The regional conference proposed in section VI-E (Recommendations) would also facilitate such exchanges.

4. *The Embassy and the Country Team*

While one encounters in the field and in Washington the conception of a "country team," it is not clear to what extent it corresponds to reality. John F. Kennedy's memo of May 29, 1961, designed to reinstate the ambassador as its head, has been, at best, imperfectly realized. A considerable portion of the mission's bureaucracy responds to two captains, and the ambassador is likely to be the less significant in the contest between him and, for example,

Agriculture, Defense, CIA and AID officials subject to dual lines of command. It should not be surprising if they are sometimes more attentive to their agency's drum beat than to the ambassador's.

Three examples suggest the nature of these relationships. At Dacca, where food aid was of critical concern in the summer of 1974, the USDA policy statement reporting Secretary Butz' calculatedly pessimistic estimates (after the Russian wheat deal) about the U.S.'s capacity to give aid, came directly to the Agricultural attache. He in turn turned them over to USIA officials who put them out through press releases to local newspapers. Neither the Agriculture nor the USIA officials cleared them with embassy political or economic officers, despite their considerable significance as a statement of U.S. policy.

In Delhi, at the same time, Ambassador Moynihan, who was taking a more skeptical view than the Defense Department of the Diego Garcia facility, on the whole managed embassy responses on this issue, and on India's nuclear explosion, without substantial input, let alone help, from local DOD representatives.

In Islamabad, the AID director, who recognized that economic policy was not to the fore in embassy planning, was nevertheless disconcerted by the omission of economic concerns from an important planning document drafted by the political officers. It was more by accident than design that the document came his way in time to permit some consideration of economic policy.

In all three locations there was agreement that some of those who sit in country team meetings, such as the DOD representative, the public affairs officer or the AID director, do not always have the same access to information as members of the country team at or near the top of the foreign service hierarchy. This, *inter alia*, limits their participation. The result is to narrow the range of issues, the dimensions of policy and available modes of action. And those who are not informed do not, in turn, always inform. But the mix varies, depending on the extent to which the mission of an agency conforms to current embassy and ambassadorial policy. In Islamabad, the defense attaches have easy access to the ambassador, are heard, and participate, in effect, in political reporting, while the AID director remains autonomous and isolated.

In Delhi, in recent years, with minimal action in either sphere, little is seen or heard from DOD or AID. The facts were different in the Bowles embassy, when the AID director and the ambassador collaborated closely.

The effectiveness of coordination in South Asia is also related to the size of the embassy. Small embassies such as those in Colombo and Dacca are sufficiently intimate to avoid the complexity that accompanies higher levels of differentiation. In Dacca, where the embassy circle is rather intimate but formal, officials regard the post as well coordinated. The size of the country team in Islamabad and Delhi precludes intimacy. Country team meetings, too large for serious discussions of policy or of the prior identification of problems that need attention, have become largely informational. The ambassador may tell the team about his latest trip to Washington or something of his recent talks with the prime minister or other high officials, and top officials may tell other top officials and a few slightly more junior ones what is going on, what is on their minds or what they think needs doing.

Coordination is also related to host country conditions. These can encourage decentralization or centralization of data gathering and political reporting. In Pakistan, Prime Minister Bhutto, like President Yahya Khan before him, chose to talk at length and individually with the U.S. ambassador, a practice that affects the pattern and style of embassy work and coordination. Ambassador Byroade played a lone hand, talking frequently and at length with the Prime Minister, preparing his reports for Washington and occasionally sharing some of his thoughts with subordinates. In India, Prime Ministers have remained more distant, sometimes very distant, from U.S. ambassadors. To know is to infer or deduce from facts and clues rather than to be told. Under such circumstances, political officers, not the host country Prime Minister, brief the ambassador.

It is not self-evident that organizational solutions short of organizational integration that eliminates most non-State personnel from embassy staffs can solidify the country team. Favorable ecological circumstances—small embassies—cannot be duplicated in all locations. Personalistic solutions are more likely. Ambassadors who are aware that career patterns, organizational location, and service ideology place FSOs in more advantageous positions than agency and service representatives can correct the balance, up to a point, by deliberate effort. By extending the distribution of critical cable information and inviting responses and by insisting on and practicing consultation, he can generate more participation and broaden his information and option base. Given the multiple channels and multiple loyalties of embassy organization, coordination under present conditions depends ultimately on the ambassador's energy, skill and personal authority.

VI. RECOMMENDATIONS

A. Context

Our recommendations assume the restoration of responsibility for the conduct of foreign policy to a smaller and revitalized Department of State whose secretary is the President's senior foreign policy advisor. The principal means to this end is the institutionalization of deliberative coordination in the context of governmental pluralism. We have discussed in Sections I and II of this report the background, evidence and reasons for a State Department-centered strategy and the meaning and benefits of deliberative coordination. Worth reiterating here is the importance of deploying professional knowledge in ways that enhance its authority and influence over policy formulation and management.

Our recommendations do not require but certainly would benefit from a variety of organizational and procedural changes.[57] Reducing substantially the size and complexity of the Department of State by eliminating functions and redundancy is one such change. The elimination of nine of its sixteen bureaus, headed by assistant secretaries (or equivalents) is a possibility that has figured in previous organizational reform proposals, notably the Hoover Task Force Report of 1949,[58] and is worth pursuing. The unprecedented boldness of Congress' recent reorganization suggests that institutional inertia can be overcome, even in the face of substantial vested interests.

We have not argued in detail the case for such changes, but we recite them briefly here to suggest the context in which our main recommendations would thrive.

Elimination of nine bureaus would leave the geographic bureaus (now five) with approximately 1000 personnel as the department's central component. A sixth bureau for multilateral affairs could absorb the functions and some of the personnel of the present Economic (EB), Oceans and International Environmental and Scientific Affairs (SCI), and International Organization (IO) bureaus. Non-redundant activities of the six remaining bureaus can be assigned to the regional and multilateral bureaus, to the secretary's office or (as we recommend below) to autonomous or multilateral agencies outside the department. The disappearance of the affected bureaus, Congressional Relations (H), Public Affairs (PA), Educational and Cultural Affairs (CU), Intelligence and Research (INR), Politico-Military Affairs (PM), and the Office of Legal Adviser (L), would eliminate superfluous and confusing mediation, often bypassed in any case, by enabling the secretary's staff and the geographic bureaus to deal directly with Congress, DOD and CIA as well as with information and law (cultural exchange will be dealt with below) through small press and legal staffs in the secretary's office.[59] Finally, we envisage the day when State will be given responsibility and commensurate authority for (1) preparing single, government-wide foreign affairs budget, and (2) for all governmental personnel sent abroad on foreign missions.[60]

The excess staffing at the secretary's level (the seventh floor) also merits attention. The chain of command over the assistant secretaries should be reduced to two, the secretary and his deputy, the under secretary. A deputy under secretary for foreign economic policy should act as the chief economic advisor to the secretary and handle the department's relations with Treasury, Commerce and other economic agencies. A second deputy under secretary for national security policy should monitor for the secretary the department's relations with DOD, CIA and the military services, including maintaining representatives on their staffs. A small secretariat able to monitor and arrange the flow of business within and outside the department and to give independent advice on day-to-day matters and a small policy planning staff, independent of but not divorced from operations and able to provide on its own initiative as well as on request independent studies and advice, should complete the staffing of the secretary's office.

Of equal importance if the Department of State and its secretary are to be the President's principal advisors and instruments in the conduct of foreign policy is the restoration of the National Security Council to something that more closely approximates Congress' legislative intent in creating it. The NSC has become a highly bureaucratized, cumbersome White House foreign office. Overweighted with representatives of military and intelligence agencies at the policy, committee and staff levels, it has shifted the concerns and objectives of foreign policy from diplomatic means and a political conception of the national interest to military means and a crisis laden conception of national security. The NSC conducts foreign policy in the context of hierarchy and imperative coordination, its staffs and committees shielded from accountability to Congress and public opinion by secrecy and executive privilege, its decisions, despite interdepartmental committees and review groups, often taken in isolation from the professional knowledge of career officials.

We envisage a small (about 20) flexible staff (divorced from policy management and operations) prepared to give and evaluate advice, to extend the President's reach by asking questions and providing information, to ensure that those who should be are heard, and to check on implementation. It would put the President's views and policies into draft form and communicate them to those for whom they are intended. Its principal officers would be an assistant for foreign and defense policy and a deputy assistant for foreign economic policy. The present elaborate structure of permanent committees, which make work and waste time, isolate the president from meaningful advice, and inhibit his capacity to direct and control, would be dismantled. The NSC itself would confine its attention and energies to topics and advice for which it was originally intended, the defense budget and military strategy, i.e., a national security, not a foreign policy, agenda. A President able and willing to foster and use a lean, coherent and revitalized State Department is likely to be a President who wants a small, personal White House staff and an NSC that confines itself to narrowly defined military and intelligence agendas.

B. Assistant Secretary Policy Planning Council

Our first recommendation is the creation of an Assistant Secretary Policy Planning Council mandated to identify national interests and formulate and manage policies in ways that take account of regional perspectives. The Council would consist of the State Department geographic assistant secretaries. It would be supported by the Secretariat (S) and by planning teams located in the bureaus. Deputy assistant secretaries would assume larger operating responsibilities so that assistant secretaries can devote the time and attention to their Council responsibilities.

The Council's proceedings would be rooted in deliberative coordination in a collegial context. It would be in a position to manage the dimensions of complexity specified in Part IV of this report in terms of levels, time, function and region. Staffed by professionals close to operations, it would be in a position to use normal diplomacy over a wide range of problems including many that count as crises under current arrangements.

Several advantages attend such a device: (a) It avoids the irrelevance and busy work that have come to characterize the National Security Council's committee and review system by relating planning to operations. Instead of adding yet another layer to those the President now struggles to control, it counters the tendency for staffs to duplicate line operations by vesting policy planning and management in line officials. (b) The Council's recommendations would capture a viewpoint different from the Policy Planning Staff whose orientation would remain to the Secretary's responsibility to advise the President about strategic diplomacy at the global level. The Council would attend to those contextual evaluations and judgments based on detailed country and regional knowledge that presidential advisors and staffs miss or ignore. (c) The Council would institutionalize and make more visible professional knowledge and experience. (d) The Council would create a collegial context of deliberation in which officials at equivalent organizational levels can freely exchange views, represent interests, and bargain.

The Council would meet regularly on an agenda of leading regional and interregional problems, including crises. The proposed deputy under secretaries for foreign economic policy and for national security policy would, ordinarily, sit with the Council to ensure liaison and coordination with the departments and agencies that fall within their responsibilities. Participants would share a regional perspective, on the one hand, but speak from divergent regional contexts, on the other. Deliberation would involve providing reasons and justifications that made sense across regions as well as in regions.

It is widely believed that operations and planning do not go well together, that planning, if it is not to be subsumed by operations, has to take place outside their framework. We are not sure whether to count this belief as an argument against giving the assistant secretaries responsibilities for policy planning and management or as a criticism of the assistant secretary role as it is now defined. If a substantial portion of the assistant secretary's operational responsibilities were given to the deputy assistant secretaries, the assistant secretary's potential as a policy planner would be enhanced.

Another objection to such a scheme is that FSO's are not suited to policy planning; neither their training nor experience prepares them for it. The operational and bilateral modes of thought and action to which they are accustomed are difficult to transcend. Difficult but not impossible. In-service mid-career training, particularly at universities, can help the right kind of officer to work effectively in the policy planning medium. Equally important would be lateral appointments from outside. In any case, we do not concede as self-evident that FSO's are constitutionally incapable of moving from "operations" to planning; it is a matter for empirical investigation whether assistant secretaries do not think like planners because their roles do not encourage them to do so or because their training and experience preclude their doing so. If getting to be an assistant secretary depended in part on showing talent in this direction it would be surprising if thinkers as well as doers did not surface on the way to the top.

C. A Southern Asia Bureau

The proposal to create an Assistant Secretary Policy Planning Council raises the question of how effectively South Asia would be represented in such a group. Are NEA and its assistant secretary the appropriate organizational form and leadership for managing the South Asia policy arena? Would an organizational arrangement other than NEA be more effective and appropriate? Our response to these questions is that the NEA should be separated into Near East and South Asia components and that South Asia be joined to South East Asia, now part of the East Asia Bureau. It is often argued that such a division would hurt South Asia by depriving it of the influence that a large and prestigious bureau provides, particularly one whose assistant secretary, even if sometimes ill-informed about or indifferent to the region, often has the caliber and standing to command a hearing laterally and upward.

Divergent career lines already separate Near East from South Asia personnel. Near East normally received the lion's share of attention in NEA; it holds six country directorates compared to two for South Asia, a ratio of 3 to 1 although the population ratio is the inverse. The assistant secretary typically is more informed about and engaged with the Middle East. Given the oil crisis and the continuing Israel-Arab confrontation, this skewing of attention and interest will increase. By the standard of the Latin American and African bureaus, which deal with regions of comparable or lesser consequence in population, military and economic terms. South Asia easily meets the test of bureau standing.

It may be that South Asia should be joined to a region other than the Near East, i.e. that NEA is not the right combination. For example, on the analogy of the European Bureau, South Asia might be joined to East Asia in a mammoth Asia Bureau. But the imbalance of such a bureau would not avoid the difficulties for South Asia that already exist in NEA and would compound them with those that trouble the European Bureau such as the proliferation of functional units that parallel those in the department and a vast array of country directorates, including one dealing with a superpower.

Another plausible option is to join South and South East Asia in a Southern Asian bureau. The transformation of China from a hostile to a friendly power, the dissolution of America's strategic commitment in South East Asia and the fact that South East Asia's economic, political and cultural characteristics are more similar to South than East Asia, all point in this direction. A Southern Asia bureau that combines scale, relatively uniform circumstances, a common geopolitical context and a good balance in country directorates makes more sense than present arrangements (NEA and EA) or than a separate South Asia Bureau. On balance, then, we recommend that South Asia be separated from NEA, South East from EA, and the two joined in a new Bureau of Southern Asian Affairs (SA).

D. Insulating Selected Programs in Multilateral and Autonomous Agencies

We have argued in Part IV-B that one of the most difficult problems associated with the time dimension of complexity is the relationship of long run and short-run interests and objectives. We noted that there is pronounced propensity to sacrifice long-run goals to the requirements of leverage and the political need for immediate gains. An organizational solution to this dilemma is the use of agencies that are insulated from the vicissitudes of short-run political circumstances and the struggle for power in domestic and international politics.

Insulation will not survive short-run political pressures if it is not grounded in good reasons that can be publicly stated and defended; if those reasons are not appreciated and defended by the President and Congress; and if they do not command public understanding and support. Among the policies and programs discussed in this report, we believe that those directed to economic growth and redistribution and people-to-people diplomacy have the kind of governmental and public support required for such a defense.

In the light of these considerations, we recommend that (1) economic aid in the form of loans and credits be concentrated in multilateral agencies such as IDA and regional development banks, (2) that cultural and educational programs now located in the State Department's Bureau of Educational and Cultural Affairs, HEW's Office of Education and in other agencies be transferred to a new autonomous agency, the Foundation for Education and Culture, described and justified in V.C (3), "Insulation in Practice: Cultural and Informational Agencies," and (3) that a people-to-people program such as the Peace Corps that relies on volunteers and operates at the grassroots level be located in an autonomous agency similar to the Foundation for Education and Culture.

E. The Regional Conference

We propose the creation of a Regional Conference designed to promote regional coordination in the field and in Washington. Regional conferences lasting two or three days would be convened quarterly at rotating centres in the region and in Washington. Conferences would be organized around topics of common interest to the region such as food and agriculture, economic development, military policy, oceanic problems, nuclear proliferation, population, trade, education and culture, and science and technology. They would be attended by approximately forty persons who would, in a concluding plenary session, review the reports of topically grouped workshops in an attempt to formulate common understandings and recommendations. Such sessions and the documents they produce could do what policy papers drawn up by NSC inter-departmental groups now attempt to do.

The objectives of the Regional Council are like those of chiefs of missions conferences but go beyond them by stressing exposure to the political environment and presenting problems of the region and by aiming to deliberate in ways that promote coordination and policy guidance. The first objective, exposure to the political environment of the host countries, can be aided by inviting as guests to plenary or workshop sessions elected or appointed officials, scholars and leaders of thought and opinion of the host country (which includes from time to time the USA).

USG participants would include not only officials whose work and qualifications relate to the topic of the conference but also ambassadors or DCMs, assistant and deputy assistant secretaries and, on occasion, the secretary, under secretary or deputy under secretaries. (We take note of Secretary Kissinger's penchant for peripatetic diplomacy and, in the Regional Conference, propose to institutionalize it.)

The Conference is also designed to promote field-Washington coordination. The operational routines, policy agendas and, most important, environmental contexts of the center and the periphery generate markedly different perspectives. Neither believes that the other is sufficiently alive to its setting, constraints and problems. The Conference exploits an underutilized resource for the conduct of foreign policy, modern means of rapid travel, to remedy these difficulties by creating new lines of discourse within the region and between it and Washington.

Conferences in Washington will expose field officials to the relevancies of bureaucratic, Congressional and national politics; to policy agendas as Washington sees them; and to political sentiment on the Hill. Such experiences will refresh their appreciation of the relatively modest domestic standing of matters that seem critical in Dacca or Islamabad.

The Regional Conference would be staffed by a small regional secretariat headed by a Regional Coordinator at the rank of Deputy Assistant Secretary. The secretariat would generate and gather information relevant to the topic and agenda of particular sessions, facilitate communication, and plan and coordinate conference agendas. Every effort should be made to prevent the regional secretariat from becoming a place where routine tasks are performed. The regional secretariat is meant to provide horizontal coordination among embassies. Its staff should know the region, have served there, and have a good command of programs, including those on the margins of the State Department and outside it.

We began this report by observing that prescriptions for administrative reform have a cyclical quality. Those that originated in the New Deal era to strengthen presidential management and leadership of the executive branch prospered and grew during and after World War II in response to America's role as a world power. In the 1960s, the need for presidential power became the dominant theme of the literature on domestic and foreign policy and in the early 1970s the principal problematic of presidential practice.

We propose in this report counter-cyclical measures designed to correct the excesses of presidential power in the conduct of foreign policy. They include proposals to counter imperative with deliberative coordination; the NSC system with a strengthened and re-organized State Department, including an Assistant Secretary Policy Planning Council and Regional Conferences; hierarchical norms and relationships with collegial ones; the general knowledge of policy intellectuals with the professional knowledge of career officials; and global-dominant view of world politics with one that gives global, regional and bilateral relations their due.

If implemented, these prescriptions will in time, no doubt, lead to other excesses, but in the historical context of the 1970s we find them appropriate remedies for the era's presenting problems.

NOTES AND REFERENCES

1. Graham Allison, *The Essence of Decision: Explaining the Cuban Missile Crisis* (Boston: Little Brown, 1971); I.M. Destler, *Presidents, Bureaucrats and Foreign Policy* (Princeton, NJ: Princeton University Press, 1972) and Morton Halperin, *Bureaucratic Politics and Foreign Policy* (Washington, D.C.: Brookings Institution Press, 1974).
2. William Barnds, *India, Pakistan and the Great Powers* (New York: Praeger, 1972).
3. We are grateful to all those who allowed themselves to be interviewed, or who participated in reviewing the cases and summary report at

various points in the life of the project. Their insights and comments were most helpful. Naturally, the opinions and conclusions expressed in this paper are those of the authors, and not necessarily of those interviewed, who participated in the review process of the Commission, or of any agency of the governments of the United States or of South Asian countries.

4. Emmet Hughes, "The Presidency as I Have Seen It," in *The Living Presidency: The Resources and Dilemmas of American Presidential Office* (New York: Coward, McCann & Geoghegan, 1973), 315.
5. See Edward S. Corwin, *The President, Office and Powers* (New York: New York University Press, 1940), p. 97ff., and Barry D. Karl, *Executive Reorganization and Reform in the New Deal: The Genesis of Administrative Management 1900-1939* (Cambridge, MA: Harward University Press, 1963).
6. Barry Karl, *Executive Reorganization and Reform*, p. 229.
7. For a systematic account of the first and second wave and their differences see Robert J. Art, "Bureaucratic Politics and American Foreign Policy: A Critique," *Policy Sciences* (1973): 467-90. The first generation includes Warner Schilling, Paul Hammond, Samuel P. Huntington and Richard Neustadt, the second Graham Allison, Morton Halperin and I.M. Destler among others.
8. Destler, *Presidents, Bureaucrats and Foreign Policy*, 89.
9. Richard Neustadt, *Presidential Power* (New York: Wiley, 1960), 9.
10. Richard Neustadt, "White House and White Hall," *The Public Interest*, 2(1966): 64.
11. Abraham F. Lowenthal, "'Bureaucratic Politics' and the United States Policy Toward Latin America: An Interim Research Report." Delivered at the American Political Association Annual Meeting, September, 1974.
12. The *New York Times*, January 6, 1972, p. 16.
13. Destler, *Presidents, Bureaucrats, and Foreign Policy*, 87.
14. Chapter 4, "The Presidential Interest," in Halperin, *Bureaucratic Politics and Foreign Policy*.
15. Destler, *Presidents, Bireaucrats and Foregn Policy*, 89-90.
16. Quoted in Henry Raymont, "Kennedy Library Documents, Opened to Two Scholars, Illuminate Politics on Cuba and Berlin," The *New York Times*, August 17, 1970.
17. Richard Neustadt in *Presidential Power* argued that to some extent the executive departments, and their heads, are by the very nature of their functions, "natural enemies" of the President.
18. Halperin, *Bureaucratic Politics and Foreign Policy*, 63 and, more generally, the facts and arguments adduced in Chapter 4, "Presidential Interests."
19. I.M. Destler, "Country Expertise and U.S. Foreign Policy Making: The Case of Japan," (Washington, D.C.: The Brookings Institution, Reprint 298); Destler, who credits the characterization, is surprised that the

experts did so well in arranging Okinawa's "reversion" to Japan, and prescribes strengthening the president's hand further even while recognizing that the State Department has "the organizational depth and breadth to bring coherence to a wide range of U.S. foreign policy."

20. See also Leon V. Sigal, *Reporters and Officials: The Organization and Politics of Newsmaking* (Lexington, MA: D.C. Heath, 1973).
21. For two different perspectives on the problem that inform our view see Destler, *President Bureaucrats and Foreign Policy*, Chapter Seven, and John F. Campbell, *The Foreign Affairs Fudge Factory* (New York: Basic Books, 1971), Part 2.
22. Jackson Subcommittee, "Basic Issues" in *Administration*, Staff Reports, p. 9, quoted in Destler, *Presidents, Bireaucrats and Foreign Policy*, 84-85.
23. The *New York Times*, October 13, 1974.
24. For the country directorate system generally, see William I. Bacchus, *Foreign Policy and the Bureaucratic Process: The State Department's Country Director System* (Princeton, NJ: Princeton University Press, 1974).
25. Interdepartmental committees active in the South Asia policy arena are depicted in the case studies appearing elsewhere in this volume, particularly those by Bjorkman, Kochanek, and Moulton.
26. For a study of the role of ambassadors and embassy officials in the Washington environment see Roger Sack and Donald L. Wyman, "Latin American Diplomacy and the United States Foreign Policy Making Process," study for the Commission on the Organization of the Government for the Conduct of Foreign Policy, December, 1974, printed in Appendix I to the Commission's Report.
27. Evidence for this findings can be found not only in the case studies of this report but also in the study by Joan Hochman, "The Suspension of Economic Assistance to India" in *Cases on a Decade of United States Foreign Economic Policy: 1965-1974*, a report submitted to the Commission on the Organization of the Government for the Conduct of Foreign Policy by Griffenhagen-Kroeger, Inc., Edward Hamilton, Principal Investigator, printed in Appendix H to the Commission's Report.
28. Chester Bowles, *Promises to Keep, My Years in Public Life, 1941-1969* (New York: Harper & Row, 1971), 552.
29. Chester Bowles, *Promises to Keep*, 557.
30. Lyndon Johnson, *The Vantage Point, Perspectives of the Presidency, 1963-1969* (New York: Holt, Rinehart and Winston, 1961), 225.
31. Bowles, *Promises*, 559.
32. Johnson, *The Vantage Point*, 226.
33. Bowles, *Promises*, 525.
34. Cited from his Journal of February 6, 1966. Bowles, *Promises*, 534.
35. Bowles, *Promises*, 525.

36. Johnson, *The Vantage Point*, p. 225.
37. See, for example, V.K.R.V. Rao, economic advisor to the GoI, who wrote at the time: "Our immediate task is to rid the country of stultifying and nationally dangerous dependence on imports for our food supplies" [GoI, *The Meaning of Self-Reliance*, November, 1965], and of course C. Subramaniam, India's Food Minister, had gained parliamentary approval for a comprehensive "self-help" policy in December, 1965.
38. William Bundy, "International Security Today," *Foreign Affairs*, 53, No. 1 (October, 1974): 38. Bundy argues for priorities that recognize that "the regions of the world have reasserted a life of their own . .." and against "pernicious abstractions" and using "universal principles as a guide."
39. The *New York Times*, January 6, 1972. All quotations of government officials addressing themselves to the Bangladesh problem are from this report, unless otherwise noted.
40. Marvin Kalb and Bernard Kalb, *Kissinger* (Boston: Little Brown, 1974), p. 262.
41. Kalb and Kalb in *Kissinger* depict Kissinger and Assistant Secretary of State for the Near East and South Asia, Joseph Sisco, as engaged in "a rip-roaring battle" over the direction of American policy. Sisco, the Kalbs report, expressed the State Department's best judgment when he argued that "India had limited ambitions in the war" and "did not want to extend the war into West Pakistan;" saw little chance of intervention by the Soviet Union or China; and advocated "a policy of cool rhetoric and calm behavior;" but "Sisco lost the battle," p. 259.
42. Unless otherwise indicated, all quotations are from the Cohen paper.
43. The reappraisal of military assistance programs was under the general supervision of Assistant Secretary of Defense for International Security Affairs, John T. McNaughton and directed by Townshend Hoopes. See Roger Sack, "United States Military Aid to the Ayub Khan Regime," a background paper for this report.
44. Ambassador to India Chester Bowles refers, in *Promises to Keep*, to USG encouragement of third country sales of tanks to Pakistan. Ensuing publicity, he believes, forced a retreat, p. 521.
45. Further, ISA/DOD "pointed out that refueling could be done more efficiently and cheaply in the Persian Gulf, that developing a U.S. facility would anger littoral states without yielding any particular benefit, and that even a small facility might be the prelude for a larger and unnecessary establishment" whose vulnerability could be used to justify additional costly aircraft carriers and might result in trapping an undue portion of the American fleet on the wrong side of the Suez Canal.
46. The World Bank's official designation is the International Bank for Reconstruction and Development or IBRD. Hereafter we refer to the World Bank as WB.

47. The Secretary of the Treasury is advised by the National Advisory Council on International Monetary and Financial Policies (NAC), an interdepartmental committee with five voting units, Treasury (which has the chair), State, Commerce, the Federal Reserve Board, and the Eximbank, and a number of "participating" non-voting units including USDA, AID, OMB, DOD, the Council of Economic Advisors (CEA) and the Council on International Economic Policy (CIEP). NAC has two "policy" levels (Secretaries as Principals and Assistant Secretaries as Alternates) and a technically oriented operating level which meets weekly to discuss agency positions on, *inter alia*, IDA proposals and to recommend position to their respective Principals who vote on the IDA Board.
48. Unless otherwise indicated, all references are to the text of Moulton's study.
49. Moulton adduces a number of other reasons including "the friendly and respectful relationship obtaining between McNamara and Kissinger" which may have "diluted" the tilt policy when applied in IDA's direction. Kissinger allegedly had intervened earlier to dissuade Nixon from attempting to dislodge McNamara from the Bank presidency.
50. All subsequent references, unless otherwise indicated, are to the Kochanek paper.
51. See Kochanek, footnotes, for personnel with office designations as of April 2, 1972. Its functions were to review and compile information relevant to potential and actual expropriation cases; to make specific findings about compensation; to recommend courses of action; and to coordinate and implement policy.
52. Section 620(e) of the Foreign Assistance Act of 1961.
53. Section 12 of the International Development Association Act.
54. Unless otherwise indicated, all references are to the Rubin paper.
55. Unless otherwise indicated, all references are to the Andersen paper.
56. As per the Agreement between the United States and India of October, 1974.
57. For a more detailed version of the assumptions, evidence, argument and prescriptions discussed below see John F. Campbell, *The Foreign Affairs Fudge Factory* (New York: Basic Books, 1971), particularly Chapter 9.
58. Harvey H. Bundy and James Grafton Rogers, *The Organization of the Government for the Conduct of Foreign Policy*, Task Force Report on Foreign Affairs (Appendix H), 1975.
59. The visa work of the Bureau of Security and Consular Affairs (SCA) can be transferred to the Immigration and Naturalization Service (INS) in the Justice Department, already responsible for the entrance of aliens and its passport responsibilities further automated. An assistant secretary for administration, responsible to the secretary and the six other assistant secretaries, can reduce substantially the 50 percent of State employees now allocated to support and housekeeping jobs.

60. A deputy under secretary for budget, replacing the deputy undersecretary for management would prepare, with the agreement and cooperation of other interested agencies and, after transferring it to State, the help of OMB's international division, an integrated foreign affairs budget for the executive branch. The regional assistant secretaries should review expenditure plans and ambassadors should justify and control expenditure in their countries.

PART III

CASE STUDIES

CASE STUDY

5

THE BREAKUP OF PAKISTAN

— Philip Oldenburg

Introduction

Chronology

The crisis of the breakup of Pakistan can be divided, in terms of U.S. participation, into roughly four major phases. The first began with the Pakistan army crackdown in the East Wing of Pakistan on the night of March 25/26, 1971.[1] This followed a three-week period of civil disobedience and the exercise of *de facto* governmental power by the Awami League led by Sheikh Mujibur Rahman. The Awami League had won an overwhelming victory in the December 1970 election for the Constituent Assembly, the climax of a movement towards greater autonomy for East Pakistan which began in 1954 or perhaps even earlier. The drive for autonomy was fueled by the economic, political and bureaucratic discrimination against East Bengal by the West Pakistan-dominated central government, exacerbated by the West Pakistani belief (held particularly by the Punjabi-dominated military) that Bengalis were culturally and racially inferior.

The crackdown, in which Sheikh Mujib was captured and thousands of Bengalis were killed—students, Hindus, and members of the police and army, particularly—precipitated a full-scale civil war, a declaration of independence by the Awami League leaders who had fled to India, and, in the view of most observers within the State Department and without, the inevitable breakup of Pakistan. As Tajuddin Ahmad, Prime Minister of the

Awami League government-in-exile, put it in April, "Pakistan is now dead and buried under a mountain of corpses."[2]

The second phase of the crisis began with the announcement of Henry Kissinger's visit to Peking (July 15) and the signing of the Indo-Soviet friendship treaty (August 9). This phase featured the build-up of guerrilla forces (the Mukti Bahini) inside East Bengal, and the increase of direct and indirect Indian support, against the backdrop of a refugee population in India of nearly ten million by November. It ended with the outbreak of full-scale war between India and Pakistan on December 3rd.

The third phase was the war, in which India, with the help of the Mukti Bahini, quickly defeated the Pakistan army in the East, and while fighting a holding action on the ground on the Western front, used air and naval power to damage Pakistan's military capability. The final phase began with the transfer of power to Sheikh Mujib on January 12, 1972 and ended with U.S. recognition of Bangladesh, on April 4, 1972.

Decision-Making and Rationales

Virtually all the decisions made by the U.S. in this crisis originated in the White House. By and large, explicit rationales for those decisions were *not* communicated to State Department officials, still less to the Congress and the public. Since the end of the crisis, some rationales have been presented, most notably by President Nixon in his "State of the World" message to Congress of February 9, 1972, but what interviewees* agreed were the *real* reasons for U.S. policy have never been publicly stated. I will discuss some of those decisions in detail below, mentioning others only briefly because of lack of information and space. Having presented what I believe the rationales of each of these decisions were, I will move to a detailed discussion divided into two parts: the facts of the case, and the implications. The study will conclude

* Much of the material in this study is drawn from interviews with government officials and private individuals, conducted in the summer of 1974. The line of argument presented is entirely my own, however, and when it is necessary to identify the source of a statement as an interview, an asterisk in parentheses is placed in the text, thus: (*).

with a brief sketch of the implications of these decision cases taken together.

Those decisions I will discuss in detail are:

(1) the decision *not* to comment on the initial "blood-bath" in East Bengal, and, later, the decision not to criticize Pakistan as the killing continued;
(2) the decision to cut off most arms aid to Pakistan, while continuing to supply some;
(3) the decision to provide humanitarian relief to refugees in India and to the people who stayed in East Bengal;
(4) the decision to pursue a political solution of the crisis with the Pakistanis, the Indians, and the exiled Bengali leadership;
(5) the decision first to attempt to prevent the outbreak of war between India and Pakistan and then to end it once it had begun.

The rationale for the first decision was that the civil war was an internal affair of Pakistan; but the reason for not letting concern for violations of human rights override that principle was the "historical coincidence" that Pakistan was the intermediary in the arrangement of the opening to China. These delicate negotiations, which were initiated in 1969[3] and had reached the stage of the exchange of notes via Pakistan by early 1971, became very serious on March 15th, and a specific invitation (in a sealed envelope) for either Kissinger or Rogers to visit China was conveyed by the Pakistan Ambassador some time before April 6th.[4] Presumably the secrecy of the negotiations, and thus the opening itself,[5] would have been jeopardized by an "unfriendly" gesture to Pakistan at the very moment a breakthrough was achieved.

The reason for not criticizing Pakistan over the violent repression in East Bengal is tied to the generally favorable position vis-a-vis Pakistan that the U.S. adopted. As stated publicly, the pro-Pakistan "tilt" was meant to retain "leverage" with President Yahya Khan. It is likely that the desire to remain the friend to China's friend contributed to the decision, as did the factor of

President Nixon's personal rapport with President Yahya, and his positive feeling towards Pakistan. (This factor has been emphasized by too many to be discounted, despite Kissinger's remark that "I do not think we do ourselves any justice if we ascribe policies to the personal pique of individuals.")[6]

The rationale for cutting off arms aid was simple: the Pakistan army was making use of them in a situation contrary to the agreement under which the U.S. supplied them. The reason for continuing a comparatively small flow of spare parts, etc. was symbolic, and was tied to the general pro-Pakistan U.S. stance. The decision to provide humanitarian relief needed no justification, but the proportions of aid given to India compared to aid earmarked for East Bengal underlined the White House position that humanitarian aid was to be the "centerpiece" of the U.S. political-diplomatic effort.

The "political solution" was juxtaposed to a military solution: if the U.S. and others did not succeed in getting a political settlement of the civil war, India in one way or the other would see that Pakistan was broken up. The rationale was that the U.S. did not wish to see the breakup of Pakistan occur, especially with outside intervention, because that would "destabilize" the region. The need to preserve Pakistan's "integrity" was even greater in view of her alliance to the U.S. and friendship with China.

The decision to exercise U.S. influence first to prevent the outbreak of war between India and Pakistan and then to end it was of course justified on the ground that war is not a way to solve international disputes (a rationale which, it should be noted, the U.N. General Assembly agreed with by a vote of 104 to 11, with 10 abstentions). A deeper rationale for the U.S. was that since India would win decisively, the "destabilization" of the subcontinent would occur. Also, the defeat of a U.S. ally would place the U.S. in a weak position vis-a-vis the USSR in upcoming summit talks. This latter reason bulks very large during the war. And underlying the "tilt" which was made explicit during the war—i.e. the war should stop because Pakistan was losing it—is the personal factor of President Nixon's attitude. In Kissinger's words at the Washington Special Action Group (hereafter WSAG;

the minutes constitute the bulk of the "Anderson Papers") meeting, ". . .the President is not inclined to let the Paks be defeated."[7]

Let me discuss briefly decisions on economic aid to Pakistan and on the recognition of Bangladesh. The focal points for Congressional action during the crisis were the Gallagher and Church/Saxbe amendments to the Foreign Aid Bill which would have cut off economic aid to Pakistan until the civil war ended. The administration not only opposed those amendments, it also dissented from the Aid-Pakistan consortium recommendation to suspend aid to Pakistan (made in the wake of the leaked World Bank report which noted that the repression in East Bengal was so severe that economic aid could not be utilized there). Again, the rationale for this policy was to preserve leverage with the Pakistanis.[8]

Finally, there was a decision to delay the recognition of Bangladesh—the U.S. recognized Bangladesh on April 4, 1972, fully two months after most of the nations of Europe had extended recognition and nearly a month after Indian troops had left Bangladesh. No plausible rationale was ever given to the State Department(*), still less the Congress,[9] but it was clearly tied to the China opening—President Nixon postponed considering it until after his trip to China (in late February 1972). Certainly, too, there was a desire to defer to Pakistan, even as the Muslim nations of the Middle East and Africa were doing.

Violent Repression; and the Register of Dissent

The Facts

After the crackdown on March 25/26, a decision was made to downplay the seriousness of the action and to avoid admitting to the facts of the "blood-bath." In the initial phase of the civil war, there was, as Senator Kennedy said on the Senate floor on April 1, 1971, "indiscriminate killing, the execution of political leaders and students, and thousands of civilians suffering and dying every hour of the day."[10] It soon became clear from press reports that Hindus were being singled out for killing,[11] and by June the London *Sunday Times* could use the title "Genocide" for its introduction to one of the best accounts of Pakistan army activities.[12] Senator Kennedy, in a news conference in New Delhi in August, called the Pakistan military action "genocide,"[13] but that word was absent from debate by public figures both before and after August.[14]

The administration was even less willing to come to terms with the possibility that "genocide" was occurring in the later phase of the civil war than they had been willing to condemn the initial violence of March. The first indication of this stance was Washington's resistance to the Dacca Consul-General's decision to have Americans evacuated from Dacca in the first week of April (*), at a time when Pakistan was claiming that the situation had already returned to normal. According to Senator Kennedy, "instead of calling it an 'evacuation'... the State Department reached into its bag of euphemisms and termed the exodus of Americans a normal 'thinning out'."[15]

The U.S. issued a statement deploring the violence at the end of the first week of April, but one view is that that actually reported a decision *not* to pressure Pakistan because it was made so late, nearly two weeks after the crackdown. U.S. officials were reluctant to make public mention of the wide-spread killing or of the facts on actions which could be labeled "genocide." Archer Blood, Consul-General in Dacca until early June, testified before Senator Kennedy's subcommittee on refugees on June 26th. Part of his testimony is worth quoting at length:

> SENATOR FONG: When the insurgents were put down, were there actions taken by the East Pakistan Army which forced the people to leave?
> MR. BLOOD: I don't see any direct relationship between the level of insurgency and the flow of refugees.
> SENATOR FONG: Then why would the refugees leave?
> MR. BLOOD: . ..An d, subsequently, many Hindus have left because of the way they were treated.
> SENATOR FONG: Did many of them leave because they say conditions were imposed on the Hindus that they thought they couldn't live with?

MR. BLOOD: I assume so, yes.
SENATOR FONG: What would those conditions be, sir?
MR. BLOOD: I wouldn't want to go into every detail, because we have reported this in the classified messages. ... I would prefer not to answer in open session. . .. [16]

The official position was that the refugee outflow was due to continued fighting and the poor economic situation. U.S. efforts were thus aimed at stopping the "fighting" (between the Pakistan army and the Mukti Bahini guerrillas) not at stopping the killing of Hindus and the destruction of their property. Official policy plus the constraints of "cliency" make it most unlikely that "genocide" ever figured in any private communication with the Pakistan government.[17]

While the Dacca consulate was urging condemnation of the violence, seconded by the New Delhi embassy, the Islamabad embassy discounted the reports from Dacca on the grounds that the consulate officials, being limited in their movements, could only be getting "partial" reports(*). The fact that the Islamabad embassy seemed to give greater credence to its Pakistan government sources than to its own officers in the field, despite close personal ties between the Deputy Chief of Mission and the Consul-General, must have hurt the morale of officers in Dacca. On the other hand, the Islamabad embassy protested on July 15 to the State Department that field reports on predictions of possible famine in East Bengal were being denied in public statements in Washington.[18]

All interviewees agreed that the "tilt" policy position of the U.S. did not affect the reporting of facts to Washington. Even after it had surfaced, during the war, Consul-General Spivack cabled details[19] of his and U.N. Assistant Secretary General Paul Marc Henry's inspection of damage and bomb-rack fragments which indicated Pakistani responsibility for the bombing of the Dacca orphanage (which was blamed on India with much publicity). The Islamabad embassy sent in a report to Washington in which the Defense Representative to Pakistan and the Defense Attache questioned Spivack's conclusion.[20]

The discounting of reports because of their tone and the presumed "cliency" bias of the drafters extended to the reporting of facts as well as to the presentation of estimates and advice on policy. (Ironically, the presumed cliency of Dacca begat cliency in Islamabad.) But the professionalism of the Foreign Service dictated that the reporting of facts known to be unpalatable not stop.

Implications

The maintenance of contact with the Pakistanis, both in the context of the opening to China and with a view towards exerting "leverage" in the future (once the situation in the East had become clear), was clearly a matter of great importance. One non-U.S. source, who discussed the findings of the leaked World Bank report of July with Yahya Khan, says the Pakistan President could not credit its finding that official violence had and was occurring in East Pakistan. The result of a U.S. decision to raise the question of "genocide" might thus have resulted in cutting off communication with the Pakistanis (and especially with Yahya Khan) rather than in changing Pakistan's policies.

Most sources agreed that almost everyone at the State Department recognized what was going on in East Bengal and would have liked to see if not a U.S. condemnation at least a dissociation of the U.S. from the Pakistan regime. The facts reached the policy-makers in the White House, although there is some difference of opinion on how forceful and articulate the presentation of State Department views were; according to one official, lower levels of State felt it could have been much better, but according to Marvin and Bernard Kalb, Assistant Secretary of State Sisco "battled" with Kissinger in WSAG meetings in December.[21]

Those within the system were apparently satisfied with the channels of dissent open to them. "Official informal" letters were seen by my sources as having considerable importance in making an impact on policy decisions in most cases (in part because they are considered leak-proof, and the leaks of dissent positions seemed to distress the dissenters as much as anyone), but it was implied, not in this crisis, because policy was being made beyond the reach of the "official informal."

No one who dissented from the U.S. policy in this crisis resigned. It would not be necessary or desirable for an FSO to threaten to resign whenever he objected strongly to a decision. But if the forceful presentation of policy alternatives is considered desirable, it might be worthwhile to make it easier for the FSO to leave the Service, by training him during his career so that he could enter a different career (e.g. university teaching, international business), or by bringing in people from outside the Service into middle-level slots.

Finally, the existence of career sub-cultures, FSOs with academic interests, for example, can provide sub-communities of knowledgeable professionals who can informally sustain the dissenter in responsible dissent. There is some evidence that the South Asia specialists—encompassing both India and Pakistan "wallahs"—constituted such a sub-community in 1971.

The Arms Aid Cut-Off Decision; and the Use of Public Statements

The Facts

A decision was made to cut-off the supply of arms to Pakistan. In a letter to Senator Kennedy, dated April 20, 1971, David Abshire, Assistant Secretary for Congressional Relations, wrote, "we have been informed by the Department of Defense that [no non-lethal military end items (of) spare parts and ammunition have] been provided to the Pakistan Government or its agents since the outbreak of fighting in East Pakistan on March 25-26, and nothing is presently scheduled for such delivery."[22] But "delivery" here meant that items contracted for and licensed for export before March 25 were considered "delivered" even though they had not left U.S. shores. This continued movement of arms to Pakistan was revealed in a *New York Times* article—presumably as the result of a leak—while the Indian Foreign Minister was returning from Washington to Delhi with what he thought were assurances that Pakistan was not receiving U.S. arms. These events contributed to Indian distrust of the U.S. (which became crucial in U.S. attempts to prevent a war; see below).

A General Accounting Office report, released on February 4, 1972,[23] revealed that not only had $3.8 million worth of Munitions List articles been exported under valid licenses, but also "Department of Defense agencies, despite departmental directives issued in April, continued to release from their stocks spare parts for lethal end-items" and "the U.S. Air Force delivered to Pakistan about $563,000 worth of spare parts between March 25 and mid-July 1971 on a priority basis using the Military Airlift Command. Some of these spare parts were needed to place inoperable aircraft, such as F-104's, into operable condition."[24] It was discovered in late August that until the practice was stopped by informal order on July 2nd and formally on August 12th, "military departments" entered into foreign military sales contracts of about $10.6 million with Pakistan. .. ,"[25] though no licenses were issued for these contracted items. On November 8th, the State Department revoked all outstanding licenses (for goods worth about $3.6 million) and the flow of arms to Pakistan ended.

There were several factors at work here. On one level, there was something of a bureaucratic "snafu" (*) in the instances of continued spare parts supply. This might of course be interpreted as deliberate effort on the part of Defense agencies to continue supplying a country they considered to be a good ally. The "business as usual" signing of new contracts was justified as proper because U.S. military supply policy was "under review." If the continued supply under valid licenses had been a "snafu" in which State Department and Defense Department signals had gotten crossed, then presumably shipments would have ceased when it was revealed in late June. But the licenses were not revoked until November—and Kissinger wondered aloud in the WSAG meetings whether that step had been wise—making it clear that the supply of a limited amount of arms to Pakistan had been U.S. policy. Christopher van Hollen, Deputy Assistant Secretary for NEA, in testimony before Senator Kennedy's sub-committee on October 4, made U.S. policy explicit:

SENATOR FONG: The administration did not feel it should revoke the licenses that had been issued?

MR. VAN HOLLEN: That is correct. The judgment was made that this would be a political sanction, and that it would not be in keeping with our efforts to maintain a political relationship with the Government of Pakistan, looking towards the achievement of certain foreign policy objectives of the United States.[26]

That is, these arms shipments were continued as part of U.S. attempts to maintain "leverage" on Pakistan.

During the December war, Jordan and possibly other countries offered to transfer U.S. supplied weapons to Pakistan. The question was discussed in two of the WSAG meetings whose minutes were leaked. State Department and Defense Department officials pointed out that it would be illegal for the U.S. to permit third country transfers, since the U.S. itself was barred from supplying arms to Pakistan. Kissinger, however, asked that King Hussein be kept in a "holding pattern," noting that the President "may want to honor" requests from Pakistan for military aid of this kind.[27] It was later reported that "military sources" disclosed that Libya and Jordan had indeed provided aircraft to Pakistan.[28]

Humanitarian Assistance; and the Role of Congress

The Facts

One interviewee told me that in August the President described the relief effort— which would be carried on, no matter what, for humanitarian reasons—as the centerpiece of the U.S. political effort vis-a-vis Pakistan. This view of U.S. policy was however not conveyed downward even to middle-level State Department officers. The decision was to provide aid both to the refugees in India and to those in the East (especially in the cyclone-affected areas) who did not leave. The threat of famine would be met and India's burden would be shared. Congress, on the other hand, wanted to give more aid for refugee relief than the administration requested, and less to the people in East Pakistan, on the grounds that with a crippled transport system and the acknowledged diversion of some relief supplies and transport vehicles to the Pakistan army, there was no guarantee that such aid would reach those for whom it was intended.[29]

The amount of U.S. assistance was consistently overstated by U.S. spokesmen, including the President, even after the crisis was over. A GAO report of June 29, 1972 listed authorized contributions for victims in India as $94.5 million, and pointed out that of the $276.7 million authorized for victims in Pakistan (and this included "old" money intended specifically for pre-March cyclone damage relief and normal bilateral food aid), *$201.2 million (73 per cent) was not implemented.* The repeated U.S. assertion that the U.S. was contributing "more than the rest of the world combined"—a formulation the Delhi embassy finally gave up protesting(*)—appears to have been a self-serving public relations effort. The World Bank's estimate of the cost of refugee relief to India was $700 million by March 1972 (India claimed in the U.N. debate in December that she was spending "3 million a day); the U.S. thus would contribute about 15 per cent of the total and the "rest of the world" about the same or more,[30] leaving India with nearly 70 per cent of the cost of refugee relief.

There was, moreover, a coordination of public utterance in this instance. Another GAO report (of April 20, 1972, but requested in July 1971 by Senator Kennedy) stated in the introduction:

> Our review efforts were impeded by Department of State and AID officials. They withheld and summarized records prior to our access and thereby limited information needed for a complete and thorough report. In connection with the GAO review, U.S. Embassy officials in Islamabad were instructed not to make available messages reporting on sensitive discussions with the GoP [Government of Pakistan], Government of India, or U.N. agencies, or certain sensitive documents relating to development of U.S. policy.

Implications

The U.S. relief effort provided a major focus for Congressional attention to the 1971 crisis. While the GAO, an arm of the Congress, was having difficulty in conducting its investigation, Senator Kennedy was able to get copies of confidential cables from Pakistan. Congressional sources I spoke with seemed satisfied with the institutional arrangements in the foreign policy field, arguing that the lack of Congressional activity during the crisis (the Foreign Relations Committee never held a public hearing, for example) reflected not the lack of power or expertise but the lack of Congressional interest in foreign policy and especially vis-a-vis South Asia.

The Congressional concern with humanitarian issues reflected the U.S. public perception of the problem—a record amount of money was contributed to refugee relief from private sources—but Congress had little impact in the face of a U.S. policy which sought first to downplay the refugee issue, then to shift the focus of concern from refugees and from "genocide" to East Pakistanis suffering because of civil strife (cause unspecified), and finally, to overstate the amount of U.S. assistance.

The Political Solution; and the "Checklist" Danger

The Facts

President Nixon in his "State of the World" message of February 9, 1972 called "the problem of political settlement between East and West Pakistan," "the basic issue of the crisis."[31] In May, in letters to President Yahya and Prime Minister Gandhi, President Nixon referred to the necessity of a "political accommodation,"[32] by summer, this was communicated to "all parties" as being a political solution "on the basis of some form of autonomy for East Pakistan."[33]

During August, September and October, eight contacts with the "Bangladesh people" in Calcutta were made, according to Kissinger.[34] And, according to President Nixon, by early November, President Yahya told us he was prepared to begin negotiations with any representatives of this group not charged with high crimes in Pakistan, or with Awami League leaders still in East Pakistan."[35] One interviewee felt that the contacts were a "sterile exercise" and another felt that they were not serious, since follow-up cross-checks were discouraged by Washington. The difficulty here was perhaps differing perceptions of what the contacts meant.

These contacts were to lead to negotiations between Pakistan "and Bangladesh representatives approved by Mujibur," according to Kissinger.[36] The negotiations never began, nor was the U.S. ever involved "on substance."[37] The next step was to establish contact with Mujib to get his approval of Awami League negotiations, and Kissinger claimed that the U.S. "had the approval of the Government of Pakistan to establish contact with Mujib through his defense lawyer," and that India had been so informed.[38] Prime Minister Gandhi, however, wrote to President Nixon on December 15th that "there was not even a whisper that anyone from the outside world had tried to have contact with Mujibur Rahman."[39] And Ambassador Keating, reacting to the news of Kissinger's backgrounder, pointed out that a move to contact Mujib had been rebuffed on December 2nd, and the initiative had been suggested on November 29th[40] (*one week after the war had begun, by President Nixon's account*).[41]

The negotiations, President Nixon admits, were to be with those not charged with "high crimes,"—i.e., the entire top leadership of the Awami League. Given the gap between "contacts" (the latest in October) and the attempted contact with Mujib (end of November), one can understand the belief that it was all a "sterile exercise."

There is also some doubt in another area, the proposal for a timetable for East Pakistan's autonomy. The U.S. claim was that "in mid-November, we informed India that we were preparing to promote discussion of an explicit timetable for Each Pakistani autonomy."[42] Kissinger told the press, "we told the Indian Ambassador .. .tha t we were prepared to discuss with them . ..a precise timetable for the establishment of political autonomy in East Bengal."[43] Ambassador Keating, relying on the news report, pointed out that he had not been informed of this "critical fact" that "Washington and Islamabad were prepared" to discuss the timetable.[44] But it seems clear from another remark by Kissinger that the U.S. was seeking a timetable from India;[45] he also said "[India] knew that we believed that political autonomy was the logical outcome of a negotiation. . . ."[46] Prime Minister Gandhi indeed wrote that "the United States recognized that ... unquestionably in the long run Pakistan must acquiesce in the direction of greater autonomy for East Pakistan. .. ."[47] There is no indication, however, that *any* timetable for political autonomy (which went beyond the scheduled restoration of civilian government in East Pakistan) was presented to Pakistan, or that the U.S. had publicly favored autonomy in a form acceptable to the Awami League.

Many officials, both in Delhi and Islamabad, believed by April that Pakistan would break up, and this assessment was supported by the intelligence community (*). Those in Islamabad felt that direct Indian intervention would be inevitable while those in the Delhi embassy felt that the guerrillas would succeed on their own (*). An interim solution of autonomy leading to independence was not ruled out as unacceptable to the Bengalis (and to India, who did not recognize an independent Bangladesh until December 6, despite considerable internal political pressure). Whether such a facade would have been acceptable to Pakistan is questionable. The Pakistan government's qualified amnesty, its willingness to accept a limited U.N. role, and the return of East Pakistan to "civilian rule" under a man totally unacceptable to the Bengalis—all pointed to as significant steps by President Nixon—were dismissed by the Awami League. The proposal to station U.N. observers on the border was called a "non-starter" by the Delhi embassy (*). Ambassador Keating dismissed the amnesty proposal in only slightly less direct terms.[48]

Implications

Ambassador Keating concluded his December 8th cable by implying that he realized he might not have been informed of some of the specific developments mentioned in the story of Kissinger's backgrounder. Several interviewees agreed that no "political solution" was pressed on Pakistan until very late, and none could say what that solution was. If indeed it was formulated as a package by the White House, it was certainly not presented as such to the State Department. The proper presentation of alternative policy proposals was frustrated in this instance by the lack of policy guidance. State Department officials seemed to have had no idea that the White House felt it was pressing a coherent strategy towards getting a political solution, and was forced to react to proposals piecemeal.

There is a danger inherent in compiling a "policy checklist" and then ticking off items as they are accomplished (or partially accomplished), because one has the illusion that the policy, overall, is then "working." The U.S. managed to get Yahya to agree to a series of steps—maybe the civilian government was not acceptable to the Awami League, but at least it was a *civilian* government; maybe Mujib would not get a public trial and would not be permitted to participate in negotiations, but at least he was *alive*; maybe the amnesty was less than complete, but at least Yahya had accepted the idea in principle; etc.—and the President and Mr. Kissinger apparently felt that progress was being made. And so they were angry (if not furious) with India for not giving Pakistan time to come to accept a political solution in such terms. But it was obvious to many officials at State that these steps came far, far too late to provide the basis for a soiution; that satisfying a number of items on the checklist did not constitute a viable policy or strategy of action.

The review process in charting policy progress must be constant: whether an objective has been achieved "too late" is the kind of judgment that demands considerable reliance on the area experts (centered on the Country Director), who have a feel for the political parameters of a situation. High-level decision-makers, especially in the White House, have neither the time nor the expertise to develop such judgment adequately. In this instance, apparently, the White House relied on its own judgment, and wound up pressing for a solution which the Bengalis would have accepted before March 25th but which would not do in the fall of 1971. The White House belief that the U.S. could play the role of honest broker seemed to fly in the face of Indian distrust of U.S.

motives and allegiance; area experts in the State Department, who did keep the situation under review, were not so sanguine. To the extent that the White House belief that a political solution was aborted by Indian actions influenced U.S. policy during the December war and after, this instance points to the failure of a White House centered system.

Prevention of War; and Policy-Making Crisis by Crisis

The Facts

The danger of India going to war against Pakistan was clear from the first phase of the crisis. On May 28, President Nixon wrote to both President Yahya and Prime Minister Gandhi urging "restraint" and warning of the danger of war.[49] In the second phase of the crisis (August-November), it seemed to be only a matter of time before war broke out. U.S. policy was to urge restraint on India and Pakistan, as part of a diplomatic effort which included humanitarian relief and the effort to broker a political solution. Specific suggestions focused on a disengagement of Indian and Pakistani troops from East Pakistan borders, and the U.S. supported a Pakistani proposal that U.N. observers be posted on the border. India rejected these moves on the grounds that the threat of war arose from the situation in East Bengal, not border confrontations.

When the war broke out on December 3rd, President Nixon apparently felt that India had not given the U.S. time to achieve a solution to the crisis, and that India was thus the "aggressor." As the war developed, officials from the U.S. ambassador to the U.N. on down followed instructions to "tilt" in favor of Pakistan. The minutes of the WSAG meeting reveal that from the outset no one believed that India would halt until she had achieved an independent Bangladesh, resolutions in the U.N. calling for a ceasefire notwithstanding. The focus of attention in WSAG was the halting of the war against West Pakistan. President Nixon reported in February that "during the week of December 6, we received convincing evidence that India was seriously contemplating the seizure of Pakistan-held portions of Kashmir and the destruction of Pakistan's military forces in the West. We could not ignore this evidence. Nor could we ignore the fact that when we repeatedly asked India and its supporters for clear assurances to the contrary we did not receive them."[50] He continued, "if we had not taken a stand against the war, it would have been prolonged and the likelihood of an attack in the West greatly increased. ... The war had to be brought to a halt."[51]

The means to this end that President Nixon mentioned was the United Nations, but it is not implausible that the U.S. did threaten to cancel the upcoming U.S.-USSR summit unless the Russians put pressure on India to stop. The sending of the *Enterprise* task force into the Bay of Bengal, after the war in the East was won, has been interpreted as a signal to the USSR and to Pakistan that the U.S. would not let an ally "go under."[52]

An important aspect of this case is the seeming gap in communication between India and the U.S. The U.S. urged "restraint" on India; India would say "yes, but only when the Pakistan army in East Bengal shows 'restraint'." More directly, after Mrs. Gandhi's trip to Washington in early November, during which she repeatedly said that India was nearing the end of her tether, she said that reports "that she and President Nixon found no common ground in their talks are entirely correct."[53] The U.S. standing vis-a-vis India, and the influence it could hope to exercise was of course seriously undercut by the clear U.S. commitment to an undivided Pakistan and its unwillingness to condemn Pakistani excesses.

Another instance of communications breakdown: President Nixon claimed that no assurances denying the report of Indian intentions to seize Pakistan-held Kashmir had been received. The CIA report which I infer had touched this off held that Mrs. Gandhi intended to "straighten out the southern border off Azad [Pakistan held] Kashmir," and to "eliminate Pakistan's armor and air force capabilities."[54] In the WSAG meeting of December 8, however, Assistant Secretary Sisco reported that India's "Foreign Minister Singh told Ambassador Keating that India has no intention of taking any Pak territory."[55] And in a public statement in New York on December 12th, Singh said India had no wish to "destroy Pakistan."[56] But, as Sisco also pointed out, "Kashmir is really disputed territory."[57] On balance, he doubted that India had any intention of breaking up West Pakistan.

President Nixon apparently wanted more ironclad assurances; the State Department spokesman reported on December 15th that "India has not replied to U.S. request for assurances it will not attack West Pakistan after defeating Pakistan in the East."[58] (General Niazi, the commander of the Pakistan army in the East, had asked the U.S. to convey his request for a ceasefire on the morning of December 14th, Washington time.) It is difficult to understand why Washington expected India *not* to attack while Pakistan continued to wage war in the West. Even before the outbreak of the war, on December 2nd, Mrs. Gandhi said: "If any country thinks that by calling us aggressors it can pressure us to forget our national interests, then that country is living in its own paradise and is welcome to it."[59] In the event, President Yahya only agreed to the Indian ceasefire offer under pressure (*). Yahya's broadcast to the nation, delivered four hours before the ceasefire was announced, in which he spoke of a fight to victory, suggests that the ceasefire was indeed hard to accept. Here, as in much of the crisis, the U.S. misunderstood both the Indian position and, probably, the intensity of Pakistani feeling.

Implications

Communication and contact between the countries involved were not impeded by cliency—the unwillingness to carry unpleasant messages to the government concerned, e.g., as it had been in the 1965 war, when Ambassador Bowles was said to have shown such reluctance—nor by any other organizational constraint. There may well have been failures in communication at even the most rudimentary level: misunderstanding Pakistani English usage, for example (*). More important is the apparent belief that conveying a message means that the recipient has digested its meaning. This dichotomy is neatly illustrated by the words of an American official in Islamabad, speaking around November 20: "we've been in it up to our necks—making suggestions, talking privately with Yahya and others night and day—but this is a closed society. They don't pay any attention—there's no flexibility left. We no longer have any reason to expect the Pakistanis to behave."[60] One suspects that India and Pakistan had similar difficulties in conveying *their* position to American officials.

There are two facets of the communication problem which relate to the U.S. effort to prevent a war. (1) The problem of ambiguity in statements and intentions, and the possibilities of "weathervaning" in analysis which this opens up, and (2) the variant definitions of the size and time dimensions of the "crisis" itself.

President Nixon and Henry Kissinger were apparently unsatisfied with Indian assurances because of the ambiguity inherent in any interpretation of a domestic political situation—they overestimated the importance of Indian "hawks" like Defense Minister Jagjivan Ram, in this instance—and in the less than sweeping nature of the assurances received (which were, to be sure, perfectly understandable from the Indian standpoint). Ambiguity can be used as a tool, however: Kissinger emphasized in the WSAG meeting of December 8th that "we cannot afford to ease India's state of mind" presumably about U.S. intentions to come to Pakistan's assistance.[61] Ambassador Keating had made it clear to Indian officials that third country transfers of weapons required U.S. approval and was told by Under Secretary of State John Irwin, on Kissinger's orders, "in view of intelligence reports spelling out military objectives in West Pakistan, we do not want in any way to ease Government of India's concerns regarding help Pakistan might received from outside sources."[62] Again, there is no reason to believe that India or Pakistan would not pursue *their* foreign policy vis-a-vis the U.S. by using the same technique.

Although, as noted above, interviewees agreed that the reporting of facts to the highest levels was not restricted, I was told that there was "weathervaning" in analysis: the preferences of the top levels were fed back to them. The ambiguity which is inherent in the communications between nations—and to a degree within one nation's foreign service—opens the way to anticipatory compliance in reporting and analysis that does not compromise professional responsibilities.

The second facet of the communication problem here has to do with the dimensions of the crisis and ideas of crisis management. The U.S. treated the threat of war and its outbreak as a separable crisis amenable to what one interviewee called the "standard crisis manual" which says "first, urge restraint; second, get the fighting stopped; third, get the parties talking." India's position was that the crisis of a threat of Indo-Pakistan war could not be and should not be separated from the overall crisis which began on March 25th.

U.S. policy towards South Asia was very much a crisis by crisis affair. From the U.S. point of view, "the crisis" did not mean the totality of events in 1971 (as it did for India and Pakistan), but rather a series of interrelated crises, like the war. Officials were taking up new posts in the summer of 1971, as is usual, and though the overall crisis was relatively subdued—no headlines, just one constant stream of refugees—they did not go into the details of previous "crises." Nor were the ex-incumbents sought out when new "crises" or decisions were encountered. Familiarity with the current file, coupled with overall expertise, was believed to be sufficient.

In 1971, decisions were made at the White House. During the "smaller" crises—the initial crackdown, the first realization of the magnitude of the refugee flow, the December war, etc.—raw intelligence reports and reports of facts direct from the field reached the highest policy-making level and probably were read. During the less active phases, analytic reports warning of the danger of continued armed violence against Hindus by Muslims reached that level (*), but there is little reason to believe that it made an impact. By the time of the crisis of the war, Indian motives might well have been difficult to descern or appreciate. A problem in an area like South Asia, which is a low priority in U.S. national interest terms, has to be more serious than in other areas before it reaches a "crisis" level, and the failure to appreciate the dimension of the crisis from the point of view of the other parties is exacerbated by the tendency to shift not only decision making *but also analysis* to levels in which expertise is severely limited. It is hardly surprising that the U.S. failed to head off war on the Indian subcontinent in 1971.

Conclusions

From the point of view of the White House, I suspect, U.S. policy in South Asia in 1971 was a qualified success. The key goal of the opening to China was not jeopardized by events on the South Asian subcontinent. The progress towards detente with the USSR was not harmed, and valuable lessons were learned on how effective ties with the Soviet Union could be. Relations with Pakistan remained firm, with all that meant for U.S. flexibility in the Middle East (recall that Middle Eastern nations, by and large, gave Pakistan considerable support during 1971). Relations with India were none too good to begin with; a further deterioration could be borne with equanimity, with the added thought, perhaps, of letting the Russians enjoy that headache for a while. Bangladesh and Sheikh Mujib—with whom the U.S. had had close ties—might well want U.S. friendship and aid to counterbalance India and the USSR.

On the other hand, of course, Pakistan had been reduced in power, though India's military development since 1965 precluded a position of parity for Pakistan in any case. A nation state, in ally, had been dismembered by its neighbor, but Pakistan was, in the view of some observers, doomed from its birth, and in the view of others, better off without the drain East Pakistan was becoming. Vigorous U.S. opposition to the war had been concurred in by almost all the nations of the world, and especially Third World nations. The U.S. was vilified in moral terms both at home and abroad, but in the context of the war in Vietnam (which was to be ended, after all, with the help of new relations with China and U.S.—USSR detente), that was hardly unusual. Moral outrage evaporates while national interests remain; even India would come around eventually.

But couldn't U.S. policy have been better? (In both senses of the word: couldn't the opening to China have been achieved *without* the costs incurred in South Asia, and *with* the U.S.

supporting a democracy instead of yet another military regime, condemning officially sanctioned violence against the civilian population and making every effort to get it stopped?) And would a different organizational structure have made any difference?

There were, on the whole, no problems in the flow of information upward, nor in the carrying out of instructions from the White House. There is no indication that President Nixon or Kissinger felt any lack in the information they received or in the responsiveness of officials in Washington or in the field (with the exception of Kissinger's famous remark in the WSAG meeting that he was "getting Hell from the President every half hour" because State Department officials were not "tilting" sufficiently towards Pakistan).[63]

There were, however, severe restrictions in the flow of information downward. Rationales for policy never reached lower levels of State. Similarly, the upward flow of analysis and advice was impeded because it had to be considered irrelevant. Until July 15, when the China opening was announced, the State Department was working in the dark—receiving no guidance on what the reasons for U.S. policy were and sending up analysis and policy advice which had to be ignored, since it could not confront the real rationale. Even after July 15, rationales for U.S. policy which took account of the China opening were not spelled out, and so meaningful alternatives could not be presented.

The secrecy of the rationale for U.S. policy meant that there was no one other than President Nixon and Kissinger who could make decisions, even on minor matters. They were the only ones able to monitor effectively the implementation of the decision, and they alone could assess its impact in terms of the goals they had set. But they also did not have the time (or the expertise) to perform those tasks well—the delay in the recognition of Bangladesh is a case in point.

Alternatives to policy were not presented effectively to decision-makers in the White House, as might be expected under the circumstances. Those sending up proposals were unaware of the "global strategy" which determined U.S. decisions. Moreover, their proposals would inevitably be framed in terms of U.S.

policy towards the region or to one country or the other, and would be discounted accordingly. Ultimately, the serious consideration of bilateral and regional dimensions of policy while global objectives are pursued—sorely needed as the U.S. dealt with South Asia in 1971—depends most on having a President or Secretary of State willing and able to work with knowledgeable professionals and with organizational arrangements that effectively represent them.

NOTES AND REFERENCES

1. All dates with no year given are from 1971. The most readily available detailed chronology for the 1971 crisis can be found under the heading "Pakistan" in the *New York Times Index 1971: A Book of Record*, pp. 1287-1310. (Cited hereafter as: *NY Times* Index.)
2. Marta Nicholas and Philip Oldenburg, compilers; Ward Morehouse, general editor, *Bangladesh: The Birth of a Nation; A Handbook of Background Information and Documentary Sources* (Madras: M. Seshachalam, 1972), p. 82. [Cited hereafter as: *Bangladesh Handbook.* This contains the "Anderson Papers" reprinted (in pp. 112-34) from the *New York Times* of January 6 and 15, 1972; the Kissinger background briefing of December 7, 1971, reprinted (in pp. 134-42) from the *Congressional Record—Senate*, December 9, 1971; Mrs. Gandhi's letter to President Nixon, reprinted (in pp. 143-45) from the *New York Times* of December 17, 1971; and other documents.]
3. G.W. Choudhury, *The Last Days of United Pakistan* (Bloomington: Indiana University Press, 1974), p. 68. Choudhury was a senior advisor to President Yahya at the time, "one of the very few whom [Yahya] took into his confidence about his top secret mission [to Peking]." (*Ibid.*, p. 70).
4. See Marvin Kalb and Bernard Kalb, *Kissinger* (Boston: Little, Brown, 1974), pp. 237-38. Unfortunately, they do not give a date, but simply set the time as cherry blossom season in Washington.
5. On President Nixon's and Kissinger's belief that secrecy was required, see I.M. Destler, "The Nixon System, a Further Look," *Foreign Service Journal*, February 1974. See also Secretary Rogers' reply to a question at the Sigma Delta Chi convention, *Department of State Bulletin*, Vol. LXV, No. 1693 (December 6, 1971), pp. 652-53.
6. Made in his background briefing of December 7th. As reprinted in Bangladesh handbook, p. 139. The remark refers to Nixon's alleged hostility to Mrs. Gandhi; in the earlier part of his reply, Kissinger denies that either he or President Nixon had a preference for Pakistan or for Pakistani leaders.

7. "Anderson Papers" as reprinted in *ibid.*, p. 125. All statements about WSAG deliberations hereafter are from this source.
8. See the study for the Commission by Joan Hochman, printed in Appendix H.
9. *Recognition of Bangladesh*, Hearings before the Committee on Foreign Relations, U.S. Senate, March 6 and 7, 1972; testimony of Christopher van Hollen, Deputy Assistant Secretary for Near East and South Asia, pp. 6-25, *passim.*
10. As reprinted in *Relief Problems in East Pakistan and India, Part I*, hearings before the subcommittee to investigate problems connected with refugees and escapees of the Committee on the Judiciary, U.S. Senate (hereafter: *Kennedy Subcommittee*), June 28, 1971, p. 87.
11. Many reports, from the onset of the crisis, mention this; see, for example, some of those reprinted in *ibid*, pp. 95ff.: Peggy Durdin, "The Political Tidal Wave That Struck East Pakistan" (reprinted from the *New York Times Magazine* of May 2, 1971), *ibid.*, pp. 95-105; Mort Rosenblum, "Army, Rebels Fight Over Ruined Pakistan" (reprinted from the *Baltimore Sun*, May [?] 1971), *ibid.*, pp. 110-11; *et al.*
12. As reprinted in *ibid*, pp. 118-20; the article introduced is by Anthony Mascarenhas, "Why the Refugees Fled," *ibid.*, pp. 120-22.
13. *New York Times Index*, p. 1296, col. 1 (original article: *New York Times*, August 16, 1971, p. 6.).
14. The International Genocide Convention (not ratified then by the U.S.), defines genocide as "acts committed with intent to destroy, in whole or in part, a national, ethnical, racial, or religious group. ..." Quoted in Michael Bowen, Guy Freeman, Key Miller (Roger Morris, Project Director), *Passing By: The United States and Genocide in Burundi, 1972* (Washington: The Carnegie Endowment for International Peace, 1973), p. 18. In addition to eyewitness testimony (see note 11, above), the fact that after May virtually all the refugees were Hindus supports the view that actions by the Pakistan army in East Bengal constituted genocide by third definition. However, the language used in public even by critics of U.S. policy did not include the word "genocide;" for instance, in Senator Kennedy's report *Crisis in South Asia*, we get only an indirect usage: "Our national leadership has yet to express one word that would suggest we do not approve of the genocidal consequences of the Pakistan Government's policy of repression and violence." (*Crisis in South Asia*, a report by Senator Edward M. Kennedy to the Kennedy subcommittee, November 1, 1971, p. 55.) Nor is there any evidence that a "demand" was made by any member of Congress, or by any FSO, to condemn Pakistan for committing "genocide." There was some indirect evidence in the interviews I had that policy positions which would have had the U.S. strongly condemn the killing—and place the blame on the Pakistan Government—were put forward within the State Department; the issue was raised, even if the word "genocide" was not used.

15. *Crisis in South Asia*, p. 56.
16. *Relief Problems in East Pakistan and India*, Part I, Kennedy subcommittee hearings, June 28, 1971, p. 46.
17. Roger Morris, "Clientism in the Foreign Service," *Foreign Service Journal*, February 1974. Ambassador Farland, while perfectly correct in his relationship with the Government of Pakistan and his superiors in Washington, did "represent" the point of view of Pakistan to Washington (*).
18. See *Crisis in South Asia*, p. 57, for excerpts from the cable.
19. Jack Anderson, with George Clifford, *The Anderson Papers* (New York: Random House, 1973), pp. 242-45.
20. *Ibid.*
21. Kalb and Kalb, pp. 258-59.
22. *Relief Problems in East Pakistan and India*, Part I, Kennedy subcommittee hearings, June 28, 1971, p. 82.
23. *Relief Problems in Bangiadesh*, Kennedy subcommittee hearings, February 2, 1972, Appendix III, pp. 85-92.
24. *Ibid.*, p. 90.
25. *Ibid.* Note that none of these shipments were illegal, nor did they violate overall U.S. policy on arms to Pakistan.
26. *Relief Problems in East Pakistan and India*, Part III, Kennedy subcommittee hearings, October 4, 1971, p. 376. Christopher van Hollen's testimony.
27. "Anderson Papers" as reprinted in *Bangladesh Handbook*, pp. 132 and 125.
28. *New York Times*, March 29, 1972, p. 1.
29. The position that the bulk of U.S. relief should go to East Pakistan was congruent with administration policy after August to portray the refugee outflow as the result of the threatened famine. But before August, the official view that all was "normal" in East Pakistan as the Government of Pakistan contended led the administration to resist Congressional efforts—especially those of Senator Kennedy—to get recognition of the danger of famine. Aid to the refugees in India, I surmise, was to case India's burden so that she would not have that excuse to go to war to stop the drain on her economy. Interviewees, however, discounted these explanations for the "humanitarian aid was centerpiece" view.
30. As of October 19, 1971, the U.S. had contributed 42 per cent of the "world's" total to refugee relief in India (and 71% of the total for East Pakistan relief). *Ibid.*, p. 40. Senator Kennedy, pointing out India's burden, concludes "we realize how little the outside world is really doing, and how paltry the American contribution is comparatively." (*Ibid.*, p. 41.).
31. *U.S. Foreign Policy for the 1970's: The Emerging Structure of Peace*, A report by President Richard Nixon to the Congress, February (9), 1972, (hereafter: *State of the World Message*), p. 159.

32. *Ibid.*, pp. 159-60.
33. *Ibid.*, p. 162.
34. Kissinger backgrounder, as reprinted in *Bangladesh Handbook*, p. 136.
35. *State of the World Message*, p. 162.
36. Kissinger backgrounder, as reprinted in *Bangladesh Handbook*, p. 140.
37. *Ibid.*, p. 141. These points only emerged from close questioning of Kissinger at the backgrounder of December 7th.
38. *Ibid.*, p. 140.
39. Kissinger backgrounder, as reprinted in *Bangladesh Handbook*, p. 144.
40. *Ibid.*, p. 134.
41. The Pakistan point of view was that the war broke out with India's large scale incursion in support of a Mukti Bahini operation on November 21st. President Nixon's phrase was "when war erupted toward the end of November" (*State of the World Message*, p. 164) This view is supported by Wayne Wilcox (*The Emergence of Bangladesh*, Foreign Affairs Study 7, American Enterprise Institute for Public Policy Research, Washington, 1973), p. 51, but a *New York Times* report of November 24th (*NY Times Index*, p. 1301, col. 3) says that "U.S. officials . .. dispute Pakistani charge that India has launched fullscale invasion," and an important Pakistani General (Farman Ali), as reported on November 26th (*Ibid*, p. 1302, col. 1), said that "field reports indicate conditions on East Pakistan border [were] returning to normal tenseness." India, of course, held that the war began with the Pakistani air attacks on 8 Indian airfields on December 3rd; most observers agree.
42. *State of World Message*, p. 162.
43. Kissinger backgrounder as reprinted in *Bangladesh Handbook*, p. 137.
44. "Anderson Papers" as reprinted in *ibid*, p. 133.
45. Kissinger backgrounder as reprinted in *ibid*, p. 138. "We were urging movement at the greatest speed that the Pakistan political process could stand. We felt that one way to resolve this would be for the Indians to give us a timetable of what they would consider a reasonable timetable. . .."
46. *Ibid.*, p. 139.
47. Mrs. Gandhi's letter to President Nixon, as reprinted in *ibid*. p. 144
48. "Anderson Papers" as reprinted in *ibid.*, p. 133.
49. *State of the World Message*, pp. 159-60.
50. *Ibid.*, p. 165.
51. *Ibid.*, p. 166.
52. Reports of the *Enterprise* task force movements first appeared on December 13th (when it went through the Straits of Malacca), when the Indian army was within artillery range of Dacca. The most detailed account of the task force deployment is in Anderson, *op. cit.*, pp. 259-69 (the chapter is titled "The Brink of World War").
53. *NY Times Index*, p. 1301 (news story of November 16).
54. "Anderson Papers" as reprinted in *Bangladesh Handbook*, p. 128.

55. *Ibid.*, p. 130.
56. *NY Times Index*, p. 1306, col. 2.
57. "Anderson Papers" as reprinted in *Bangladesh Handbook*, p. 130.
58. *NY Times Index*, p. 1307, col. 1.
59. Quoted in Robert Shaplen, "The Birth of Bangladesh—II," *The New Yorker*, February 19, 1972; as reprinted in *Relief Problems in Bangladesh*, Kennedy subcommittee hearings, February 2, 1972, p. 117.
60. *Ibid.*, p. 114.
61. "Anderson Papers" as reprinted in *Bangladesh Handbook*, p. 132.
62. Anderson, *op. cit.*, p. 228.
63. "Anderson Papers" as reprinted in *Bangladesh Handbook*, p. 115.

CASE STUDY

6

PUBLIC LAW 480 AND THE POLICIES OF SELF-HELP AND SHORT-TETHER

Indo-American Relations, 1965-68

— James Warner Bjorkman

American agricultural abundance offers a great opportunity for the United States to promote the interests of peace in a significant way.

— John Fitzgerald Kennedy, 1958

Food is power and the basis of a happier world.

— George S. McGovern, 1962

Food, and the ability to produce it, and the means of teaching others to produce it, are the most powerful weapons that America possesses.

— Orville L. Freeman, 1966

We know that a grain of wheat is a potent weapon in the arsenal of freedom.

— Lyndon Baines Johnson, 1968

I. INTRODUCTION

The politics of food and agricultural aid has become an increasingly large component of American foreign policy. Unlike traditional foreign policy concerns like diplomacy, espionage and war, food policy deals with a very prosaic subject. But it is a vital subject on which the strength of nations, both morally and physically, depends. Since *Famine 1975!* (Paddock and Paddock, 1967) and *The Limits to Growth* (Meadows *et al.*, 1972), the imperatives of agricultural production and distribution systems have become increasingly apparent to policy-makers, both here and abroad.

The Achilles heel of writings on contemporary problems is the seeming impossibility of political prediction, and evaluations of a particular decision's consequences are likewise unlikely. Although retrospectives often seem passé, a historical case example permits judicious estimates of such causes and consequences. No single study can discuss all the issues involved in the political economy of foodaid, but an example focused on Public Law 480 can illuminate the operation of US food policies towards the Republic of India. The time-period selected for detailed examination lies in the mid-sixties and coincides with the troubled presidency of Lyndon Baines Johnson. The period was selected because it spans the revision of ground-rules for American food policy and because it illustrates the vulnerability of a seemingly well-insulated program to presidential manipulation. It also marked a reorientation of India's strategy for economic development, even as Indo-American relations cooled.

Two broad decisions within the PL-480 ambit have been selected for special consideration. These are the requirements that India demonstrate sincere efforts at 'self-help' before foodaid would be granted, and LBJ's 'short-tether' on food shipments during the latter half of the 1965-67 drought. The self-help provisions include a discussion of their origin, the negotiating of their terms, and the monitoring of their implementation. And the short-tether policy includes its source, its coordination with other nations, and its political effects.

After the background of PL-480, its shifting complex of players, and its mechanisms for coordination and surveillance have been discussed, a narrative history will be presented of PL-480 programs in Indo-American relations and how they affected bureaucratic politics in the respective countries. This history indicates how an incremental policy affected by many players was abruptly placed under close presidential supervision, and describes some effects of this changed situation on the US policy-making system. The essay ends with brief observations and recommendations about coordinating American foreign policies.

II. BACKGROUND OF A WELL-INSULATED PROGRAM

The Agricultural Trade Development and Assistance Act of 1954 authorized the "sale" of American farm surpluses to other countries on concessional terms. These terms included payments in foreign currency, reduced rates of interest, and grace-periods before repayments began. Proceeds from these commodity sales were deposited in special local currency accounts. Other than a small percentage transferred to the United States Government (USG) for use by its in-country agencies, the counterpart funds in these accounts belong to the recipient country.[1] The USG cannot spend this balance because "in essence, with the exception of the portion set aside for US uses, counterpart is a conditional grant—the condition being agreement by the United States on the final uses of the funds" (Galdi, 1974: 5).

The 1954 Act had several goals which can be rank-ordered. First, it sought to protect and sustain standing patterns of American agricultural commerce or, in other words, to ensure the profitable disposal of American farm produce; second, to expand old markets and develop new ones for US agricultural goods; and third, to help other countries to grow to the point of economic self-sufficiency. No specific assistance, however, would be allowed that jeopardized America's international or domestic commercial interests.

Furthermore, PL-480—as this Act of the 83rd Congress came to be called—included non-agricultural aims. It authorized the purchase of goods and services on behalf of other countries, the promotion of trade, and the financing of international educational exchange. Like the successive Mutual Security Acts of the 1950s, PL-480 also sought to purchase materials for the US strategic stockpile, pay US obligations overseas, and provide military equipment, materials, or facilities. Over time, amendments and extensions added other aims to Section 104.[2]

The Act is administered through the Commodity Credit Corporation (CCC) under a remarkably flexible financial arrangement. US domestic agricultural policy is committed to a price-support program and, therefore, to a type of national subsidy for agriculture. In order to respond to market forces, CCC was designed to operate independently of the Congress since market fluctuations made it impractical to put line-items for specific commodities in the annual budget. Thus, in 1949, Congress

still be paid for and then reallocated as foreign aid. In simple terms, the *appropriations committees* are interested in keeping government expenditures, and therefore taxes, down. Give-away programs (other than porkbarrel projects) have never been popular with these committees, even when the proceeds go to the powerful agricultural barons.

Finally, the *Government of India* (GoI) had a considerable stake in the PL-480 program. The GoI received the food supplies necessary to maintain political stability while it devoted its slim resources to industrial investments (the Nehru-Mahalanobis strategy of development). And in fact, by allowing India to concentrate on industrialization, PL-480 indirectly helped US firms to sell India capital goods. Furthermore, at a time of general inflation, Nehru in particular repeatedly pointed with pride to the cheap-food policy of his government.[6] While price indices of all other commodities kept rising, the prices of wheat and other foodgrains were held in check through 1963 by PL-480 imports (Bhatnagar, 1969: 250-59). As under the old CCC strategy in the US, economic analyses indicated that the price of wheat in India varied more with government wheat-stocks than with domestic production, so ample PL-480 imports were desirable. Fortunately, payments for the American-provided grainstocks could be deferred to the distant future through 'credit sales' while reaping immediate benefits. Of course, like all governments, the GoI was not monolithic. Its *Finance Ministry* worried about the inflation caused by additional rupee-revenue flowing through the economy, while the *Ministry of Food and Agriculture* sought the contradictory policies of cheap food for the consumers and better prices for the producers.

Thus, in the period examined, a pattern of interests emerged among those playing an active role in PL-480 decisions. These interests involved three sets of basic issues: economic, budgetary-finance, and political, which were of varying concern to the many participants as PL-480 policy evolved over time.

Economic issues concerned the transfer of real resources from the US into the Indian economy, the actual terms of individual agreements, the US balance of payments, and transfers within the

US to the agricultural sector. Until about 1964, AID wanted to free up indigenous resources and precious foreign exchange for India's industrial undertakings and the large-scale projects necessary to build up an infrastructure for future development. The GoI wanted the same as well as an adequate supply of grain to keep food prices down.

USDA had originally want to dispose of its surplus commodities and secondarily to develop or expand markets. Later, when reserve stocks of commodities grew scarce and claims could only be made on America's long-range agricultural production capacity, USDA wanted assurance that accidental over-runs in production could be absorbed by CCC. In the latter post-1964 period, USDA also sought to stimulate agricultural development in India in order to wean India from its increasing dependency on US grain reserves and to strengthen India's ability to purchase US products commercially. In both periods, USDA sought to ensure price stability and economic well-being for its primary domestic constituency, the American farmers.

Meanwhile, the Department of the Treasury became increasingly concerned about the adverse balance of payments and regarded PL-480 "sales" as a drain on America's potential hard-currency assets. The same issue (but for obviously different reasons) agitated other producer nations which earn a substantial portion of their foreign exchange from agricultural exports. Through the United Nations' Food and Agriculture Organization (FAO), such countries as Australia, Argentina, Canada, the Netherlands and Denmark (plus, recently, other members of the European Economic Community) kept track of American PL-480 negotiations and shipments so that the usual marketing patterns in world agricultural trade were not disrupted.

Budgetary-finance issues dealt with taxation and the internal contours of the American budget. The Bureau of the Budget (BoB) and the Congress knew that PL-480 costs real dollars, which have to be appropriated in order to pay for agricultural commodities. Since 1964 when the CCC appropriation peaked at $1.6 billion, about one billion dollars have annually been allocated to the CCC for financing Titles I and II of PL-480. Appropriations for this budget item entail taxation to pay for government expenditures, curtail other domestic programs, and place a drain on the US Treasury.

In addition to the natural Treasury and BoB interests in fiscal responsibility, the Appropriations Committees are concerned. As Galdi (1974: 8-9) reports, "the fact that the local currencies obtained are not dollars and not convertible is frequently misunderstood, especially when it comes time to spend them." The original relevance of the 1966 Mondale-Poage amendment[7] was that the US Executive could use PL-480 funds for certain purposes without undergoing the appropriations process.

The GoI was also concerned about the domestic fiscal effects of PL-480 agreements, since the rupees they generated were permitted to have an inflationary effect on the Indian economy. Such inflation was caused not only by expenditures of blocked rupees through loans and grants but also by the multiplicative effects of an increased money supply in the central budget. The US goods supplied under each PL-480 Agreement were, in turn, sold by the Food Corporation of India and the proceeds, after committing about ten per cent to USG use, were added to the annual GoI budget.[8]

Political issues comprise the more traditional concerns of US foreign policy, although there was a growing concern for the US balance of payments during the latter half of the decade. The State Department and the President usually wanted *quid pro quos* of support for (or, at minimum neutrality towards) American diplomatic positions, both bilaterally and through international organizations. Treasury and BoB had greater interest in improving American leverage over international commerce in order to correct the shortfalls in the US balance of payments. Meanwhile, PL-480 Agreements automatically meant involvement in and interference with a recipient country's internal affairs. As the conditions of each Agreement became more explicit and more oriented towards self-help, PL-480 became a lever to redirect and restructure the Indian domestic economy. This leverage was of critical interest to AID and to USDA for their development projects and strategy. It was also of increasing concern to the Government of India, which regarded such conditions as an infringement on its national sovereignty. At the same time, within the GoI were competing factions who were respectively weakened or strengthened by US decisions about PL-480 and the resources it provided.

IV. MECHANISMS FOR COORDINATION AND SURVEILLANCE: THE AGREEMENT PROCESS

Including the Executive Office of the President and five major Cabinet Departments as well as various committees of the US Congress, PL-480 had ramifications throughout much of American government. The oldest of the formal coordinating devices for PL-480 is the Interagency Staff Committee (ISC) which has operated since 1954. Chaired by USDA, the ISC has representatives from State/AID (two masquerading as one), Treasury, Commerce, Defense, and the Bureau of the Budget (now Office of Management and Budget). Other departments and agencies which are concerned with specific phases of Title I programs and with uses of foreign currencies but which are not voting members of the ISC include the Office of Emergency Planning, the US Information Agency, the National Science Foundation, the Department of the Interior (for fisheries) the Library of Congress, the Smithsonian Institution, and the Department of Health, Education, and Welfare.

The ISC is a working-level committee whose members, all career bureaucrats, proceed only through consensual decision-making. If problems cannot be resolved in ISC deliberations, decisions are deferred until representatives can consult with their parent agencies. Or the decisions may be taken by other agency personnel on a bilateral basis at an appropriately high level, reaching up to and including the Department Secretaries themselves. In recent years, as commodities have become more scarce, higher-level decision-making has become more common; and in 1973, a more permanent committee was convened under the chairmanship of OMB's Associate Director. During the mid-1960s, however, although BoB became more important as the Planning, Program, and Budgeting System (PPBS) was increasingly adopted by the federal government, only the ISC provided working-level coordination of PL-480 on a sustained basis.

The extension of PL-480 (PL88—638) in 1964 established a Joint Executive-Congressional Advisory Committee to review Title I currency uses and to consult about loans, sales agreements, and convertibility terms. The House in particular wanted more systematic knowledge about PL-480 operations. In 1966, PL89-808, which completely restructured PL-480, expanded the joint committee to include the Secretaries of State and Treasury, as well as four additional Congressional members from the agricultural committees. These latter four were dropped again in 1968. Chaired by its Congressional members on a rotational basis, the Joint Committee has met but twice since 1966. Many interviewees mentioned that the Joint Committee's large size and high-status personnel made its meetings exceedingly difficult to arrange.

Congressional supervision of PL-480 programs, particularly towards India, is poor. The Congress is not a unified actor in PL-480 affairs and is characterized by jurisdictional disputes. Its Committees spend as much time squabbling among themselves as overseeing the Executive Branch. Also, Congress is understaffed and over-crowded with only a spasmodic interest in and knowledge about the PL-480 program. To expect the Congress to monitor the PL-480 program is probably like asking blind a man to describe an elephant. Furthermore, knowledge of and sympathy for India is rare on Capitol Hill. Most Congressmen, Senators, and staff regard Indians as poor, inept and arrogant. Their concern for the region is minimal and declining in an era of accelerated non-interventionism.

The relative importance of these coordinating devices varies at different phases of the process for contracting a PL-480 Agreement, a process which has changed over the years towards increasingly formalized procedures. At first, contacts were informal and could start during a luncheon engagement between USG and GoI officials. Later the USG began to ask the GoI to provide a formal request and a justification, and then would try to supply its needs. Finally by the late '60s. PL-480 was drawn into the planning-programing-budgeting process. The program's procedures became particularly rigid under LBJ who required pre-clearance for any agreement with ten selected countries receiving the bulk of US economic aid.

During the mid-60s, the standardized procedures for contracting a PL-480 agreement with India were as follows:

(1) India would approach the US Embassy in Delhi with a request for food aid, along with a justification. Informal consultations among Embassy personnel and GoI bureaucrats generated the contours of most requests. Often the Embassy took the initial initiative.

(2) The Embassy would transmit the request back to Washington for submission to the Interagency Staff Committee. In addition, the Embassy staff collected relevant information about the country's needs and prospects, to accompany the request. There seems to have been as many channels for transmitting information as there were attaches and administrators in Delhi although all were formally responsible to the Ambassador. That is, despite most information being transmitted through the State Department's cables. Treasury, AID, and USDA could and did receive information independently of one another.

(3) The broad outlines of the potential agreement were generated by the ISC. Decision-making in that body was consensual and, if disagreements occurred, the problem was passed to superior levels of government. After 1966 and coincident with ISC's initial discussion about each individual agreement, the State Department through its Food for Freedom Division in the Economic Bureau alerted other producer-nations about the pending negotiations and potential "sale." Usual Marketing Requirements were calculated on the past five years' average and advice was solicited.

(4) When the ISC had agreed on the outlines of an agreement and no objections had been received or acknowledged

from the big three producers (Canada, Australia and Argentina—with the EEC being added in later years), the US Embassy in Delhi was authorized to commence negotiations with GoI representatives. The ISC document served as the basic negotiating instrument. At this time, the Consultative Subcommittee on Surplus Disposal of the Food and Agriculture Organization's Committee on Commodity Problems was notified in order to alert the rare country that might not already have been consulted.

(5) Negotiations took place in Delhi with varying numbers of participants. The larger the individual Agreement proposed or the more comprehensive its terms, the higher the ranks of the players involved. The American Ambassador and the AID Mission Director might well consult with members of the Indian Council of Ministers. In exceptional cases, special delegations from Washington would join the negotiations. The negotiation of self-help provisions in particular required, or at any rate inspired, participation by USDA experts.

Within the GoI, foreign aid negotiations were highly coordinated. The Ministry of Finance served as focal point and all other ministries, including the Food and Agriculture Ministry deferred to its lead. The Delhi venue for negotiating PL-480 terms made the US Embassy a critical link in the government-to-government relations that characterized PL-480 programs.[9] In the American Embassy, the Minister for Political and Economic Affairs headed the American negotiating team, under ambassadorial guidance. He relied heavily on a staff team comprised of AID, USDA, and Treasury representatives. The Agricultural Attache in particular was a major participant, although as an agent of USDA, he often was motivated more by the interests of American commercial agriculture than by general foreign policy considerations.

(6) When the terms of an Agreement had been mutually devised, the Agreement required formal approval by both

governments. Signing ceremonies were often regarded as major diplomatic events so their sites alternated between national capitals.

V. PL-480 IN THE MID-SIXTIES: SELF-HELP AND THE POLITICS OF AN ERA

The Washington Scene

Prior to becoming Secretary of Agriculture, Orville Freeman had expressed an interest in the agricultural economies of less-developed countries (LDCs). Freeman believed that American agriculture could make considerable contributions to the rest of the world and one of his conditions for taking up JFK's offer was a chance to stress this developmental theme. The pragmatic basis of his reasoning was later borne out by USDA studies which demonstrated that to the extent a country absòrbs PL-480 aid and grows economically, that country comes to purchase more and more US goods. Trade relations are built up, and what begins as concessional sales later shifts into straight agricultural commerce. Taiwan, Spain, Japan, Israel and Korea are all cited as examples of a successful market development policy. It, therefore, made good business sense to American agriculture to see that LDCs develop to the point where they could pay for American goods with cash.

Furthermore, it was clear to USDA economists, if not to many in AID, that most LDCs were neglecting agriculture in favor of industrialization. Certainly, such a skewed development strategy characterized India during the Nehru era. Whether Freeman sought to improve India's agricultural base enough to permit future commercial sales or just wanted to end the assumption that the US was obligated to supply India's food needs on a concessional basis, he bade for control over agricultural development in the LDCs. The problem was that responsibility for economic development aid had previously been almost completely within the Agency for International Development or its predecessors.

Freeman entered the bureaucratic battle with several advantages. First, he already had an instrument in the PL-480 program which was a direct avenue into the LDCs. Concessional sales, originally stimulated to dispose of unwanted American surpluses, had been underway since the mid-1950s. Second, by virtue of PL 83-690, the Agriculture Attaches in US embassies, while nominally subject to the Ambassador as head of the country-team, were actually USDA personnel rather than in the Foreign Service. Third, USDA had a powerful domestic constituency which the State Department did not. And fourth, the Secretary had a good friend in the White House both before and after 23 November 1963.

Perhaps because of his Vietnam burden, LBJ became the even better friend. The quarrels between LBJ and Fulbright over foreign policy were not secret and were increasingly evident in the annual foreign aid bills, over which the Foreign Relations Committee had jurisdiction. Agricultural aid, however, was a large and enlarging portion of total economic aid and PL-480 was the major source of food-aid. Since PL-480 was under the jurisdiction of the agricultural committees and since the deployment of PL-480 commodities was decided by the ISC chaired by USDA, Fulbright's influence over foreign policy could be diminished if the agricultural component of foreign aid were shifted elsewhere. Freeman was a trusted lieutenant, with an acceptable ideological position, who aspired for control over US policy towards agriculture in LDCs. And in addition, Freeman shared LBJ's conviction—at least vis-a-vis India—that only a strong dose of self-help would ensure the type of national commitment necessary to remove LDCs from excessive dependence on US grain-bins.[10]

The origin of the 'self-help' concept in agriculture is somewhat disputed, but the drive towards its implementation is generally conceded to have come from USDA. State/AID did not need to be converted about self-help's value, but there was a question of its priority among other goals. During the early 1960s, for example, it was often erroneously assumed that capital investments achieve a higher payoff in industry than in agriculture (Singh, 1963, quoted by Lindblom, 1964b: 8). Therefore, Freeman argued that only agricultural experts could really specify a less developed country's agricultural needs. The State Department was too concerned with diplomacy and AID with industrial projects to pay sufficient attention to the agricultural basis of an LDC's economy.

At the same time, the importance of self-help in agriculture was being promoted in India by various non-governmental agents as well as by technocrats within the Ministry of Food and Agriculture (if not in the Planning Commission). Public and private research organizations such as the Indian Council of Agricultural Research, the Ford Foundation, and the Rockefeller Foundation repeatedly stressed the value of developing India's agricultural sector and had offered practical schemes to improve production. Leading nationalist economists such as V.K.R.V. Rao, M.L. Dantawala, K.N. Raj, V.M. Dandekar and Gyan Chand also supported a strategy of "self-reliance" in agriculture.[11] Furthermore, agricultural technocrats such as M.S. Swaminathan, B.P. Pal, M.S. Randhawa, and especially N. Sivaraman, who staffed the GoI's Department of Agriculture, argued forcefully for greater emphasis on agricultural development. Until the 1965 confrontations with Pakistan and the subsequent cut-off of US aid painfully demonstrated India's vulnerability, however, the Planning Commission continued to favor investments in the industrial sector.

The campaign for "self-help" proceeded slowly and by a circuitous route. In 1961, when the International Cooperation Administration was reconstituted into the Agency for International Development, the Food for Peace Program was not assigned to the new agency. Agricultural pressures were marshalled to keep PL-480's Title I "sales" in USDA while promotional responsibilities for its Title II grants and donations through voluntary agencies were assigned to a newly created post in the Executive Office of the President. The Office of Food for Peace was mainly a publicity vehicle as well as a safe haven for George McGovern, the defeated Congressman from South Dakota, until the 1962 Senate race.

In 1964 and again in 1965, PL-480 was marginally amended to extend the USDA Secretary's powers over counterpart funds. And in early 1966, a complex inter-agency agreement was signed which exchanged USDA and AID personnel and strengthened the former's role in planning, implementing and evaluating technical assistance in agriculture overseas. But despite these marginal successes, Freeman's original aspiration seemed stymied in the bureaucratic jungle of jurisdictional dickering.

In fact, through an administrative maneuver, USDA almost lost its international food-aid program in 1965. The problem of PL-480 in foreign policy had been, and is, that no single agency is administratively responsible for it. The ISC coördinates among many interested parties, but it cannot take authoritative decisions. This peculiar "headless" administrative arrangement was devised by one of Eisenhower's Executive Orders which is still operational. In 1965, some members of the ISC thought they had agreed on a new Executive Order which would assign responsibility for PL-480 to the newly created "War on Hunger" office within AID. That draft order went to LBJ for his signature but on Freeman's (rumored) advice, the President decided not to sign it. Rather LBJ decided to coordinate the program himself and required that all PL-480 Agreements with the ten major recipient countries be cleared by him personally.

Presumably, LBJ did not want to augment the powers of State/AID, to which he had already transferred the White House's Office of Food for Peace established by JFK.[12] In contrast to his predecessor, LBJ did not really like State Department types or even foreign policy. He felt ill-at-ease on international affairs (especially towards Europe) and much preferred domestic policies and their intuitively understandable protective interests. Furthermore, in LBJ's particular conception of politics, there were international and domestic payoffs in wielding PL-480, which he did not want to relinquish. Thus the foundation for the "short-tether" policy had been laid considerably before it was applied.

In February 1966, LBJ sent Congress a special message to pass his Food for Freedom Program and thereby drastically restructure PL-480.[13] Since US grain stocks had peaked in 1960, economic reasons to dispose of surplus commodities were no longer pressing. Through a combination of acreage controls, large PL-480 shipments, and expanding commercial exports, grain stocks had been almost halved (Schnittker, 1966) and the annual storage costs had been substantially reduced. Indeed, a number of Congressmen claimed the well-being of the US was threatened because grain reserves were so low. Their fear, while premature in 1966, has become more valid today.

Interviewees note that USDA drafted the bill revising PL-480 in order to get a major share of the action. In large measure, USDA was successful although its success must be qualified. PL-480/808 retained its conventional statement of intent "to increase the consumption of United States agricultural commodities in foreign countries, to improve the foreign relations of the United States, and for other purposes." But a new preamble to the Act read:

> "The Congress hereby declares it to be the policy of the United States to expand international trade; to develop and expand export markets for US agricultural commodities; to use the abundant agricultural productivity of the United States to combat hunger and malnutrition, and to encourage economic development in the developing countries, with particular emphasis on assistance to those countries that are determined to improve their own agricultural production; and to promote in other ways the foreign policy of the United States." (7 U.S.C. 1691)

In order to promote these developmental goals, a new Title IV specifically enhanced USDA's role in international affairs without, however, assigning it exclusive responsibility. In his special message on the Food for Freedom Program, LBJ had emphasized that "the Departments of State and Agriculture and the Agency for International Development will work together even more closely than they have in the past in the planning and implementation of coordinated programs." He sought to reassign

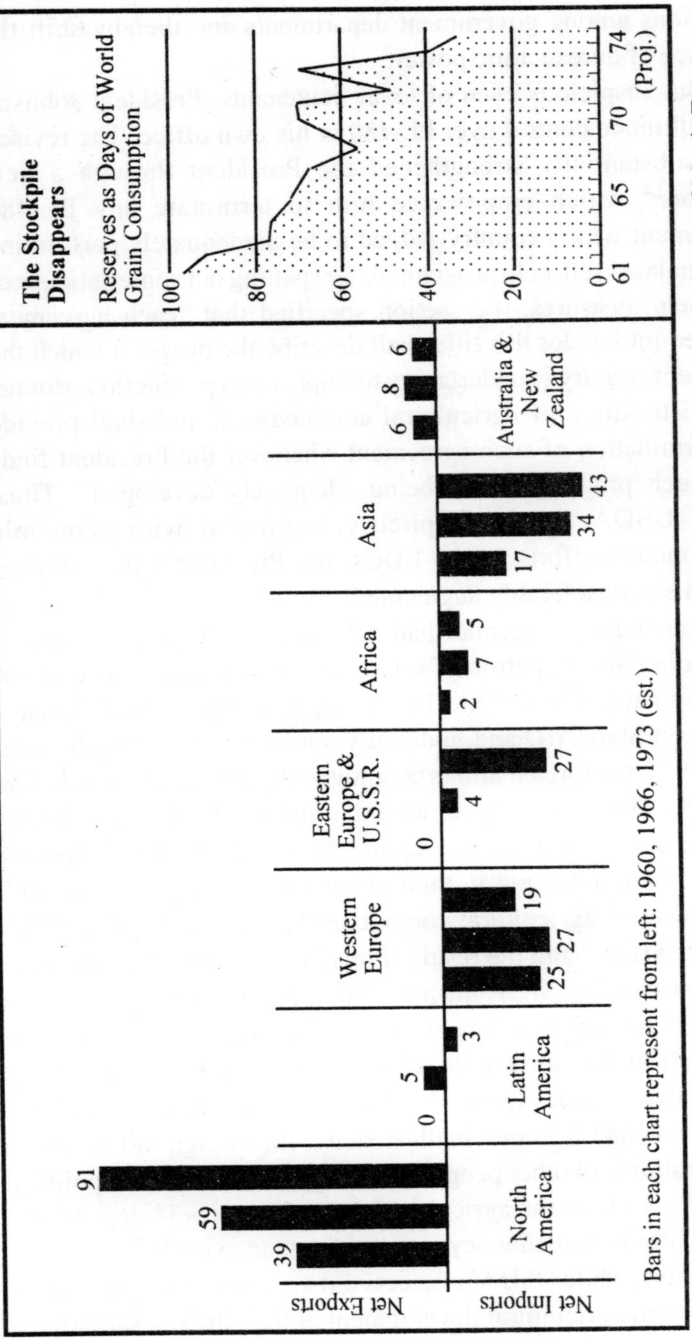

FIG. 9.1: North America's Emergence as the World's Bread Basket. Numbers in Bars represent Millions of Metric Tons

Source: Brown and Eckholm, 1974a: 6—E. As based on U.S. Dept. of Agricultural data.

functions among government departments and thereby shift the balance of bureaucratic power.

But suspicious even of loyal lieutenants, President Johnson kept ultimate control over PL-480 in his own office. The revised Act substantially strengthened the President through a new section[14] which empowered him to terminate any PL-480 agreement with a country judged to be inadequately performing its stipulated self-help program. After spelling out some anticipated self-help measures, the section specified that "each agreement entered into under this title shall describe the program which the recipient country is undertaking to improve its production, storage and distribution of agricultural commodities; and shall provide for termination of such agreement whenever the President finds that such program is not being adequately developed." Thus, while USDA became explicitly associated with economic development efforts in the LDCs, the President's own powers were also considerably augmented.

Nonetheless, Freeman had achieved a qualified success in expanding his department's role in international agricultural development. With White House support, USDA had stolen a march on State/AID and, indirectly, on Fulbright. The following year, 1967, the foreign affairs committees tried to assert jurisdiction over PL-480 by placing agricultural and food aid in the annual foreign aid bill but, as one senior staffer of the House Foreign Affairs Committee put it, their attempt was a "total nonstarter." The powerful agricultural committees had approved of USDA's enhanced role[15] and the result of this jurisdictional dispute was a foregone conclusion. By the mid-1960s, problems began to appear in the US balance of payments and a messy war in Southeast Asia was well underway which went unsupported by those nations rebuilt two decades before by American capital and knowhow. Americans had become disillusioned with foreign aid and with the ingratitude of other peoples so that, unlike the staunch political support on which the agricultural committees could depend, the foreign affairs constituency was weaker than ever.[16]

In short, while USDA's success did not amount to total control over foreign agricultural development policy, the revised bill did strengthen Freeman's authority over the quantity of PL-480 commodities available for any country and did establish some new USDA programs in the international field.[17] And perhaps USDA's greatest accomplishments lay in reorienting AID's development strategy and in sharing the planning and execution of the revised strategy's agricultural component. Under Eisenhower, USDA was not connected in the affairs of the International Cooperation Administration. Ezra Taft Benson, the previous Secretary of Agriculture, regarded PL-480 as just a messy method for disposing of agricultural surpluses and was not interested in development *per se*. Neither, to a great extent, were the State Departments of Dulles and Herter.

Even after 1961 and Freeman's avowed interest in international development issues, AID did not draw upon USDA's resources. One reason lay in reciprocal jurisdictional jealousies, for the Food for Peace Program had been kept outside the new agency. Another was that AID concentrated primarily on a strategy of industrial development. When David Bell became Administrator, AID's relationship with USDA improved but he still tried to duplicate expertise already available in USDA. Senator Humphrey of Minnesota then introduced an amendment to an annual AID bill which, while emphasizing that AID was the "operating agency" for international agricultural development efforts, arranged for 'cooperative agreements' between USDA and AID. In 1964, in order to fulfill these cooperative arrangements under which AID financed a series of teams contracted from USDA, Freeman established the International Agriculture Development Service.

This contractual arrangement, while an improvement over the vacuum of the past, was still unsatisfactory to Freeman. As he testified in 1966 on behalf of revising PL-480 (*Hearings*, 1966: 47-48):

> The Secretary of Agriculture will need to take into account the foreign policy aspects of food aid and the degree of success of self-help efforts in recipient countries before he can make final determination about commodity programs.

★ ★ ★ ★ ★

> The new Food for Freedom Program contemplates closer coordination of food aid with other assistance programs directed towards food and agriculture in recipient countries.
>
> ★ ★ ★ ★ ★
>
> The Department of Agriculture and the AID have for several years been developing closer working relationships with each other in the food aid part of US assistance programs. But the kind of unified efforts to which the President referred means that Agriculture will also be called upon to participate in the planning of agricultural assistance activities and in reviewing the progress made in agricultural development.
>
> This means that we are called upon to develop closer interagency operating relationships that will involve the Department of Agriculture in a shared concern for not only the food component of assistance programs but also that part of economic assistance that relates to self-help in the agriculture related sectors of developing nations.
>
> This planning is primarily the responsibility of the AID ... [but] Mr. Bell has indicated his hope that the USDA will be increasingly helpful in this area. We have just signed a new interagency agreement under which AID seeks to—'enlist as fully and effectively as possible on a partnership basis the pertinent resources of the Department in planning, executing and evaluating those portions of the foreign assistance program in which it has special competence'.

Members of the Senate Committee then interrupted to cross-examine Freeman on these cooperative arrangements:

> SENATOR YOUNG. May I ask a question at this point, Mr. Chairman?
>
> THE CHAIRMAN. Yes, sir.
>
> SENATOR YOUNG. To what agency would the costs of this program be charged, the cost of assisting other countries to produce more?
>
> SECRETARY FREEMAN. To the AID Agency in the State Department.

SENATOR YOUNG. But not to Agriculture?
SECRETARY FREEMAN. Not to Agriculture.
THE CHAIRMAN. Why was it necessary to enter this agreement that you speak of? I thought there was always full cooperation among the agencies in respect to Agriculture and AID. Weren't you consulted in the past by the AID Agency as to food production abroad?
SECRETARY FREEMAN. Some.
THE CHAIRMAN. Not too much?
SECRETARY FREEMAN. No.

The Congress did oblige by enhancing both USDA's control over food-aid and its role in international agricultural development policy. But USDA's influence over the latter was due more to its resident expertise than its formal responsibility.

Once associated with foreign agricultural policy, USDA began to relax its battle on behalf of "self-help." True, self-help provisions were written into every subsequent PL-480 Agreement[18] whose fulfilment was purportedly the basis for allowing further concessional sales. But the criteria of "self-help" actions were not explicit and, when objectified, were not closely monitored. Some typical criteria were (1) proportion of national budget allocated to agriculture; (2) emphasis on provision of chemical fertilizers, either through foreign imports or domestic production (which opened an avenue to foreign investment); and (3) extension of power generation and electrification, provided the rate-structure was modified to remove subsidies and make the user pay appropriate costs. AID devised "check-list" against which to measure a country's performance but such monitoring was unimpressive. Instead of holding countries to their targets, US decision-makers were satisfied with a country's "best efforts."

By the end of LBJ's administration, "self-help" had been considerably de-emphasized. The State Department had always contended that self-help requirements could never really be enforced without some sharp political repercussions, and USDA soon agreed. In the field the US Embassy and the AID Mission were responsible for assessing the progress towards self-help and the recipient country had to submit reports on its performance twice each year. USDA assigned responsibility for evaluating the information compiled to the International Agriculture Development Service, which was abolished in 1969. Since then, as a further demotion, evaluations of "self-help" efforts have been conducted by the Foreign Development Division of the Economic Research Service. The USDA's Assistant Secretary for International Affairs and Commodity Programs once again emphasized commercial trade almost exclusively.

The problems with "self-help" and the coordination it presumed were evident in all phases of PL-480 in India. Officials of the New Delhi Embassy from that period suggest that the ISC's formal instructions for each PL-480 Agreement contained one item of essential information and a lot of "boiler-plate." The essential item was the amount of specific commodities to be authorized under the Agreement and the balance included the conditions soughts as *quid pro quos*. The latter "boiler-plate" were not too meaningful a set of requirements, a conclusion supported by a ranking member of the AID policy planning team in Washington at that time. Few new commitments to agricultural development were ever extracted from the GoI since the terms in the Agreements were usually projects already about to get underway.

The AID planner further observed that "the idea of self-help provisions is a reasonable one, and the recipient countries agreed. But the teeth in those agreements were often quite weak. India, for example, had 'food zones' which obstructed the movements of its own commodities from surplus to short-fall areas. Overall efficiency would suggest that these zones be abolished, and one indicator that self-help was really underway would have been to require the elimination of these zones by a fixed date. But such blatant interference was impossible because it raised questions of national sovereignty." As the AID official quipped, "you can't have a report card for a country." And so "self-help" increasingly became mere window-dressing rather than an enforceable criterion for action.[19]

Even granting that self-help may have been a temporary touchstone for US foreign agricultural policy after 1966, it was poorly coordinated and suffered the drawbacks of any dyarchy. Responsibility for it resided in AID, but the necessary expertise lay in USDA. Progress reports by recipient countries and the American field personnel were evaluated by a relatively low office in USDA and by AID's Washington bureaus, but in reality these evaluations rarely surfaced. The results of these investigations were seldom brought before the ISC during its deliberations on subsequent PL-480 Agreements. And since USDA remained primarily interested in maintaining and developing its hard-currency foreign markets (a position much appreciated by the Treasury and by BoB), the "self-help" provisions were more an excuse to diminish shipments of food-aid and end Indian dependency on US supplies. As one wag put it, "there is never enough self-help!" And then, of course, there were the extra-regional policy considerations to the east.

An Indian Chronology

Before discussing LBJ's "short-tether" policy on PL-480 shipments, some developments in India should be reviewed which are relevant to self-help and the struggle between USDA and State/AID. American foreign policy-making does not occur in a vacuum, and changes in India affected the fates of bureaucratic players in Washington. Furthermore, there is some evidence that through PL-480 the USG tried to influence the Indian Cabinet's composition and general policies.

Under Nehru and his economic advisor, P.C. Mahalanobis, the Government of India had pursued a heavy-industries strategy of economic development. PL-480 shipments were welcomed as a cushion in years of agricultural shortfalls and, as a perfectly rational reason not to invest scarce resources in rural development schemes. They also helped to ensure that urban food prices remained low. During a 1961 world-trip, a member of Freeman's staff asked a ranking Indian official about India's grain reserves and received the ingenuous reply: "Oh, they're in Kansas."

As Ministers of Food and Agriculture, neither S.K. Patil[20] nor his successor, Swaran Singh, were particularly interested in agriculture *per se*, a fact that attests to the low salience of agricultural policy in the Nehruvian years. Shortly before Nehru's death in May, 1964, Freeman again visited Delhi and found Swaran Singh noncommittal about "self-help" proposals. Freeman did, however, leave behind a standing offer to provide whatever help he could to solve India's food problems, should the GoI so desire. And the Bowles Embassy continued to press for a shake-up of Indian thinking on agricultural policy.

After Nehru's death, a period of collective and confused political leadership occurred. Then in July 1964, Prime Minister Shastri had a mild heart attack and the collective leadership decided that Nehru's practice of reserving the External Affairs Ministry along with a number of other portfolios for the Prime Minister, was too great a task for the ailing Lal Bahadur. Swaran Singh, who had gained minor diplomatic experience in 1963 as Nehru's surrogate in a series of discussions[21] with the Pakistani Foreign Minister, then Zulfikar Ali Bhutto, became Minister of External Affairs. And in the same cabinet reshuffle, Chidambaram Subramaniam became Food Minister. The latter's appointment was yet another example of the low salience of domestic agricultural policy in India, since Subramaniam was a relatively junior member of the Cabinet. At the same time Subramaniam, who had previously served as Minister of Steel and Heavy Industries, was recognized as an accomplished administrator and technocrat.

Subramaniam soon expressed interest in Freeman's offers, which had been supplemented and supported by Bowles and the AID Mission. Most American participants from the period credit the turn-around on agricultural policy in India to him. Like Freeman, Subramaniam was not an agriculturalist but he was an experienced politician who knew how to get things done. Subramaniam began to push for the modernization of agriculture through the application of new high-yielding seeds, the expansion of fertilizer production, farm mechanization, and the spread of irrigation facilities and electricity. Since its First Five-Year Plan and the Community Development program, India had sought to expand its agricultural production but only at a modest rate of about five-to-ten per cent. Agricultural accomplishments measured up to these goals, but Subramaniam sought to double and triple crop-yields with the new techniques.

The path to increased agricultural production was not, however, easy. The year of 1965 proved to be one of turbulence and trouble for India. In January, language riots occurred in Madras over the mandatory shift to Hindi as the national language. Subramaniam submitted his resignation over this issue, but Shastri refused to accept it. From April through June, India confronted Pakistan in the Rann of Kutch incident, while the Chinese increased tensions on the northern border. Then the main monsoon failed and by late July, the country's food situation began to deteriorate. Furthermore, on September 1st, Pakistan attacked the Chamb sector of Kashmir and by 6th Ayub Khan broadcast: "We are at war with India." Two days later the US suspended all military and economic aid to both belligerents. A ceasefire was arranged in less than a month and Shastri and Ayub agreed to January discussions under Soviet auspices in Tashkent.

Given these dilemmas, the Indian Cabinet belatedly reemphasized its agriculture-first strategy of development. Subramaniam was authorized to accept standing offers of American technical aid and to reach an understanding with Freeman in order to ensure adequate supplies of grain. The unfolding effects of the drought were most pronounced in the Hindi-heartland of northern India, which had always been the sheet-anchor of the Congress Party. Concessional rates would allow the GoI to provide cheap food to the masses in the Indo-Gangetic plain, so US food shipments were a guarantee of political stability in India and indirectly underwrote its Congress government.

On 25 November 1965, Subramaniam and Freeman met in Rome to hammer out an agricultural package for India. Both agreed on the importance of self-help, and Subramaniam made it clear that American pressures for self-help would help him in the Indian Parliament as well as supply needed leverage on his own

Cabinet colleagues. He returned to India armed with a package of promises and penalties. The situation also allowed Freeman, back in Washington, to emphasize the importance of USDA in stimulating agricultural development. "Self-help" helped to advance the careers of two political bureaucrats in their respective countries and became as well as code-word for re-orienting the GoI's development strategy. On 7 December 1965, the GoI announced its new farm program, and LBJ immediately ordered a speed-up in the shipping of 1.5 million tons of wheat to India to meet the food crisis. Thereafter, says LBJ in *The Vantage Point* (1971: 226), he gave Freeman the ball to carry. Within seven months, he retrieved it on a rebound.

In January 1966, Shastri signed the Tashkent Declaration and then died of a heart attack. Eight days later, Indira Gandhi became Prime Minister. As India's food shortage worsened, she immediately appealed to other countries for assistance, and the American Embassy in Delhi supported her request with extensive documentation on the disaster confronting India. In February, Vice-President Humphrey traveled to New Delhi to announce new loans totaling $150 million for purchasing essential raw materials for industry and also for fertilizer imports. And LBJ revived his invitation to the Indian Prime Minister for a state visit.

In March, Indira Gandhi came to Washington for formal discussions, just as India and the USSR signed an agreement in Delhi about building the Bokaro Steel plant. After their meeting, LBJ sent Congress a special message about emergency food aid for India, and also lobbied actively and personally among the Senators and Representatives. Johnson's rhetoric was passionate and inspiring:

> India is a good and deserving friend. Let it never be said that "bread should be so dear and flesh and blood so cheap" that we turned in indifference from her bitter need.

The Congress obliged almost immediately with a unanimous joint resolution, and favorable exchanges between the USG and the GoI became fairly common.

In the following three months, in response to the World Bank's Bell Report and as articulately promoted by Indian civil servants and politicians like L.K. Jha, I.G. Patel, S. Bhoothalingam and Ashok Mehta, the GoI's policy of limited economic liberalization was underway. The GoI changed its foodzone policy (slightly); liberalized its import requirement; delicensed a number of industries; signed a pact with the American International Oil Company for a Madras fertilizer plant; and on 5 June announced the devaluation of the rupee by over one-third.

The United States, in turn, agreed to send India 3.5 million more tons of foodgrains under PL-480; committed another $50 million to expanding Indian power generation plants; and loaned the GoI $33 million for the Beas Dam Project. In July, even as evidence accumulated that for a second straight year the monsoon played fickle with India, the US signed another $150 million loan for industrial and agricultural production, while the Government of India accepted in principle the recommendations of the Swaminathan Committee on industrial development procedures, and delicensed still more industries.

Operation Short-Tether

Then a critical event occurred which derailed the entire train of events. On a July 1966 state visit to Moscow, Prime Minister Gandhi signed a communique which criticized the "imperialists in South East Asia." The communique was allegedly written by a very young Indian Foreign Service officer and was signed, unread.

Indian comments on Vietnam may have been a necessary trade-off between sovereignty (in foreign policy) and dependency (in agricultural aid) and therefore a type of symbolic horse-trading for domestic consumption. The relationship should have been intuitively obvious to a consummate politician, but President Johnson did not always appreciate the democratic imperatives of other countries. LBJ was infuriated and descriptions of his reaction range from the violent to the obscene. He was particularly angry since Shastri's last message to him from Tashkent had praised LBJ's "determined effort ...to bring about a peace in Vietnam."

Despite the grim drought, ironically coupled with floods, LBJ strictly applied the short-tether policy on grain shipments to India from August onwards.

The justification for short-tether had been laid earlier, and mildly practiced. On 30 June 1965, the four-year PL-480 agreements signed under JFK with both India and Pakistan terminated. During July and August, negotiations were underway to provide another agreement, but for one month's duration only. LBJ's stated aim was to keep recipients on a short leash in order to force their attentions towards domestic agriculture. His instructions to the bureaucracy, in the rcollections of one AID official, were: "don't be easy on them; let them get cracking and show they seriously mean business in boosting food-production." Furthermore, during the 1965 Executive Order issue, LBJ had drawn the many strings of PL-480 into his own hands and assumed direct control for some ten major recipient countries. By March 1966, when testifying on the proposed revision of the Act, Freeman also argued against multi-year agreements and advocated a shortened—although not arbitrarily tight—tether on PL-480 agreements:

> The new Food for Freedom Program can truly be an instrument under which the millions of lives that are now threatened by famine under present trends can be saved. But this will result only if it proves effective in changing those trends by stimulating, encouraging, and if necessary, insisting on effective self-help measures. This may mean agreements for no longer than one year, with provisions for periodic reviews of progress made towards self-reliance.

In November 1966, LBJ obtained Congressional action on his Food-for-Freedom message and signed PL-89-808 into law. Then Freeman, with a formally acknowledged role in foreign economic affairs, sent several USDA experts to estimate India's harvest. In November, LBJ also told Freeman and others that he had decided to end the "giveaway" days and would not move on PL-480 without Congressional agreement.

Furthermore, in contrast to his earlier instructions to the bureaucracy, LBJ's public explanation for short-tether was to force other countries to share the burden of food-aid for India. He wanted Canada, Australia, and other major wheat producers to supply some of the grain needed. Thus, when in March 1967 he did send another message to Congress on behalf of Indian food-aid, he sent Freeman and Eugene Rostow to testify that the US wanted a 50-50 principle of sharing the burden with other countries. In December 1966, LBJ persuaded Congress to send a fact-finding delegation to India, and that team subsequently recommended 1.8 million tons of PL-480 grain for the February-April shipments. LBJ, however, refused to send more than half that amount as America's share.

The international response was not overwhelming. India's estimated food needs for 1967 were ten million tons of imports, towards which the US had already committed 3.6 million tons of PL-480 grain. In mid-December, Canada announced a grant of about 200,000 tons of wheat to India and, after extensive diplomatic pressure, Australia announced a grant of 150,000 tons. The US was startled and angered to learn, however, that the Indian High Commission in Canberra and the Australian Wheat Board had also concluded a hard-currency sale of another 150,000 tons. The Soviet Union contributed 200,000 tons of emergency food aid, too.

But LBJ wanted more action on the 5.7 million tons deficit which India still needed. He asked the World Bank President, George Woods, to organize as many nations as possible into a food-aid consortium for India, and Woods agreed. LBJ also sent Eugene Rostow, Under Secretary of State for Political Affairs, around the world to generate support for India's food needs. Pledges worth about $200 million were grudgingly obtained, although many countries bluntly felt that "twenty people are being saved today so that forty can starve tomorrow."

India in 1967 was like a ship adrift. The Government of India continued to delicense additional industries but its policy of economic liberalism was flagging. Indira Gandhi had been strongly criticized by many older leaders for devaluing the rupee, especially since exports did not rise as anticipated. Bhagwati and Desai (1970: 487-490) describe numerous reasons why the experiments with economic liberalism did not work, but by early 1967 the GoI began to sign economic cooperation pacts and trade protocols, with Soviet-bloc nations. The strategy of administrative markets revived in Indian economic planning.

Despite India's food needs, Indo-American relations grew increasingly distant. During the Six-day War in West Asia, India strongly criticized Israel and took over US-UAR relations after they were severed. Greetings were also sent to Ho Chi Minh in Hanoi on his 77th birthday and in November Indira Gandhi attended the 50th anniversary celebrations of the Russian Revolution in Moscow. LBJ grudgingly authorized repeated PL-480 shipments but only after holding every one up long enough to indicate his displeasure. During 1967, agreements totaling over six million tons were authorized, along with several loans for fertilizer imports. But LBJ was clearly unhappy with India as well as increasingly absorbed by his Vietnam policies.

LBJ's short-tether policy, which others have dubbed "the great hold-up" or "the tight-rope tether," illustrates the pernicious effects of excessive coordination. It also illuminates how a program, well-insulated from Congressional supervision and control, can be wielded as a weapon of executive policy. The bureaucratic politics paradigm of behavior is adequate up to a point, and has revealed reasons and methods by which self-help provisions got written into law. But the paradigm loses applicability as soon as the highest elected official takes a direct interest in whatever the subject is at hand.

The views, moods and actions of a President of the United States are subject to a different calculus than that applied to other players. With reference to the subcontinent of South Asia, LBJ, like many of his former peers in Congress, disliked Indians and admired Pakistanis. LBJ's associates often comment how he anthropomorphized politics for, rather than seeing nations of people, the President saw countries in terms of discrete personalities. Based on his assessment of selected leaders, LBJ regarded Indians as weak and indecisive. And although he had vowed to "help that girl" after his first meeting with Indira Gandhi, he reportedly had also concluded that she was a "typical woman in politics" who tended towards the opaque if not the vacuous.[22] His lack of confidence in the Prime Minister's ability or that of her colleagues, presaged Myrdal's classification of India among the "soft states" of the world, but LBJ's view had considerably more impact.

LBJ's personal dislike for Indians would not have explained his behavior, however, because as his domestic policies demonstrate, he had great compassion for the poor and the unfortunate. But LBJ was infuriated at Indian pronouncements on Vietnam and American policies there. In retrospect, Mrs. Gandhi could have been much more vocal in leading Asian opposition to the war, and her remarks sound more like products for domestic consumption than like leverage on the international scene. But LBJ was excessively preoccupied with and sensitive about his policies towards Southeast Asia. And while by now this explanation has a hackneyed flavor, it still seems accurate.

The self-help policy, which was objectively sensible and necessary for balanced economic development, became tainted as an American strategy foisted upon India. The technological package of hybrid seeds, chemical fertilizers, electrified irrigation and easy credit required sustained application over the long-term rather than on a month-to-month basis. LBJ's tether was clearly tied more to political events than to economic performance. Consequently, like the whole strategy of economic liberalization of which it was a part, the self-help policy was discredited in India as a device for systematic national humiliation. In the long run, LBJ's short-tether policy and his lack of respect for the Indian leadership were political mistakes.

Short-tether did have a salutary effect on American government, however, for it managed to unite USDA, the State Department, AID, and the Congress in favor of an uninterrupted flow of foodstuffs to India. Many interviewees commented that previously warring interests learned to cooperate against Johnson in order to release the food shipments for India, a unity which LBJ interpreted as proof that his subordinates were all soft-headed.

More seriously, the short-tether policy reduced LBJ's own credibility as a competent guardian of American interests. Tying everything to his Vietnam policy was damaging enough in itself, but the President also discredited pro-American forces within the Indian establishment. Two cases illustrate the ill-effects of trying to coordinate policy at the White House level, when its occupant has more pressing concerns elsewhere.

The most blatant example dealt with Subramaniam, a very competent Minister skilled in combining political insights and administrative ability. Subramaniam had become clearly identified with technological attitudes and pro-American affiliations, but he was also a man getting things done. Although under considerable pressure within India, Subramaniam maintained his progressive policies towards India's agricultural problems. Then one day in May 1966, LBJ unceremoniously and imperiously summoned Freeman and Subramaniam to his Texan ranch—Subramaniam all the way from India. Right up to the presidential press conference, nobody, including Freeman, knew the President's intentions. His decision, announced with great pride, was to approve a new PL-480 Agreement. This decision, in itself, was fine but the circumstances of its announcement made Subramaniam look like an American puppet and weakened him further at home. His 1967 electoral defeat was probably due more to linguistic quarrels than his American connections, but Subramaniam's power within the Cabinet had eroded considerably.

The second case dealt with those Indian bureaucrats who consistently advocated economic liberalism, a policy regularly promoted by the US government. Their prescriptive recommendations failed for many reasons—some would say they were never really tried—but the decision to devalue was predicated upon an expectation that sufficiently large doses of economic capital would be forthcoming to provide the big push. The World Bank's Bell Report of 1965 had led the GoI to assume that massive foreign aid commitments from the Aid-Consortium would follow upon changes in the rupee's exchange rate, relaxation of administrative market controls, and re-emphasis on the agricultural sector. The successive droughts in themselves were probably sufficient to prevent success, but along with the short-tether food policy came a mere trickle of foreign aid. Part of the problem surely lays in India's inadequate absorptive capacities for the Consortium's first installment of $900 million, but perhaps the US also cannot afford extensive involvement in more than one Asian country at a time, if that. The choice actually made between a peripheral state of Southeast Asia and a major state of South Asia bore decidedly recurrent ill-consequences.

VI. CONCLUDING OBSERVATIONS AND COMMENTS

As representative American policies towards agricultural and food aid, self-help and short-tether suggest the merit of moderation in all things. Neither succeeded fully, although both had identifiable effects at home as well as in India. On reflection perhaps self-help, and certainly short-tether, violated the first rule of diplomacy, namely that nations should never threaten actions which they are not prepared to back up.

The rationale for both policies' objectives had been fairly well thought out. LDCs, with development strategies skewed towards industrialization, had to rebalance their industrial projects with agricultural investments. Self-help was a code-word for such reorientation. And in terms of yearly evaluations of performance, short-tether was a reasonable condition for external assistance. Application of a shorter-tether in periods of crisis in order to encourage other countries to share the burden of food-aid is somewhat less reasonable or realistic.

The adoption of self-help as a US policy was a slow process, but the trend was based on extensive and accurate information about agricultural development. The options of indiscriminately continuing US food-aid policies and of ending food-aid altogether had been considered and properly rejected. The latter was inhumane and the former would lead to excessive dependency and future disaster. Consequently, in the phase of policy-formulation, self-help seems to have been thought through, while short-tether was not. The former calculated the range of relevant issues, consulted most appropriate participants, and was assigned to middle-level government agencies capable of executing the policy. The latter, in all cases, was the reverse. It sought very short-term payoffs, was basically a presidential whim, and was decided at the rarefied pinnacle of the governmental hierarchy.

Parenthetically, the analyses above indicate that Lyndon Baines Johnson was the prime actor in PL-480 during the mid-sixties. By asserting presidential control over a semi-insulated program, LBJ required his personal clearance for all shipments of food to major recipients. And as Chester Bowles' memoirs also indicate, LBJ's erratic and capricious behavior in sometimes withholding, sometimes releasing shipments authorized under PL-480, complicated most of the natural dilemmas. His method of control disrupted normal program operations because officials in both countries were unable to deal with each other on the basis of minimally confident expectations. Evidently, Johnson's preoccupation with Vietnam led him to withhold economic aid elsewhere as the war absorbed increasing amounts of America's wealth. At the same time, the Congress whittled down its appropriations for development loans, many of which were understood to be destined for India. The general conclusion emerges that India's trial of a liberal economic policy failed in large part because the anticipated, if not explicitly promised, support was forthcoming neither from the US nor from the World Bank as a whole.

By its implementation phase, because self-help took so long to adopt, most participants understood its intent. The series of reports and consultative committees envisaged suggested that those responsible for self-help activities would be thoroughly supervised, but operational difficulties and jurisdictional rivalries made such monitoring inadequate. US-AID, for example, often appreciated self-help as an idea but not for the leverage it gave USDA over agricultural development. On the other hand, despite some prior intimations, the application of the short-tether was abrupt and surprised many of those affected. Short-tether was, however, extensively monitored in the sense that the President alone was responsible for the decision and its implementation. Ironically, the resources of presidential authority and interest devoted to short-tether were commensurate to the task set forth, while the resources devoted to self-help were not.

Assessments of the outcomes of the two policies and the participating organizations were provided *inter alia* above. But in brief summation, self-help did have an impact on re-orienting Indian agricultural strategy, although other pressures, both internal and international, led to the GoI's 1965 decision as well. In the long run, the well-intended US pressures and requirements for a public Indian profession of faith in a pro-agriculture development strategy had considerable political costs. Even when advice is correct, nations like people don't like to accept it and implicitly admit past errors.*

Furthermore, some issues require more insulation than others. Like population programs and environmental issues, food problems necessarily involve higher costs if and when they are sacrificed to short-run political goals. These social issues need longer gestation periods and time perspectives, attainable only by a degree of insulation from direct control by Presidents and their political appointees. But since much visible foreign policy deals with political problems and crises of a short-run nature, programs with longer-term objectives are at a disadvantage. Too much insulation, of course, may entail neglect and ultimate asphyxiation because every viable program requires a real constituency. The question is, what domestic costs and benefits are associated with any particular program or policy. Rather than prescribing a series of autonomous but centralized programs, insulation may best be achieved through a loosely articulated process of decision-making with multiple access-points and considerable slippage.

The principal bureaucratic players involved in self-help were USDA, AID, and the State Department, in descending order of interest and commitment. Other actors and agencies participated much more minimally, although USDA drew considerably on the system of land-grant universities and their institutes of agriculture.

---

* Editor's Note: In retrospect, India's relative inattention to agricultural investment up to 1966-67 coincided with non-availability of new agricultural technology. Investment began after new technology made substantial returns possible.

The principal players were not, however, well-coordinated; and the relations between overseas and Washington-based units in each agency were not strong. Congress had an overall interest in whatever impact self-help would have on American agricultural exports for hard-currency and thereby on the US balance of payments. Congressional interest, however, declined in proportion to the diminishing stock of surplus commodities.

Short-tether also had an impact: it discredited the sensible US policies towards Indian agricultural development and towards the general Indian economy. Its postulated aim of encouraging other nations to share in the burden of providing food-aid was not achieved either, but it did serve to diminish the moral standing of the United States overseas. The short-tether participants can be summed up in a simple dichotomy: LBJ versus the rest. Even loyal lieutenants like Freeman and Rusk ended up opposing an increasingly crotchety President in order to release the badly needed foodgrains. The American people, Congress, and bureaucracy came to regard LBJ's short-tether as an ill-disguised halter systematically choking Indo-American relations. While the US may be ambivalent towards South Asia, its actions since 1950 of offering India over $4 billion in economic aid and supplying over $4 billion of foodgrains against soft-currency payments, suggest some understanding of India's importance in a stable, friendly South Asia.

In conclusion, the case study above suggests considerable merit in an incremental and somewhat disjoined system for administering US food and agricultural policies. There are times when rapid and coordinated actions are needed, but past events have indicated the ability of the current distribution of offices and responsibilities to cope with such crises. During the drought years, the ISC had worked well-enough in obtaining the necessary food supplies and expediting their shipment. Despite presidential harassment, the ISC and supplementary task forces had resolved the formidable technical problems in one of history's largest relief programs. Consequently, the best approach to self-help would probably have been to pass the word among participating departments that the Congress and the President wanted agricultural development promoted at all possible opportunities because, given the subtleties of international relations and of persuasive pressurizing, a decentralized system is more appropriate than a sharply articulated hierarchy.

In any case, when an issue is important enough to merit unflagging attention by the occupant of the White House, constitutional provisions are still sufficient to allow the Chief Executive maximal participation. In crisis conditions, the most that bureaucrats can do is present necessary information and choices, argue the alternatives and consequences cogently, and then abide by the legitimate policy-makers' decisions—or else publicly resign with a reasoned explanation of why the policy-makers are wrong. At times, executive leadership is necessary; at times, reforms are required to strengthen the bureaucracy and thereby brake determined but short-sighted leaders. But theories of democratic government require active, involved political leadership even though it occasionally rejects the best professional advice from knowledgeable specialists. Short of a platonic state, there is no solution to this creative tension. And notwithstanding any of the above, in food and agricultural aid as well as in other policies of economic development, American foreign policy-makers might well heed Hirschman's long-standing advice (1964: 54): "We must recognize that there are tasks that simply exceed the capacities of a society, no matter to whom they are being entrusted."

NOTES AND REFERENCES

1. Through 1971 when PL-480 shipments to India were interrupted, 87 per cent of PL-480 receipts had been earmarked for use in India (63 per cent for loans, 18 per cent for grants, and six per cent for the so-called 'Cooley loans' to American business ventures) and the remaining 13 per cent had been allocated for use by USG agencies (Veit, no date: 4).
2. See Annex A.
3. Although CCC is formally within the jurisdiction of USDA, the negotiations for the ultimate signing ceremony of the Soviet-American wheat deal occurred in the US Department of Commerce. However, recent presidential interventions in CCC operations and their

consequences for domestic inflation and American investments in Siberia are beyond the scope of this case-study.

4. In contrast to previous presidencies, the Ford Administration's strategy for making the US merchant marine more competitive entails subsidies for ship-construction and for flying the American flag rather than the imposition of cargo-preference requirements. While the American shipping fleet and the maritime unions are both well-entrenched interests in US politics, GOP administrations tend to favor the former and Democratic administrations the latter.
5. One experienced interviewee observed that during the Marshall Plan, to the disgust of domestic American agriculture, the State Department persistently slighted US exports in favor of European-grown agricultural produce. Thus when PL-480 was drafted in 1954, it was specifically designed for USDA's interests. The bill's basic intent was to move surplus commodities but not to interfere with commercial trade.
6. The success of the GoI's cheap-food policy until 1963 and the dilemmas thereafter are indicated by the index numbers of December wholesale prices for Indian food articles:

1952 = 100.0	1964 = 166.0	1969 = 227.3
1960 = 117.0	1965 = 173.2	1970 = 235.6
1961 = 117.8	1966 = 204.1	1971 = 241.1
1962 = 122.8	1967 = 239.3	1972 = 287.9
1963 = 136.1	1968 = 227.3	

Source: Agricultural Situation in India, Department of Economics and Statistics, Ministry for Food and Agriculture, Government of India (various years).

7. See Section 104(k) of Annex A.
8. The Khusro Report (1968) also correctly predicted that inflation would worsen when the PL-480 shipments ceased and the buffer stocks in the Food Corporation of India declined.
9. Almost 100 per cent (and never less than 93 per cent) of all American agricultural exports to India occurred through official governmental channels; the private grain trade was virtually nil.
10. As a basic foreign policy aim, all countries seek to keep others mildly dependent in order to influence their behavior. But there are always questions about the appropriate mix of independence and dependence, as well as questions of what lever works best when trying to deflect or halt another country's unwanted policies. Food supplies are, unfortunately, a crude and ugly weapon to use among nations. Human malnutrition and starvation are conditions guaranteed to soften all but the hardest hearts, for the strong humanitarian streak in the American character, however ungraciously acknowledged or delivered, tempers its more materialistic and realpolitik aims. Allowing people to go hungry when food supplies are available is not a 'clean' instrument of foreign policy, either in world or domestic public opinion.

11. See, for example, Chand, 1965; Rao, 1965; Raj, 1966; Dandekar, 1967; as well as the entire collection of articles from *Yojana*, 1965, entitled "The Meaning of Self-Reliance."
12. The White House office, which had been renamed Food for Freedom in line with LBJ's manipulation of verbal symbols, should not be confused with the operational office of Food for Peace, which was transferred to the 'War on Hunger'. That FFF office is, apparently, the predecessor of the division now found in the State Department's Economic and Business Bureau, which is responsible for furnishing a delegate to the FAO's Consultative Subcommittee on Surplus Disposal.
13. The nomenclature expressed a symbolic squabble between Congress and the Executive PL-480 had come to be known as 'Food for Peace' but LBJ wanted 'freedom' to be the hallmark of his foreign policy. For a time there was a tug-of-war between FFP and FFF—both complicated by the 'War on Hunger'—but FFP ultimately won the day. Congress does have greater staying power than a President, and also the earlier phrase had taken firm root in the media. FFF still exists in one anachronistically titled office in the State Department, where bets are occasionally taken about its prospective longevity.
14. Annex B provides the full text of Section 109.
15. Pithy evidence from a 1966 Senate hearing on the "Food for Freedom Program and Commodity Reserves" is provided in Annex C.
16. It has also been suggested that Senator Fulbright, being equally interested in relieving the rice-glut of that year which plagued his Arkansan constituents, did not press the fight for jurisdictional reassignment very hard.
17. See, respectively Sections 401 and 406 of Annex D. Ironically, the annual funds authorized for Section 406 programs were *not* appropriated by Congress during Freeman's final two years in office.
18. Annex E presents a representative example of a PL-480 Agreement with 'self-help' provisions contracted between the United States and India.
19. Much more contributory to meaningful American help for Indian agricultural development were the monthly "world problem-solving luncheons" regularly held in Delhi by representatives of USDA (the Agriculture Attaches and an Economic Research Service man), AID, the Rockefeller Foundation, the Ford Foundation, Peace Corps, and CLUSA (the Cooperative League of the USA). Informal consultations, it is commonly agreed, produced more coordinated leverage on Indian agriculture than all the public PL-480 pronouncements and requirements.
20. In Washington, D.C. on 4 May 1960, Patil and Eisenhower had signed a PL-480 Agreement for 17 million tons of foodgrain, the largest Agreement ever signed. At a time when US farm surpluses were still accumulating, the deal made economic sense to USDA. It also established a well-insulated crutch for India that justified the remark about Kansan reserves and also allowed Patil to neglect the agricultural sector for the

next four years. Patil, it should be noted, was political boss of Bombay, the great metropolis of Western India, and had greater interests in industry and commerce than in the rural sector. Patil was concerned, however, about ensuring cheap food-stuffs for the urban consumer.

21. President Kennedy, in hopes of resolving the Kashmir dispute, had persuaded the two belligerents to conduct these meetings. The Sino-Indian conflict of 1962 had placed a new dimension on this old problem.

22. In contrast to this characterization by a White House insider, Bhatia (1974: 193) comments that "the President told Ambassador to India Chester Bowles that he had been 'particularly impressed by the political astuteness she displayed' during those parleys." And according to other hearsay, LBJ likened Indira to a "cross between Barbara Ward and Lady Bird," which surely indicated high praise. But these interpretations seem less consonant with his subsequent behavior, especially when the following year LBJ and the Congress gave exaggerated attention to Indira's domestic rival, Morarji Desai, on his official visit to Washington, D.C.

ANNEX A

Uses of Foreign Currencies: Section 104 of PL 83-480 (As Amended)

Sec. 104*. Notwithstanding any other provision of law, the President may use or enter into agreements with foreign countries or international organizations to use the foreign currencies, including principal and interest from loan repayments, which accrue in connection with sales for foreign currencies under this title for one or more of the following purposes:

(a) For payment of United States obligations (including obligations entered into pursuant to other legislation);

(b) For carrying out programs of United States Government agencies to—

(1) help develop new markets for United States agricultural commodities on a mutually benefiting basis. From sale proceeds and loan repayments under this title not less than the equivalent of 5 per centum of the total sales made each year under this title shall be set aside in the amounts and kinds of foreign currencies specified by the Secretary of Agriculture and made available in advance for use as provided by this paragraph over such period of years as the Secretary of Agriculture determines will most effectively carry out the purpose of this paragraph: *Provided*, That the Secretary of Agriculture may release such amounts of the foreign currencies so set aside as he determines cannot be effectively used for agricultural market development purposes under this section, except that no release shall be made until the expiration of thirty days following the date on which notice of such proposed release is transmitted by the President to the Senate Committee on Agriculture and Forestry and to the House Committee on Agriculture, if transmitted while Congress is in session, or sixty days following the date of transmittal if transmitted

* Public Law 85-128, 71 Stat: 345, approved 13 August 1957 (7 U S C, 1704a), provides that "within sixty days after any agreement is entered into for the use of any foreign currencies, a full report thereon shall be made to the Senate and House of Representatives of the United States and to the Committees on Agriculture and Appropriations thereof."

while Congress is not in session. Provision shall be made in sale and loan agreements for the convertibility of such amount of the proceeds thereof (not less than 2 per centum) as the Secretary of Agriculture determines to be needed to carry out the purpose of this paragraph in those countries which are or offer reasonable potential of becoming dollar markets for United States agricultural commodities. Such sums shall be converted into the types and kinds of foreign currencies as the Secretary deems necessary to carry out the provisions of this paragraph and such sums shall be deposited to a special Treasury account and shall not be made available or expended except for carrying out the provisions of this paragraph. Notwithstanding any other provision of law, if sufficient foreign currencies for carrying out the purpose of this paragraph in such countries are not otherwise available, the Secretary of Agriculture is authorized and directed to enter into agreements with such countries for the sale of agricultural commodities in such amounts as the Secretary of Agriculture determines to be adequate and for the use of the proceeds to carry out the purpose of this paragraph. In carrying out agricultural market development activities, non-profit agricultural trade organizations shall be utilized to the maximum extent practicable. The purpose of this paragraph shall include such representation of agricultural industries as may be required during the course of discussions on trade programs relating either to individual commodities or groups of commodities;

(2) finance with not less than 2 per centum of the total sales proceeds received each year in each country activities to assist international educational and cultural exchange and to provide for the strengthening of the resources of American schools, colleges, universities, and other public and nonprofit private educational agencies for international studies and research under the programs authorized by Title VI of the National Defense Education Act, the Mutual Educational and Cultural Exchange Act of 1961, the International Education Act of 1966, the Higher Education Act of 1965, the Elementary and Secondary Education Act of 1965, the National Foundation on the Arts and the Humanities Act of 1965, and the Public Broadcasting Act of 1967;

(3) collect, collate, translate, abstract, and disseminate scientific and technological information and conduct research and support scientific activities overseas including programs and projects of scientific cooperation between the United States and other countries such as coordinated research against diseases common to all of mankind or unique to individual regions of the globe, and promote and support programs of medical and scientific research, cultural and educational development, family planning, health, nutrition, and sanitation;

(4) acquire by purchase, lease, rental, or otherwise, sites and buildings and grounds abroad, for United States Government use including offices, residence quarters, community and other facilities, and construct, repair, alter, and furnish such buildings and facilities;

(5) finance under the direction of the Librarian of Congress, in consultation with the National Science foundation and other interested agencies, (A) programs outside the United States for the analysis and evaluation of foreign books, periodicals, and other materials to determine whether they would provide information of technical or scientific significance in the United States and whether such books, periodicals, and other materials are of cultural or educational significance, (B) the registry, indexing, binding, reproduction, cataloging, abstracting, translating, and dissemination of books, periodicals, and related materials determined to have such significance; and (C) the acquisition of such books, periodicals, and other materials and the deposit thereof in libraries and research centers in the United States specializing in the areas to which they relate;

(c) To procure equipments, materials, facilities and services for the common defense including internal security;*

---

* Section 505(e) of the Foreign Assistance Act of 1961, as added by the Foreign Assistance Act of 1966, Public Law 89-583, 80 Stat. 803, approved September 19, 1966, and redesignated by the Foreign Assistance Act of 1967, Public Law 90-137, 81 Stat. 459, approved November 14, 1967, provides as follows: "(e) From and after the sixtieth day after the date of enactment of the Foreign Assistance Act of 1966, no assistance shall be provided under this chapter to any country to which sales are made under title I of the Agricultural Trade Development and Assistance Act of 1954

(d) For assistance to meet emergency or extraordinary relief requirement other than requirements for food commodities: *Provided*, That not more than a total amount equivalent to $5,000,000 may be made available for this purpose during any fiscal year;

(e) For use to the maximum extent under the procedures established by such agency as the President shall designate for loans to United States business firms (including cooperatives) and branches, subsidiaries, or affiliates of such firms for business development and trade expansion in such countries, including loans for private home construction, and for loans to domestic or foreign firms (including cooperatives) for the establishment of facilities for aiding in the utilization, distribution, or otherwise increasing the consumption of, and markets for, United States agricultural products: *Provided however*, That no such loans shall be made for the manufacture of any products intended to be exported to the United States in competition with products produced in the United States and due consideration shall be given to the continued expansion of markets for United States agricultural commodities or the products thereof. Foreign currencies may be accepted in repayment of such loans;

(f) To promote multilateral trade and agricultural and other economic development, under procedures, established by the President, by loans or by use in any other manner which the President may determine to be in the national interest of the United States, particularly to assist programs of recipient countries designed to promote, increase, or improve food production, processing, distribution, or marketing in food-deficit countries friendly to the United States, for which purpose the President may utilize to the extent practicable the services of nonprofit voluntary agencies registered with and approved by the Advisory

---

Contd.

until such country has entered into an agreement to permit the use of foreign currencies accruing to the United States under such Title I to procure equipment, materials, facilities, and services, for the common defense including internal security, in accordance with the provisions of Section 104(c) of such Title I." [22 U.S.C. 2314(e).]

Committee on Voluntary Foreign Aid: *Provided*, That no such funds may be utilized to promote religious activities;

(g) For the purchase of goods or services for other friendly countries;

(h) For financing, at the request of such country, programs emphasizing maternal welfare, child health and nutrition, and activities, where participation is voluntary, related to the problems of population growth, under procedures established by the President through any agency of the United States, or through any local agency which he determines is qualified to administer such activities. Not less than 5 per centum of the total sales proceeds received each year shall, if requested by the foreign country, be used for voluntary programs to control population growth;

(i) For paying, to the maximum extent practicable, the costs outside the United States of carrying out the program authorized in Section 406 of this Act;

(j) For sale of dollars to United States citizens and non-profit organizations for travel or other purposes of currencies determined to be in excess of the needs of departments and agencies of the United States for such currencies. The United States dollars received from the sale of such foreign currencies shall be deposited to the account of the Commodity Credit Corporation; and

(k) For paying, to the maximum extent practicable, the costs of carrying out programs for the control of rodents, insects, weeds, and other animal or plant pests; *Provided*, That—

(1) Section 1415 of the Supplemental Appropriation Act, 1953,* shall apply to currencies used for the purposes specified in subsections (a) and (b), and in the case of currencies to be used for the purposes specified in paragraph (2) of subsection(b) the Appropriation Act may specifically authorize the use of such

* Section 1415 of the Supplemental Appropriation Act, 1953, provides that "Foreign credits owed to or owned by the United States Treasury will not be available for expenditure by agencies of the United States after June 30, 1953, except as may be provided for annually in appropriation Acts and provisions of the utilization of such credits for purposes authorized by law are hereby authorized to be included in general appropriation Acts." Public Law 547, 82nd Congress, 66 Stat. 662 approved July 15, 1952 (31 U.S.C. 724).

currencies and shall not require the appropriation of dollars for the purchase of such currencies,

(2) Section 1415 of the Supplemental Appropriation Act, 1953, shall apply to all foreign currencies used for grants under subsections (f) and (g), to no less than 10 per centum of the foreign currencies which accrue pursuant to agreements entered into on or before December 31, 1964, and to not less than 20 per centum in the aggregate of the foreign currencies which accrue pursuant to agreements entered into thereafter: *Provided, however*, That the President is authorized to waive such applicability of Section 1415 in any case where he determines that it would be inappropriate or inconsistent with the purposes of this title,

(3) No agreement or proposal to grant any foreign currencies [except as provided in subsection (c) of this section], or to use (except pursuant to Appropriation Act) any principal or interest from loan repayments under this section shall be entered into or carried out until the expiration of thirty days following the date on which such agreement or proposal is transmitted by the President to the Senate Committee on Agriculture and Forestry and to the House Committee on Agriculture, if transmitted while Congress is in session or sixty days following the date of transmittal if transmitted while Congress is not in session,

(4) Any loan made under the authority of this section shall bear interest at such rate as the President may determine but not less than the cost of funds to the United States Treasury, taking into consideration the current average market yields on outstanding marketable obligations of the United States having maturity comparable to the maturity of such loans, unless the President shall in specific instances after consultation with the advisory committee established under Section 407 designate a different rate: *Provided, further*, That paragraphs (2), (3), and (4) of the foregoing proviso shall not apply in the case of any nation where the foreign currencies or credits owned by the United States and available for use by it in such nation are determined by the Secretary of the Treasury to be in excess of the normal requirements of the departments and agencies of the United States for expenditures in such nations for the two fiscal years following

the fiscal year in which such determination is made. The amount of any such excess shall be devoted to the extent practicable and without regard to paragraph (1) of the foregoing proviso, to the acquisition of sites, buildings, and grounds under paragraph (4) of subsection (b) of this section and to assist such nation in undertaking self-help measures to increase its production of agricultural commodities and its facilities for storage and distribution of such commodities. Assistance under the foregoing provision shall be limited to self-help measures additional to those which would be undertaken without such assistance. Upon the determination by the Secretary of the Treasury that such an excess exists with respect to any nation, the President shall advise the Senate Committee on Agriculture and Forestry and the House Committee on Agriculture of such determination; and shall thereafter report to each such Committee as often as may be necessary to keep such Committee advised as to the extent of such excess, the purposes for which it is used or proposed to be used, and the effects of such use. (7 U.S.C. 1704.)

ANNEX B

Self-Help Measures: Section 109 of PL 83-480 (as Amended)

Sec. 109 (a). Before entering into agreements with developing countries for the sale of United States agricultural commodities on whatever terms, the President shall consider the extent to which the recipient country is undertaking wherever practicable self-help measures to increase per capita production and improve the means for storage and distribution of agricultural commodities, including:

(1) devoting land resources to the production of needed food rather than to the production of nonfood crops—especially nonfood crops in world surplus;
(2) development of the agricultural chemical, farm machinery and equipment, transportation and other necessary industries through private enterprise;
(3) training and instructing farmers in agricultural methods and techniques;
(4) constructing adequate storage facilities;
(5) improving marketing and distribution systems;
(6) creating a favorable environment for private enterprise and investment, both domestic and foreign, and utilizing available technical knowhow;
(7) establishing and maintaining Government policies to ensure adequate incentives to producers;
(8) establishing and expanding institutions for adaptive agricultural research;
(9) allocating for these purposes sufficient national budgetary and foreign exchange resources (including those supplied by bilateral, multilateral and consortium aid programs) and local currency resources (resulting from loans or grants to recipient governments of the proceeds of local currency sales);
(10) carrying out voluntary programs to control population growth.

(b) Notwithstanding any other provisions of this Act, in agreements with nations not engaged in armed conflict against Communist forces or against nations with which the United States has no diplomatic relations, not less than 20 per centum of the foreign currencies set aside for purposes other than those in Sections 104 (a), (b), (e), and (j) shall be allocated for the self-help measures set forth in this section.

(c) Each agreement entered into under this title shall describe the program which the recipient country is undertaking to improve its production, storage, and distribution of agricultural commodities; and shall provide for termination of such agreement whenever the President finds that such program is not being adequately developed. (7 U.S.C. 1709.)

ANNEX C

Transcript on Interagency Relationships in Foreign Agricultural Development Policy

Participants: Senator Allen J. Ellender of Louisiana, Chairman of the Committee on Agriculture and Forestry, United States Senate; and the Honorable Orville L. Freeman, Secretary of Agriculture, United States Department of Agriculture.

THE CHAIRMAN. Have you any kind of agreement between the State Department and you?

SECRETARY FREEMAN. Yes, I have had long discussions with Mr. Bell in connection with this, and he has volunteered and urged, and since he has been in the AID agency he has advocated a stronger working relationship, and it has improved very significantly since he became Administrator of the program.

And one of the ways to make it work more efficiently has been for them to contract with the Department to take on a special project or in some cases possibly in the agricultural development in a country. Then the appropriation goes to AID. They contract with Agriculture. We then carry out to meet the contracted objective. We have been learning how to use this device and it is becoming more and more important.

THE CHAIRMAN. I presume you are not giving up any of your authority. I hope.

SECRETARY FREEMAN. No. sir.

THE CHAIRMAN. Neither to AID nor the State Department?

SECRETARY FREEMAN. No. Quite the contrary. This means that we will be more intimately involved in both the planning and the evaluation of the results. I might just add, to be sure the record is straight, that the so-called PASA's are merely an effort to formulate more effectively the effort we have tried to try over a long period of time.

THE CHAIRMAN. It is my hope that the Department of Agriculture will remain at the top of the heap instead of at the bottom in handling such a program as you are now proposing.

SECRETARY FREEMAN. I believe the Department has an important contribution to make.

THE CHAIRMAN. We will see that happens as far as I am concerned.

SOURCE: Hearing on "Food for Freedom Program and Commodity Reserves" on 2 June 1966 (Washington: U.S. Government Printing Office), p. 49.

ANNEX D

Selected Sections of Title IV of PL 83-480 (As Amended)

Sec. 401. After consulting with other agencies of the Government affected and within policies laid down by the President for implementing this Act, and after taking into account productive capacity, domestic requirements, farm and consumer price levels, commercial exports, and adequate carryover, the Secretary of Agriculture shall determine the agricultural commodities and quantities thereof available for disposition under this Act, and the commodities and quantities thereof which may be included in the negotiations with each country. No commodity shall be available for disposition under this Act if such disposition would reduce the domestic supply of such commodity below that needed to meet domestic requirements, adequate carryover, and anticipated exports for dollars as determined by the Secretary of Agriculture at the time of exportation of such commodity. (7 U.S.C. 1731.)

Sec. 403. These are hereby authorized to be appropriated such sums as may be necessary to carry out this Act including such amounts as may be required to make payments to the Commodity Credit Corporation, to the extent the Commodity Credit Corporation is not reimbursed under Sections 104 (j) and 105, for its actual cost incurred or to be incurred. In presenting his budget, the President shall classify expenditures under this Act as expenditures for international affairs and finance rather than for agriculture and agricultural resources. (7 U.S.C. 1733.)

Sec. 405. The authority and funds provided by this Act shall be utilized in a manner that will assist friendly countries that are determined to help themselves towards a greater degree of self-reliance in providing enough food to meet the needs of their people and in resolving their problems relative to population growth. (7 U.S.C. 1734.)

Sec. 406. (a) In order to further assist friendly developing countries to become self-sufficient in food production, the Secretary of Agriculture is authorized, notwithstanding any other provision of law:

(1) To establish and administer through existing agencies of the Department of Agriculture a program of farmer-to-farmer assistance between the United States and such countries to help farmers in such countries in the practical aspects of increasing food production and distribution and improving the effectiveness of their farming operations;

(2) To enter into contracts or other cooperative agreements with, or make grants to, land-grant colleges and universities and other institutions of higher learning in the United States to recruit persons who by reason of training, education, or practical experience are knowledgeable in the practical arts and sciences of agriculture and home economics, and to train such persons in the practical techniques of transmitting to farmers in such countries improved practices in agriculture, and to participate in carrying out the program in such countries including, where desirable, additional courses for training or re-training in such countries.

(3) To consult and cooperate with private nonprofit farm organizations in the exchange of farm youth and farm leaders with developing countries and in the training of farmers of such developing countries within the United States or abroad;

(4) To conduct research in tropical and subtropical agriculture for the improvement and development of tropical and subtropical food products for dissemination and cultivation in friendly countries;

(5) To coordinate the program authorized in this section with the activities of the Peace Corps, the Agency for International Development, and other agencies of the United States and to assign, upon agreement with such agencies, such persons to work with and under the administration of such agencies: *Provided*, That nothing in this section shall be construed to infringe upon the powers or functions of the Secretary of State;

(6) To establish by such rules and regulations as he deems necessary the conditions for eligibility and retention in and dismissal from the program established in this section, together with the terms, length and nature of service, compensation, employee status, oaths of office, and security clearances, and such persons shall be entitled to the benefits and subject to the responsibilities applicable to persons serving in the Peace Corps pursuant to the provisions of Section 612, volume 75 of the Statutes at Large, as amended; and

(7) (a) To the maximum extent practicable, to pay the costs of such program through the use of foreign currencies accruing from the sale of agricultural commodities under this Act, as provided in Section 104(i).

(b) These are hereby authorized to be appropriated not to exceed $33,000,000 during any fiscal year for the purpose of carrying out the provisions of this section. (7 U.S.C. 1736.)

Sec. 407. There is hereby established an Advisory Committee composed of the Secretary of State, the Secretary of Treasury, the Secretary of Agriculture, the Director of the Bureau of the Budget,* the Administrator of the Agency for International Development, the chairman and the ranking minority member of both the House Committee on Agriculture and the House Committee on Foreign Affairs, and the chairman and the ranking minority member of both the Senate Committee on Agriculture and Forestry and the Senate Committee on Foreign Relations. The Advisory Committee shall survey the general policies relating to the administration of the Act, including the manner of implementing the self-help provisions, the uses to be made of foreign currencies which accrue in connection with sales for foreign currencies under title I, the amount of currencies to be reserved in sales agreements for loans to private industry under Section 104(e), rates of exchange, interest rates, and the terms under which dollar credit sales are made, and shall advise the President with respect thereto. The

* Office of Management and Budget.

Advisory Committee shall meet not less than four times during each calendar year at the call of the Acting Chairman of such Committee who shall preside in the following order: The chairman of the House Committee on Agriculture, the chairman of the Senate Committee on Foreign Relations, the chairman of the Senate Committee on Agriculture and Forestry, and the chairman of the House Committee on Foreign Affairs.* (7 U.S.C. 1736a.)

---

* Amended by PL90—436, 82 Stat. 451, approved 29 July 1968.

ANNEX E

Representative PL-480 Agreement with India, Signed 20 February 1967

1. The two governments have consulted on the problems arising out of the gap between food production and food consumption. India has launched strong programs of economic and agricultural development accompanied by appropriate measures of import liberalization, which this agreement is designed to support.

2. The two Governments are agreed that planning for food sufficiency is an integral part of the development process and necessarily the first priority in economic planning. Nevertheless programs to achieve food sufficiency will be self-defeating if they are achieved at the expense of development in other sectors of the economy.

3. The Indian Government, as a part of its overall development program for the fiscal year beginning April 1967, is giving priority to its programs to improve production, storage and distribution of agricultural commodities, particularly food crops. Subject to the overall development of the economy and the availability of adequate amounts of foreign exchange, the following general targets were established for 1967-68 within the framework of the draft outline of the Fourth Five Year Plan of the Indian Government.

(a) Fertilizer production—535,000 nutrient tons of nitrogen (N), 250,000 nutrient tons of phosphate (P_2O_5).

(b) Fertilizer imports—850,000 nutrient tons of N, 250,000 nutrient tons of P_2O_5 and 300,000 nutrient tons of potassium (K_2O).

(c) Acreage to be placed under new varieties of seeds:

Rice	6,000,000 acres
Wheat	3,500,000 acres
Maize, Bajra, and Jowar	5,500,000 acres

(d) Crop protection—125 million acres to be sprayed.

(e) Irrigation—an increase in minor irrigation of 3 million acres, of which 2.4 million will be new command areas, 300,000 acres improvement in existing systems and 300,000 acres provided with supplementary irrigation; and concentration on use of irrigation for intensive production.

(f) Agricultural credit—an increase of over Rs. 1,000 million in agricultural credit—short, medium and long-term—administered through government agencies, cooperatives and land develop-ment banks.

(g) Storage—owned by the Food Department and the Food Corporation of India will increase from 2 million tons capacity to 2.5 million tons. The Central and State Warehousing Corporations will increase their modern storage capacity by 0.35 million ton (to 1.8 million tons) and the States and co-operative societies will increase their facilities on modern construction designs by 0.5 million ton (to 2.5 million tons).

4. Further the following is also recognized:

(a) With respect to pricing, the timely announcement of the food grain price support at levels sufficient to encourage greater production is important so that the cultivator will base his cropping pattern on certain knowledge of the return of his expenditure, and

(b) With respect to distribution, a satisfactory distribution policy is heavily dependent on the availability of stocks under the control of the Central Government, and it is the intention of the Indian Government to increase the end of year grain stocks through implementation of price support and food distribution policies.

(c) With respect to investment, implementation of the targets set forth in paragraph 3 above and of the general agricultural development program calls for a significantly larger investment in agriculture in 1967-68 than in the previous year.

5. The Indian Government has announced its intention of accelerating domestic production capacity for fertilizer and other industrial inputs for agriculture. The Indian Government has also announced its determination to call on all possible sources of financing for these undertakings, including private investment, and has declared that it recognizes in the context the importance of policies designed to secure a favorable investment climate.

Agreement Signed 24 June 1967 (1st Supplementary)

1. As part of its efforts to increase the domestic production of fertilizer needed to achieve its target of food sufficiency and to reduce the demand for foreign exchange, the Government of India is accelerating its efforts to assess and if feasible develop indigenous sources of phosphate rock.

2. The Government of India has also announced its determination to give high priority to the implementation of a massive countrywide family planning program in order to limit the growth of population and ensure a better standard of living for its people.

3. The Government of India has announced that it is undertaking measures to systematically reduce the rate of foodgrain losses due to pests, particularly insects and rodents.

4. The Government of India anticipates that foodgrain acreage will increase by about 10 million acres by 1970-71 over the total area in 1964-65, while the area under cotton is expected to remain unchanged during the same period. In seeking to increase foodgrain production; the Government of India is developing and implementing a policy of announced incentive prices, improved information and extension programs, and other appropriate means.

Source: Food for Freedom, New Emphasis on Self-Help, The Annual Report of the President on Activities Carried Out under Public Law 480, 83rd Congress, as Amended, during the Period January 1 through December 31, 1967; 90th Congress, 2nd Session, House Document No. 296 (Washington, D.C.: U.S. Government Printing Office, 1968), pp. 72-73.

ANNEX F

Suggested Readings

Abel, Martin E., *The 1966 Amendments to Public Law 480,* Washington: Economic Research Service, US Department of Agriculture (November, 1966).

Allison, Graham T., *Essence of Decision: Explaining the Cuban Missile Crisis*, Boston: Little, Brown and Company, 1971.

Allison, Graham T. and Morton H. Halperin, *Bureaucratic Politics: A Paradigm and Some Policy Implications*, Washington: The Brookings Institution, Reprint No. 246, 1972.

Analyst, "Politics of PL-480," A four part discussion in *Mainstream* (an Indian leftist weekly) on 16, 23 and 30 October and 13 November, 1965.

———, "Trading Freedom for US Wheat: Aid with Chains," *Mainstream*, 25 February, 1967, 9-11.

Barnds, William, *India, Pakistan, and the United States*, New York: Praeger, 1971.

Bhagwati, Jagdish N. and Padma Desai, *India: Planning for Industrialization: Industrialization and Trade Policies Since 1951*, London: Oxford University Press, 1970.

Bhardhan, Kalpana, "Do Foodgrain Imports Affect Production?" *Economic and Political Weekly*, I, 1966, 541.

Bhatia, Krishan, *The Ordeal of Nationhood: A Social Study of India Since Independence, 1947-1970*, New York: Atheneum, 1971.

_____, *Indira: A Biography of Prime Minister Gandhi*, New York: Praeger Publishers, 1974.

Bhatnagar, Satvir K., "An Analysis of Wheat Prices in India, 1954-67, With Particular Reference to PL-480," *Indian Journal of Economics*, X, 1969, 249-65.

Brown, Lester R. and Erik P. Eckholm, "Grim Reaping: This Year the Whole World is Short of Grain," *The New York Times*, 15 September, 1974, 6-E.

———, *By Bread Alone*, New York: Praeger Publishers, 1974.

Bowles, Chester, *Promises to Keep: My Years in Public Life, 1941-1969*. New York: Harper & Row, Publishers, 1971.

Chand, Gyan, "Food and Self-reliance," *Mainstream*, 4 December, 1965, 9-11.

Cochrane, Willard W., *Food and Agricultural Policy for India*, Report by the Consultant on Agricultural Planning to the Ford Foundation, New Delhi, 24 April, 1968.

Dandekar, V.M., "Food and Freedom," A two part article in *Mainstream* on 25 March and 1 April, 1967.

Destler, I.M., *Presidents, Bureaucrats, and Foreign Policy*, Princeton: Princeton University Press, 1972.

Eldridge, P.J., *The Politics of Foreign Aid in India*, Delhi: Vikas Publications, 1969.

Galdi, Theodor, *The Availability and Use of Local Currencies in U.S. Foreign Aid Programs*, A report prepared for the Committee on Foreign Affairs, 93rd Congress, First Session, by the Foreign Affairs Division of the Congressional Research Service, Library of Congress, Washington: U.S. Government Printing Office, 1974.

Ghosh, Arun, *A Recipient Country Looks at Food Aid—Its Benefits and Problems*, Statement by the delegate for India at the ninetyninth meeting of the Consultative Subcommittee on Surplus Disposal of the Committee on Commodity Problems, Food and Agriculture Organization of the United Nations, 20 February, 1964.

Hrischman, Albert O., *Strategy of Economic Development*, New Haven: Yale University Press, 1964.

Hunter, Robert E. and John E. Reilly, *Development Today: A New Look at US Relations with the Poor Countries*, editors, New York: Praeger Publishers, 1972.

Jacobson, Jerome, *PL-480 Consultation Procedures*, A statement by the Deputy Assistant Secretary of State for Economic Affairs, before the Subcommittee on Surplus Disposal of the Committee on Commodity Problems, Food and Agriculture Organization of the United Nations, at its 110th meeting, 9 February, 1965.

Jain, A.P., "For a New Food Policy," *Mainstream*, 25 July, 1964, 9-11.

Johnson, Lyndon Baines, "Feeding the Hungry: India's Food Crisis," *The Vantage Point: Perspectives of the Presidency, 1963-1969*. New York: Holt, Rinehart & Winston, 1971, 222-31.

Johnson, Nicholas, Letter of 19 November from the Maritime Administrator to Senator Paul H. Douglas of Illinois, Chairman of the Subcommittee on Federal Procurement and Regulation, of the Joint Economic Committee. The letter is included in a report entitled "The Impact of Government-Generated Cargo on the U.S.-Flag Foreign Trade Fleet for Calendar Year 1964," prepared by the Maritime Administration of the Department of Commerce for the subcommittee, 89th Congress, First Session. Washington: U.S. Government Printing Office, 1965.

Kalra, O.P., *Agricultural Policy in India*, Bombay: Popular Prakashan, 1973.

Khusro, A.M., *et al. Report of the Expert Group on the Monetary Impact of PL-480 Transactions*, New Delhi: Department of Economic Affairs, Ministry of Finance, Government of India (December 1968).

Krishnanath, *Impact of Foreign Aid on India's Foreign Policy, Economic and Political Development and Cultural Change*, Hyderabad: Rammanohar Lohia Samata Vidyalaya Nyas, 1971.

Lelyveld, Joseph, "U.S. and India: Some Mutual Irritations over Food," *New York Times*, 11 June, 1967.

———, "A Case Study in Disillusion: U.S. Aid Effort in India," *New York Times*, 25 June, 1974, 6.

Lewis, John P., *Quiet Crisis in India: Economic Development and American Policy*, Anchor Books edition, Garden City, New York: Doubleday and Company, Inc., 1964.

———, "Continuity and Change in U.S. Economic Aid," *Commerce*, annual number, 1966, 89-90.

Lindblom, C.E., "Has India an Economic Future?" *Foreign Affairs*, XLIV, 1964, 239-52.

———, "Five Problems in Foodgrain Production: Memorandum to Ambassador Chester Bowles," New Delhi: U.S. Embassy (April, 1964), mimeographed.

———, "India's Economic Prospects," *Ventures: Magazine of the Yale Graduate School*, VII: 1 (Spring, 1968).

Lukas, Anthony, "India Tastes Politics in Food form U.S.," *New York Times*, 12 February, 1967.

Mackey, George, "Consultative Subcommittee on Surplus Disposal: Adaptation to Changing Conditions," Report to the Committee on Commodity Problems of the Food and Agriculture Organization of the United Nations, 31 July, 1974.

Meadows, Dennis *et al.*, *The Limits to Growth: A Report of the Club of Rome's Project on the Predicament of Mankind*, New York: Universe Books, 1972.

Mehta, Balraj, "Reverse Gear in Agriculture: Spotlight on Subramaniam Plan," *Mainstream*, 25 December, 1965, 8-9.

Paddock, William and Paul Paddock, *Famine 1975! America's Decision: Who Will Survive?* Boston: Little, Brown and Company, 1967.

Raj, K.N., "Food, Fertilizer and Foreign Aid," *Mainstream*, 30 April 1966, 10-12.

Rao, V.K.R.V., "Agricultural Production," *Yojana*, 24 October, 1965.

Reserve Bank of India, *Report on Currency and Finance*, issued annually, Bombay: The Examiner Press, 1961-1973.

Schertz, Lyle P., "World Food: Prices and the Poor," *Foreign Affairs*, LII, 1974, 511-37.

Schnittker, John A., "U.S. Food and Agriculture Act of 1965," Remarks by the Under Secretary of Agriculture at the 119th meeting of the Consultative Subcommittee on Surplus Disposal of the Committee on Commodity Problems, Food and Agriculture Organization of the United Nations, 10 January, 1966.

Sen, A.K., "PL-480 and India," *Now*, 12 November, 1965.

Singh, Har Pal, "Capital and Labour Inputs in Agriculture," *The Economic Weekly*, XV, 1963, 1963-64.

Srivastava, U.K., "PL-480 and the Indian Economy," *Asian Economic Review*, XI (February, 1969).

Sundaram, K., "PL-480 Imports—Efficiency in Purchase and Distribution," *Economic and Political Weekly*, II, 1967, 487.

———, "The Relationship between PL-480 Transactions, Money Supply with the Public, and Prices: An Analysis," *Indian Economic Review*, V: 1 (April, 1970).

USDA Economic Research Service, *Changes in Agriculture in 26 Developing Nations, 1948 to 1963*. Foreign Agricultural Economic Report No. 27, 1965.

Veit, Lawrence, "The Economic and Political Ramifications of Local Currency (Rupee) Finance," Unpublished appendix to chapter six of his forthcoming book from the Council of Foreign Relations, New York.

Yojana, "The Meaning of Self-Reliance," Delhi: Publications Division, Ministry of Information and Broadcasting, Government of India, 1965.

Hearings Before Congress

"Discriminatory Ocean Freight Rates and the Balance of Payments." Before the Joint Economic Committee on 20-21 June, 9-10 October, and 19-20 November 1963 and on 25-26 March, 88th Congress, first and second sessions, 1964.

"Extension of Public Law 480—Titles I and II." Before the Subcommittee on Foreign Agricultural Operations of the Committee on Agriculture, House of Representatives, 88th Congress; second session, 18-20 and 28 February, 1964.

"Extension of Public Law 480, 83rd Congress." Before the Committee on Agricultural and Forestry, United States Senate, 88th Congress, second session, 12 August, 1964.

"Discriminatory Ocean Freight Rates and the Balance of Payments." A Report of the Joint Economic Committee, Congress of the United States, 6 January, 89th Congress, first session, 1965.

"Discriminatory Ocean Freight Rates and the Balance of Payments." Before the Subcommittee on Federal Procurement and Regulation of the Joint Economic Committee, Congress of the United States, 89th Congress, first session, 7-8 April, 1965.

"Food and Agriculture Act of 1965." Before the Committee on Agriculture and Forestry, United States Senate, 89th Congress, first session, 16-18, 21-25, and 28-29 June and 15 July, 1965.

"Emergency Food Relief for India." Before the Committee on Agriculture and Forestry, United States Senate, 89th Congress, second session, 5 April, 1966.

"Discriminatory Ocean Freight Rates and the Balance of Payments." Before the Subcommittee on Federal Procurement and Regulation of the Joint Economic Committee, Congress of the United States, 89th Congress, second session, 6 and 19 May, 1966.

"Food for Freedom Program and Commodity Reserves." Before the Senate Committee on Agriculture and Forestry, United States Senate, 89th Congress, second session, 2-4, 7-8, and 15 June, 1966.

"Extension of Public Law 480, 83rd Congress." Before the Committee on Ağriculture and Forestry, United States Senate, 90th Congress, second session, 13-15 March, 1968.

"Cargo Preference Provision of the Export Expansion and Regulation Act." Before the Committee on Banking and Currency, United States Senate, 91st Congress, first session, 10 July, 1969.

Annual *Reports on Public Law 480* by the President to the Congress of the United States, 1966-1972.

INDEX

reluctantly agreed to allot CCC a blanket authorization against which annual appropriations are requested. Other than the comparable example of the Tennessee Valley Authority, CCC's authority is unique in American government.

In order to finance commodity "sales" abroad, the funding arrangements for PL-480 provide an annual ceiling between $1.5 and $3 billion with which to pay the CCC for its surplus commodities. Since CCC goods cost cash dollars, Congressional appropriations are required to pay for the commodities purchased. Appropriations, of course, entail taxation to pay for government expenditures, which put a strain on the normal domestic US budget. In turn, the US Treasury accepts foreign currencies as payment for the PL-480 goods overseas, although after 1971 most sales were shifted into freely convertible currencies.

In addition to the annual appropriations for PL-480, there are "reflows" which come back from overseas agreements. These reflows now total about $200 million per year and can be carried over to subsequent years. As a consequence of these cumulative reflows, the CCC budget for PL-480 can always facilitate the export of US agricultural commodities. Furthermore, CCC is empowered to purchase commodities on credit, using its reflows and annual appropriations as security collateral. In 1975 Title I had about $10.8 billion on tap for underwriting concessional sales while Title II, which authorizes the outright donation of surplus commodity stocks through voluntary agencies, had about $1.4 billion.

These funding arrangements through CCC have always provided the PL-480 program with considerable fiscal autonomy. It is not subject to quick Congressional leverage since the purse-strings cannot be drawn shut very easily—a situation which is perhaps the *sine qua non* of a well-insulated program. Until the Soviet wheat deal of 1972,[3] the Commodity Credit Corporation had operated prudently and responsibly within the increasingly restrictive constraints of the American executive budget. Since that deal, the problem confronting PL-480 operations has not been one of funds to cover exports but the availability of the commodities themselves.